To Drink and To Eat

Tastes and Tales from a French Kitchen

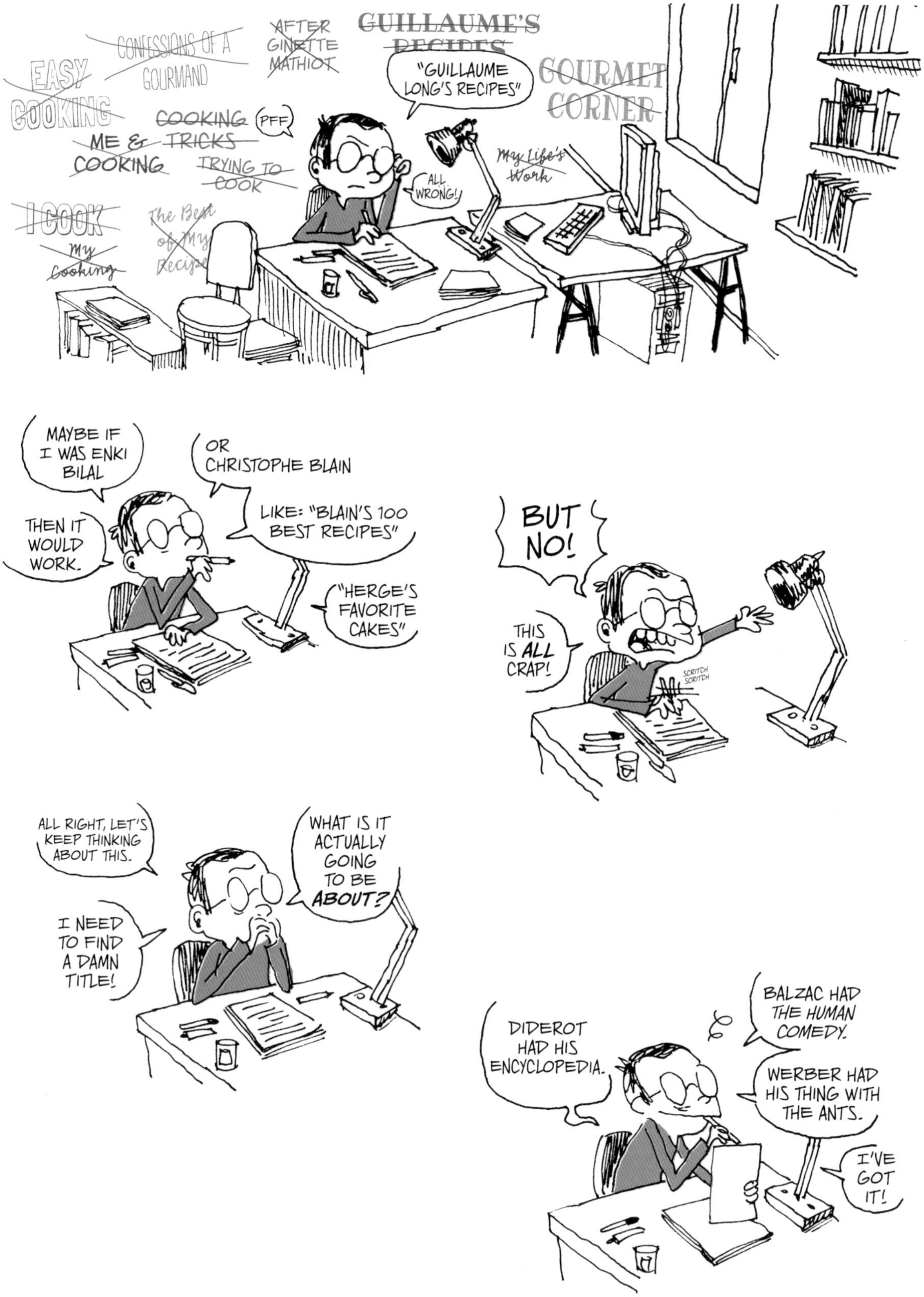
EASY COOKING
CONFESSIONS OF A GOURMAND
AFTER GINETTE MATHIOT
GUILLAUME'S RECIPES
"GUILLAUME LONG'S RECIPES"
GOURMET CORNER
COOKING TRICKS
PFF
ME & COOKING
TRYING TO COOK
My Life's Work
ALL WRONG!
I COOK
My Cooking
The Best of My Recipes
MAYBE IF I WAS ENKI BILAL
THEN IT WOULD WORK.
OR CHRISTOPHE BLAIN
LIKE: "BLAIN'S 100 BEST RECIPES"
"HERGE'S FAVORITE CAKES"
BUT NO!
THIS IS ALL CRAP!
SCRITCH SCRITCH
ALL RIGHT, LET'S KEEP THINKING ABOUT THIS.
I NEED TO FIND A DAMN TITLE!
WHAT IS IT ACTUALLY GOING TO BE ABOUT?
DIDEROT HAD HIS ENCYCLOPEDIA.
BALZAC HAD THE HUMAN COMEDY.
WERBER HAD HIS THING WITH THE ANTS.
I'VE GOT IT!

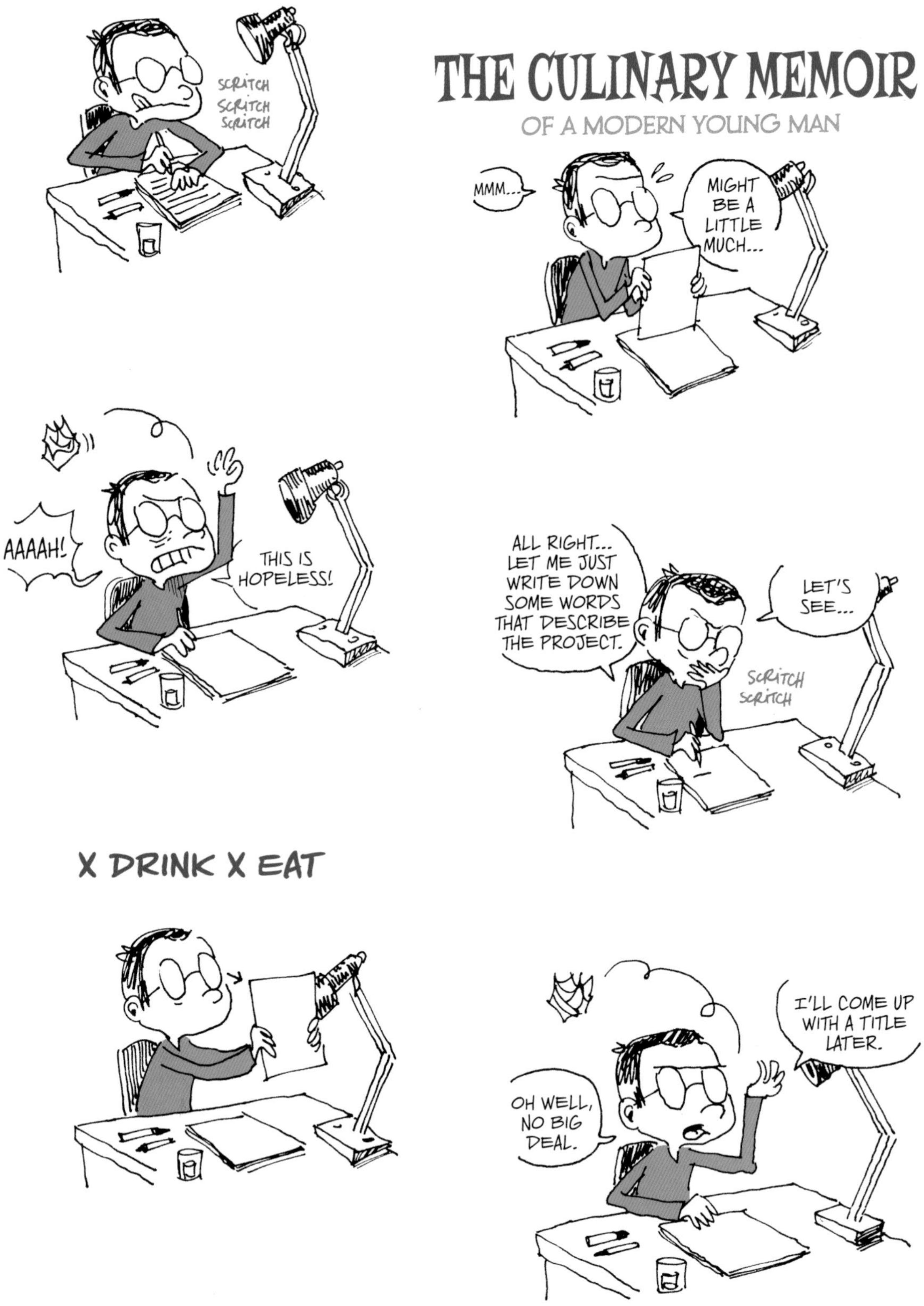
SCRITCH
SCRITCH
SCRITCH
THE CULINARY MEMOIR
OF A MODERN YOUNG MAN
MMM...
MIGHT BE A LITTLE MUCH...
AAAAH!
THIS IS HOPELESS!
ALL RIGHT... LET ME JUST WRITE DOWN SOME WORDS THAT DESCRIBE THE PROJECT.
LET'S SEE...
SCRITCH
SCRITCH
X DRINK X EAT
OH WELL, NO BIG DEAL.
I'LL COME UP WITH A TITLE LATER.

To Drink and To Eat

Tastes and Tales from a French Kitchen

GUILLAUME LONG

Colors Mélanie Roubineau
and Guillaume Long

This book is dedicated to all the people with whom I shared a pleasant moment over drinks or a good meal.

G. L.

Thank you to Céline Badarous Denizon for her invaluable help coloring this comic.

The Pépé Roni strips are the work of the artist Mathis Martin and first appeared in the magazine *French Cuisine.*

English Translation by Jeremy Melloul
Lettering by AndWorld Design's DC Hopkins
Editing and Localization by Amanda Meadows and Grace Bornhoft
Front Cover by Guillaume Long
Jacket Design by Annie Monette

ISBN: 978-1-5493-0320-3

Library Congress Control Number: 2018958120

To Drink and to Eat, Volume 1, published 2019 by The Lion Forge, LLC. Originally published in French under the following title: À boire et à manger

10 9 8 7 6 5 4 3 2 1

Preface

He likes: Bialetti coffee makers, garlic mills, copper saucepans, the escargot with parsley from Le Bistrot de la Tournelle in Arbois, freshly-hatched eggs, cherries from a tree, beefsteak tomatoes, Yirgacheffe coffee from Ethiopia, dry martelli pasta, lobster from the Rialkto market in Venice, the apple strudel from Ruszwurm in Budapest, and the soup at Chez Xu's in Lausanne.

He dislikes: sugar in coffee (or in tea), breaded fish, tomatoes from supermarkets, plastic strainers, the grater that slices vegetables into vermicelli, Zander from Lake Baraton when it's poorly cooked, the aftertaste of Chinese pine nuts, sharing his dish of raclette, and drawing anchovy fillets. I don't know much about Guillaume Long. But one thing I learned from this culinary profile was that he's a man of good taste. In reading through the pages to come, you'll be happy to get to know him and his talents, too.

A talent for eating. Gourmet, gourmand, gastronomy, glutton . . . Guillaume falls somewhere in between these four *g*'s, with a preference for nontraditional cooking (ah, bear's garlic and dandelions!), and small plates that pack a big punch, like his feta-watermelon salad or his black radish soup (tasted and approved).

A talent for drawing. Lively, impulsive, enthusiastic, ready to take a bite out of life, with a fresh, joyful perspective and a deliciously naive style, a collection of tomatoes, the fetishized products in his pantry, or his own face, drooling with ecstasy at the sight of a grilled chicken roasting.

A talent for writing, too. A large serving of dark humor, a pinch of craziness, a zest of the absurd, small parentheticals, asides, and post-scripts that sparkle all over, not to mention a good helping of sweetness. Over the course of a story that's extremely well told, Guillaume has the talent to make you salivate, laugh, smile, shiver with emotion, and even shed a nostalgic tear . . . often just a few balloons apart.

Take the last two pages of this comic: he evokes, with a touching, shy sense of humor, a memory of a rack of lamb cooked with garlic and his grandfather's parsley. In the end, it's a real treat, one to savor, after you've greedily devoured the 133 pages that precede it. You'll drink every last drop and eat every last crumb of *To Drink and To Eat*. It's just that kind of comic.

François-Régis Gaudry

François-Régis Gaudry is a food critic and co-editor in chief of The Express, *producer and host of the show* On Va Déguster (Let's Taste) *on France* (a major French public radio channel) *and the host of* Tres Tres Bon (Very Very Good) *on Paris Premiere* (a French TV channel).

Contents

Manual

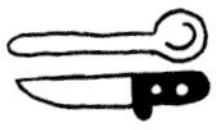

Level 1 : Recipes requiring no cooking experience. Quick, with no actual cooking involved.

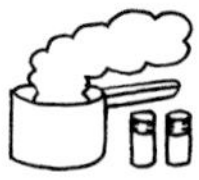

Level 2 : Recipes that are slightly more involved, take some time, and require some cooking.

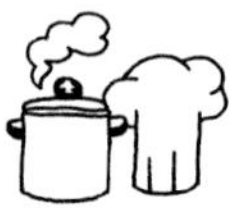

Level 3 : Recipes that are very difficult to make (only sometimes; I'm mainly joking).

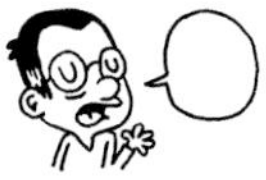

Egotrip : Stories about myself.

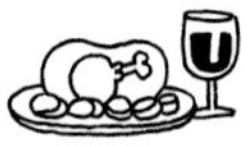

Restaurant : Stories of meals in places I like.

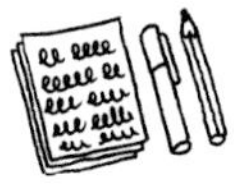

Inventory : Useful lists for foodies.

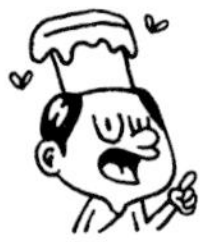

Joël Reblochon : Cooking tips and history presented by the late Joël Reblochon.

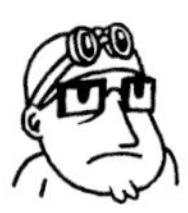

New Friend : Cooking commentary provided by my friend Florian.

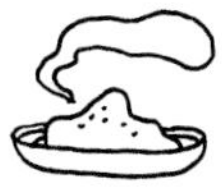

Leftovers : Everything that doesn't fit in one of the other categories in this book.

Spring

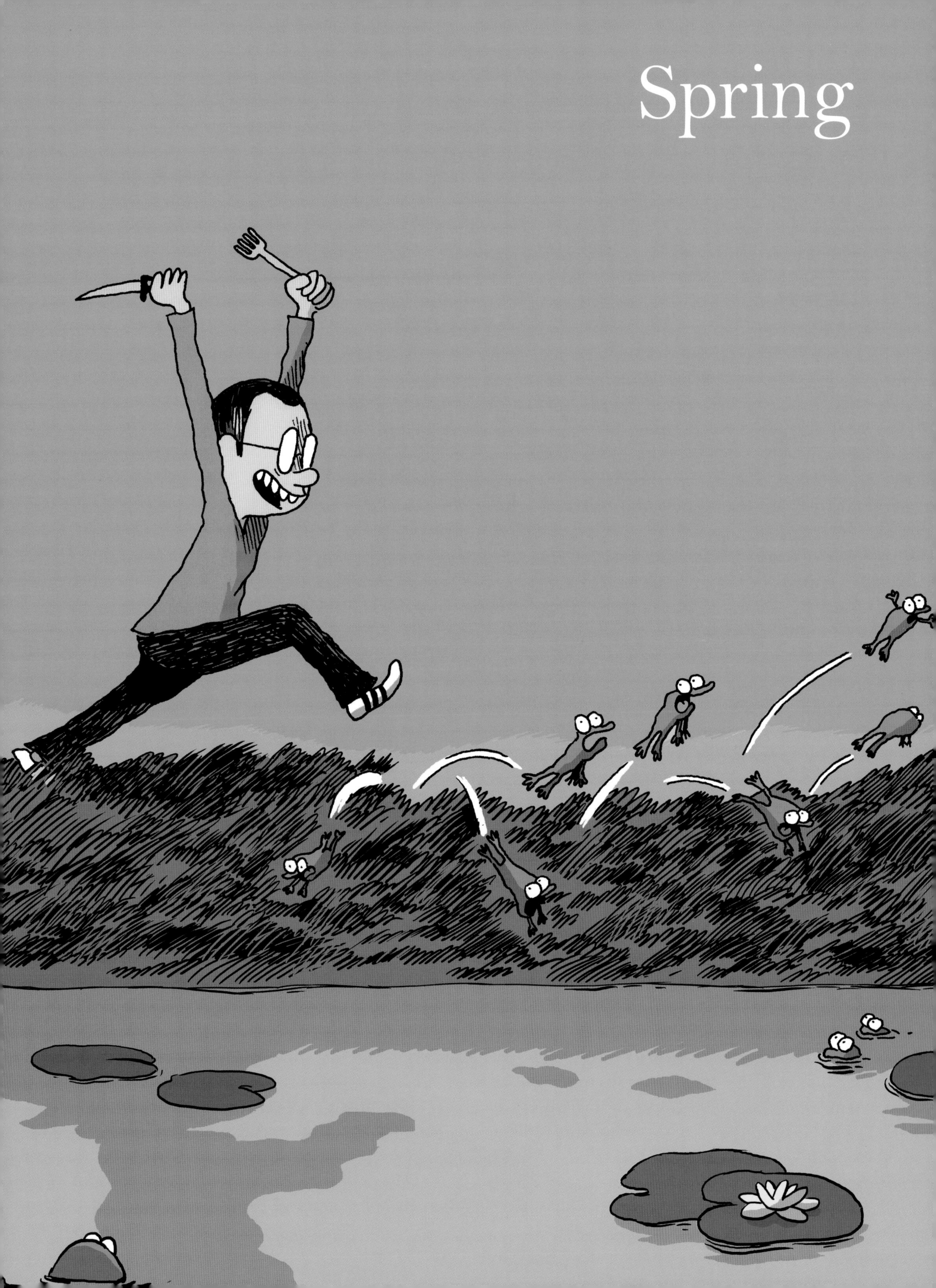

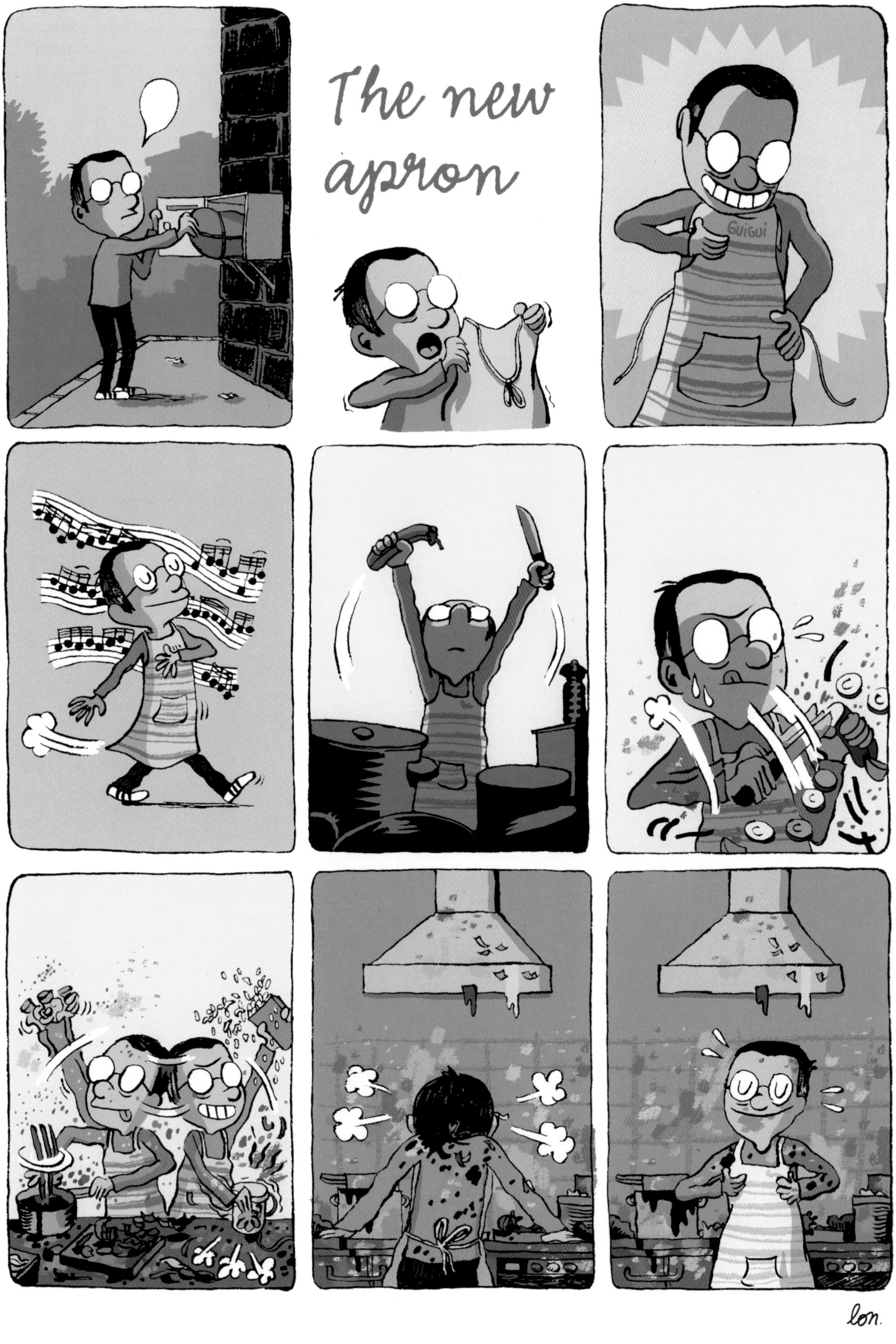
The new apron
GUIGUI
lon.

Playing on the lawn

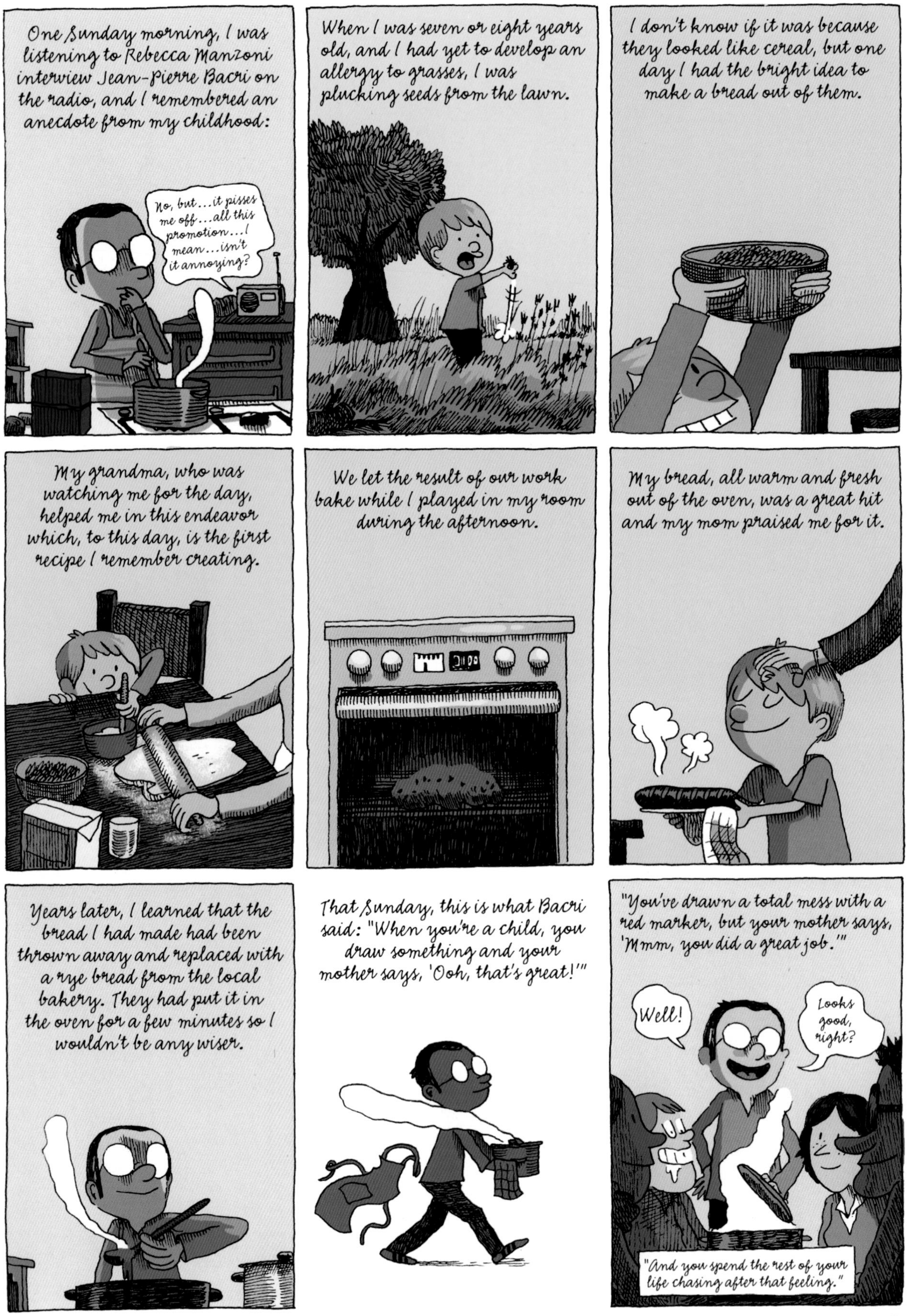
One Sunday morning, I was listening to Rebecca Manzoni interview Jean-Pierre Bacri on the radio, and I remembered an anecdote from my childhood:
No, but...it pisses me off...all this promotion...I mean...isn't it annoying?
When I was seven or eight years old, and I had yet to develop an allergy to grasses, I was plucking seeds from the lawn.
I don't know if it was because they looked like cereal, but one day I had the bright idea to make a bread out of them.
My grandma, who was watching me for the day, helped me in this endeavor which, to this day, is the first recipe I remember creating.
We let the result of our work bake while I played in my room during the afternoon.
My bread, all warm and fresh out of the oven, was a great hit and my mom praised me for it.
Years later, I learned that the bread I had made had been thrown away and replaced with a rye bread from the local bakery. They had put it in the oven for a few minutes so I wouldn't be any wiser.
That Sunday, this is what Bacri said: "When you're a child, you draw something and your mother says, 'Ooh, that's great!'"
"You've drawn a total mess with a red marker, but your mother says, 'Mmm, you did a great job.'"
Well!
Looks good, right?
"And you spend the rest of your life chasing after that feeling."

lon.

A GOOD COFFEE

MAKING GOOD COFFEE? HMM, THAT'S A BIG QUESTION THAT DESERVES ITS OWN BOOK...

BUT I'LL TRY TO BREAK IT DOWN.

SLRRRRP.

WHERE TO START? LET'S SEE... YOU NEED COFFEE, OF COURSE. AND WATER. A FLYSWATTER AND, MOST IMPORTANTLY, A COFFEE MAKER.

A **REAL** ONE.

FORGET ABOUT NESPRESSO® AND THE OTHER FAKERS...

TCHIII

THEY MIGHT BE COOL AND PRODUCE DECENT COFFEE, BUT THEY ALL TASTE THE SAME.

AND DROP THE FANTASY OF SOMEDAY HAVING A CONA COFFEE MAKER.

FWIP FWIP

THEY'RE OVERKILL-- AND WAY TOO EXPENSIVE. THE TYPE OF THING YOU ONLY USE ONCE.

AS FOR YOUR ELECTRIC COFFEE MAKER, SELL IT OR JUST THROW IT AWAY. THEY'RE SO UGLY.

KRR-RRR

WHAT A HORRIBLE SOUND

THE COFFEE THAT IT MAKES IS SAD AND, IF YOU'RE NOT AWARE, CAUSES ABSCESSES BETWEEN YOUR TOES.

IGNORE YOUR BODUM ®, TOO.

...

BECAUSE... WELL, JUST TRUST ME. AND ANYWAY, MAKING GOOD COFFEE REQUIRES A HEALTHY DOSE OF SUPERSTITION.

YOU CAN START BY GETTING...

An Italian Coffee Maker

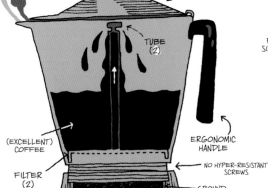

DECORATION →

LID

TUBE (2)

(EXCELLENT) COFFEE

FILTER (2)

FILTER (1)

ERGONOMIC HANDLE

NO HYPER-RESISTANT SCREWS

GROUND COFFEE

SAFETY VALVE

TUBE (1)

BOILING WATER

(UNNECESSARY SECTIONAL VIEW OF POT FOR EFFECT.)

I HAVE THREE AT HOME:

FOUR CUPS, SIX YEARS OLD

SIX CUPS, THREE YEARS OLD

SIX CUPS, NEWBORN

I LOVE THEM; I SPOIL THEM. I COULD'VE PROBABLY EVEN NAMED THEM...

FOR SOME PEOPLE IT'S CARS, FOR ME IT'S COFFEE MAKERS.

THE POINT IS TO HAVE ONE FOR THE REST OF YOUR LIFE... OVER TIME, THE COFFEE IT MAKES BECOMES EVEN MORE DELICIOUS...

SO, MAKE YOUR CHOICE CAREFULLY.

IF ONLY I HAD KNOWN!

HELL OF A BREW.

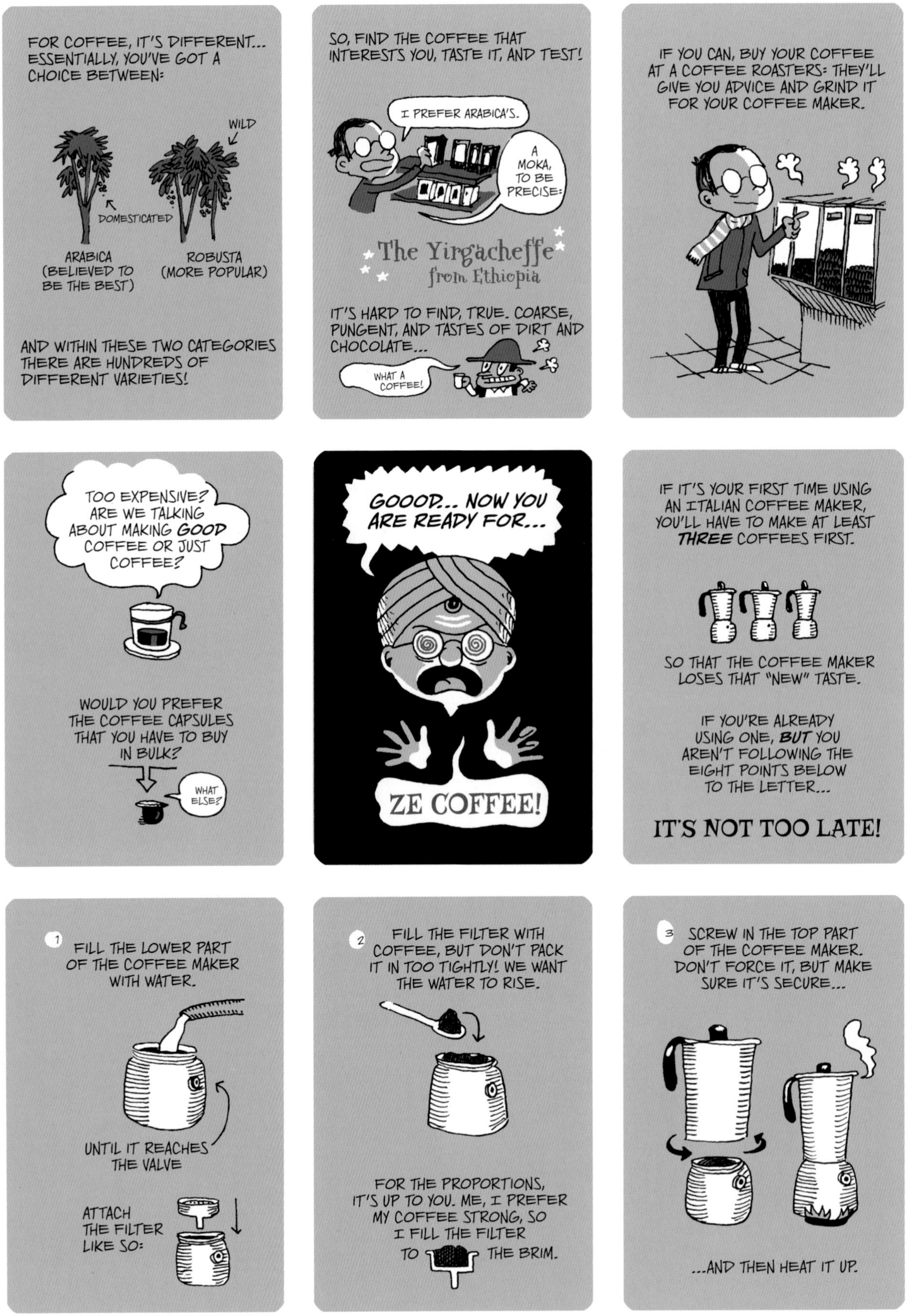
FOR COFFEE, IT'S DIFFERENT... ESSENTIALLY, YOU'VE GOT A CHOICE BETWEEN:
WILD
DOMESTICATED
ARABICA (BELIEVED TO BE THE BEST)
ROBUSTA (MORE POPULAR)
AND WITHIN THESE TWO CATEGORIES THERE ARE HUNDREDS OF DIFFERENT VARIETIES!
SO, FIND THE COFFEE THAT INTERESTS YOU, TASTE IT, AND TEST!
I PREFER ARABICA'S.
A MOKA, TO BE PRECISE:
The Yirgacheffe from Ethiopia
IT'S HARD TO FIND, TRUE. COARSE, PUNGENT, AND TASTES OF DIRT AND CHOCOLATE...
WHAT A COFFEE!
IF YOU CAN, BUY YOUR COFFEE AT A COFFEE ROASTERS: THEY'LL GIVE YOU ADVICE AND GRIND IT FOR YOUR COFFEE MAKER.
TOO EXPENSIVE? ARE WE TALKING ABOUT MAKING GOOD COFFEE OR JUST COFFEE?
WOULD YOU PREFER THE COFFEE CAPSULES THAT YOU HAVE TO BUY IN BULK?
WHAT ELSE?
GOOOD... NOW YOU ARE READY FOR...
ZE COFFEE!
IF IT'S YOUR FIRST TIME USING AN ITALIAN COFFEE MAKER, YOU'LL HAVE TO MAKE AT LEAST THREE COFFEES FIRST.
SO THAT THE COFFEE MAKER LOSES THAT "NEW" TASTE.
IF YOU'RE ALREADY USING ONE, BUT YOU AREN'T FOLLOWING THE EIGHT POINTS BELOW TO THE LETTER...
IT'S NOT TOO LATE!
1 FILL THE LOWER PART OF THE COFFEE MAKER WITH WATER.
UNTIL IT REACHES THE VALVE
ATTACH THE FILTER LIKE SO:
2 FILL THE FILTER WITH COFFEE, BUT DON'T PACK IT IN TOO TIGHTLY! WE WANT THE WATER TO RISE.
FOR THE PROPORTIONS, IT'S UP TO YOU. ME, I PREFER MY COFFEE STRONG, SO I FILL THE FILTER
TO THE BRIM.
3 SCREW IN THE TOP PART OF THE COFFEE MAKER. DON'T FORCE IT, BUT MAKE SURE IT'S SECURE...
...AND THEN HEAT IT UP.

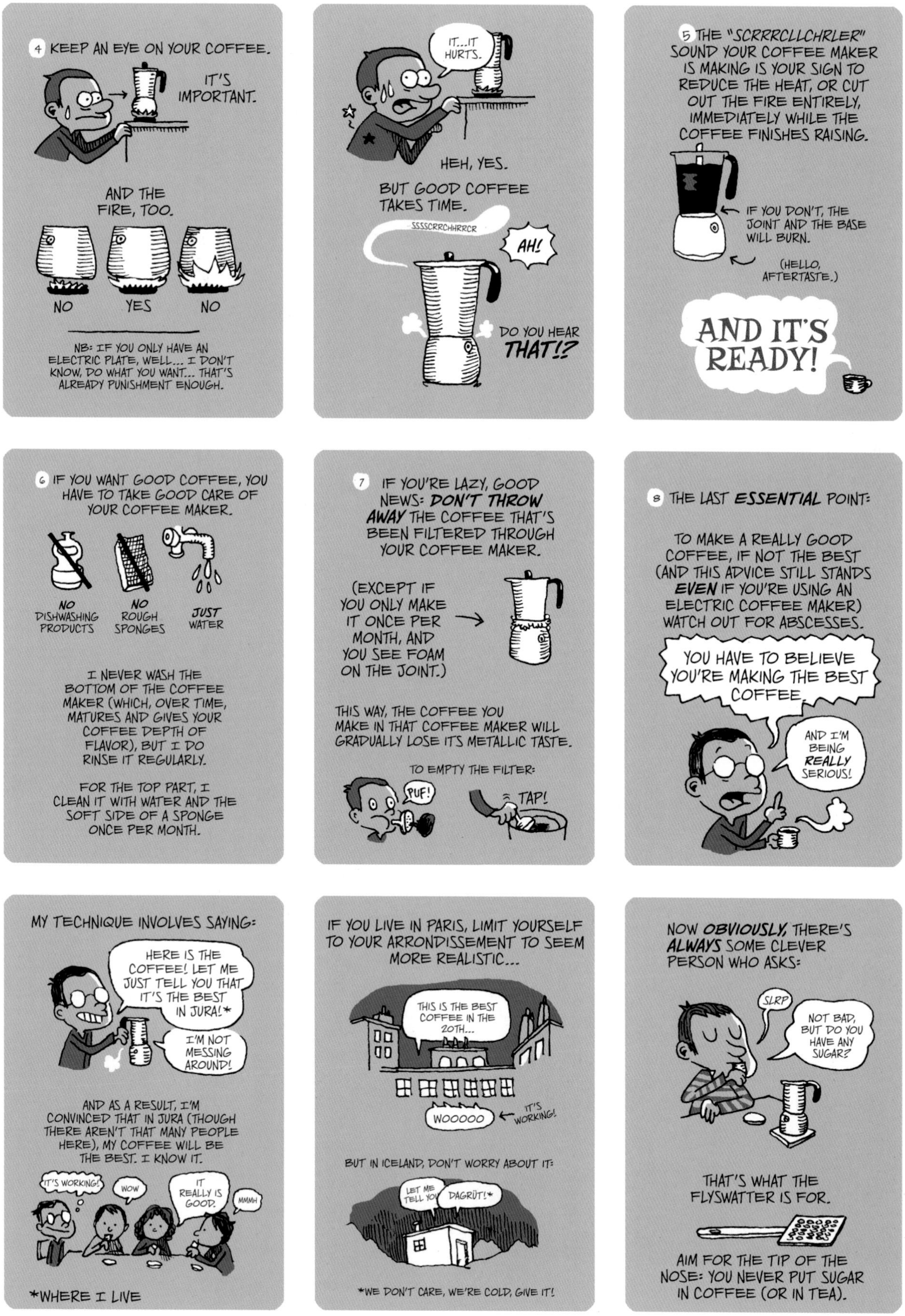
4 KEEP AN EYE ON YOUR COFFEE.
IT'S IMPORTANT.
AND THE FIRE, TOO.
NO
YES
NO
NB: IF YOU ONLY HAVE AN ELECTRIC PLATE, WELL... I DON'T KNOW, DO WHAT YOU WANT... THAT'S ALREADY PUNISHMENT ENOUGH.
IT... IT HURTS.
HEH, YES.
BUT GOOD COFFEE TAKES TIME.
SSSSCRRCHHRRCR
AH!
DO YOU HEAR THAT!?
5 THE "SCRRRCLLCHRLER" SOUND YOUR COFFEE MAKER IS MAKING IS YOUR SIGN TO REDUCE THE HEAT, OR CUT OUT THE FIRE ENTIRELY, IMMEDIATELY WHILE THE COFFEE FINISHES RAISING.
IF YOU DON'T, THE JOINT AND THE BASE WILL BURN.
(HELLO, AFTERTASTE.)
AND IT'S READY!
6 IF YOU WANT GOOD COFFEE, YOU HAVE TO TAKE GOOD CARE OF YOUR COFFEE MAKER.
NO DISHWASHING PRODUCTS
NO ROUGH SPONGES
JUST WATER
I NEVER WASH THE BOTTOM OF THE COFFEE MAKER (WHICH, OVER TIME, MATURES AND GIVES YOUR COFFEE DEPTH OF FLAVOR), BUT I DO RINSE IT REGULARLY.
FOR THE TOP PART, I CLEAN IT WITH WATER AND THE SOFT SIDE OF A SPONGE ONCE PER MONTH.
7 IF YOU'RE LAZY, GOOD NEWS: DON'T THROW AWAY THE COFFEE THAT'S BEEN FILTERED THROUGH YOUR COFFEE MAKER.
(EXCEPT IF YOU ONLY MAKE IT ONCE PER MONTH, AND YOU SEE FOAM ON THE JOINT.)
THIS WAY, THE COFFEE YOU MAKE IN THAT COFFEE MAKER WILL GRADUALLY LOSE ITS METALLIC TASTE.
TO EMPTY THE FILTER:
PUF!
TAP!
8 THE LAST ESSENTIAL POINT:
TO MAKE A REALLY GOOD COFFEE, IF NOT THE BEST (AND THIS ADVICE STILL STANDS EVEN IF YOU'RE USING AN ELECTRIC COFFEE MAKER) WATCH OUT FOR ABSCESSES.
YOU HAVE TO BELIEVE YOU'RE MAKING THE BEST COFFEE.
AND I'M BEING REALLY SERIOUS!
MY TECHNIQUE INVOLVES SAYING:
HERE IS THE COFFEE! LET ME JUST TELL YOU THAT IT'S THE BEST IN JURA!*
I'M NOT MESSING AROUND!
AND AS A RESULT, I'M CONVINCED THAT IN JURA (THOUGH THERE AREN'T THAT MANY PEOPLE HERE), MY COFFEE WILL BE THE BEST. I KNOW IT.
IT'S WORKING!
WOW
IT REALLY IS GOOD.
MMMH
*WHERE I LIVE
IF YOU LIVE IN PARIS, LIMIT YOURSELF TO YOUR ARRONDISSEMENT TO SEEM MORE REALISTIC...
THIS IS THE BEST COFFEE IN THE 20TH...
WOOOOO
IT'S WORKING!
BUT IN ICELAND, DON'T WORRY ABOUT IT:
LET ME TELL YOU
DAGRÜT!*
*WE DON'T CARE, WE'RE COLD, GIVE IT!
NOW OBVIOUSLY, THERE'S ALWAYS SOME CLEVER PERSON WHO ASKS:
SLRP
NOT BAD, BUT DO YOU HAVE ANY SUGAR?
THAT'S WHAT THE FLYSWATTER IS FOR.
AIM FOR THE TIP OF THE NOSE: YOU NEVER PUT SUGAR IN COFFEE (OR IN TEA).

Lon.

✦ ASIDE ✦

IN *MULHOLLAND DRIVE* BY DAVID LYNCH, THERE'S A TENSE SCENE WHERE WE SEE PEOPLE NEGOTIATE A CONTRACT FOR A MOVIE.

ADAM · RAY · MR. DARBY · LUIGI

THEN, AT ONE POINT, A GUY (LUIGI) ORDERS A COFFEE, AND WE CAN TELL HE'S NOT HERE TO MESS AROUND:

ESPRESSO

NAPKIN

HE TAKES A SINGLE SIP, AND THEN HE STARTS SPITTING IT OUT INTO HIS NAPKIN!

HE SAYS:

IT'S SHIT!!

AND HE:

FLPFLPF

AND THEN HE GETS UP, EXTREMELY ANGRY. THE MEETING IS RUINED, AND THE TWO GUYS (RAY AND MR. DARBY) START TO APOLOGIZE:

I'M SORRY

THAWASHIGHLY RECOMM--

WHICH PROVES TWO THINGS:

1) IF YOU'RE NOT USING AN ITALIAN COFFEE MAKER, THEN YOU'RE MAKING CRAPPY COFFEE!

PIECE OF SHIT!

2) IF THE TWO GUYS HAD SAID THAT IT WAS THE BEST COFFEE IN THE WORLD (NOT ONE OF THE BEST, BUT THE BEST!) **BEFORE** SERVING THE COFFEE, WELL I BET THAT LUIGI WOULD'VE LOVED IT!

BUT THE SCENE WOULDN'T HAVE BEEN AS INTERESTING...

LYNCH KNEW.

lon.

Pépé Roni's Good Advice: skimming

n° 278

You can't confuse "skimming over the ocean"

"and skimming a soup.

BECAUSE ANYONE CAN MAKE MISTAKES!

Skimming: Removing, with the help of a skimmer, the foam or scum that forms on the surface of a dish when it is cooked.

YOU PLAYED WITH IT WHEN YOU WERE A CHILD.
YOU BARELY PAY ATTENTION TO IT IN THE STREET.
YOU SEE IT FROM TIME TO TIME FROM YOUR CAR.
Dandelions, are a little like life...
I am poetry
In springtime, they symbolize hope and renewal for us...
AND NOW YOU'RE GOING TO EAT IT!
AND NOT BY THE ROOTS!
HE HE!
THE DANDELION
But its bitterness is a good reminder of how hard life can be sometimes....
EW!
MHM HM
And that you need to season it properly if you want to appreciate it.
a delicious dandelion salad
OLIVE OIL
RED WINE VINEGAR
ANCHOVIES
SALT
NUT OIL
PEPPER
EGGS
DANDELION FLOWERS
MUSTARD
PORK BELLY
1 GATHER SOME DANDELIONS, BUT BE CAREFUL: ONLY THE YOUNG ONES THAT HAVE YET TO FLOWER (IN OTHER WORDS, HARVEST THE ONES THAT ARE TENDER).
WELL, THIS WON'T MAKE A PRETTY BOUQUET.
MOM!
NEMO!
2 THIS IS THE LONGEST AND MOST ANNOYING PART: CAREFULLY WASH THE LEAVES, SORT THEM, AND REMOVE THE ROOTS.
YOU CAN KEEP THE BULBS
FINALLY, SOAK THEM FOR FIVE MINUTES IN A BASIN OF WATER WITH TWO TABLESPOONS OF VINEGAR.
IT KILLS MICROBES.
OF COURSE, STEPS (1) AND (2) ARE USELESS IF YOU'RE BUYING YOUR DANDELIONS. BUT WHY WOULD YOU PAY FOR BAD HERBS (ESPECIALLY WHEN THEY'RE USUALLY EXPENSIVE)?
YEAH, BUT I'M USED TO THE CITY.
I'M NOT GOING ALL THE WAY TO THE COUNTRY JUST FOR DANDELIONS.
3 MAKE SOME HARD-BOILED EGGS (ONE PER PERSON IS GOOD).
WAIT EXACTLY NINE MINUTES
OPEN UP A BOX OF ANCHOVIES.
OR FRY THE SMOKED PORK BELLY IN SLICES.
TSHH
4 PREPARE A SPICY VINAIGRETTE TO BALANCE THE DANDELION SALAD'S BITTERNESS.
THEY'RE FAR MORE BITTER THAN PINE NUTS EXCEPT THAT THE AFTERTASTE DOESN'T LAST A WEEK.
FOR EVERY TWO SPOONS OF OIL (OLIVE OR OTHERWISE), ADD HALF AS MUCH MUSTARD, TWO SPOONS OF VINEGAR, ONE SPOON OF NUT OIL, AND SALT AND PEPPER.
5 MIX THE SALAD TOGETHER AND TASTE IT:
KRRRRK DAMN!
IT'S SO BITTER.
AND, IF NEEDED, ADD A LITTLE BIT OF NORMAL SALAD, EVEN IF IT'S LESS "GREEN."
LET'S KICK SOME BUTT!
YEAH!
YEAH!
6 ON A PLATE, DRESS THE SALAD, AND SPRINKLE SOME GRILLED PORK OR ANCHOVIES, OR BOTH.
WOOO, FATTY!!
THEN TOP WITH AN EGG, CUT IN FOUR:
IT REALLY IS BITTER.
OR IS IT JUST ME?
ALL THOSE ANCHO-VIES.
len.

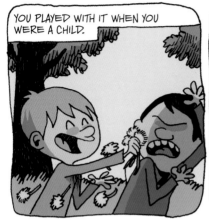

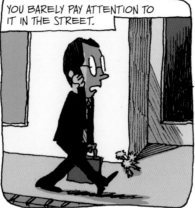

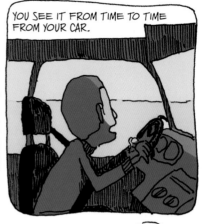

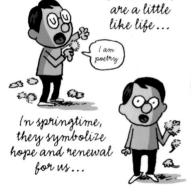

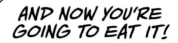

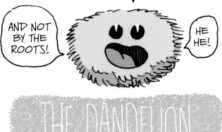

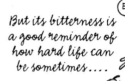

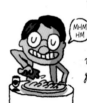

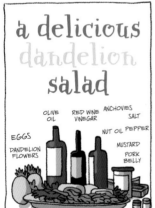

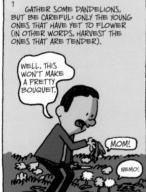

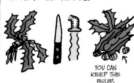

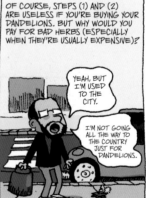

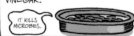

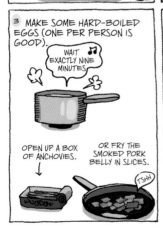

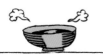

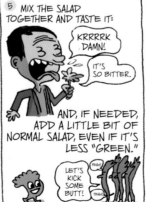

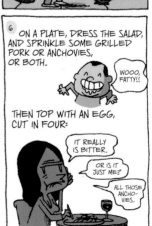

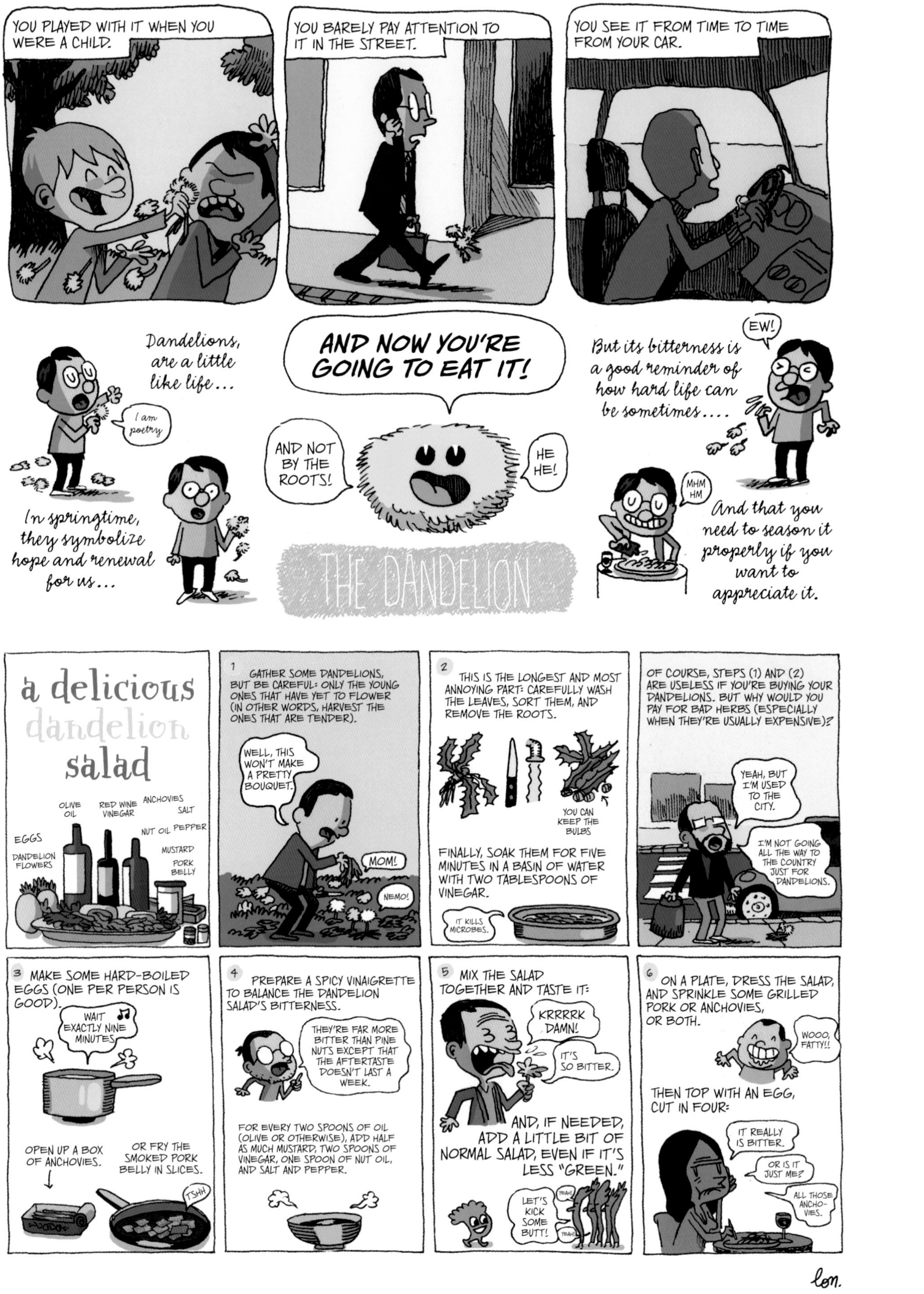

Egg heist I

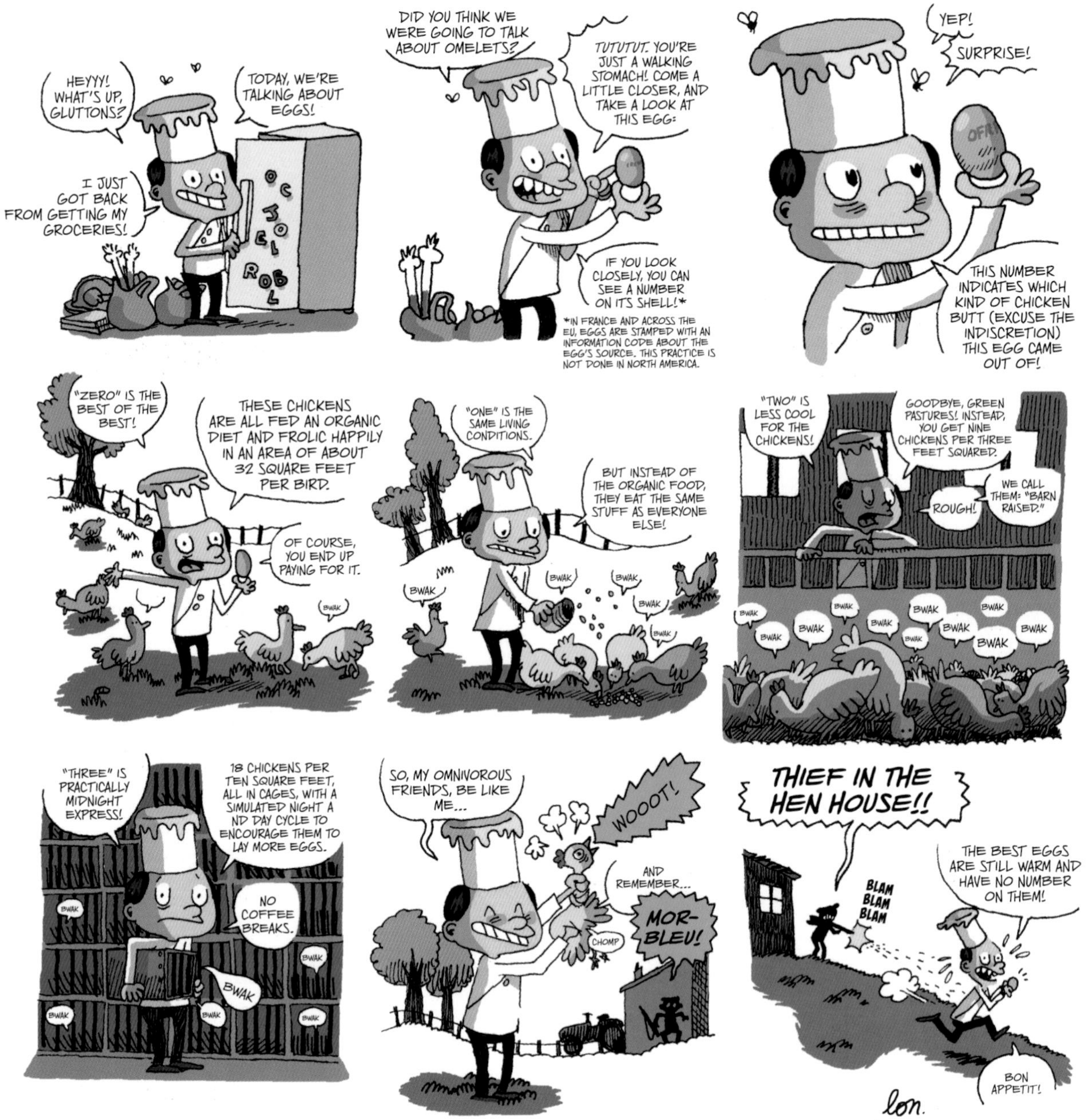
HEYYY! WHAT'S UP, GLUTTONS?
TODAY, WE'RE TALKING ABOUT EGGS!
I JUST GOT BACK FROM GETTING MY GROCERIES!
DID YOU THINK WE WERE GOING TO TALK ABOUT OMELETS?
TUTUTUT. YOU'RE JUST A WALKING STOMACH! COME A LITTLE CLOSER, AND TAKE A LOOK AT THIS EGG:
IF YOU LOOK CLOSELY, YOU CAN SEE A NUMBER ON ITS SHELL!*
*IN FRANCE AND ACROSS THE EU, EGGS ARE STAMPED WITH AN INFORMATION CODE ABOUT THE EGG'S SOURCE. THIS PRACTICE IS NOT DONE IN NORTH AMERICA.
YEP!
SURPRISE!
THIS NUMBER INDICATES WHICH KIND OF CHICKEN BUTT (EXCUSE THE INDISCRETION) THIS EGG CAME OUT OF!
"ZERO" IS THE BEST OF THE BEST!
THESE CHICKENS ARE ALL FED AN ORGANIC DIET AND FROLIC HAPPILY IN AN AREA OF ABOUT 32 SQUARE FEET PER BIRD.
OF COURSE, YOU END UP PAYING FOR IT.
BWAK
"ONE" IS THE SAME LIVING CONDITIONS.
BUT INSTEAD OF THE ORGANIC FOOD, THEY EAT THE SAME STUFF AS EVERYONE ELSE!
BWAK
"TWO" IS LESS COOL FOR THE CHICKENS!
GOODBYE, GREEN PASTURES! INSTEAD, YOU GET NINE CHICKENS PER THREE FEET SQUARED.
ROUGH!
WE CALL THEM: "BARN RAISED."
BWAK
"THREE" IS PRACTICALLY MIDNIGHT EXPRESS!
18 CHICKENS PER TEN SQUARE FEET, ALL IN CAGES, WITH A SIMULATED NIGHT A ND DAY CYCLE TO ENCOURAGE THEM TO LAY MORE EGGS.
NO COFFEE BREAKS.
BWAK
SO, MY OMNIVOROUS FRIENDS, BE LIKE ME...
WOOOT!
AND REMEMBER...
MORBLEU!
CHOMP
THIEF IN THE HEN HOUSE!!
BLAM BLAM BLAM
THE BEST EGGS ARE STILL WARM AND HAVE NO NUMBER ON THEM!
BON APPETIT!
lon.

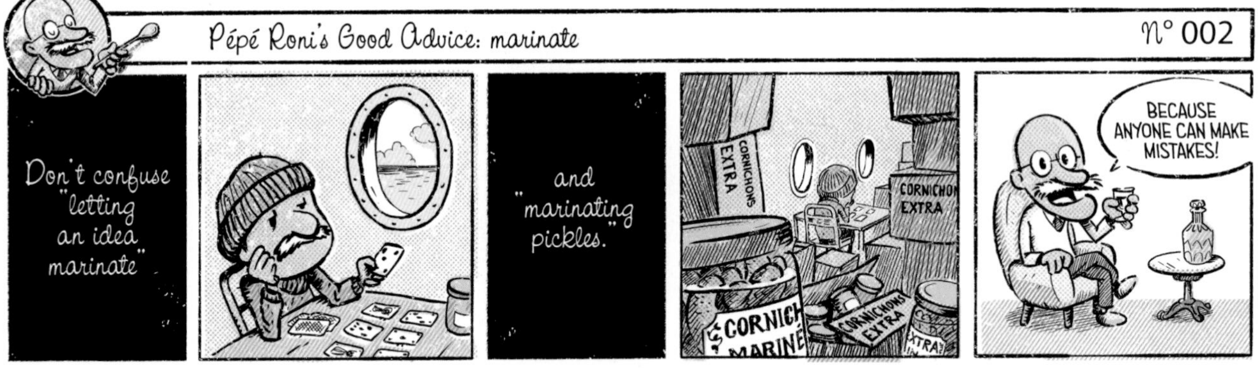
Pépé Roni's Good Advice: marinate
N° 002
Don't confuse "letting an idea marinate"
and "marinating pickles."
CORNICHONS EXTRA
CORNICHONS EXTRA
BECAUSE ANYONE CAN MAKE MISTAKES!

Marinate: Soaking a food item into a marinade to tenderize it and give it flavor.

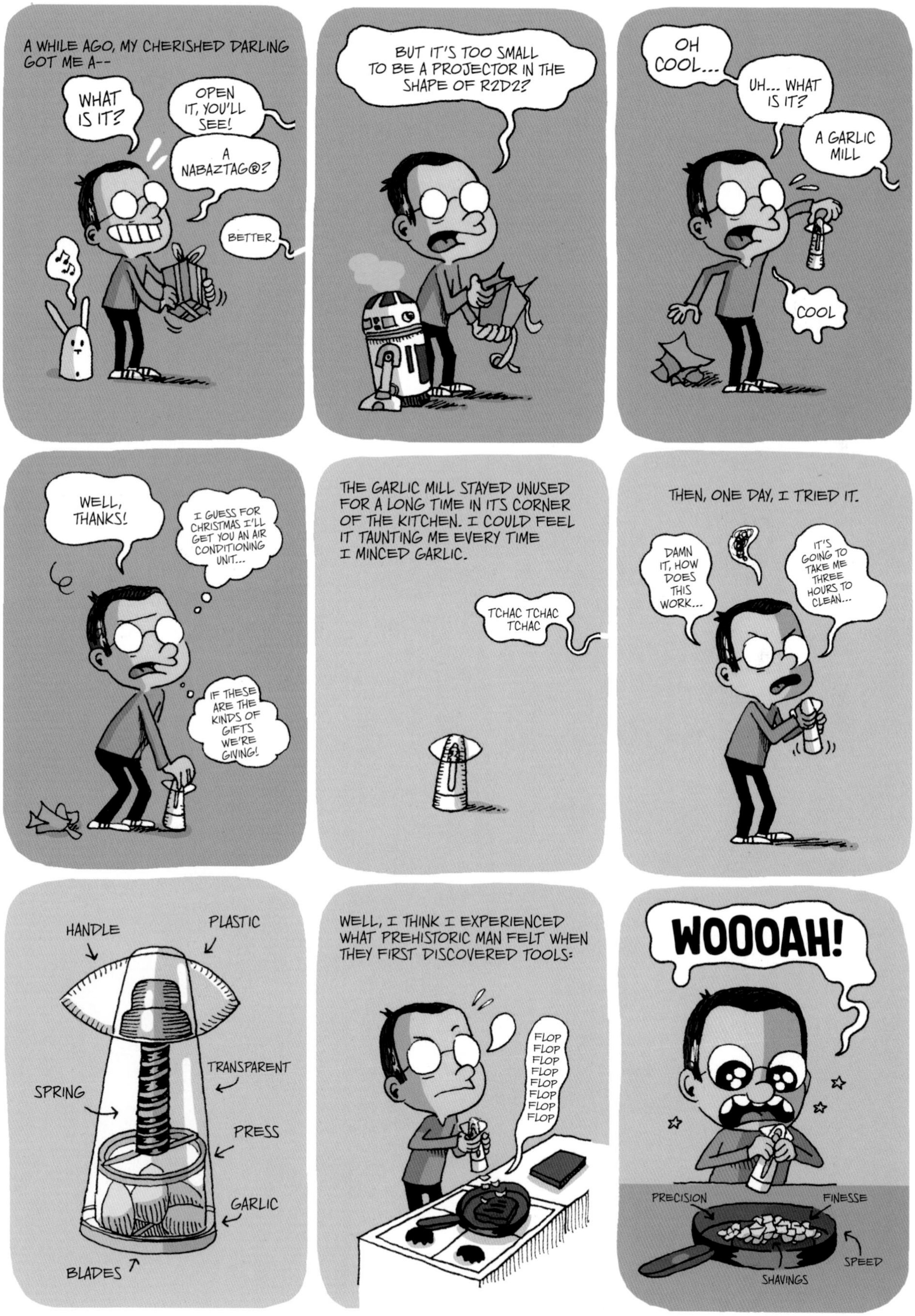
A WHILE AGO, MY CHERISHED DARLING GOT ME A--
WHAT IS IT?
OPEN IT, YOU'LL SEE!
A NABAZTAG®?
BETTER.
BUT IT'S TOO SMALL TO BE A PROJECTOR IN THE SHAPE OF R2D2?
OH COOL...
UH... WHAT IS IT?
A GARLIC MILL
COOL
WELL, THANKS!
I GUESS FOR CHRISTMAS I'LL GET YOU AN AIR CONDITIONING UNIT...
IF THESE ARE THE KINDS OF GIFTS WE'RE GIVING!
THE GARLIC MILL STAYED UNUSED FOR A LONG TIME IN ITS CORNER OF THE KITCHEN. I COULD FEEL IT TAUNTING ME EVERY TIME I MINCED GARLIC.
TCHAC TCHAC TCHAC
THEN, ONE DAY, I TRIED IT.
DAMN IT, HOW DOES THIS WORK...
IT'S GOING TO TAKE ME THREE HOURS TO CLEAN...
HANDLE
PLASTIC
TRANSPARENT
SPRING
PRESS
GARLIC
BLADES
WELL, I THINK I EXPERIENCED WHAT PREHISTORIC MAN FELT WHEN THEY FIRST DISCOVERED TOOLS:
FLOP FLOP FLOP FLOP FLOP FLOP FLOP FLOP
WOOOAH!
PRECISION
FINESSE
SPEED
SHAVINGS

Cooking for geeks I

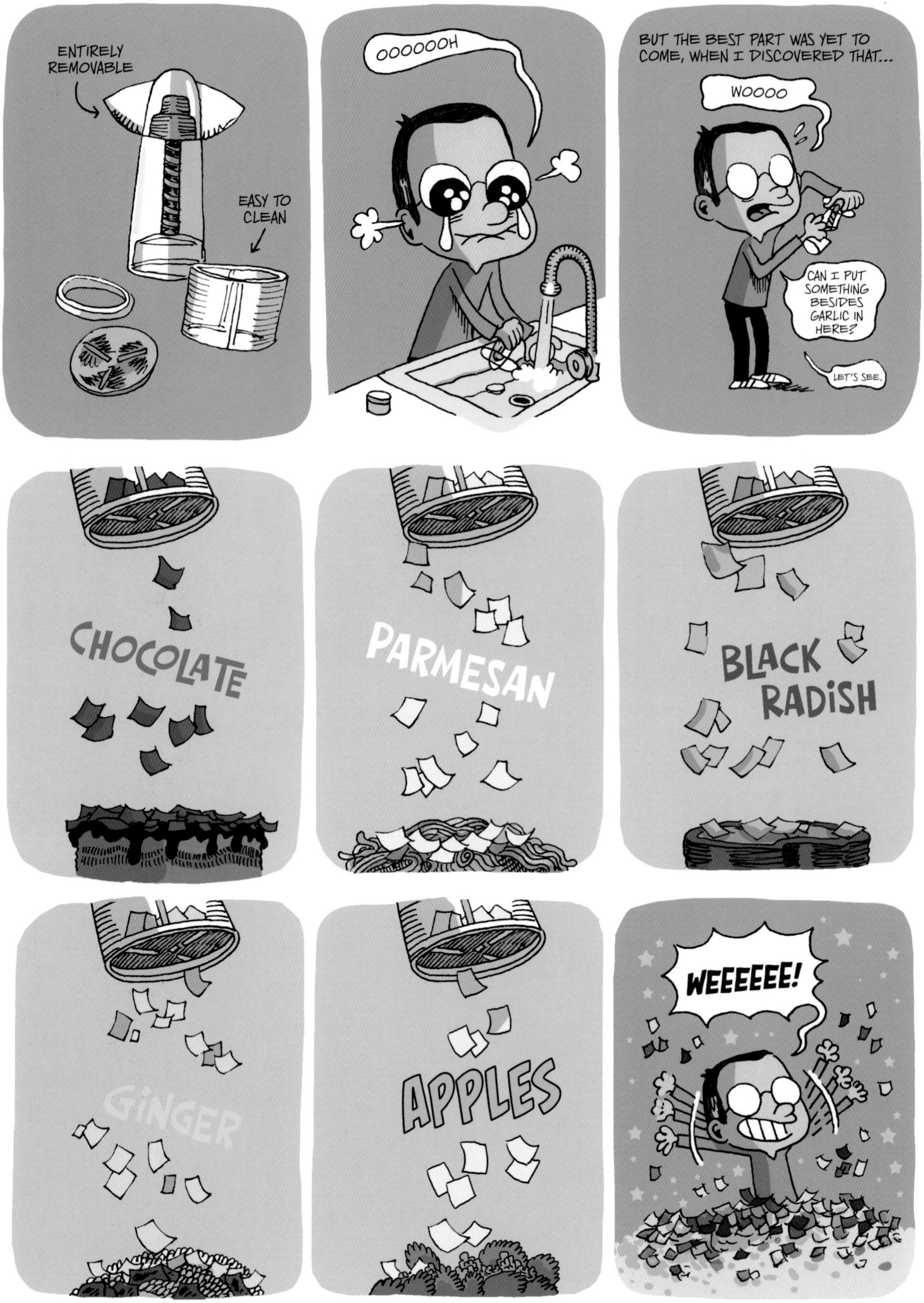
ENTIRELY REMOVABLE
EASY TO CLEAN
OOOOOOH
BUT THE BEST PART WAS YET TO COME, WHEN I DISCOVERED THAT...
WOOOO
CAN I PUT SOMETHING BESIDES GARLIC IN HERE?
LET'S SEE.
CHOCOLATE
PARMESAN
BLACK RADISH
GINGER
APPLES
WEEEEEE!

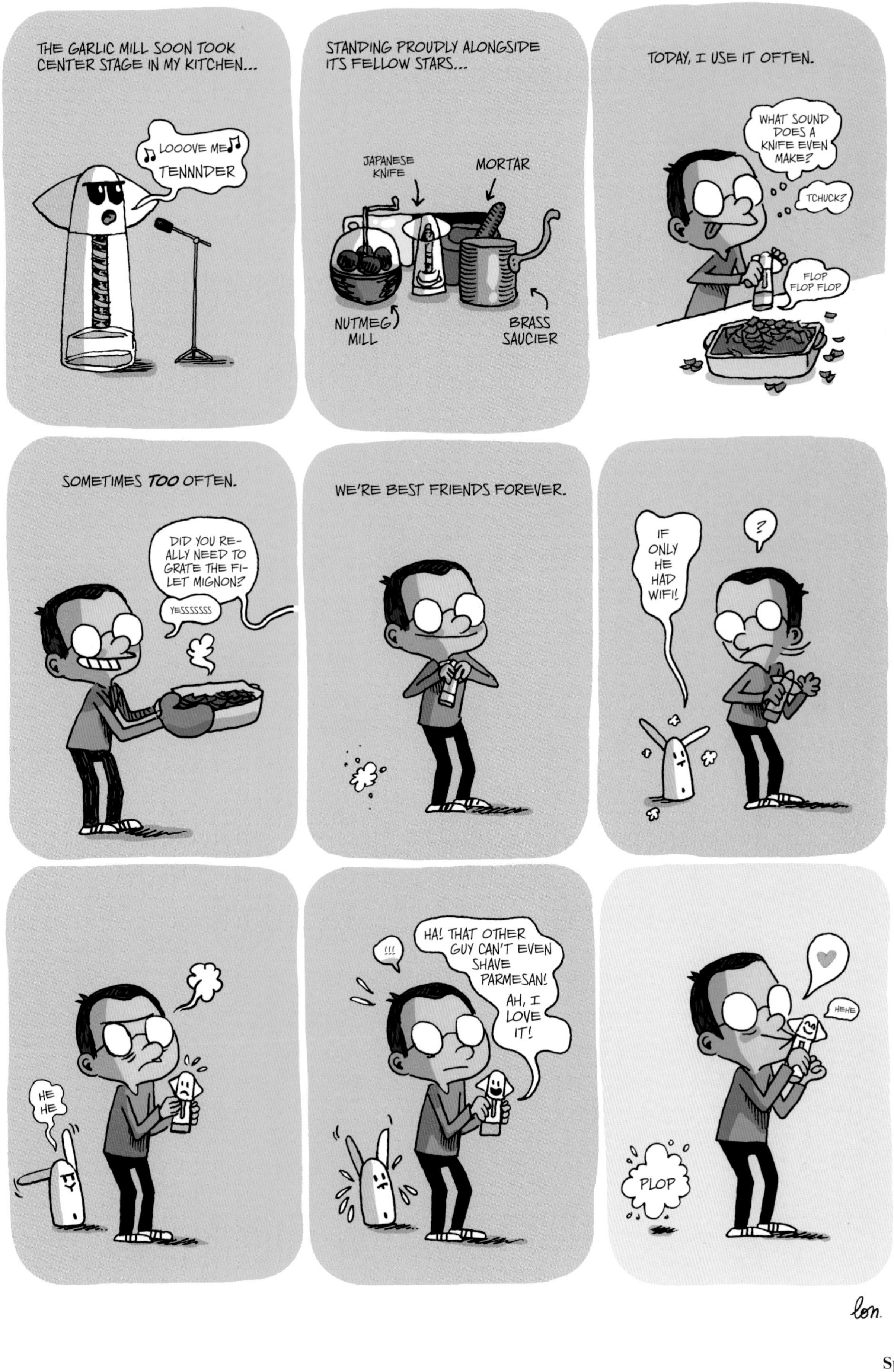
THE GARLIC MILL SOON TOOK CENTER STAGE IN MY KITCHEN...
LOOOVE ME TENNNDER
STANDING PROUDLY ALONGSIDE ITS FELLOW STARS...
JAPANESE KNIFE
MORTAR
NUTMEG MILL
BRASS SAUCIER
TODAY, I USE IT OFTEN.
WHAT SOUND DOES A KNIFE EVEN MAKE?
TCHUCK?
FLOP FLOP FLOP
SOMETIMES TOO OFTEN.
DID YOU REALLY NEED TO GRATE THE FILET MIGNON?
YESSSSSSS
WE'RE BEST FRIENDS FOREVER.
IF ONLY HE HAD WIFI!
?
HE HE
!!!
HA! THAT OTHER GUY CAN'T EVEN SHAVE PARMESAN!
AH, I LOVE IT!
HEHE
PLOP
lon.

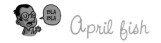

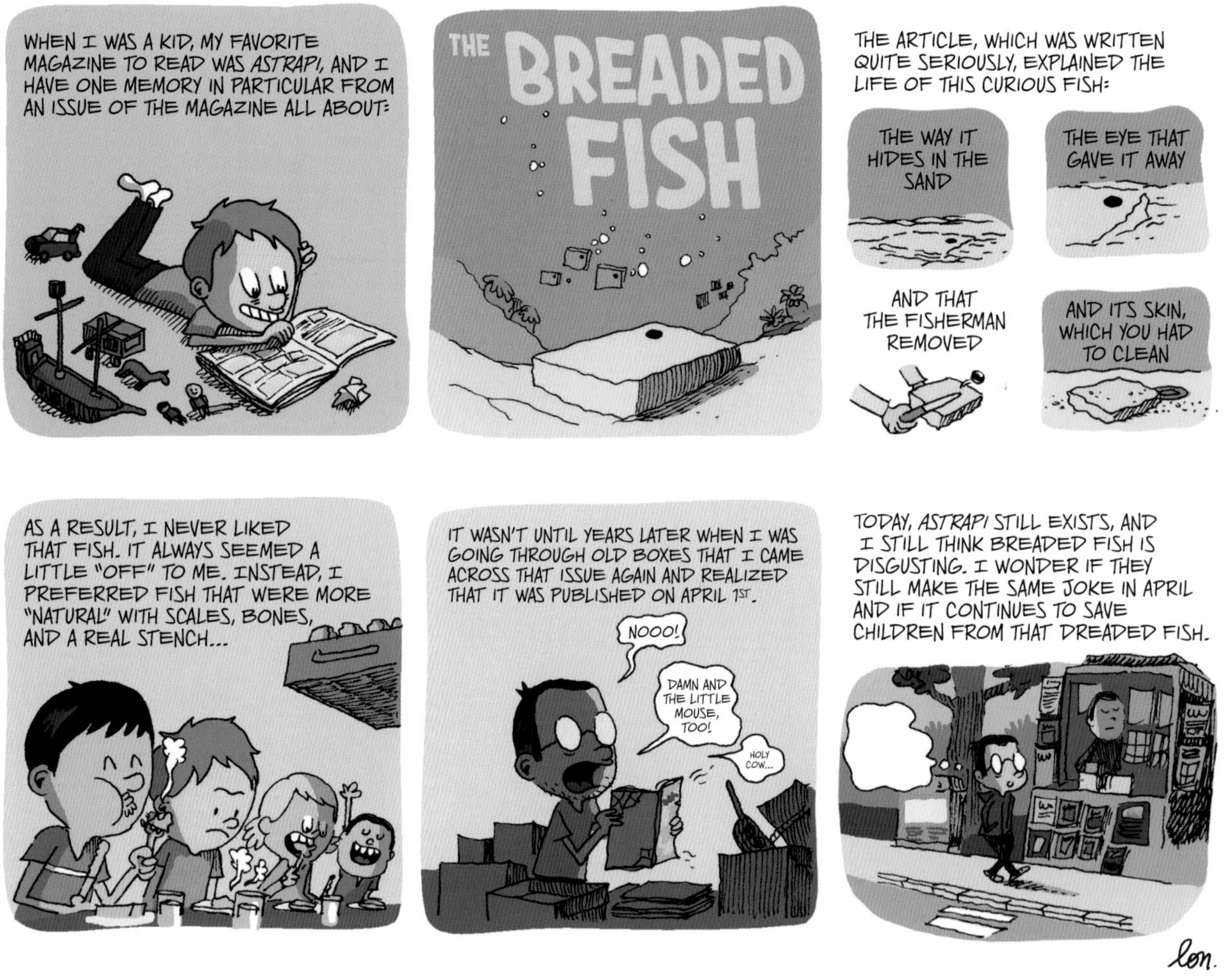
WHEN I WAS A KID, MY FAVORITE MAGAZINE TO READ WAS *ASTRAPI*, AND I HAVE ONE MEMORY IN PARTICULAR FROM AN ISSUE OF THE MAGAZINE ALL ABOUT:
THE BREADED FISH
THE ARTICLE, WHICH WAS WRITTEN QUITE SERIOUSLY, EXPLAINED THE LIFE OF THIS CURIOUS FISH:
THE WAY IT HIDES IN THE SAND
THE EYE THAT GAVE IT AWAY
AND THAT THE FISHERMAN REMOVED
AND ITS SKIN, WHICH YOU HAD TO CLEAN
AS A RESULT, I NEVER LIKED THAT FISH. IT ALWAYS SEEMED A LITTLE "OFF" TO ME. INSTEAD, I PREFERRED FISH THAT WERE MORE "NATURAL" WITH SCALES, BONES, AND A REAL STENCH...
IT WASN'T UNTIL YEARS LATER WHEN I WAS GOING THROUGH OLD BOXES THAT I CAME ACROSS THAT ISSUE AGAIN AND REALIZED THAT IT WAS PUBLISHED ON APRIL 1ST.
NOOO!
DAMN AND THE LITTLE MOUSE, TOO!
HOLY COW...
TODAY, *ASTRAPI* STILL EXISTS, AND I STILL THINK BREADED FISH IS DISGUSTING. I WONDER IF THEY STILL MAKE THE SAME JOKE IN APRIL AND IF IT CONTINUES TO SAVE CHILDREN FROM THAT DREADED FISH.
lon.

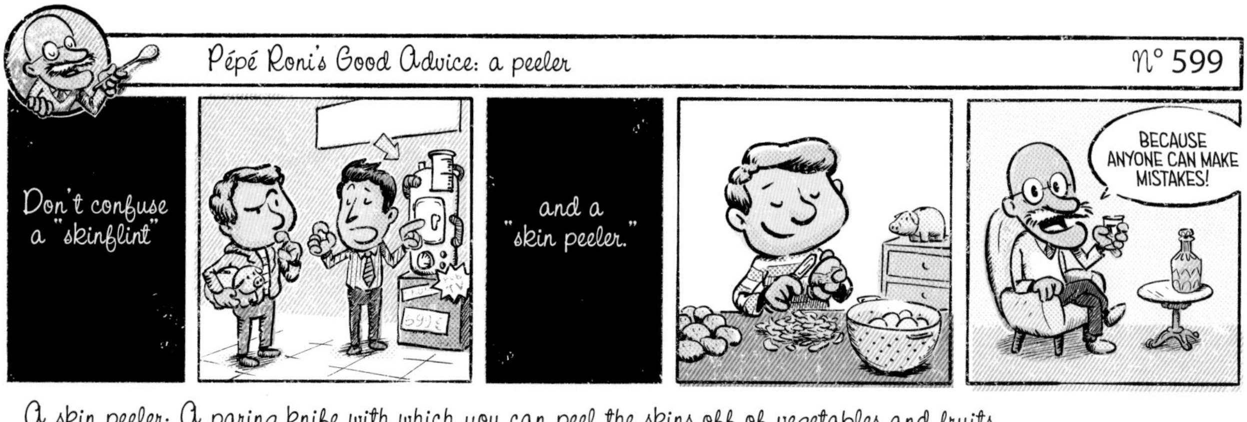
Pépé Roni's Good Advice: a peeler
N° 599
Don't confuse a "skinflint"
and a "skin peeler."
BECAUSE ANYONE CAN MAKE MISTAKES!

A skin peeler: A paring knife with which you can peel the skins off of vegetables and fruits.

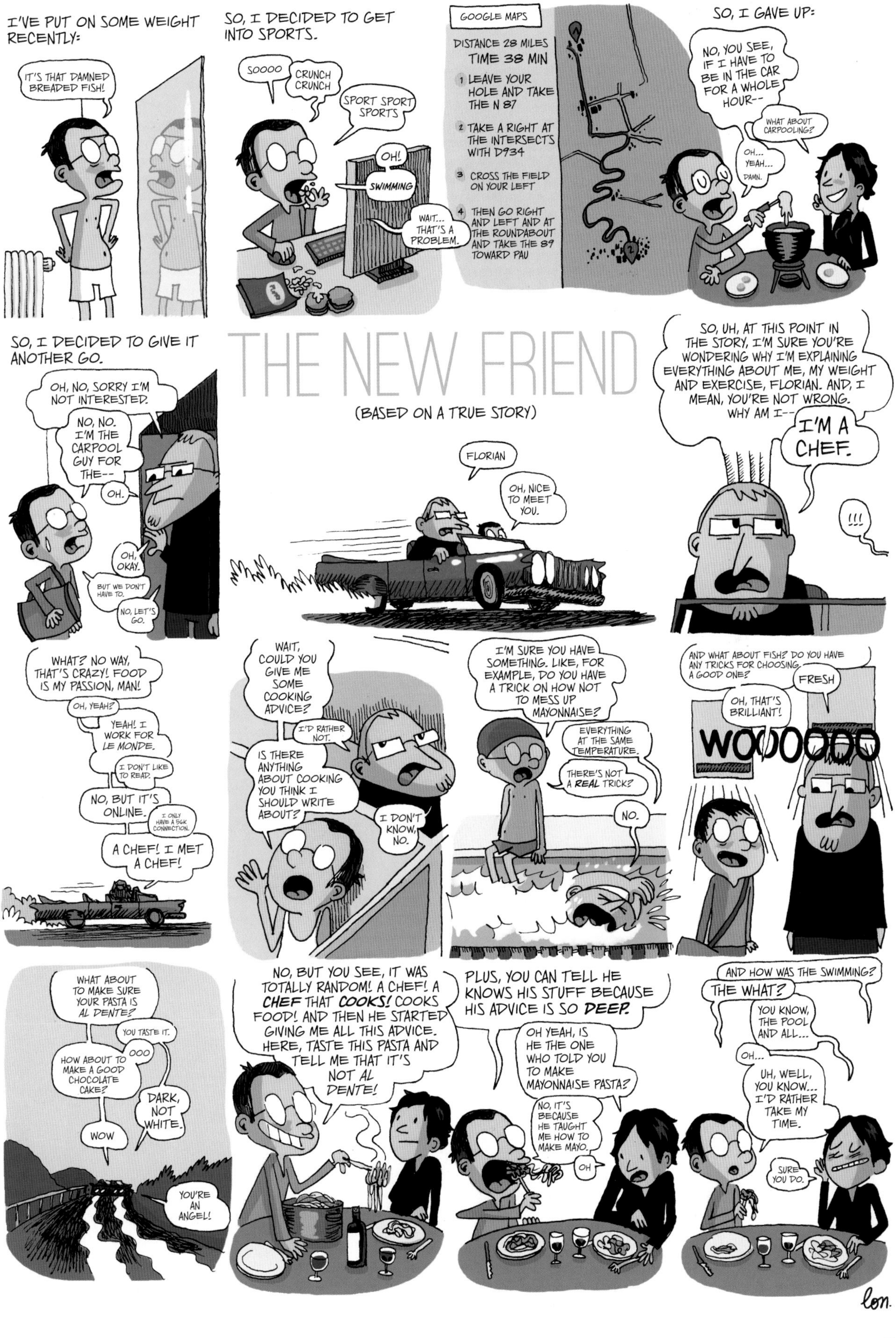
I'VE PUT ON SOME WEIGHT RECENTLY:
IT'S THAT DAMNED BREADED FISH!
SO, I DECIDED TO GET INTO SPORTS.
SOOOO
CRUNCH CRUNCH
SPORT SPORT SPORTS
OH!
SWIMMING
WAIT... THAT'S A PROBLEM.
GOOGLE MAPS
DISTANCE 28 MILES
TIME 38 MIN
1 LEAVE YOUR HOLE AND TAKE THE N 87
2 TAKE A RIGHT AT THE INTERSECTS WITH D934
3 CROSS THE FIELD ON YOUR LEFT
4 THEN GO RIGHT AND LEFT AND AT THE ROUNDABOUT AND TAKE THE 89 TOWARD PAU
SO, I GAVE UP:
NO, YOU SEE, IF I HAVE TO BE IN THE CAR FOR A WHOLE HOUR--
WHAT ABOUT CARPOOLING?
OH... YEAH...
DAMN.
SO, I DECIDED TO GIVE IT ANOTHER GO.
OH, NO, SORRY I'M NOT INTERESTED.
NO, NO. I'M THE CARPOOL GUY FOR THE--
OH.
OH, OKAY.
BUT WE DON'T HAVE TO.
NO, LET'S GO.
THE NEW FRIEND
(BASED ON A TRUE STORY)
FLORIAN
OH, NICE TO MEET YOU.
SO, UH, AT THIS POINT IN THE STORY, I'M SURE YOU'RE WONDERING WHY I'M EXPLAINING EVERYTHING ABOUT ME, MY WEIGHT AND EXERCISE, FLORIAN. AND, I MEAN, YOU'RE NOT WRONG. WHY AM I--
I'M A CHEF.
!!!
WHAT? NO WAY, THAT'S CRAZY! FOOD IS MY PASSION, MAN!
OH, YEAH?
YEAH! I WORK FOR LE MONDE.
I DON'T LIKE TO READ.
NO, BUT IT'S ONLINE.
I ONLY HAVE A 56K CONNECTION.
A CHEF! I MET A CHEF!
WAIT, COULD YOU GIVE ME SOME COOKING ADVICE?
I'D RATHER NOT.
IS THERE ANYTHING ABOUT COOKING YOU THINK I SHOULD WRITE ABOUT?
I DON'T KNOW, NO.
I'M SURE YOU HAVE SOMETHING. LIKE, FOR EXAMPLE, DO YOU HAVE A TRICK ON HOW NOT TO MESS UP MAYONNAISE?
EVERYTHING AT THE SAME TEMPERATURE.
THERE'S NOT A REAL TRICK?
NO.
AND WHAT ABOUT FISH? DO YOU HAVE ANY TRICKS FOR CHOOSING A GOOD ONE?
FRESH
OH, THAT'S BRILLIANT!
WOOOOOO
WHAT ABOUT TO MAKE SURE YOUR PASTA IS AL DENTE?
YOU TASTE IT.
OOO
HOW ABOUT TO MAKE A GOOD CHOCOLATE CAKE?
DARK, NOT WHITE.
WOW
YOU'RE AN ANGEL!
NO, BUT YOU SEE, IT WAS TOTALLY RANDOM! A CHEF! A CHEF THAT COOKS! COOKS FOOD! AND THEN HE STARTED GIVING ME ALL THIS ADVICE. HERE, TASTE THIS PASTA AND TELL ME THAT IT'S NOT AL DENTE!
PLUS, YOU CAN TELL HE KNOWS HIS STUFF BECAUSE HIS ADVICE IS SO DEEP.
OH YEAH, IS HE THE ONE WHO TOLD YOU TO MAKE MAYONNAISE PASTA?
NO, IT'S BECAUSE HE TAUGHT ME HOW TO MAKE MAYO.
OH
AND HOW WAS THE SWIMMING?
THE WHAT?
YOU KNOW, THE POOL AND ALL...
OH...
UH, WELL, YOU KNOW... I'D RATHER TAKE MY TIME.
SURE YOU DO.
lon.

YOU TOOK YOUR NISSAN PATROL©, YOUR QUECHUA TENT©, YOUR VICTORINOX© SWISS KNIFE, DRESSED IN YOUR CAMEL TROPHY EXPLORER'S OUTFIT. AND EVEN AN RPG-7 YOU FOUND ON EBAY© THAT'S IN YOUR TRUNK.

BEAR'S GARLIC

I... I DID IT!

ALL BECAUSE, FOR THE FIRST TIME, YOU'RE GOING TO GATHER RAMSONS--OR BEAR'S GARLIC--AND BECAUSE, IN YOUR MIND, YOU THINK IT'LL BE LIKE:

SO, IT'S A LITTLE SHOCKING WHEN YOU REALIZE THAT YOU CAN ACTUALLY FIND RAMSONS IN ALMOST ANY UNDERGROWTH IN LARGE QUANTITIES:

OH WOW.

ACTUALLY, YOU CAN EVEN PAY A LOT OF MONEY TO BUY 3.5 OZ WORTH AT THE LOCAL ORGANIC GROCERY STORE:

YEAH, YEAH WE GET IT! SHEESH.

YOU DECIDE TO TRY TO MAKE A NUTRITIOUS PUREE FOR YOUR SON.

TCHAC TCHAC TCHAC TCHAC

UNFORTUNATELY: YOU CONFUSE RAMSONS WITH LILY OF THE VALLEY (EXTREMELY POISONOUS):

NO, DON'T... YUMM SLURRP 100 Toxic Plants

OKAY, WELL AT LEAST YOUR SECOND TRY AT THE SOUP IS BOUND TO BE A SUCCESS WITH YOUR WIFE:

HONEY, I'VE GOT TO TELL YOU SOMETHING... BUT LET'S EAT FIRST!

OH, UH, SORRY! YOU DIDN'T KNOW THAT COLCHICUM HAD THE SAME LEAVES, BUT JUST IN A LARGER SIZE?

THIS IS STARTING TO BE A LITTLE MUCH JUST FOR AN AROMATIC HERB... DAMN BEAR'S GARLIC

WELL, IT'S ALL RIGHT. YOU CAN FIND SOME ACTUAL BEAR'S GARLIC PICKED BY PEOPLE WHO KNOW WHAT THEY'RE DOING FOR SALE AT A REALLY HIGH PRICE AT THE LOCAL ORGANIC MARKET.

AH, BEAR'S GARLIC! YES, YOU REALLY SHOULDN'T GET IT WRONG... I MEAN, WELL, IT DOES SMELL OF GARLIC WHEN YOU CRUSH IT, AND IT COVERS THE UNDERGROWTHS WITH SMALL WHITE FLOWERS.

OH, SPEAKING OF... ARE YOU SURE THERE'S NO RISK OF ECHINOCOCCOSIS WHERE YOU--

ECHINO-CO-WHAT?

I... I...

SHEESH, THIS KOUNEN BROTHERS FILM ISN'T GREAT...

BEAR'S GARLIC IS REALLY GOOD AND NOT THAT COMPLICATED TO PREPARE SAFELY-- LIKE IN A PESTO, FOR EXAMPLE...

FOR A
Bear's Garlic Pesto

① YOU NEED A HANDFUL OF HERBS YOU'VE WASHED **VERY** WELL.

THEN YOU PUT THEM IN A POT OF BOILING WATER, FOR ONE OR TWO MINUTES.

FLPFLOP

③ ONCE YOU'VE DRAINED THEM AS MUCH AS POSSIBLE, YOU MIX THE LEAVES WITH OLIVE OIL:

BVV VRVV VRR

WHICH SHOULD GIVE YOU A SORT OF SLIGHTLY LIQUID, GREEN PASTE WHICH YOU SEASON WITH SALT AND PEPPER.

② THEN YOU DRAIN IT AND RINSE WITH COLD WATER AND ICE CUBES TO STOP THE LEAVES FROM COOKING AND TO HELP SET THE COLOR OF THE LEAVES:

AND THAT'S IT! YOU CAN KEEP IT IN THE FRIDGE FOR A WEEK, AND YOU CAN PUT IT IN PASTA, A RISOTTO, OR A SALAD!

AND IT'S DELI-CIOUS!

SEE YOU NEXT TIME, AND BON APPÉTIT!

Flowers

Stem

Leaves

Bulbs

Bear's garlic

lon.

YOU'RE PROBABLY PART OF THE

52%

OF FRENCH PEOPLE

WHO BELIEVE THEY EAT TOO MUCH MEAT, IN GENERAL, AND SAY THAT THEY PREFER FISH AND THAT IT'S BETTER FOR THEIR HEALTH.

EXACTLY THE SAME AMOUNT OF PEOPLE WHO ARE AGAINST--

NOW HOLD ON A MINUTE!

THAT'S NOT NORMAL, YOU KNOW!

OR ELSE YOU OPEN THE DOOR TO A LOT OF OTHER THINGS.

AND IT'S TOTALLY NORMAL TO BE AGAINST THAT!

EVEN IF IT HAS **NOTHING** TO DO WITH IT.

HOWEVER, EVEN IF YOU BELONG TO THIS MAJORITY, YOU (BERNARD) DON'T ACT ACCORDINGLY WHEN BUYING GROCERIES.

BECAUSE EVEN THOUGH YOU MIGHT KNOW YOUR STUFF IN THE MEAT SECTION...

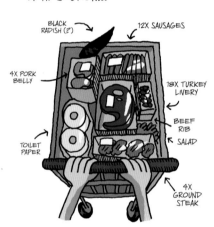

BLACK RADISH (?) · 12X SAUSAGES · 4X PORK BELLY · 18X TURKEY LIVERY · BEEF RIB · SALAD · TOILET PAPER · 4X GROUND STEAK

IN THE FRESH FISH SECTION...

HERE'S THE TRUTH

OH SHIT, WHAT DO I DO?

ONLY REMEMBERS HOW TO COOK BREADED FISH

FISHMONGER WHO SAW YOU AND IS GOING TO ASK YOU WHAT KIND OF FISH YOU WANT

THE FILETS DANCE A BALLET IN FRONT OF YOU.

RED SNAPPER · CATFISH · BLUEFISH · BASS · POLLOCK · MACKEREL · PIKE · GUPPY · ESCOLAR · DRUM

A THOUSAND DIFFERENT NAMES ALL PRONOUNCED EXOTICALLY!

FOR A SECOND, YOU THINK ABOUT RUNNING AWAY TO THE ORGANIC FOOD ISLE AND BUYING TOFU INSTEAD...

WITH STEAMED BROCCOLI? WHAT A TREAT!

BUT YOU STILL HAVE YOUR DIGNITY!

FORTUNATELY *A SOLUTION EXISTS*

NO MORE HUMILIATION

NO MORE UNKNOWN NAMES

NO MORE MUSTACHE

YOU CAN HOLD YOUR HEAD UP HIGH WITH YOUR FISHMONGER THANKS TO...

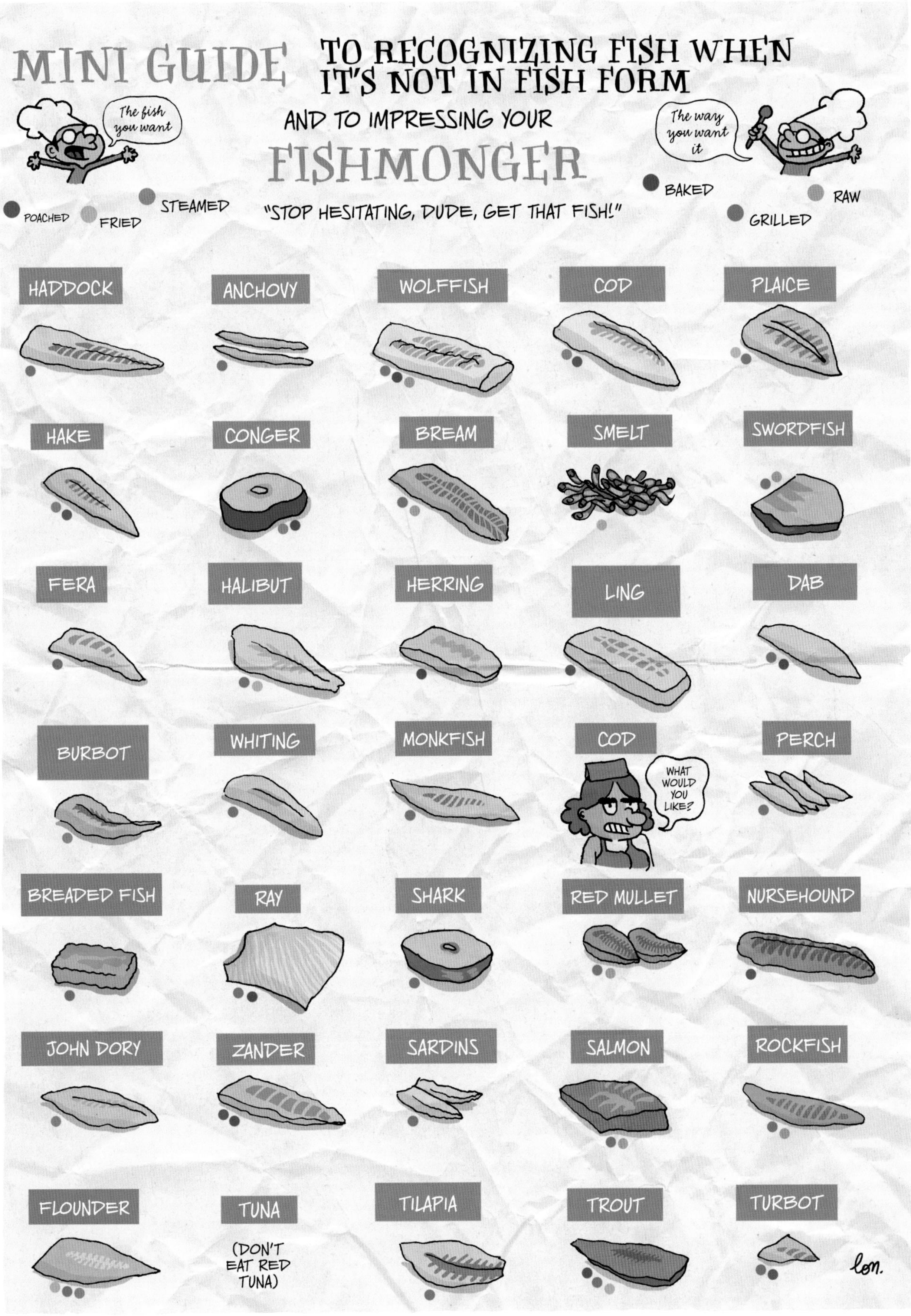
MINI GUIDE
TO RECOGNIZING FISH WHEN IT'S NOT IN FISH FORM
AND TO IMPRESSING YOUR
FISHMONGER
The fish you want
The way you want it
"STOP HESITATING, DUDE, GET THAT FISH!"
POACHED
FRIED
STEAMED
BAKED
GRILLED
RAW
HADDOCK
ANCHOVY
WOLFFISH
COD
PLAICE
HAKE
CONGER
BREAM
SMELT
SWORDFISH
FERA
HALIBUT
HERRING
LING
DAB
BURBOT
WHITING
MONKFISH
COD
WHAT WOULD YOU LIKE?
PERCH
BREADED FISH
RAY
SHARK
RED MULLET
NURSEHOUND
JOHN DORY
ZANDER
SARDINS
SALMON
ROCKFISH
FLOUNDER
TUNA
(DON'T EAT RED TUNA)
TILAPIA
TROUT
TURBOT
lon.

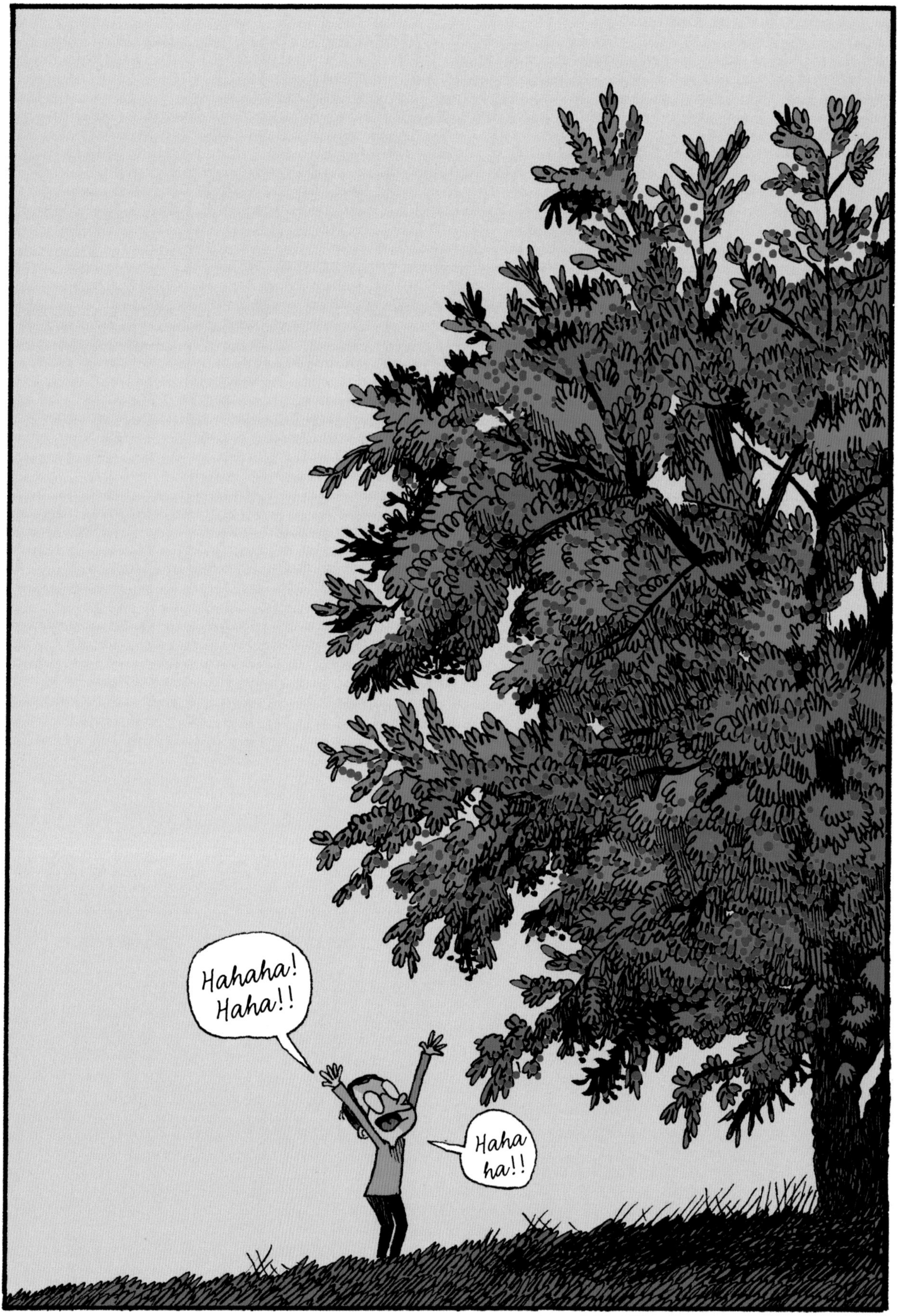
Hahaha! Haha!!
Haha ha!!

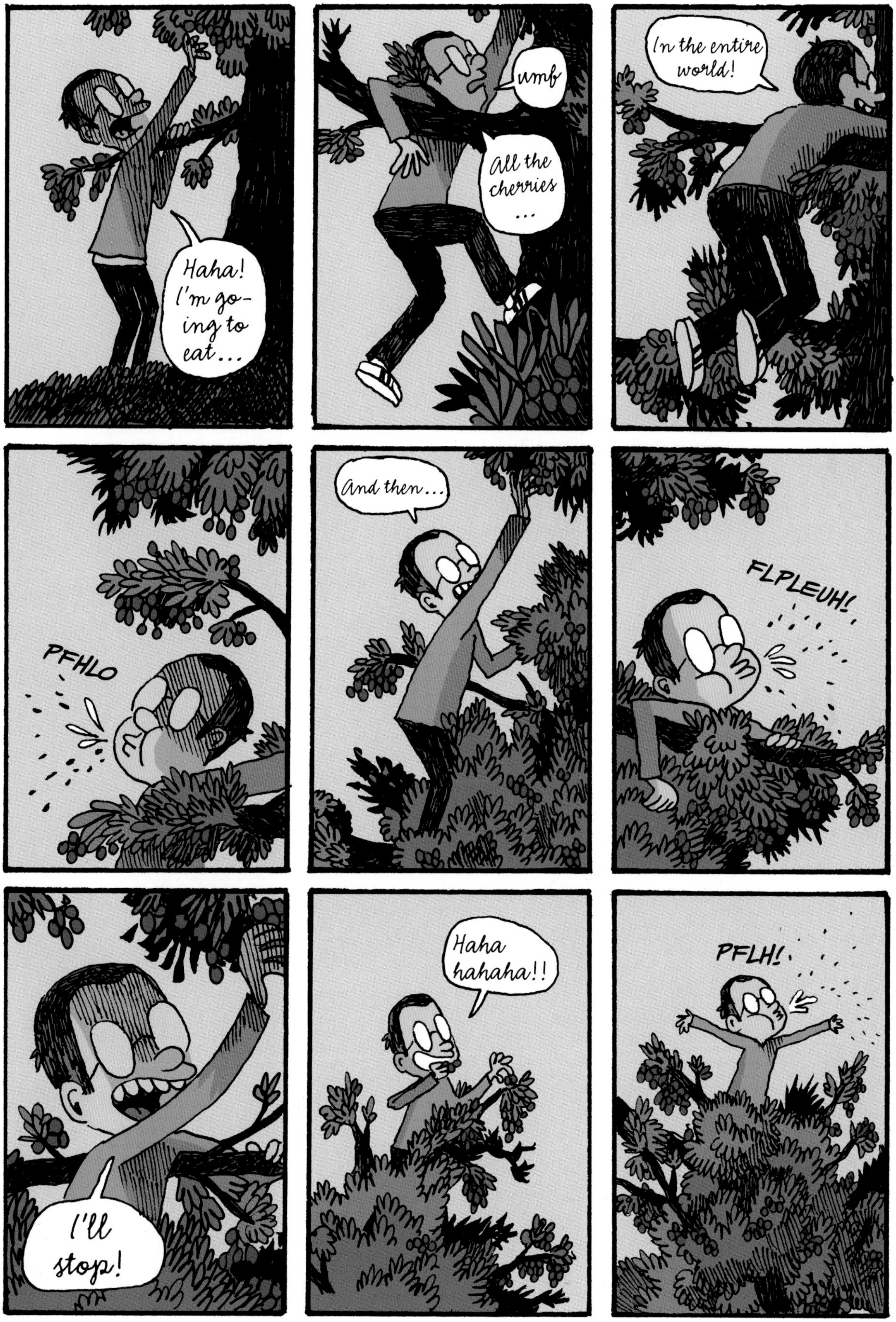
Haha! I'm go- ing to eat...
umf
All the cherries ...
In the entire world!
PFHLO
And then...
FLPLEUH!
I'll stop!
Haha hahaha!!
PFLH!

Cherry time

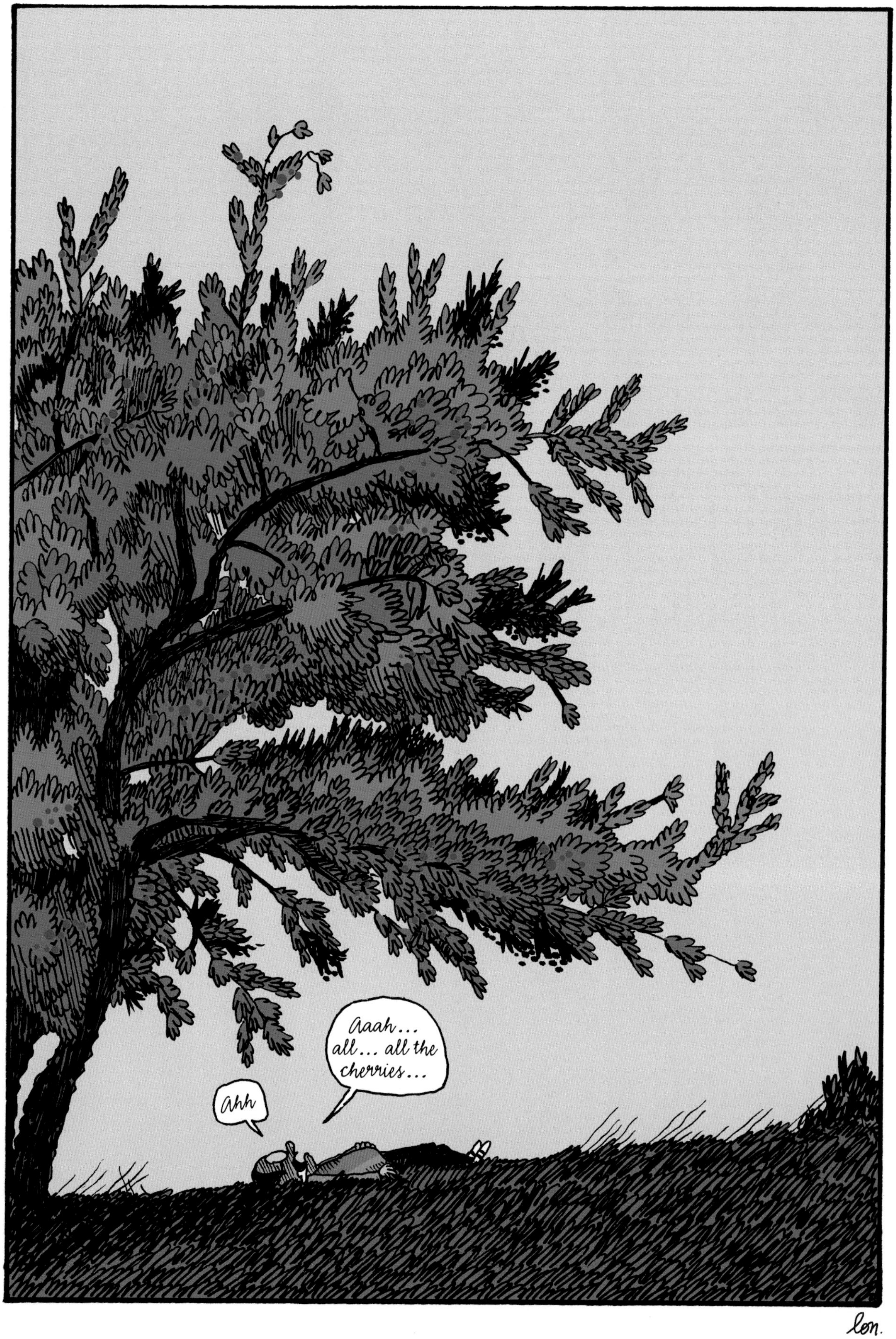
Ahh
Aaah... all... all the cherries...
lon.

EVERYTHING STARTED THE OTHER DAY, WHEN I WAS BUYING FISH...

HELLO...

I'D LIKE A FILET OF PLAICE...

TO... FRY.

HOW IS HE DOING THAT? *WHAT* IS THAT PAPER?

EVERYTHING WAS GOING WELL, AND THEN...

HE SAID THE FOLLOWING:

NO PROBLEM...

ARE YOU GOING TO FLOUR IT?

GOT HIM.

YOU COULD'VE JUST FRIED YOUR FILLET LIKE YOU PLANNED.

BUT YOU HAVE TO ADMIT...

FLOURED FISH IS DELICIOUS.

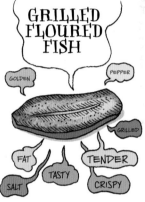

GRILLED FLOURED FISH

GOLDEN   PEPPER

GRILLED

FAT   TENDER

SALT   TASTY   CRISPY

YOU FIND YOURSELF WITH A FILET IN THE AIR, YOUR HAND READY TO PLUNGE INTO THE FLOUR LIKE AL PACINO IN *SCARFACE* SHOVING HIS FACE INTO A MOUNTAIN OF COKE.

HAHA HAHA!

DON'T FUCK WITH ME!

I'M TONY MONTANA!

WELL, THERE'S A MUCH SIMPLER WAY TO FLOUR A FISH!

THOUGH IT MIGHT BE A LITTLE LESS DRAMATIC.

HAHAHA!

TAKE A RANDOM PLASTIC BAG.

NOT A HUGE ONE.

YOU KNOW, A SMALL ONE LIKE YOU MIGHT FIND IN NATURE...

DRIFTING AWAY FROM THEIR SUPERMARKET HOMES.

THE SMALL ONES LIKE FROM A SUPERMARKET.

THE ONES YOU PAY FOR WHEN YOU FORGET TO BRING YOUR OWN BAGS (TOTALLY YOUR FAULT).

OPEN IT AND PUT A FEW SPOONS OF FLOUR INSIDE.

BUT NOT TOO MUCH.

SEASON THE FISH WITH SALT AND PEPPER, AND PUT IT IN THE BAG!

I HOPE, FOR YOUR SAKE, THAT YOUR BAG DOESN'T HAVE ANY HOLES.

CLOSE THE BAG TIGHTLY, AND THEN SHAKE IT HARD.

GNNY

RUSSIAN TONY MONTANA

FLFL FLFL

AND VOILA. YOU HAVE A BEAUTIFUL FILET, WELL-FLOURED, READY TO FRY, WITHOUT MAKING A MESS OF YOUR KITCHEN.

SHAKE OFF THE EXCESS FLOUR.

FRY IT UP WITH A LITTLE BIT OF FAT.

FCCHHHH

PSHIII

SOME LEMON TO DELGAZE IT.

AND REUSE THE PLASTIC BAG AS TRASH.

EEEK!

I FOLLOWED ALL THE STEPS, AND I BURNED IT!

I FORGOT: IF YOU'RE USING GROCERY BAGS, MAKE SURE YOU'VE REMOVED THE RECEIPT BEFORE FLOURING YOUR FISH.

AND ENJOY YOUR MEAL!

SHIT... IT BURNS!

leon.

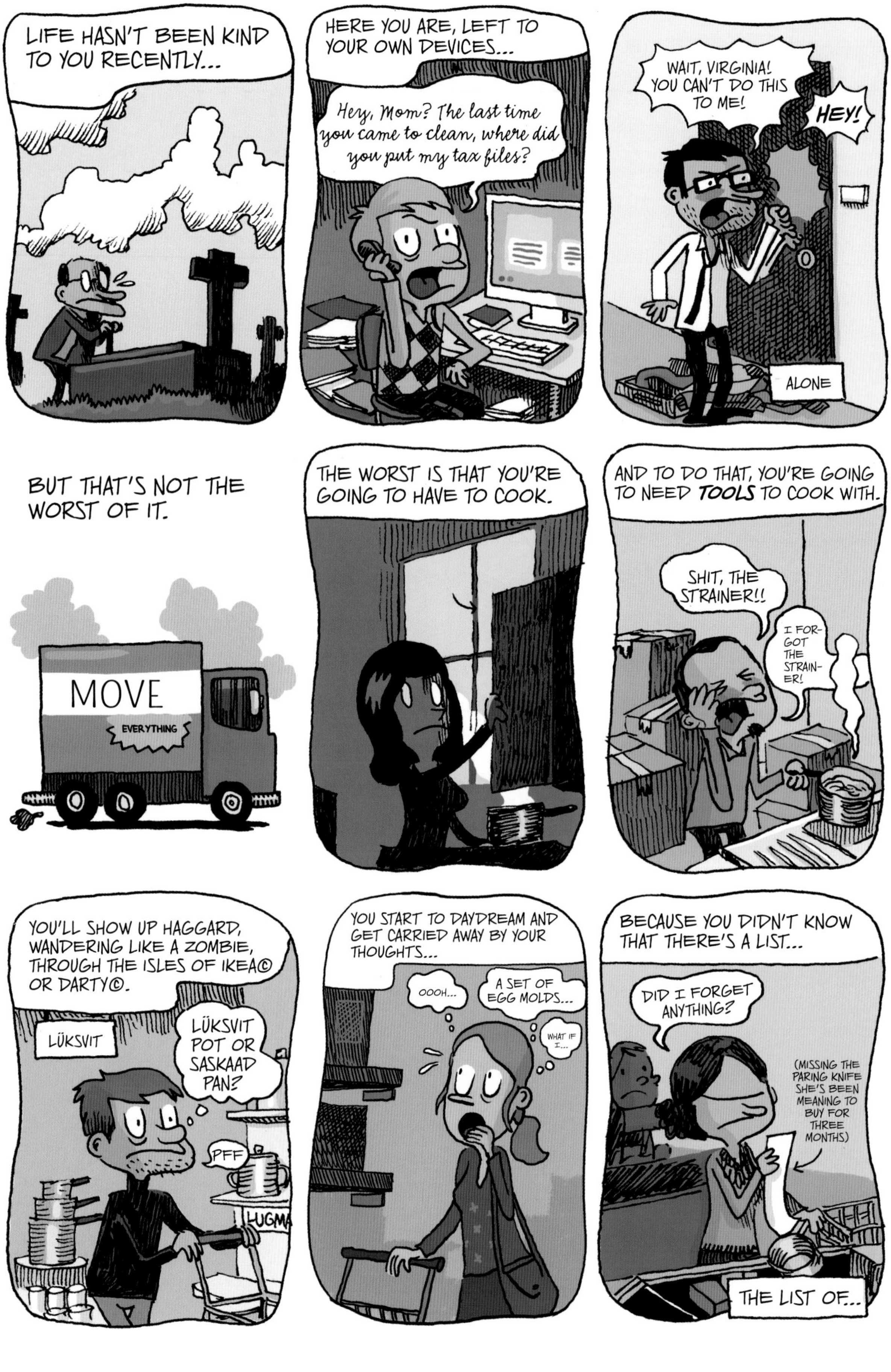
LIFE HASN'T BEEN KIND TO YOU RECENTLY...
HERE YOU ARE, LEFT TO YOUR OWN DEVICES...
Hey, Mom? The last time you came to clean, where did you put my tax files?
WAIT, VIRGINIA! YOU CAN'T DO THIS TO ME!
HEY!
ALONE
BUT THAT'S NOT THE WORST OF IT.
MOVE
EVERYTHING
THE WORST IS THAT YOU'RE GOING TO HAVE TO COOK.
AND TO DO THAT, YOU'RE GOING TO NEED TOOLS TO COOK WITH.
SHIT, THE STRAINER!!
I FORGOT THE STRAINER!
YOU'LL SHOW UP HAGGARD, WANDERING LIKE A ZOMBIE, THROUGH THE ISLES OF IKEA© OR DARTY©.
LÜKSVIT
LÜKSVIT POT OR SASKAAD PAN?
PFF
LUGMA
YOU START TO DAYDREAM AND GET CARRIED AWAY BY YOUR THOUGHTS...
OOOH...
A SET OF EGG MOLDS...
WHAT IF I...
BECAUSE YOU DIDN'T KNOW THAT THERE'S A LIST...
DID I FORGET ANYTHING?
(MISSING THE PARING KNIFE SHE'S BEEN MEANING TO BUY FOR THREE MONTHS)
THE LIST OF...

A FEW USEFUL TOOLS FOR YOUR KITCHEN

NO MORE FORGETTING!

INK INK!

① TWO SHARP KNIVES ARE A GOOD START:

ONE SMALL

ONE BIG, WHILE YOU'RE AT IT

② A CUTTING BOARD MIGHT NOT SEEM LIKE MUCH, BUT IS SUPER PRACTICAL:

LUXURY MODEL WITH A GROOVE TO KEEP ANY JUICES FROM LEAKING

③ A PEELER OR PARING KNIFE TO PEEL VEGETABLES:

MY PREFERRED MODEL

ANOTHER KIND

④ A GRATER FOR VARIOUS PEELED VEGETABLES:

THIS ONE IS PRACTICAL BUT ANNOYING TO CLEAN

⑤ A SAUCEPAN, BUT NOT ONE MADE OUT OF TIN--THEY STICK:

DECENT SIZE

SOLID HANDLE

⑥ A PAN OR A WOK, IF NOT BOTH:

LARGE DIAMETER, EASY TO HANDLE

DEEP, USEFUL FOR BIG DISHES

⑦ A LARGE POT FOR FAMILY STYLE DISHES:

GOOD HANDLES

MADE OF STAINLESS STEEL, LIGHT AND HANDY

A DURABLE CAST-IRON ONE THAT WILL LAST

⑧ A LARGE LID:

GROOVES TO FIT POTS OF ANY SIZE

NON-STICK COATING, USEFUL FOR FLIPPING OMELETS.

⑨ A MEASURING CUP, FOR BAKING:

IN GLASS, CLASSY BUT FRAGILE

IN PLASTIC, NOTHING TO FEAR (MINE IS TEN YEARS OLD)

⑩ A SCALE WHILE YOU'RE AT IT, ELECTRONIC OR MECHANICAL:

OLD SCHOOL

PRECISE MEASUREMENTS

⑪ A SALAD BOWL, FOR MIXING:

(NOTHING SPECIAL TO SAY HERE)

⑫ A WHISK OR ELECTRIC BEATER, IF NOT BOTH:

PRACTICAL FOR REMOVING LUMPS

BEST FOR WHIPPING EGG WHITES

⑬ A WOODEN SPOON AND A SPATULA:

FOR TOSSING

TO GRIP AND FLIP

⑭ A STRAINER, BUT NOT A PLASTIC ONE, THEY SUCK:

(SEE COMMENTS ON SALAD BOWL)

⑮ A CORKSCREW:

THE "DE GAULE" MODEL THAT RAISES ITS ARMS

I UNDER- STAND YOU!

VINEYARD MODEL, RUSTIC STYLE

⑯ A LADLE AND SKIMMER:

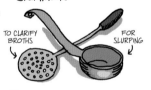

TO CLARIFY BROTHS

FOR SLURPING

⑰ A BAKING DISH:

ONE WITH HANDLES IS BEST

⑱ A PIE AND CAKE MOLD:

PYREX ONES ARE GREAT FOR PIZZA

SILICONE IS IDEAL

⑲ A CITRUS PRESS:

YOU CAN GET AN ELECTRIC ONE

...BUT A LITTLE EXERCISE NEVER HURT ANYONE

⑳ AN ELECTRIC MIXER:

SIMPLER MODEL

INDUSTRIAL FACTORY STYLE

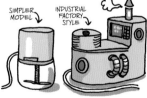

㉑ A PAIR OF SCISSORS:

TO CUT PACKAGING AND STRINGS...

㉒ A GARLIC MILL:

THE HOLY GRAIL OF ALL CHEFS

㉓ A BRASS SAUCIER, NOT REQUIRED BUT VERY CLASSY:

IDEAL FOR BASIL SAUCES

㉔ A PESTLE:

STONE

METAL

WOOD

lon.

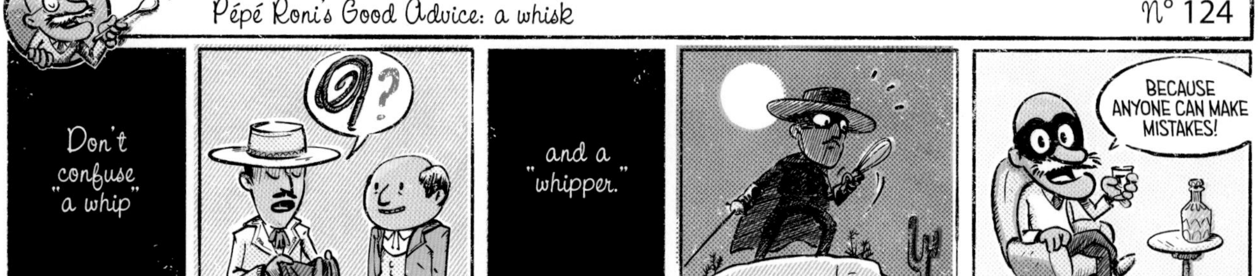
Pépé Roni's Good Advice: a whisk
N° 124
Don't confuse "a whip"
and a "whipper."
BECAUSE ANYONE CAN MAKE MISTAKES!

Whisk: A tool to whip, beat, or mix food items.

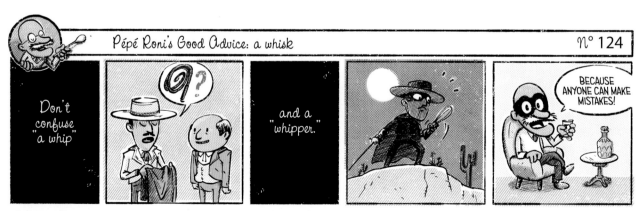

JOURNAL FROM BUDAPEST

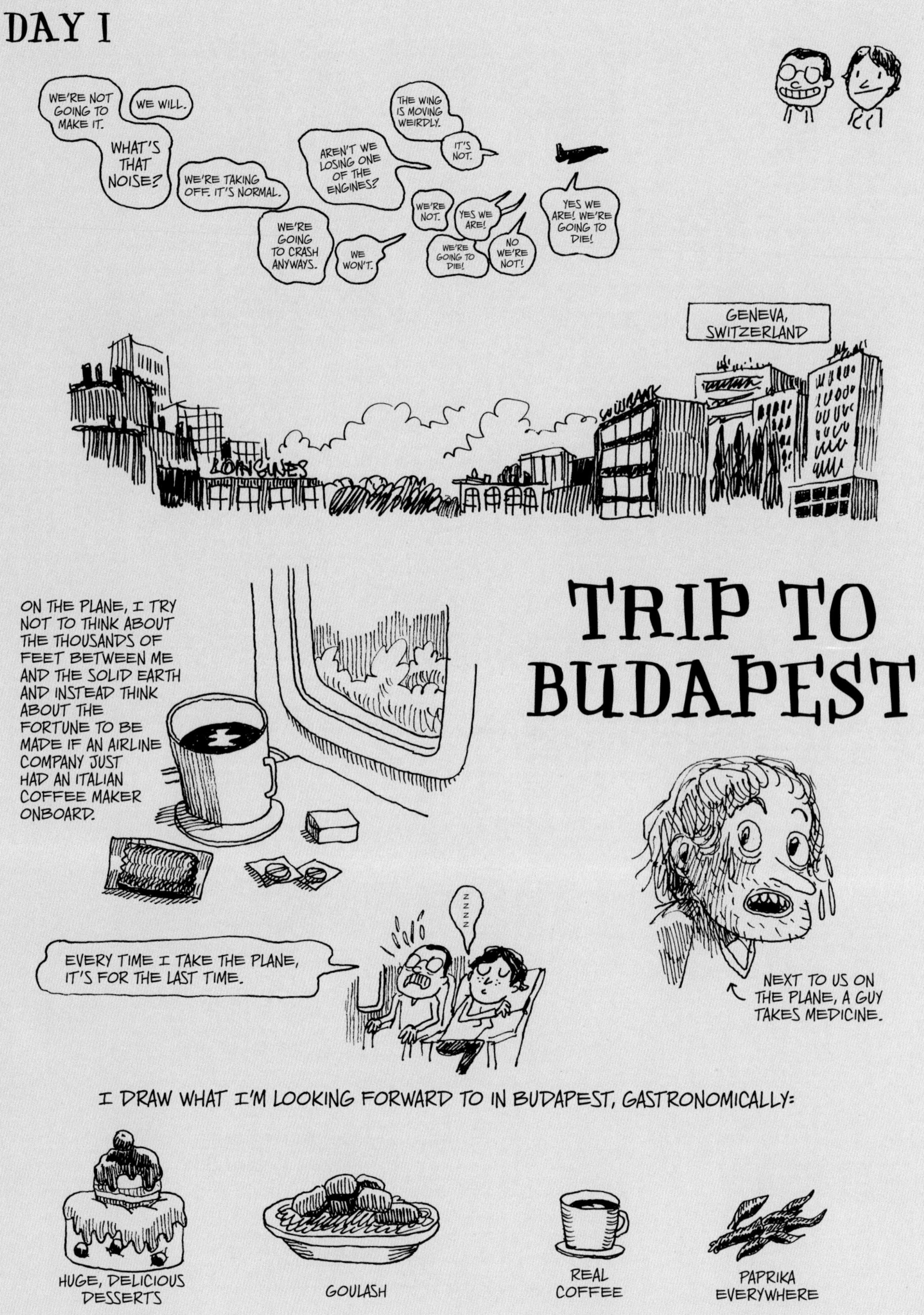
DAY I
WE'RE NOT GOING TO MAKE IT.
WE WILL.
WHAT'S THAT NOISE?
WE'RE TAKING OFF. IT'S NORMAL.
WE'RE GOING TO CRASH ANYWAYS.
WE WON'T.
AREN'T WE LOSING ONE OF THE ENGINES?
WE'RE NOT.
YES WE ARE!
WE'RE GOING TO DIE!
NO WE'RE NOT!
THE WING IS MOVING WEIRDLY.
IT'S NOT.
YES WE ARE! WE'RE GOING TO DIE!
GENEVA, SWITZERLAND
TRIP TO BUDAPEST
ON THE PLANE, I TRY NOT TO THINK ABOUT THE THOUSANDS OF FEET BETWEEN ME AND THE SOLID EARTH AND INSTEAD THINK ABOUT THE FORTUNE TO BE MADE IF AN AIRLINE COMPANY JUST HAD AN ITALIAN COFFEE MAKER ONBOARD.
EVERY TIME I TAKE THE PLANE, IT'S FOR THE LAST TIME.
ZZZZ
NEXT TO US ON THE PLANE, A GUY TAKES MEDICINE.
I DRAW WHAT I'M LOOKING FORWARD TO IN BUDAPEST, GASTRONOMICALLY:
HUGE, DELICIOUS DESSERTS
GOULASH
REAL COFFEE
PAPRIKA EVERYWHERE

WORDS TO KNOW:

KÁVÉHÁZ = CAFÉ (THE PLACE)

ÉTTEREM = RESTAURANT

KÖSZÖNÖM = THANKS

HALLO = HELLO, HEY

HAZANCZKY UT

KEUSSEUNEUM.

APPARENTLY, HUNGARIANS DON'T LIKE THE FRENCH.

FIRST MEAL IN HUNGARY AT THE GERLOCZY KÁVÉHÁZ, FIRST ENCOUNTER WITH LOCAL CUISINE:

OKAY, SO WHEN WE ORDER GOULASH WE GET A GOULASH *SOUP*.

WE HAVE TO ASK FOR PÖRKÖLT INSTEAD.

BREAKFAST (PRETTY GOOD, SPECIAL MENTION TO THE GOULASH SOUP) IN A SUNLIT PATIO BY A TREE. NANCY ORDERS SOME SORT OF CHICKEN STUFFED WITH CHEESE.

A TREE WITH HANGING BRANCHES AND POMPOMS OF FLOWERS ↗

SERVICE

NYMLÖGÖTZ PLÖKTMENKT WÜGLÖNGÖT

KEUSSEUNEUM, DUDE

PUGÖ, TRUKUL

IGÉN, IGÉN

15%

WHEN YOU RECEIVE THE CHECK (USUALLY A NICE SURPRISE, AROUND 20 EUROS FOR TWO, EVEN WITH A GLASS OF WINE), YOU USUALLY HAVE TO LEAVE 10% TO 15% OF THE COST OF THE MEAL AS A TIP FOR THE SERVICE (TO BE PRECISE: IF THE SERVICE WAS GOOD).

WRÖLÖ TENEM

AND BECAUSE THE WAIT STAFF ARE GENERALLY VERY NICE, WE'RE USUALLY MORE THAN HAPPY TO PAY FOR THE SERVICE.

IF WE DID THE SAME THING IN PARIS, THE WAITERS WOULDN'T GET A DIME FOR THEIR SERVICE!

SERIOUSLY

(LIVED IN PARIS FOR 5 YEARS)

AT NIGHT, A FORGETTABLE DINNER AT THE DARSHAN, NEAR THE HOTEL. THE DECOR IS WEIRD--STUCK SOMEWHERE BETWEEN INDIA AND AFRICA. THEY SERVE EVERYTHING HERE: PIZZAS, GREEK SALADS, TANDOORI CHICKEN, AND STEAK TARTAR. SO, AS EXPECTED, EVERYTHING'S PRETTY AVERAGE.

DAY 2

A TRAP FOR THE SWEET-TOOTHED... WE SPEND SEVERAL HOURS INSIDE ONE OF THE TEMPLES OF HUNGARIAN PASTRIES...

A SORT OF PREAMBLE →

OH... WELL A REALLY SMALL SLICE THEN...

DESSERTS AREN'T REALLY MY THING, EXCEPT FOR MOM'S APPLE TARTS AND MOLTEN LAVA CAKE, OF COURSE...

IT LOOKS GOOD...

I JUST DON'T HAVE MUCH OF A SWEET TOOTH.

PLENTY OF CAKES HERE!

ANNO 1858 — GERBEAUD — BUDAPEST

THEY'LL DRIVE YOU CRAZY!

NANCY, I CAN'T...

YES, YOU CAN!

← CHOCOHOLIC

GERBEAUD, A SORT OF CATNIP FOR WOMEN

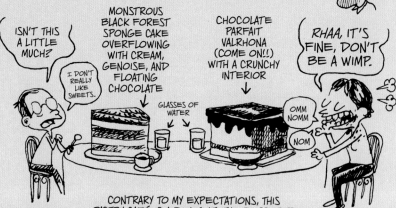

ISN'T THIS A LITTLE MUCH?

I DON'T REALLY LIKE SWEETS.

MONSTROUS BLACK FOREST SPONGE CAKE OVERFLOWING WITH CREAM, GENOISE, AND FLOATING CHOCOLATE

GLASSES OF WATER

CHOCOLATE PARFAIT VALRHONA (COME ON!!) WITH A CRUNCHY INTERIOR

RHAA, IT'S FINE, DON'T BE A WIMP.

OMM NOMM NOM

CONTRARY TO MY EXPECTATIONS, THIS PASTRY CAFÉ IS A DELIGHT: THE DESSERTS ARE EXCELLENT (SPONGE CAKE) AND AS FULL OF CREAM AS THEY ARE LIGHT IN YOUR STOMACH, NO JOKE. DIDN'T EVEN MAKE ME SICK!

HINHIN! COFFEE! IN HUNGARY! HUHU!

SLRRRRP

WOW. THAT'S GOOD.

REALLY GOOD.

NANSS TAKES A TRUE WOMAN'S COFFEE, A "MADEMOISELLE," WITH A PRONOUNCED TASTE OF CARAMEL TOPPED WITH A HEAPING PORTION OF WHIPPED CREAM. IT'S DELICIOUS.

YOU CAN TELL YOU'RE HAVING **GOOD COFFEE** BY THE FACT THAT IT'S ALWAYS SERVED WITH A GLASS OF WATER.

THE NIGHT

DINNER AT NÁROLY ETTEREM, NAROLY UT.

WE EAT DINNER IN A REALLY GREAT RESTAURANT, WITH A WONDERFUL BUDAPEST-STYLE DECOR: ARCHITECTURAL ARCHES, PAINTINGS, ORNAMENTS, AND A REDDISH-BROWN TINT.

YOU HAVE TO TAKE A PATH FROM THE STREET (UTCA) AND YOU ARRIVE IN A CHARMING INTERIOR HALL WHERE THE RESTAURANT IS.

THE DINNER STARTS OFF WELL WITH A DEER SOUP!! IT'S SERVED IN A BREAD BOWL-- A GREAT IDEA. THE SOUP IS FULL OF FLAVOR, WELL SPICED AND GAMEY (THOUGH I'VE NEVER HAD DEER BEFORE). IT'S ACCOMPANIED BY A GLASS OF TOKAJ WINE. I LIKE IT SO FAR.

THEN, I ORDER A ZANDER FILET WITH POTATOES...

BLACK BREAD FULL OF SOUP...

THE PROMISE

HUNGARIAN ZANDER STRAIGHT FROM THE BALATON!! ZANDER IS ALREADY A STAR AMONG FRESHWATER FISH, WITH A THIN FLESH, A GREAT SMELL, A TENDER TEXTURE, AND AN IVORY COLOR! ZANDER! FRESH ZANDER! FROM LAKE BALATON! HAND-FISHED!

← NANCY ON HER SIDE

MMH, THIS IS DELICOUS! A CHICKEN FILET IN A POTATO CREPE. BUT I REALLY CAN'T HAVE A DESSERT.

THE REALITY

MY GOD

I'M SO DIS-APPOINTED

SO DIS-APPOINTED

THE ZANDER IS HERE, GLOOMY, TASTELESS, LYING DEAD IN THE MIDDLE OF THE PLATE WITH A MOUNTAIN OF WATERY, UNDERCOOKED POTATOES. IT'S PRACTICALLY CARDBOARD AND DOESN'T DESERVE TO BE CALLED FISH.

NO, YOU SEE, THE BEST WAY TO HAVE REAL, FRESH, SPINY LOBSTERS IS TO FRY THEM UP ON THE BARBECUE, LIKE THIS!

YOU PUT JUST A LITTLE BIT OF GARLIC ON TOP, AND A DROP OF OLIVE OIL.

LOOK AT THAT GOLDEN SKIN...

SMELL THAT!

LOOK AT THIS JUICY PIECE!

A LITTLE SLICE OF LEMON, SOME SALT... HERE, THIS PIECE IS CALLING FOR YOU.

PLOP

GNEEEEIN?

OH DAMN IT. COME ON...

TODAY, I'M GOING TO TRY TO COMPLETE TWO CHALLENGES:

(OH YES, I SHOULD PROBABLY TALK ABOUT THE HOTEL AND BREAKFAST... MAYBE TOMORROW?)

DETERMINED

CRUNCH CRUNCH

BUDAPEST DAY THREE

challenge no 1 :

Explain in English to a Hungarian the joke of Mr. and Mrs. "GariansinmybathroomwhatcanIdo" who have a son*, in its entirety while in a bath:

(the main reason for this trip, joke wise)

* Gideon

OKAY IT'S MR AND MRS "GARIANSINMYBATHROOMWHATCANIDO" AND THEY HAVE A SON...

NO? IT'S AEVON ! I-HAVE-HUN

I HAVE HUNGARIANS IN MY BATHROOM WHAT...

WELL

SHAME

IT WORKS BETTER IN FRENCH

BUT DIFFICULT TO EXPLAIN

challenge no2:

Try to leave a restaurant without paying for the bill

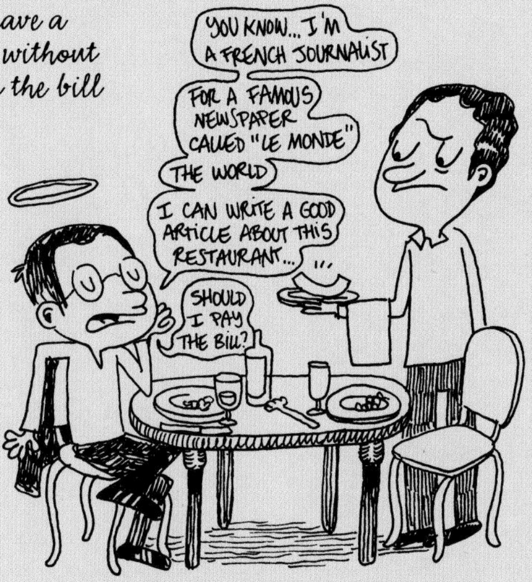

YOU KNOW... I'M A FRENCH JOURNALIST
FOR A FAMOUS NEWSPAPER CALLED "LE MONDE"
THE WORLD
I CAN WRITE A GOOD ARTICLE ABOUT THIS RESTAURANT...
SHOULD I PAY THE BILL?

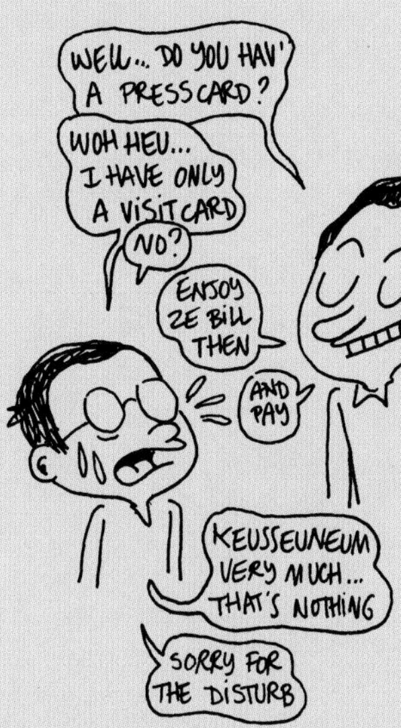

WELL... DO YOU HAV' A PRESSCARD?
WOH HEU... I HAVE ONLY A VISIT CARD
NO?
ENJOY ZE BILL THEN
AND PAY
KEUSSEUNEUM VERY MUCH... THAT'S NOTHING
SORRY FOR THE DISTURB

IN ADDITION, **KOLEVES** (KAZINCZY UTCA) WAS REALLY GOOD. IT WAS IN THE OLD JEWISH GHETTO IN BUDAPEST. IT LOOKS LIKE A BISTRO AND ALL THE WAITERS WERE YOUNG.

I ORDER AN ARTICHOKE CREAM SOUP AND SOME PINK DUCK BREAST WITH AN APPLE AND POTATO PUREE.

THE PROMISE

THERE ARE LAMPS MADE FROM IKEA GRATERS AND THESE REALLY NICE DRAWINGS AND PAINTINGS EVERYWHERE. VERY COOL!

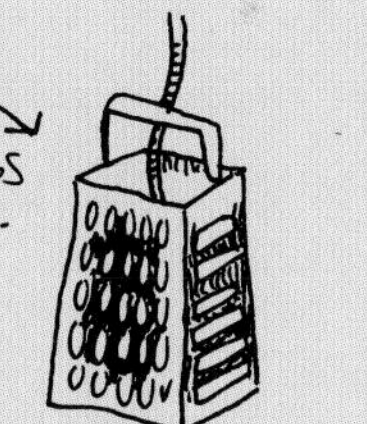

AND WHAT DO I GET? WELL, ***EXACTLY*** WHAT I ORDERED. IT'S DELICIOUS AND LOOKS GREAT, ***EXCEPT*** THAT I HADN'T ENVISIONED IT BEING QUITE SO...

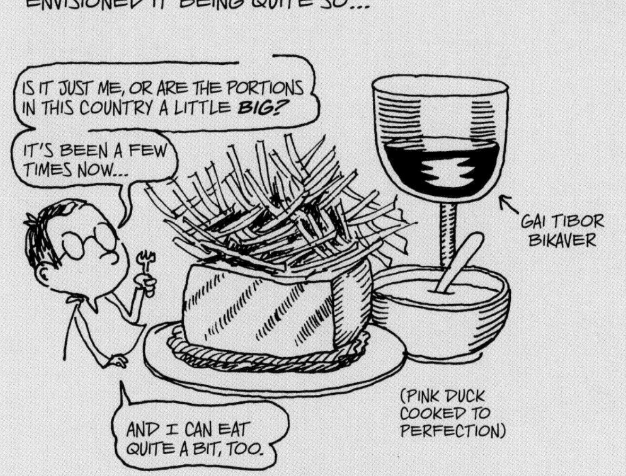

IS IT JUST ME, OR ARE THE PORTIONS IN THIS COUNTRY A LITTLE *BIG?*
IT'S BEEN A FEW TIMES NOW...
GAI TIBOR BIKAVER
(PINK DUCK COOKED TO PERFECTION)
AND I CAN EAT QUITE A BIT, TOO.

THE REALITY

WHEN WE PAY WITH A CREDIT CARD IN THE RESTAURANTS HERE, YOU CAN READ THIS AT THE BOTTOM OF YOUR RECEIPT:

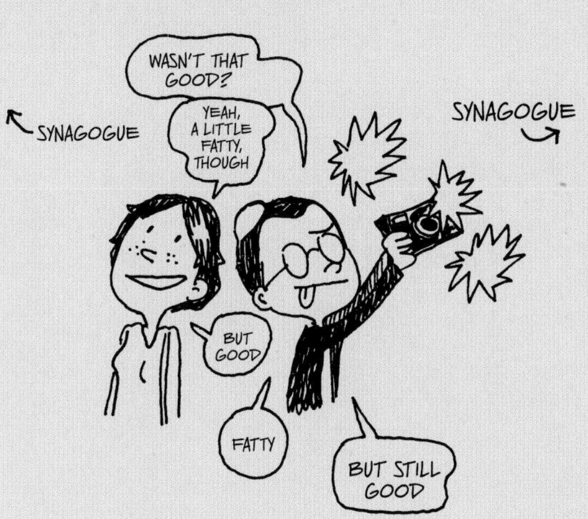

WASN'T THAT GOOD?
YEAH, A LITTLE FATTY, THOUGH
SYNAGOGUE
SYNAGOGUE
BUT GOOD
FATTY
BUT STILL GOOD

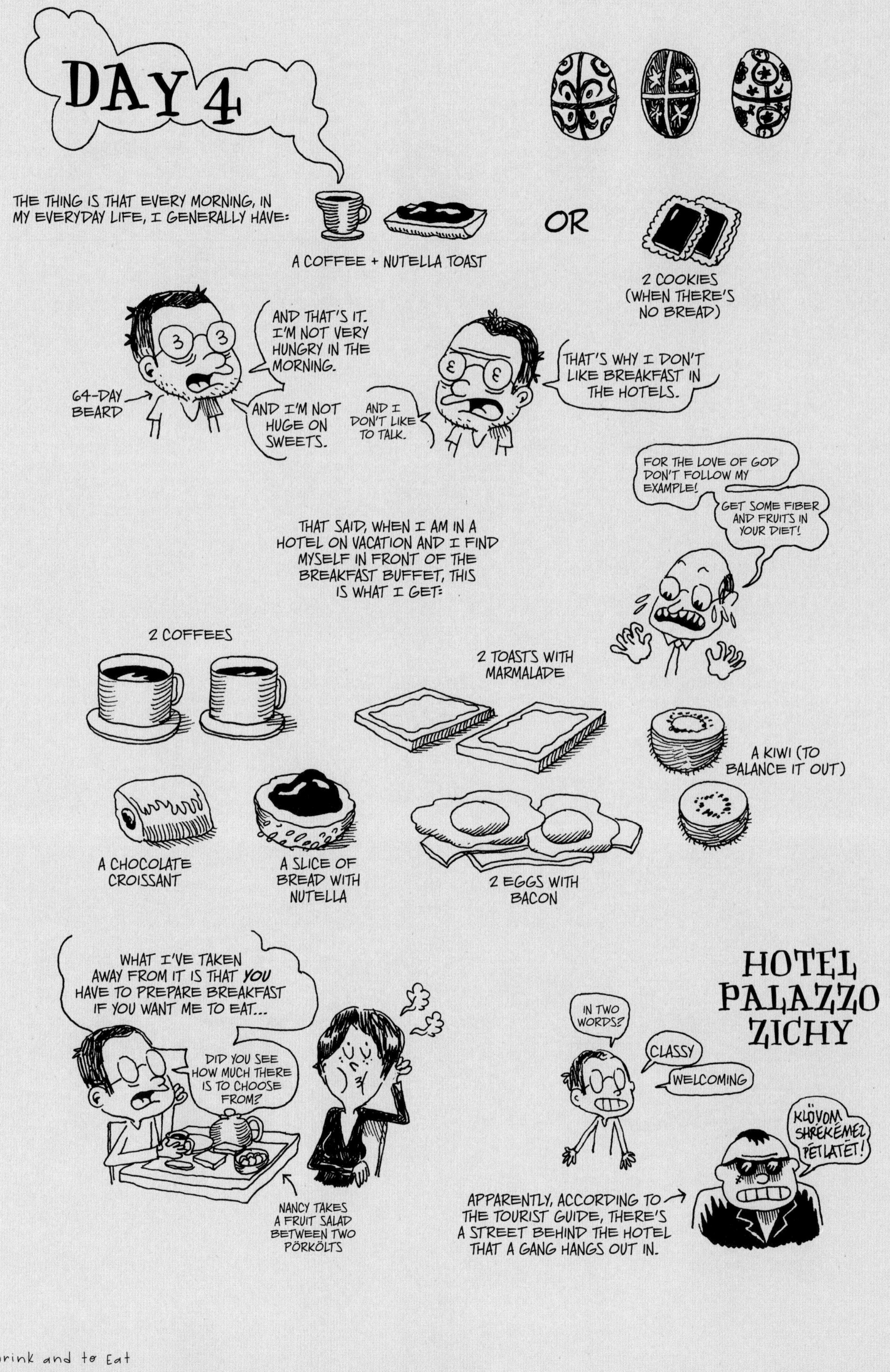
DAY 4
THE THING IS THAT EVERY MORNING, IN MY EVERYDAY LIFE, I GENERALLY HAVE:
A COFFEE + NUTELLA TOAST
OR
2 COOKIES (WHEN THERE'S NO BREAD)
AND THAT'S IT. I'M NOT VERY HUNGRY IN THE MORNING.
AND I'M NOT HUGE ON SWEETS.
64-DAY BEARD
AND I DON'T LIKE TO TALK.
THAT'S WHY I DON'T LIKE BREAKFAST IN THE HOTELS.
FOR THE LOVE OF GOD DON'T FOLLOW MY EXAMPLE!
GET SOME FIBER AND FRUITS IN YOUR DIET!
THAT SAID, WHEN I AM IN A HOTEL ON VACATION AND I FIND MYSELF IN FRONT OF THE BREAKFAST BUFFET, THIS IS WHAT I GET:
2 COFFEES
2 TOASTS WITH MARMALADE
A KIWI (TO BALANCE IT OUT)
A CHOCOLATE CROISSANT
A SLICE OF BREAD WITH NUTELLA
2 EGGS WITH BACON
WHAT I'VE TAKEN AWAY FROM IT IS THAT YOU HAVE TO PREPARE BREAKFAST IF YOU WANT ME TO EAT...
DID YOU SEE HOW MUCH THERE IS TO CHOOSE FROM?
NANCY TAKES A FRUIT SALAD BETWEEN TWO PÖRKÖLTS
HOTEL PALAZZO ZICHY
IN TWO WORDS?
CLASSY
WELCOMING
KLÖVOM SHRÉKÉMEZ PÉTLATÉT!
APPARENTLY, ACCORDING TO THE TOURIST GUIDE, THERE'S A STREET BEHIND THE HOTEL THAT A GANG HANGS OUT IN.

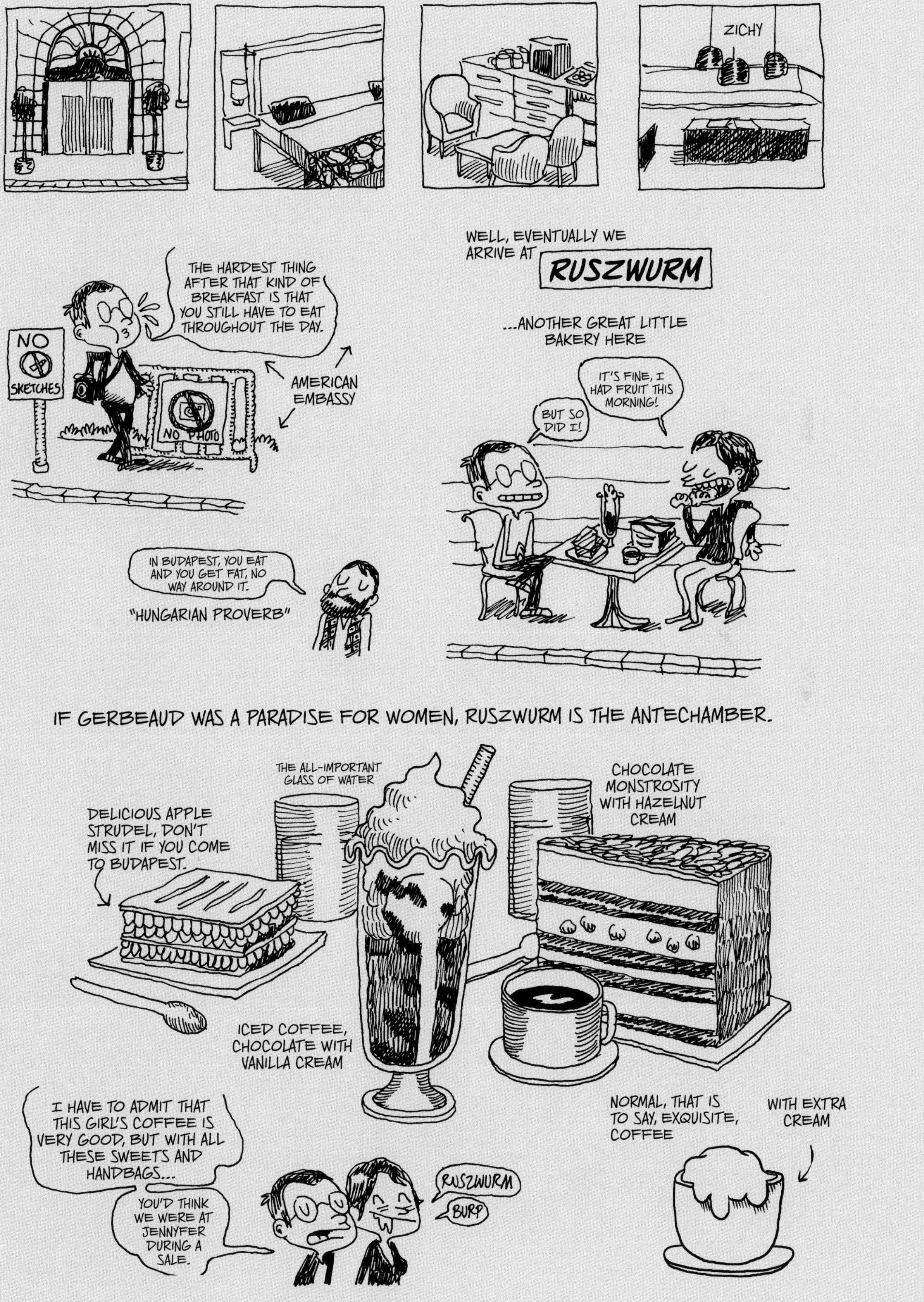
ZICHY
THE HARDEST THING AFTER THAT KIND OF BREAKFAST IS THAT YOU STILL HAVE TO EAT THROUGHOUT THE DAY.
NO SKETCHES
NO PHOTO
AMERICAN EMBASSY
IN BUDAPEST, YOU EAT AND YOU GET FAT, NO WAY AROUND IT.
"HUNGARIAN PROVERB"
WELL, EVENTUALLY WE ARRIVE AT
RUSZWURM
...ANOTHER GREAT LITTLE BAKERY HERE
IT'S FINE, I HAD FRUIT THIS MORNING!
BUT SO DID I!
IF GERBEAUD WAS A PARADISE FOR WOMEN, RUSZWURM IS THE ANTECHAMBER.
THE ALL-IMPORTANT GLASS OF WATER
DELICIOUS APPLE STRUDEL, DON'T MISS IT IF YOU COME TO BUDAPEST.
CHOCOLATE MONSTROSITY WITH HAZELNUT CREAM
ICED COFFEE, CHOCOLATE WITH VANILLA CREAM
I HAVE TO ADMIT THAT THIS GIRL'S COFFEE IS VERY GOOD, BUT WITH ALL THESE SWEETS AND HANDBAGS...
YOU'D THINK WE WERE AT JENNYFER DURING A SALE.
RUSZWURM
BURP
NORMAL, THAT IS TO SAY, EXQUISITE, COFFEE
WITH EXTRA CREAM

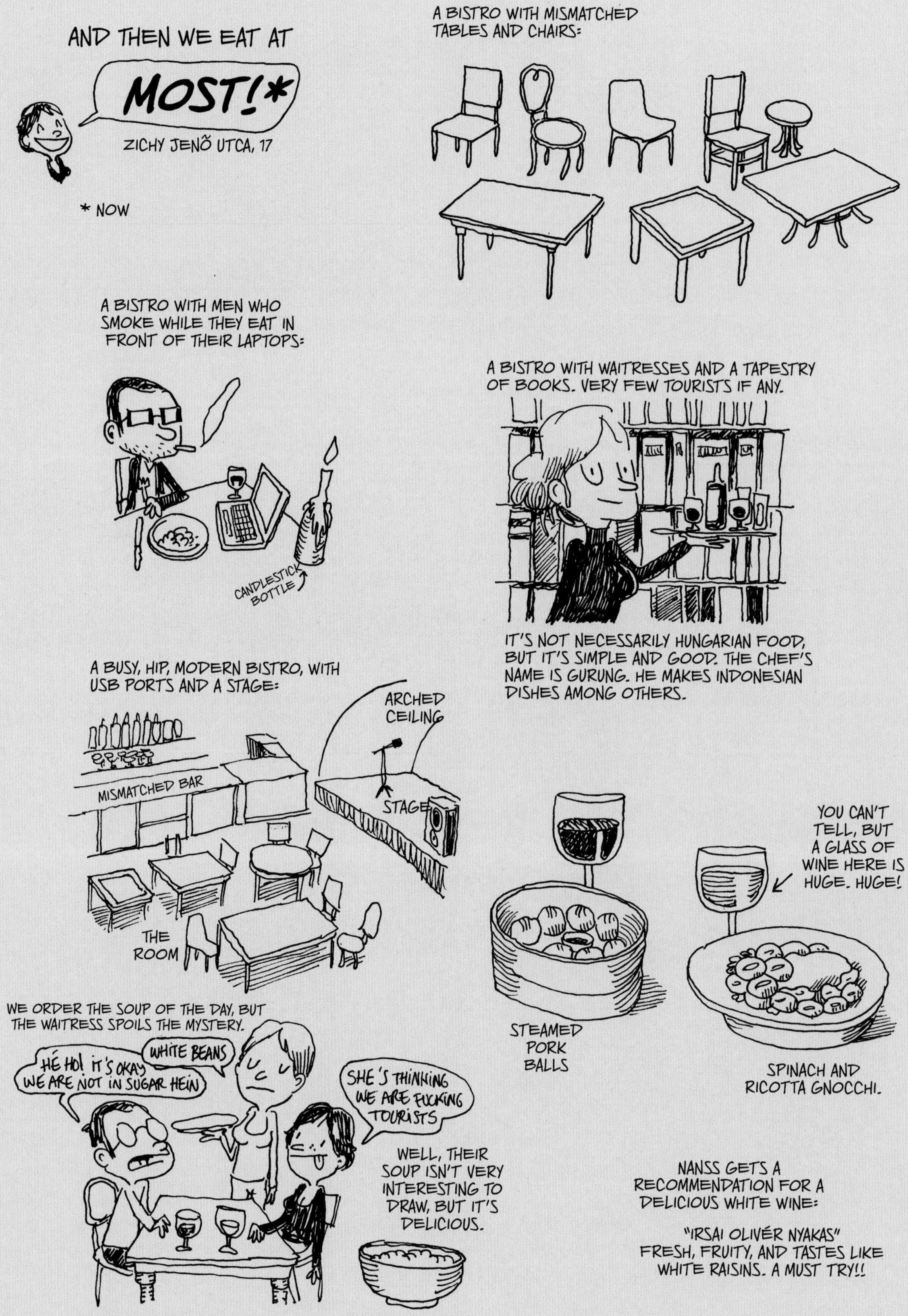
AND THEN WE EAT AT
MOST!*
ZICHY JENŐ UTCA, 17
* NOW
A BISTRO WITH MISMATCHED TABLES AND CHAIRS:
A BISTRO WITH MEN WHO SMOKE WHILE THEY EAT IN FRONT OF THEIR LAPTOPS:
CANDLESTICK BOTTLE
A BISTRO WITH WAITRESSES AND A TAPESTRY OF BOOKS. VERY FEW TOURISTS IF ANY.
IT'S NOT NECESSARILY HUNGARIAN FOOD, BUT IT'S SIMPLE AND GOOD. THE CHEF'S NAME IS GURUNG. HE MAKES INDONESIAN DISHES AMONG OTHERS.
A BUSY, HIP, MODERN BISTRO, WITH USB PORTS AND A STAGE:
ARCHED CEILING
MISMATCHED BAR
STAGE
THE ROOM
YOU CAN'T TELL, BUT A GLASS OF WINE HERE IS HUGE. HUGE!
STEAMED PORK BALLS
SPINACH AND RICOTTA GNOCCHI.
WE ORDER THE SOUP OF THE DAY, BUT THE WAITRESS SPOILS THE MYSTERY.
HÉ HO! IT'S OKAY WE ARE NOT IN SUGAR HEIN
WHITE BEANS
SHE'S THINKING WE ARE FUCKING TOURISTS
WELL, THEIR SOUP ISN'T VERY INTERESTING TO DRAW, BUT IT'S DELICIOUS.
NANSS GETS A RECOMMENDATION FOR A DELICIOUS WHITE WINE:
"IRSAI OLIVÉR NYAKAS" FRESH, FRUITY, AND TASTES LIKE WHITE RAISINS. A MUST TRY!!

DAY 5

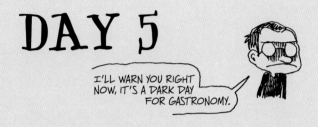

I'LL WARN YOU RIGHT NOW, IT'S A DARK DAY FOR GASTRONOMY.

ON THIS DAY, MY STOMACH EXPERIENCED ITS OWN APOCALYPSE.

WHAT? ? HUH?

IT DIDN'T START THAT WAY, THOUGH...

NAGY VASARCSARNOK
(CENTRAL MARKET, NA'MHA'Z, KÖRÜT, 1-3)

WOOOAH IT'S SO COOL!

CAN YOU GET UP NOW?

THOUSANDS OF SQUARE FEET ON TWO FLOORS MADE OF IRON AND GLASS, ENTIRELY DEDICATED TO FOOD!! IT REMINDS ME OF THE ENORMOUS MARKET IN BARCELONA (SAINT JOSEPH'S).

CHARCUTERIE, SPICES, VEGETABLES. ALL LIVING TOGETHER IN PACKED STALLS. THERE'S A WHOLE ETIQUETTE TO IT IN HUNGARY THAT I HAVE NO CLUE ABOUT, BUT I DON'T MIND.

ON THE UPPER FLOOR, WE EAT SIDE BY SIDE WITH HUNGARIANS AND OTHER TOURISTS. PEOPLE SMOKE. THE FOOD IS FATTY AND RICH. IT'S BEAUTIFUL.

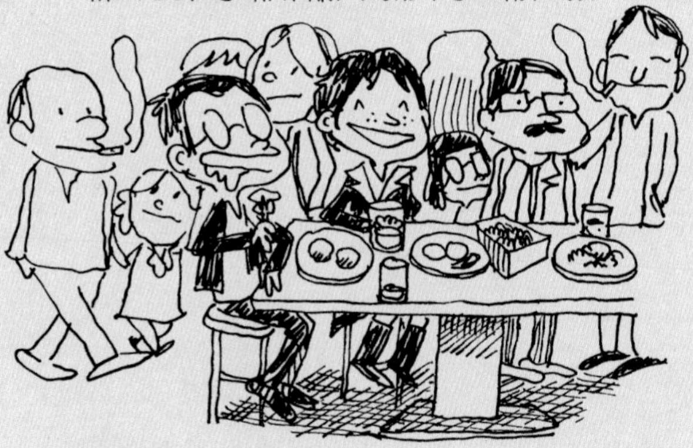

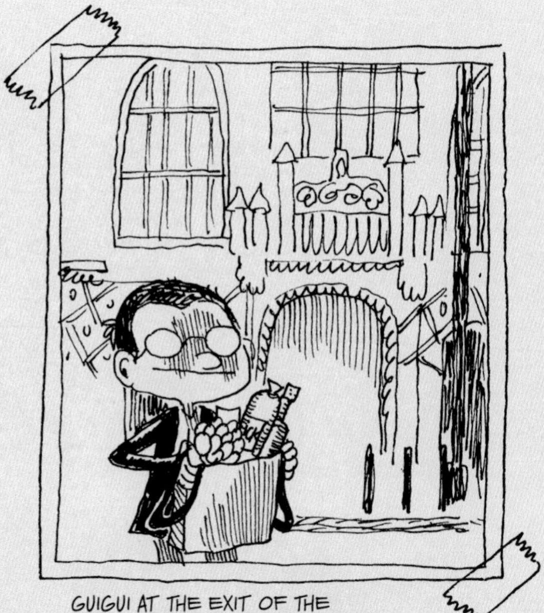

GUIGUI AT THE EXIT OF THE MARKET IN BUDAPEST WITH SOME SALAMI, RADISHES, TOKAJ, AND SPICES. (A FEW HOURS BEFORE THE ORDEAL)

ON OUR PLATES, MEATBALLS MADE WITH SOME SORT OF UNKNOWN MEAT, RICE SPICED WITH PAPRIKA, AND MYSTERY CROQUETTES. I WOULDN'T SAY IT WAS GOOD, I WOULD SAY IT WAS FATTY AND THAT IT LACKED TASTE.

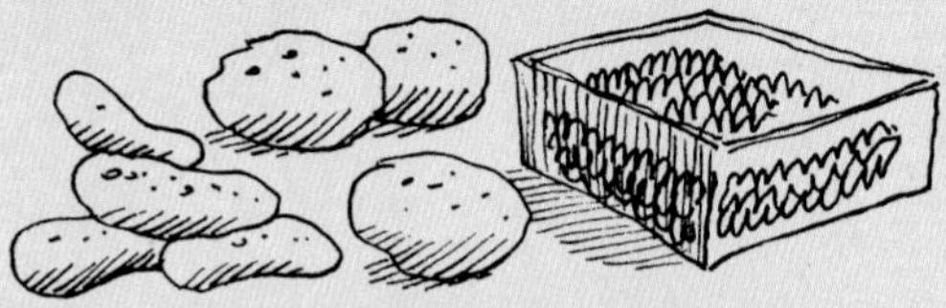

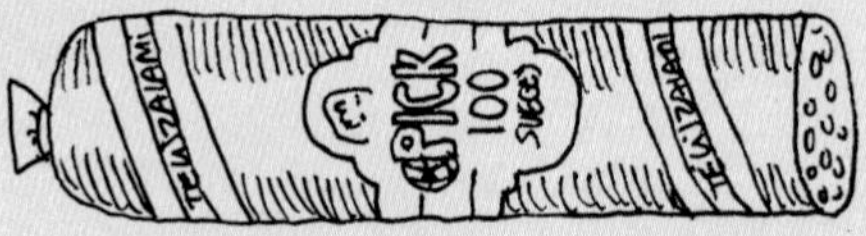
PICK

"KRÚJMÜT VLAPÖ PICK SKIYSCNYÉLT"*

* PICK, SIMPLY THE BEST

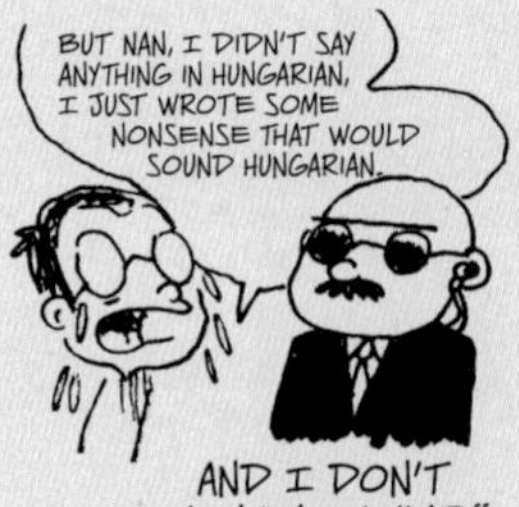
BUT NAN, I DIDN'T SAY ANYTHING IN HUNGARIAN, I JUST WROTE SOME NONSENSE THAT WOULD SOUND HUNGARIAN.

AND I DON'T EVEN KNOW VLAPÖ, HOW COULD I HAVE TOLD HIM TO GO SHOVE A SALAMI UP HIS ASS?

THE GOOD TIMES CONTINUED WELL INTO

CENTRAL KÁVÉHÁZ

CRAZY DECOR ALL AROUND, VERY 19TH CENTURY

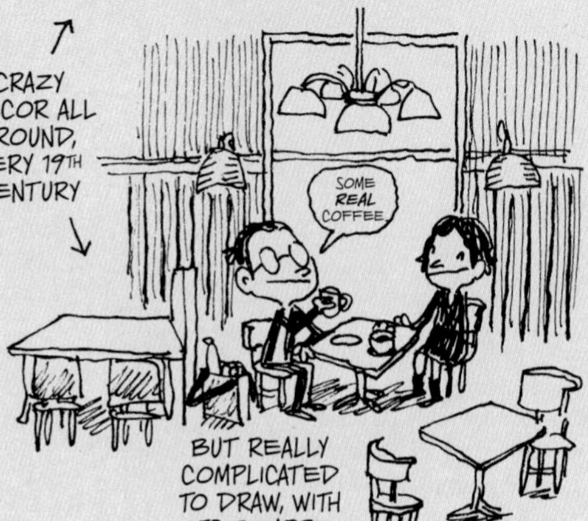
SOME REAL COFFEE

BUT REALLY COMPLICATED TO DRAW, WITH ITS BIZARRE PERSPECTIVE

WE HAD AN ESPRESSO PEPPERINO (COFFEE, CHOCOLATE AND PEPPER-- KILLER!) AND A KAPUCINER, WHICH ACTUALLY MADE ME APPRECIATE CAPUCCINO AS A COFFEE.

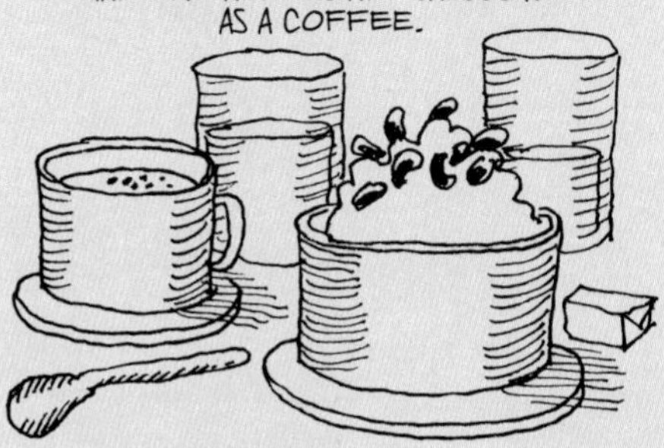

NO... THE HORROR OF MY CULINARY VIETNAM TRULY STARTED WITH...

HORGASZTANYA*

IT STARTS LIKE ORGASM, BUT IT FINISHES LIKE TENIA* *TAPEWORM

* THE FISHERMAN'S FARM, FÖ UTCA 27

THINGS STARTED OUT WELL, AT FIRST:

DEAL

HIGHLY RECOMMENDED BY THE PEOPLE HERE, AND MY GUIDE SAYS THAT THE FISH SCALE SOUP IS DELICIOUS!

EFFECTIVELY:

WE ORDER A CATFISH SOUP AND IT'S DELICIOUS. IT'S NOT TOO FILTERED SO IT'S KIND OF LIKE A BOUILLABAISSE, AND THERE ARE LARGE PIECES OF FISH INSIDE!

THE RESTAURANT'S DECOR IS A LITTLE KITSCH, IT'S FUNNY... THERE ARE A BUNCH OF FISHING TOOLS, OPTICAL ILLUSIONS, NETTING...

DID YOU SEE THE BOAT ON THE CEILING?

SEEMS LIKE A POPULAR PLACE.

BUT EVERYTHING TOOK A TURN FOR THE WORSE WHEN WE DECIDED TO:

LIVING A DREAM →

OOOOH THERE'S A DISH WITH PERCH, ZANDER, CARP, AND CATFISH!

FOR TWO...

CAN WE TRY IT?

HAVE SOME GNOCCHI* WITH IT.

EEEH! I'M GOING TO DIE!!!

* IN HUNGARY, GNOCCHI ARE SPÄTZLE

THE PROMISE

THE BEST FRESHWATER FISH ALL TOGETHER IN A SINGLE DISH! FRESHLY FISHED FROM LAKE BALATON! THE DREAM OF EVERY AMATEUR FISH-LOVER COME TRUE, SERVED ON A SILVER PLATTER!

THE REALITY

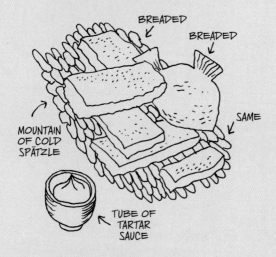

BREADED

BREADED

SAME

MOUNTAIN OF COLD SPÄTZLE

TUBE OF TARTAR SAUCE

I'M GOING TO DIE.

NO YOU WON'T, GIVE IT A SHOT.

I ALREADY KNOW WHAT BREADED FISH TASTES LIKE

NOT IN HUNGARY...

I THINK I'M GOING TO THROW UP.

GROO

GROO

CAMERA OF THE INSIDE OF MY STOMACH:

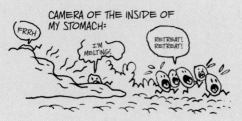

FRRH

I'M MELTING!

RETREAT! RETREAT!

SO... HOW SHOULD I PUT THIS... WELL, IF YOU PULLED OFF THE SIDE OF A HIGHWAY AND ORDERED FOUR PLATES OF BREADED FISH THAT YOU THEN DROWNED IN OIL AND RANDOMLY DUSTED WITH SUGAR (SERIOUSLY!), AND THEN ON THE SIDE YOU TOOK A POT OF COLD, UNSALTED SPÄTZLE, YOU'D GET APPROXIMATELY THE SAME END RESULT.

IT WASN'T GOOD. AT ALL. IT WAS SO BAD THAT IT TOOK AWAY MY DESIRE TO LIVE. IT KILLS ME TO HAVE FISH COOKED THAT WAY. I LEFT THREE-QUARTERS OF IT ON THE PLATE.

LATER...

DAMN IT. I... I'M GETTING OLDER.

NO YOU'RE NOT.

I'M... SCARED...

I... I CAN FEEL IT.

RELAX.

STOP MAKING A BIG DEAL OUT OF EVERYTHING.

AND STOP QUOTING KUBRICK. IT'S ANNOYING.

(BEHIND US, THE DANUBE ALL LIT UP)

EVEN LATER...

YOU'RE NOT GOING TO DIE.

I'M GOING TO DIE.

IT WASN'T THAT BAD.

YOU THOUGHT IT WAS GOOD?

IT WAS POPULAR.

I'M GOING TO DIE.

STOP IT...

I... I FEEL COLD.

WE WON.

I DON'T THINK THERE'S ANYTHING WORSE THAN BEING DISAPPOINTED BY A RESTAURANT. ACTUALLY, MAYBE MESSING UP A DINNER YOU COOK FOR YOUR GUESTS. BUT THAT'S IT.

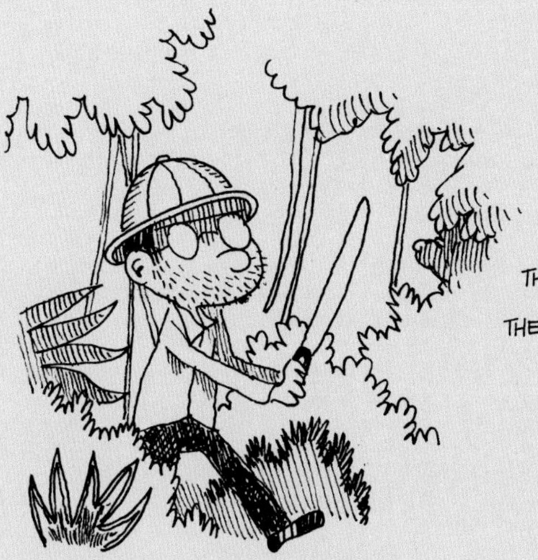

57TH DAY: IT'S BEEN ALMOST TWO MONTHS SINCE I LANDED IN HUNGARY. THE ELEMENTS HAVE BEEN PARTICULARLY ACTIVE THESE LAST FEW WEEKS AND I'VE BEEN LOSING MY MEMORY EVER SINCE I ATE A PARTICULAR BITTER DISH OF BREADED FISH... THE CLIMATE AND FOOD GOT THE BEST OF MY BELOVED, I BURIED HER LAST WEEK. I WALK DEEPER INTO THE HUNGARIAN JUNGLE, ON THE HUNT FOR PÖRKÖLT, DRINKING FROM THE PUDDLES OF THE TOKAJ, BUT STILL ALIVE.

I NOTICED THAT THE HUNGARIANS WEAR A SORT OF GLASS CAGE AROUND THEIR HEADS, WHICH MAKES IT IMPOSSIBLE FOR THEM TO COMMUNICATE.

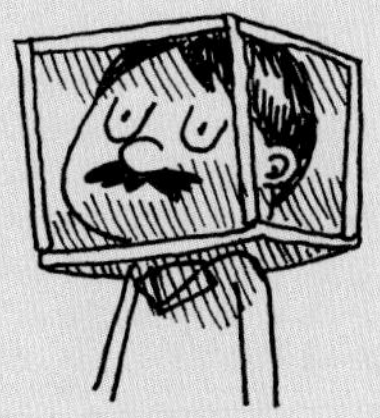

FORTUNATELY, I MANAGED TO FIND A HAMMER TO BREAK THE GLASS, AND UNDERNEATH DISCOVERED A VERY CHARMING PEOPLE.

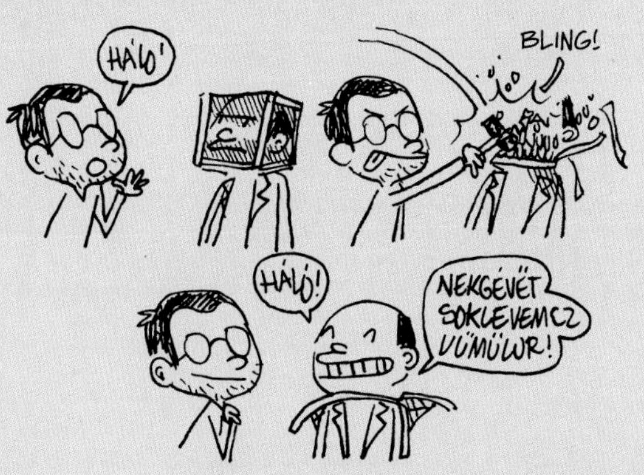
HÁLÓ!
BLING!
HÁLÓ!
NEKGÉVÉT SOKLEVEMCZ VÜMÜWR!

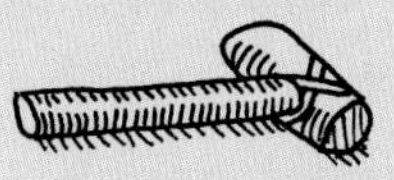

I USE THIS TECHNIQUE QUITE OFTEN, MOST NOTABLY IN A SMALL SHOP WHERE I BOUGHT SOME MEDICINE FOR INDIGESTION.

HOLLO MUHELY

VIKTOVICS MIHA'LY UTCA, 12. CENTRAL PEST

A REALLY, REALLY COOL, UNDERAPPRECIATED, ARTISANAL STORE WHERE I MET LÁSZLÓ HOLLÓ, A GUY WHO PAINTS EGGS AND OTHER OBJECTS WITH A HUNGARIAN MOTIF. HE EVEN HAS A LITTLE WORKSHOP CONNECTED TO HIS SHOP. WE SPOKE IN A SORT OF BROKEN ENGLISH, ABOUT HOW HARD IT IS TO LIVE AN ARTISTIC LIFE, AND INDULGED IN A LITTLE NOSTALGIA FOR A TIME THAT WAS LESS... CAPITALIST.

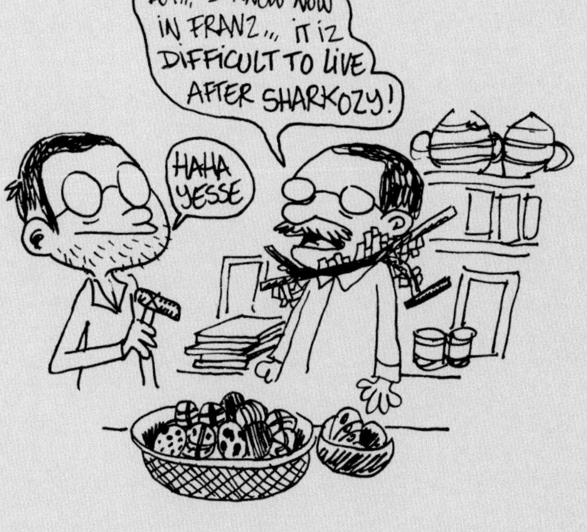
BUT... I KNOW NOW IN FRANZ... IT IZ DIFFICULT TO LIVE AFTER SHARKOZY!
HAHA YESSE

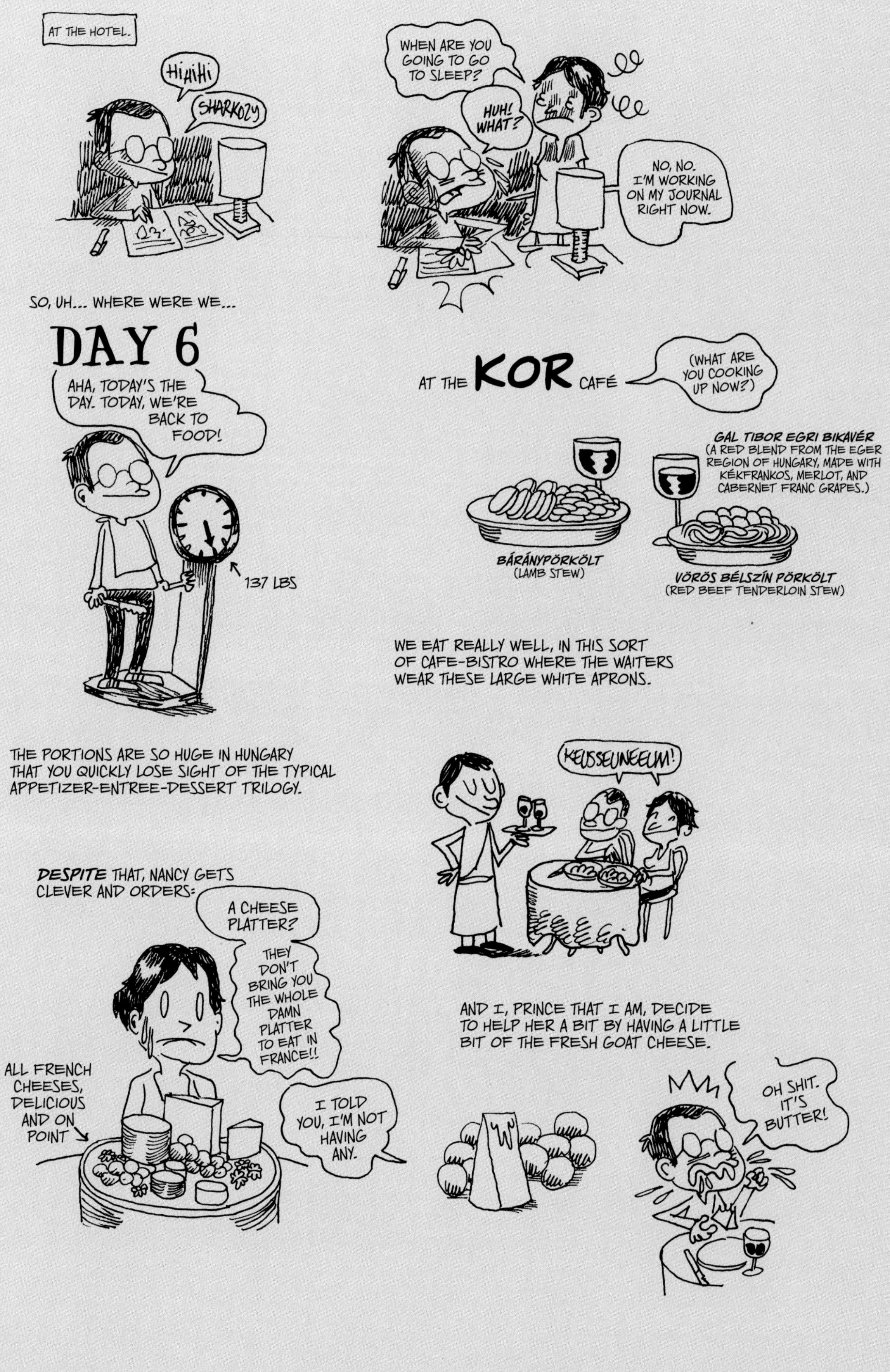
AT THE HOTEL.
HI HI HI
SHARKOZY
WHEN ARE YOU GOING TO GO TO SLEEP?
HUH! WHAT?
NO, NO. I'M WORKING ON MY JOURNAL RIGHT NOW.
SO, UH... WHERE WERE WE...
DAY 6
AHA, TODAY'S THE DAY. TODAY, WE'RE BACK TO FOOD!
137 LBS
AT THE KOR CAFÉ
(WHAT ARE YOU COOKING UP NOW?)
GAL TIBOR EGRI BIKAVÉR
(A RED BLEND FROM THE EGER REGION OF HUNGARY, MADE WITH KÉKFRANKOS, MERLOT, AND CABERNET FRANC GRAPES.)
BÁRÁNYPÖRKÖLT
(LAMB STEW)
VÖRÖS BÉLSZÍN PÖRKÖLT
(RED BEEF TENDERLOIN STEW)
WE EAT REALLY WELL, IN THIS SORT OF CAFE-BISTRO WHERE THE WAITERS WEAR THESE LARGE WHITE APRONS.
THE PORTIONS ARE SO HUGE IN HUNGARY THAT YOU QUICKLY LOSE SIGHT OF THE TYPICAL APPETIZER-ENTREE-DESSERT TRILOGY.
KEUSSEUNEEUM!
DESPITE THAT, NANCY GETS CLEVER AND ORDERS:
A CHEESE PLATTER?
THEY DON'T BRING YOU THE WHOLE DAMN PLATTER TO EAT IN FRANCE!!
ALL FRENCH CHEESES, DELICIOUS AND ON POINT
I TOLD YOU, I'M NOT HAVING ANY.
AND I, PRINCE THAT I AM, DECIDE TO HELP HER A BIT BY HAVING A LITTLE BIT OF THE FRESH GOAT CHEESE.
OH SHIT. IT'S BUTTER!

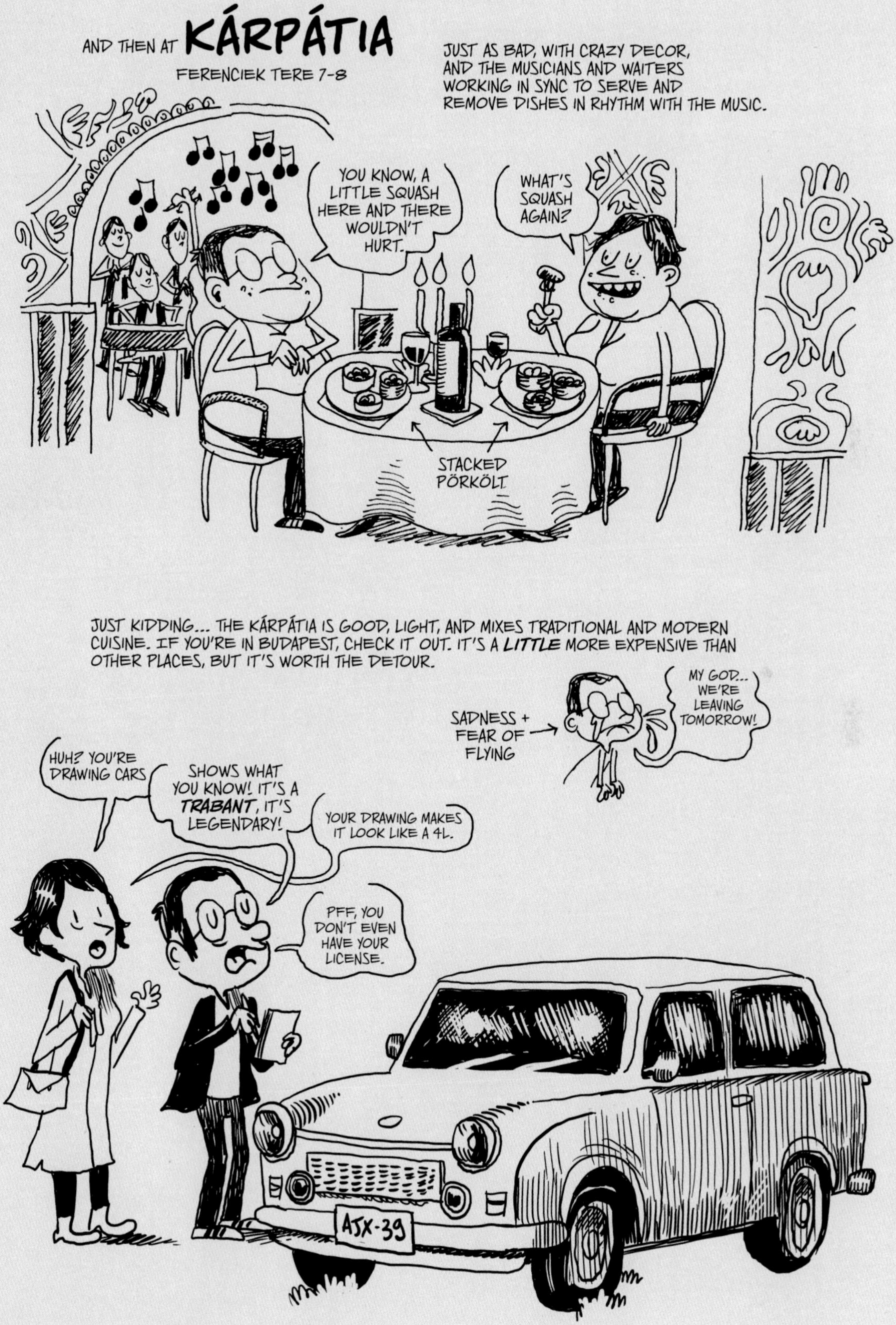
AND THEN AT KÁRPÁTIA
FERENCIEK TERE 7-8
JUST AS BAD, WITH CRAZY DECOR, AND THE MUSICIANS AND WAITERS WORKING IN SYNC TO SERVE AND REMOVE DISHES IN RHYTHM WITH THE MUSIC.
YOU KNOW, A LITTLE SQUASH HERE AND THERE WOULDN'T HURT.
WHAT'S SQUASH AGAIN?
STACKED PÖRKÖLT.
JUST KIDDING... THE KÁRPÁTIA IS GOOD, LIGHT, AND MIXES TRADITIONAL AND MODERN CUISINE. IF YOU'RE IN BUDAPEST, CHECK IT OUT. IT'S A *LITTLE* MORE EXPENSIVE THAN OTHER PLACES, BUT IT'S WORTH THE DETOUR.
SADNESS + FEAR OF FLYING
MY GOD... WE'RE LEAVING TOMORROW!
HUH? YOU'RE DRAWING CARS
SHOWS WHAT YOU KNOW! IT'S A *TRABANT*, IT'S LEGENDARY!
YOUR DRAWING MAKES IT LOOK LIKE A 4L.
PFF, YOU DON'T EVEN HAVE YOUR LICENSE.
AJX-39

DAY 7

IN OTHER WORDS, THE SEVENTH DAY. WHEN WE REFLECT ON THE WORK WE'VE DONE AND SEE THAT IT WAS GOOD...

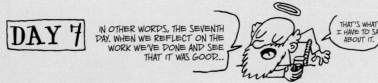

THAT'S WHAT I HAVE TO SAY ABOUT IT.

FINALLY, WHAT'S A **PÖRKÖLT?**

A week of study.

(1) GOOD, SIMPLE INGREDIENTS

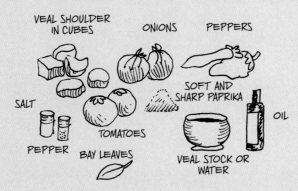

VEAL SHOULDER IN CUBES

ONIONS

PEPPERS

SOFT AND SHARP PAPRIKA

SALT

PEPPER

TOMATOES

BAY LEAVES

OIL

VEAL STOCK OR WATER

(2) MINCE THE ONIONS AND SWEAT THEM WITH OIL IN A PAN UNTIL THEY BECOME TRANSLUCENT.

TSCHHH

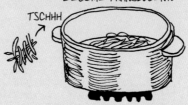

(3) THEN LOWER THE HEAT TO THE MINIMUM AND ADD ALL THE VEAL AND SHARP PAPRIKA, UNTIL THE MEAT TAKES COLOR...

IF YOU BURN THE PAPRIKA, IT'LL BECOME BITTER.

BAY LEAF

SO SLOWLY.

THE MORE PAPRIKA YOU ADD, THE THICKER YOUR SAUCE WILL BE.

(4) AND THEN COVER IT ALL WITH THE STOCK, ADD A LITTLE SALT AND PEPPER, AND LET IT SIMMER FOR AN HOUR ON A LOW FIRE.

THE MEAT HAS TO COOK IN THE STOCK FOR THE SAUCE TO THICKEN.

FLOP FLOP FLOP

(5) ADD THE DICED TOMATOES, THE PEPPERS IN LARGE PIECES, AND THEN LET IT SIMMER FOR ANOTHER HOUR WHILE MAKING SURE THERE'S ENOUGH STOCK THAT NOTHING STICKS TOGETHER.

(6) SERVE IT UP NICE AND HOT, SEASON WITH A LITTLE BIT OF SOFT PAPRIKA, WITH SOME BOILED OR BAKED POTATOES.

WELL, THAT'S IT. A NICE, FILLING DISH. NOTHING PARTICULARLY AMAZING. SIMPLE AND DELICIOUS. BUT IT'S NOTHING TO ROLL ON THE FLOOR OVER.

JADED AFTER 10,000 PÖRKÖLTS.

AND THEN AT THE

BORSSÓ
BISTRO
(KIRALYIPAL UTCA, 14)

WE'RE ROLLING ON THE FLOOR!

IT'S SO GOOD!

GROOO

I THINK IT'S THE BEST RESTAURANT I ATE AT HERE... HUNGARIAN CUISINE REINVENTED, A DECONSTRUCTED PÖRKÖLT, A BURST GOULASH. WELL, IT WAS INCREDIBLE.

FORGOT THAT HE HAS TO TAKE A PLANE IN A FEW HOURS.

GREAT PRESENTATION, DELICIOUS FLAVORS

LAMB PÖRKÖLT WITH CREPES

KIRALY PAUL IXERKÁBORUM LIKE THE ALBIS WINES

GÜJNER ÖROGAROK NADÁRKA THAT TASTES LIKE LICORICE AND PEPPER

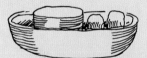

VEAL MEDALLION AND VEGETABLE CROQUETTES

AFTER EVERYTHING ELSE, IT'S TIME FOR DESSERT:

DARK CHOCOLATE VOLCANO CAKE

EPILOGUE

WE TAKE THE PLANE HOME IN THE AFTERNOON. A CLOUDY SKY. WE'RE GOING TO DIE. THE STEWARDESS IS SMILING WEIRDLY. EVERY TIME THE PLANE SHAKES IS MY LAST TIME. FEELING LIKE WE'RE GOING TO CRASH LIKE LOST...

PLANE THAT'S FLOWN A THOUSAND TIMES

SPONGE CAKE

WITH A LOT OF CREAM

2000 MILES FROM HERE, A VOLCANO ERUPTED, PARALYZING ALL AIR TRAFFIC IN EUROPE FOR A WEEK... TOO BAD, I COULD'VE EASILY SPENT A FEW EXTRA DAYS HERE, AND WE COULD'VE TAKEN THE TRAIN INSTEAD.

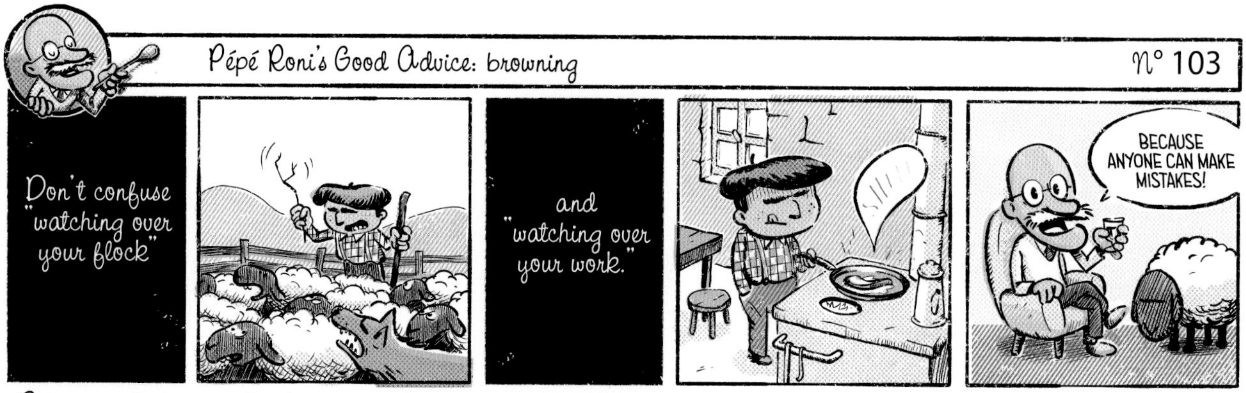
Pépé Roni's Good Advice: browning
N° 103
Don't confuse "watching over your flock"
and "watching over your work."
BECAUSE ANYONE CAN MAKE MISTAKES!

Browning: to bring color to an ingredient in a heated fat, generally before further cooking.

Summer

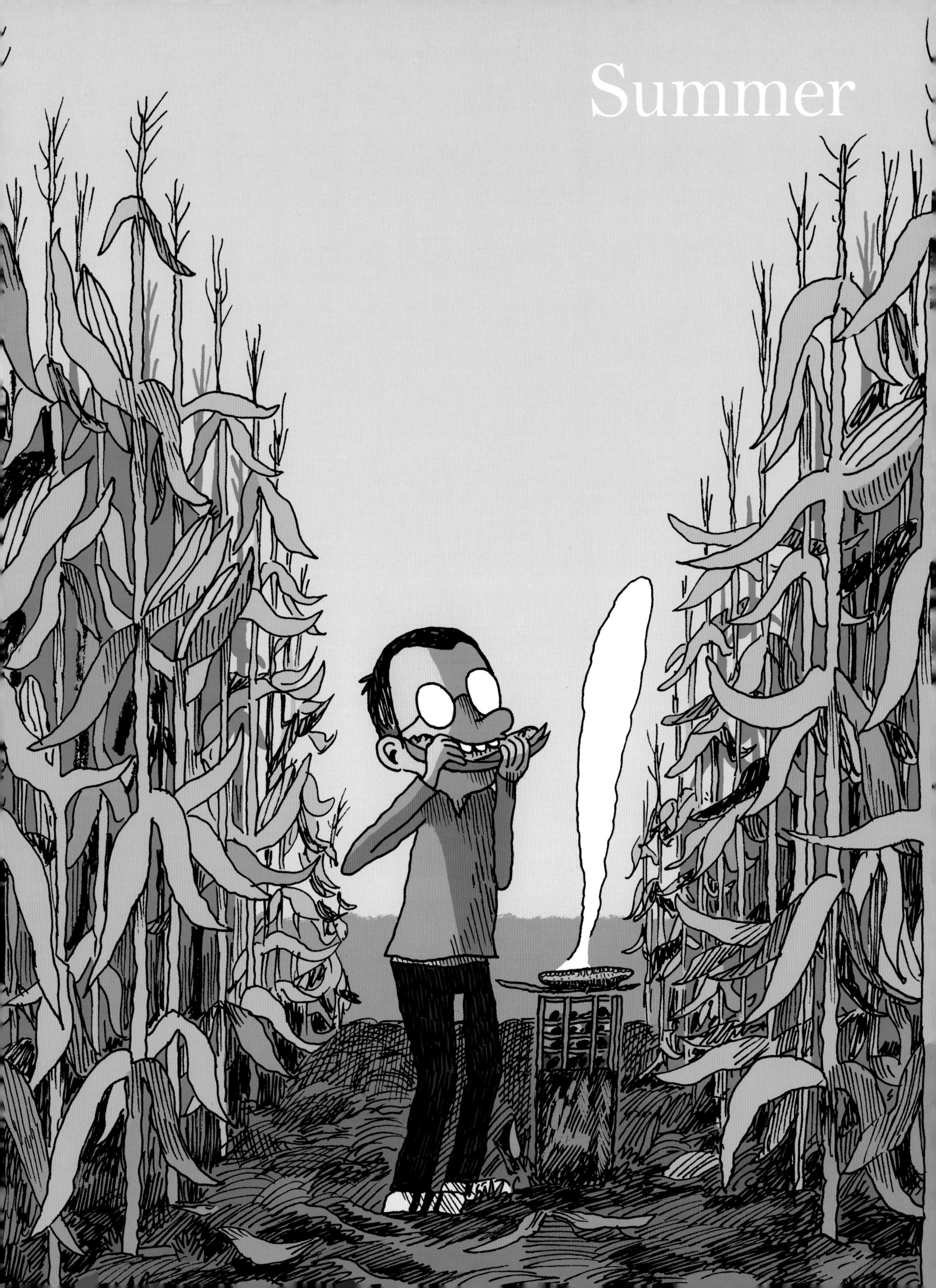

THE TOMATOES
THAT I'VE TASTED

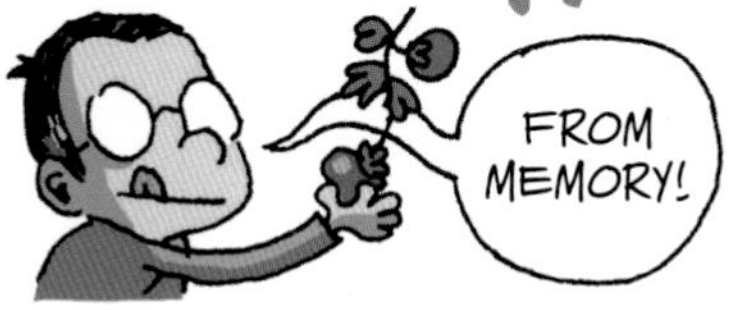
FROM MEMORY!

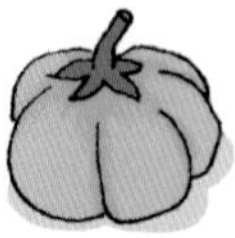

PINEAPPLE

A YELLOW TOMATO. BESIDES ITS COLOR, WHICH IS THE REASON I BOUGHT IT IN THE FIRST PLACE, I HAVE NO OTHER MEMORABLE THINGS TO SHARE ABOUT THIS FRUIT.

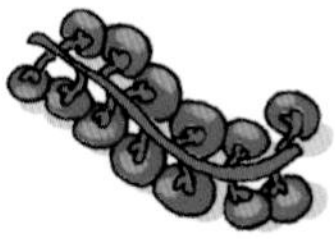

CHERRY

THE BEST APPETIZER TOMATO. PRETTY ACIDIC. CURIOUSLY, IT'S DELICIOUS REGARDLESS OF WHETHER YOU GET IT FROM A SUPERMARKET OR GROW THEM YOURSELF.

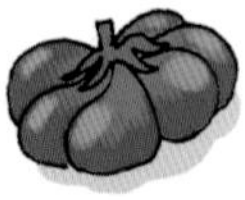

BEEFSTEAK

I'VE ALWAYS BEEN DISAPPOINTED BY THESE MOSTLY TASTELESS TOMATOES WHEN I'VE BOUGHT THEM. IF YOU GET THEM FROM A GARDEN, THOUGH, THEY'RE KILLER!

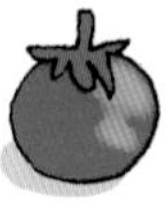

DIPLOM F1

THE FIRST TOMATO I GREW AND HARVESTED, SO IT'S OBVIOUSLY A TOMATO I LOOK BACK UPON FONDLY.

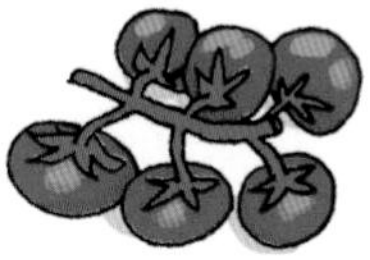

GRAPE

OFTEN BOUGHT IN SUPERMARKETS. I FIND THESE REALLY TASTE LIKE TOMATOES. THOUGH CURRENTLY PRETTY POPULAR, I'VE FOUND THEIR QUALITY TO BE DECREASING.

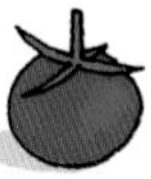

KUMATO

A TOMATO THAT'S BROWN AND PRETTY EXPENSIVE, WHICH MADE ME REALLY WANT TO TRY IT AT THE TIME. IN THE END, IT'S NO BETTER THAN A GRAPE TOMATO, THIS REALLY ISN'T "THE" TOMATO.

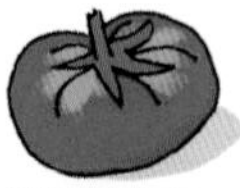

MARMANDE TOMATO

REALLY EASY TO GROW. THESE FRUITS ARE LARGE AND SMELL GREAT. THEY'RE PERFECT FOR MAKING BAKED TOMATOES.

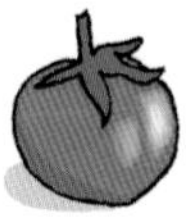

MONTFAVET

I BARELY REMEMBER THIS ONE, BUT I'M SURE I'VE HAD IT BEFORE.

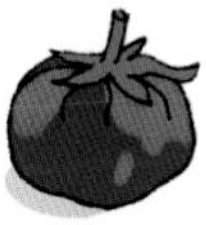

BLACK KRIM

REALLY DELICIOUS GARDEN TOMATO, SOFT, WITH A FULL FLESH.

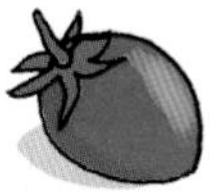

PLUM

I RECENTLY DISCOVERED THIS TOMATO IN SALADS. IT'S GREAT FOR SAUCES AND HAS A LIGHT TASTE OF PEPPER.

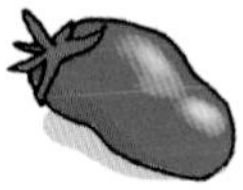

ROMA

ANOTHER SAUCE TOMATO WITH A LOT OF PULP. A VERY ITALIAN STYLE, LIKE OUT OF A BARILLA®.

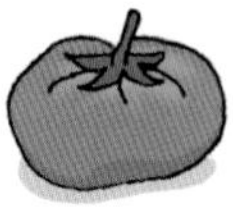

ROSE DE BERNE

A TOMATO SO PINK YOU WONDER IF IT'S EVER GOING TO RIPEN. IT'S NAME MAKES IT SOUND LIKE SOMETHING OUT OF A BARBARA CARTLAND NOVEL. SOFT AND SWEET.

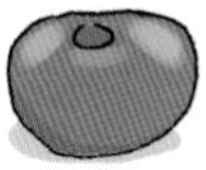

ROUND

AS DELICIOUS TO TASTE AS IT WAS FUN TO DRAW... THAT IS TO SAY, NOT VERY. I ONLY KNOW THEM FROM SUPERMARKETS AND, FOR A LONG TIME, THOUGHT I DIDN'T LIKE TOMATOES BECAUSE OF THEM.

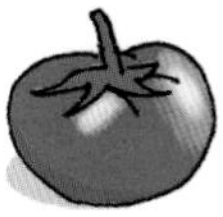

SAINT-PIERRE

A GOOD, BIG TOMATO. VERY PLUMP AND REWARDING TO GROW IN YOUR OWN HERB GARDEN.

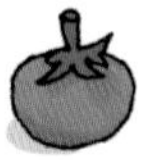

SARDINIA

THE BEST TOMATO I'VE EVER HAD! VERY FIRM WITH AN ACIDIC TASTE. YOU SHOULD EAT IT WHEN IT'S STILL GREEN. YOU CAN FIND THEM IN SUPERMARKETS IN SWITZERLAND. THEY'RE EXPENSIVE, BUT WORTH EVERY PENNY. THEY'RE BEST TO HAVE IN A SALAD.

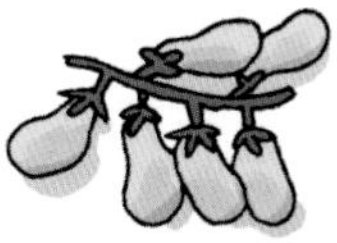

YELLOW PEAR

ANOTHER APPETIZER TOMATO, RELATIVELY SWEET, AND GREAT FOR DECORATING YOUR DISHES WITH A LITTLE COLOR.

lon.

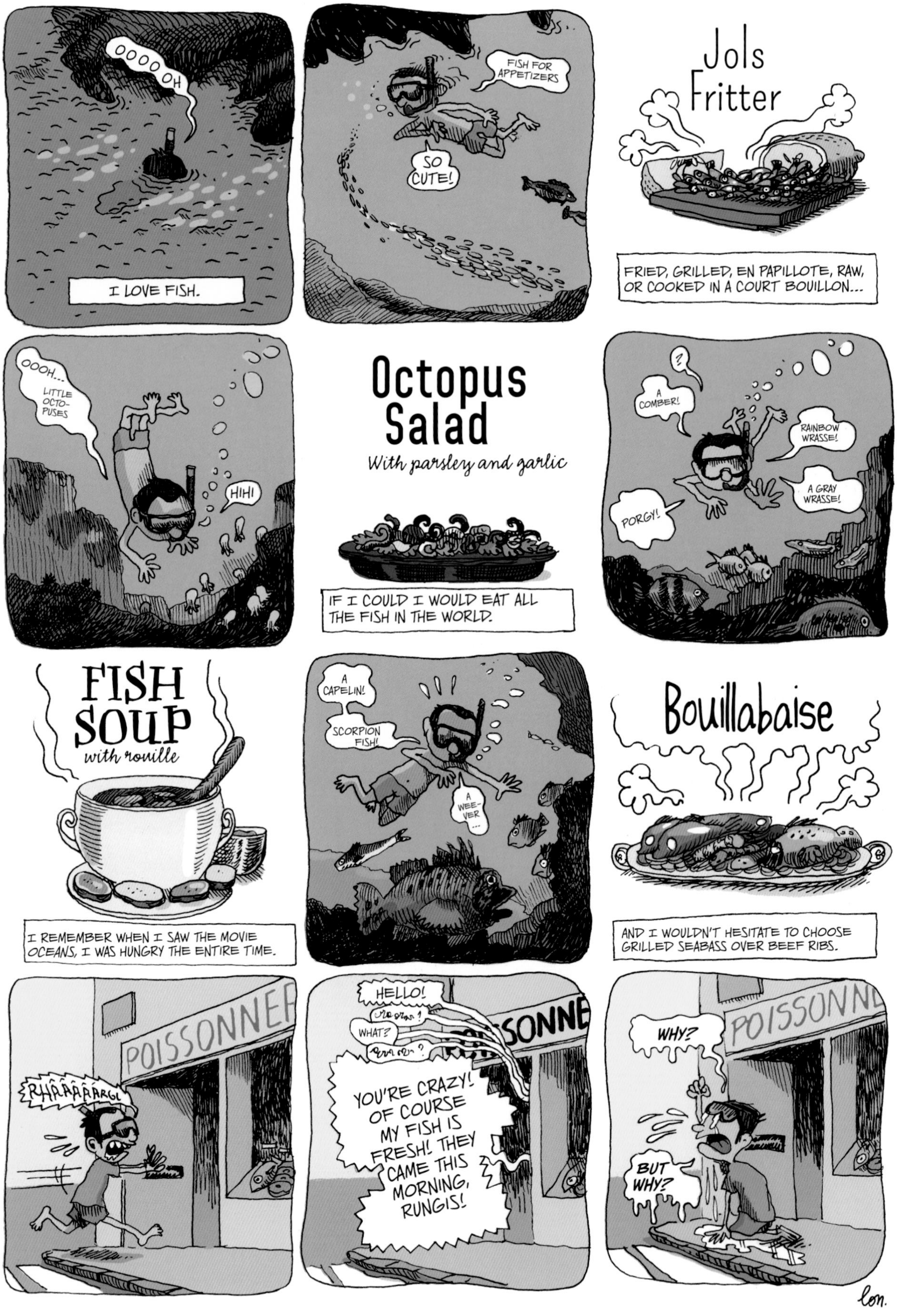
OOOO OH
I LOVE FISH.
FISH FOR APPETIZERS
SO CUTE!
Jols Fritter
FRIED, GRILLED, EN PAPILLOTE, RAW, OR COOKED IN A COURT BOUILLON...
OOOH... LITTLE OCTO-PUSES
HIHI
Octopus Salad
With parsley and garlic
IF I COULD I WOULD EAT ALL THE FISH IN THE WORLD.
?
A COMBER!
RAINBOW WRASSE!
A GRAY WRASSE!
PORGY!
FISH SOUP
with rouille
I REMEMBER WHEN I SAW THE MOVIE OCEANS, I WAS HUNGRY THE ENTIRE TIME.
A CAPELIN!
SCORPION FISH!
A WEE-VER ...
Bouillabaise
AND I WOULDN'T HESITATE TO CHOOSE GRILLED SEABASS OVER BEEF RIBS.
POISSONNER
RHÂÂÂÂÂRGL
HELLO!
WHAT?
YOU'RE CRAZY! OF COURSE MY FISH IS FRESH! THEY CAME THIS MORNING, RUNGIS!
POISSONN
WHY?
BUT WHY?
lon.

YOU MIGHT HAVE NOTICED IT IN RESTAURANTS, CAFES, OR EVEN TEA HOUSES...

DISTINGUISHED PEOPLE ALWAYS KEEP THEIR PINKIES RAISED.

WELL, IT MIGHT LOOK NICE, BUT IT'S NOT PART OF ANY SORT OF ELEGANT TRADITION! QUITE THE OPPOSITE IN FACT!

OH? IS THAT SO?

LET US REWIND A BIT THROUGH HISTORY... TO A TIME WHEN SITTING AT THE TABLE WAS AN ADVENTURE UNTO ITSELF.

THE FIRST RULE OF ELEGANCE WAS TO EAT CLEANLY AND TO KEEP YOUR PINKY RAISED:

BURRRP

THE SECOND RULE OF ELEGANCE WAS TO AVOID GETTING FOOD ALL OVER YOURSELF, KEEPING YOUR PINKY IN THE AIR.

MIOM GLUP   SLURP BRÖT

THE THIRD RULE... WELL, CAN WE REALLY STILL TALK ABOUT ELEGANCE AT THIS POINT? HOPEFULLY YOU HAVEN'T MISSED THAT THIS PIG...

CHOMPSLI BOOFE

HAS KEPT HIS PINKY IN THE AIR!

HUHU! HU!

BUT WHY?

WELL... WHEN YOU EAT A NICE TURKEY LEG WITH YOUR HANDS, AND THEY GET COVERED IN FAT...

BUT... I... I NEVER... I...

HAVE YOU EVER TRIED TO SERVE YOURSELF SOME SALT, OR MUSTARD, OR SPICES?

THAT'S WHY HAVING YOUR PINKY DRY BECAME A COMMON PRACTICE!

AND IT'S GREAT FOR SCRATCHING OUR EAR, TOO!   TIME FOR A LITTLE PAPRIKA   WOW, I'M A MESS!

SO INSTEAD OF ADOPTING THESE BOORISH MANNERS, WHY NOT LET YOURSELF GO A LITTLE...

CHÄÄRLES!!   SUGAR FOR TABLE 12!

MA'AM

THAT SAID, BEWARE OF IMITATIONS.

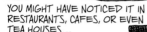

SOME "PEOPLE" DON'T KEEP THEIR PINKY RAISED OUT OF TRADITION...

CH-CHARLES. WHY... WHY ARE YOU LOOKING AT ME LIKE THAT?

CHARLES?

leon.

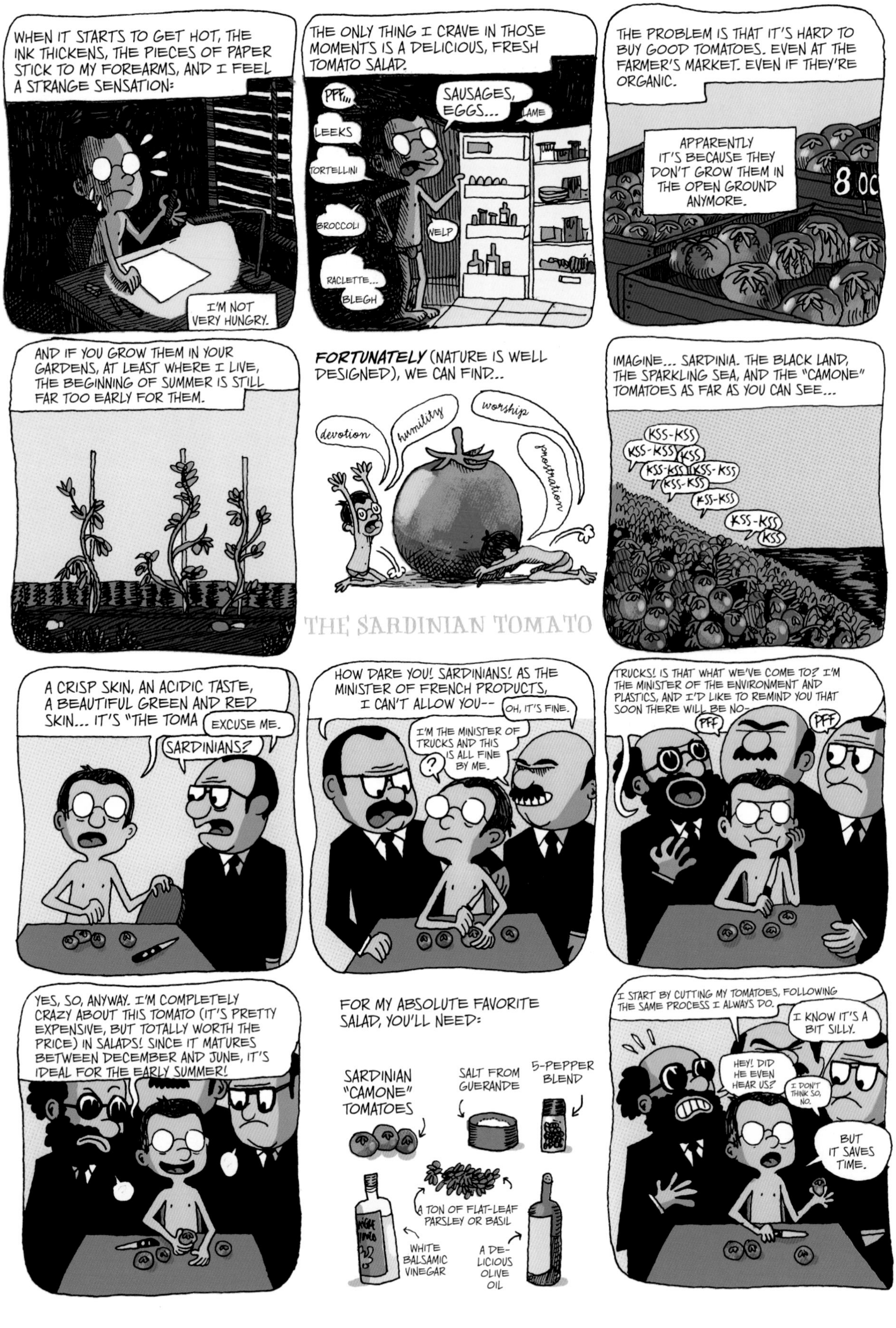
WHEN IT STARTS TO GET HOT, THE INK THICKENS, THE PIECES OF PAPER STICK TO MY FOREARMS, AND I FEEL A STRANGE SENSATION:
I'M NOT VERY HUNGRY.
THE ONLY THING I CRAVE IN THOSE MOMENTS IS A DELICIOUS, FRESH TOMATO SALAD.
PFF...
SAUSAGES, EGGS...
LAME
LEEKS
TORTELLINI
BROCCOLI
WELP
RACLETTE...
BLEGH
THE PROBLEM IS THAT IT'S HARD TO BUY GOOD TOMATOES. EVEN AT THE FARMER'S MARKET. EVEN IF THEY'RE ORGANIC.
APPARENTLY IT'S BECAUSE THEY DON'T GROW THEM IN THE OPEN GROUND ANYMORE.
AND IF YOU GROW THEM IN YOUR GARDENS, AT LEAST WHERE I LIVE, THE BEGINNING OF SUMMER IS STILL FAR TOO EARLY FOR THEM.
FORTUNATELY (NATURE IS WELL DESIGNED), WE CAN FIND...
devotion
humility
worship
prostration
THE SARDINIAN TOMATO
IMAGINE... SARDINIA. THE BLACK LAND, THE SPARKLING SEA, AND THE "CAMONE" TOMATOES AS FAR AS YOU CAN SEE...
KSS-KSS
KSS-KSS
KSS
KSS-KSS
KSS-KSS
KSS-KSS
KSS-KSS
KSS-KSS
KSS
A CRISP SKIN, AN ACIDIC TASTE, A BEAUTIFUL GREEN AND RED SKIN... IT'S "THE TOMA
EXCUSE ME.
SARDINIANS?
HOW DARE YOU! SARDINIANS! AS THE MINISTER OF FRENCH PRODUCTS, I CAN'T ALLOW YOU--
OH, IT'S FINE.
I'M THE MINISTER OF TRUCKS AND THIS IS ALL FINE BY ME.
?
TRUCKS! IS THAT WHAT WE'VE COME TO? I'M THE MINISTER OF THE ENVIRONMENT AND PLASTICS, AND I'D LIKE TO REMIND YOU THAT SOON THERE WILL BE NO-
PFF
PFF
YES, SO, ANYWAY. I'M COMPLETELY CRAZY ABOUT THIS TOMATO (IT'S PRETTY EXPENSIVE, BUT TOTALLY WORTH THE PRICE) IN SALADS! SINCE IT MATURES BETWEEN DECEMBER AND JUNE, IT'S IDEAL FOR THE EARLY SUMMER!
FOR MY ABSOLUTE FAVORITE SALAD, YOU'LL NEED:
SARDINIAN "CAMONE" TOMATOES
SALT FROM GUERANDE
5-PEPPER BLEND
A TON OF FLAT-LEAF PARSLEY OR BASIL
WHITE BALSAMIC VINEGAR
A DELICIOUS OLIVE OIL
I START BY CUTTING MY TOMATOES, FOLLOWING THE SAME PROCESS I ALWAYS DO.
I KNOW IT'S A BIT SILLY.
HEY! DID HE EVEN HEAR US?
I DON'T THINK SO, NO.
BUT IT SAVES TIME.

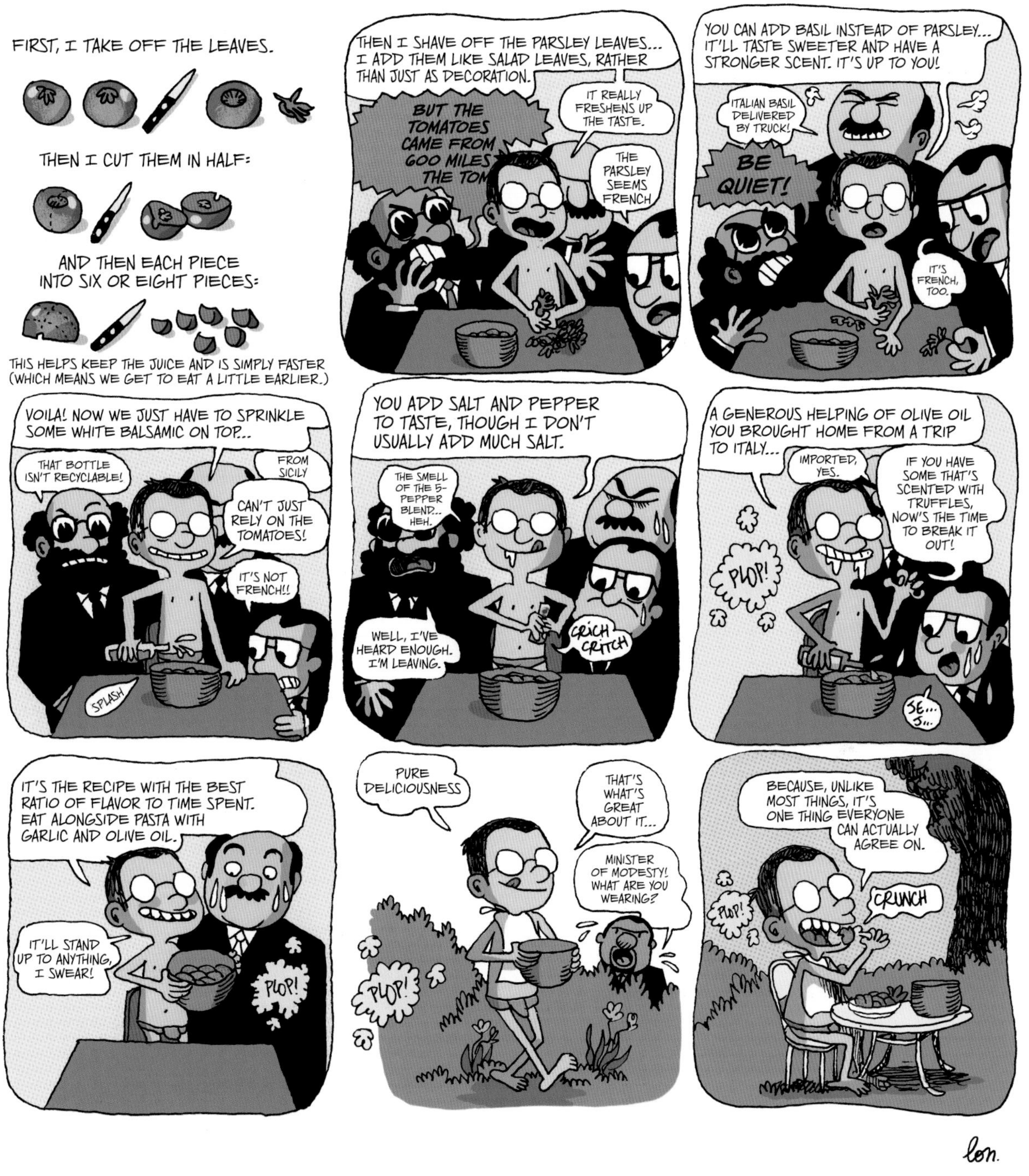
FIRST, I TAKE OFF THE LEAVES.
THEN I CUT THEM IN HALF:
AND THEN EACH PIECE INTO SIX OR EIGHT PIECES:
THIS HELPS KEEP THE JUICE AND IS SIMPLY FASTER (WHICH MEANS WE GET TO EAT A LITTLE EARLIER.)
THEN I SHAVE OFF THE PARSLEY LEAVES... I ADD THEM LIKE SALAD LEAVES, RATHER THAN JUST AS DECORATION.
BUT THE TOMATOES CAME FROM 600 MILES THE TOM
IT REALLY FRESHENS UP THE TASTE.
THE PARSLEY SEEMS FRENCH
YOU CAN ADD BASIL INSTEAD OF PARSLEY... IT'LL TASTE SWEETER AND HAVE A STRONGER SCENT. IT'S UP TO YOU!
ITALIAN BASIL DELIVERED BY TRUCK!
BE QUIET!
IT'S FRENCH, TOO.
VOILA! NOW WE JUST HAVE TO SPRINKLE SOME WHITE BALSAMIC ON TOP...
THAT BOTTLE ISN'T RECYCLABLE!
FROM SICILY
CAN'T JUST RELY ON THE TOMATOES!
IT'S NOT FRENCH!!
SPLASH
YOU ADD SALT AND PEPPER TO TASTE, THOUGH I DON'T USUALLY ADD MUCH SALT.
THE SMELL OF THE 5-PEPPER BLEND... HEH.
WELL, I'VE HEARD ENOUGH. I'M LEAVING.
CRICH CRITCH
A GENEROUS HELPING OF OLIVE OIL YOU BROUGHT HOME FROM A TRIP TO ITALY...
IMPORTED, YES.
IF YOU HAVE SOME THAT'S SCENTED WITH TRUFFLES, NOW'S THE TIME TO BREAK IT OUT!
PLOP!
JE... J...
IT'S THE RECIPE WITH THE BEST RATIO OF FLAVOR TO TIME SPENT. EAT ALONGSIDE PASTA WITH GARLIC AND OLIVE OIL.
IT'LL STAND UP TO ANYTHING, I SWEAR!
PLOP!
PURE DELICIOUSNESS
THAT'S WHAT'S GREAT ABOUT IT...
MINISTER OF MODESTY! WHAT ARE YOU WEARING?
PLOP!
BECAUSE, UNLIKE MOST THINGS, IT'S ONE THING EVERYONE CAN ACTUALLY AGREE ON.
PLOP!
CRUNCH
lon.

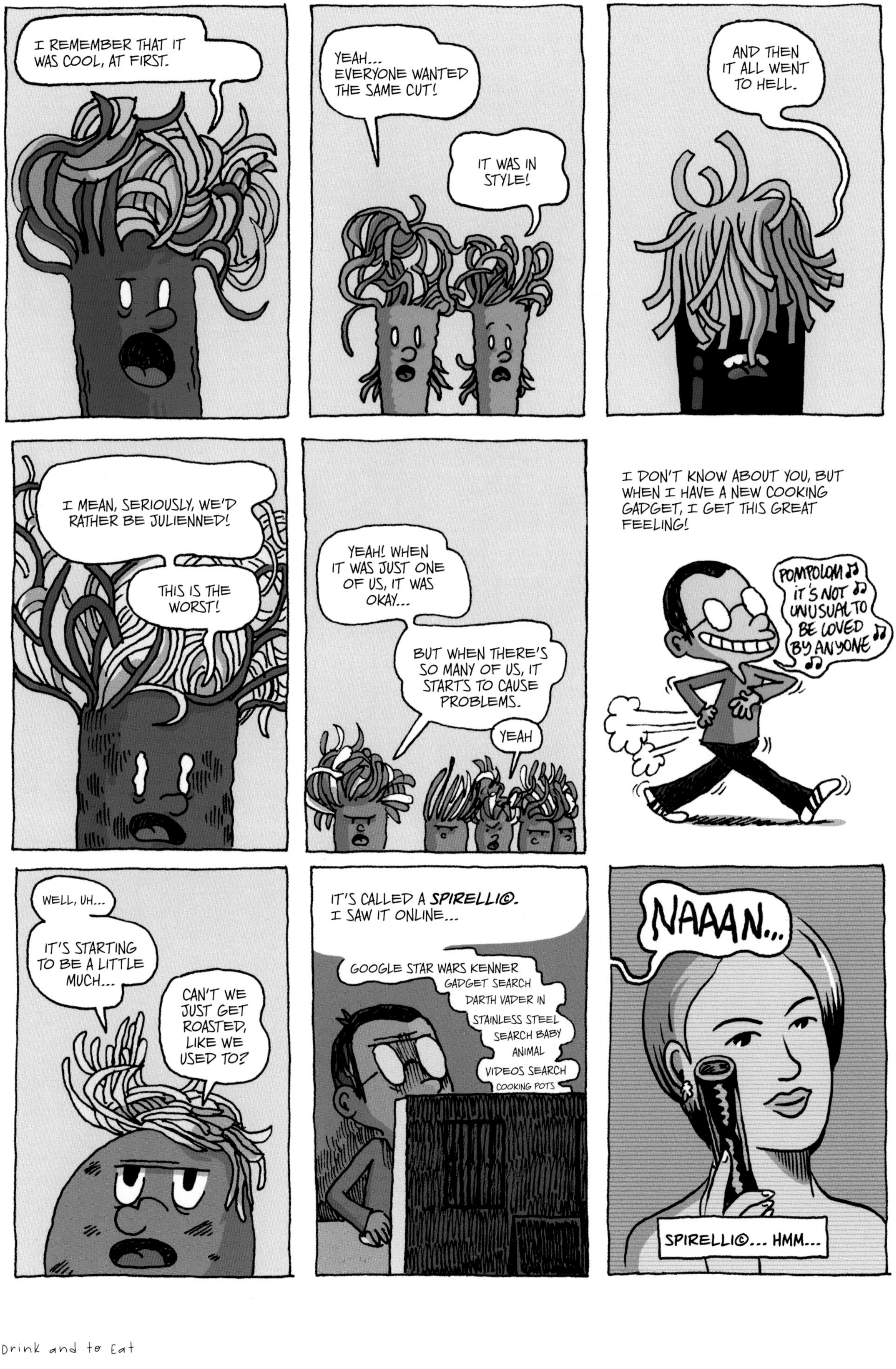
I REMEMBER THAT IT WAS COOL, AT FIRST.
YEAH... EVERYONE WANTED THE SAME CUT!
IT WAS IN STYLE!
AND THEN IT ALL WENT TO HELL.
I MEAN, SERIOUSLY, WE'D RATHER BE JULIENNED!
THIS IS THE WORST!
YEAH! WHEN IT WAS JUST ONE OF US, IT WAS OKAY...
BUT WHEN THERE'S SO MANY OF US, IT STARTS TO CAUSE PROBLEMS.
YEAH
I DON'T KNOW ABOUT YOU, BUT WHEN I HAVE A NEW COOKING GADGET, I GET THIS GREAT FEELING!
POMPOLOM ♫ IT'S NOT ♫ UNUSUAL TO BE LOVED ♫ BY ANYONE ♫
WELL, UH...
IT'S STARTING TO BE A LITTLE MUCH...
CAN'T WE JUST GET ROASTED, LIKE WE USED TO?
IT'S CALLED A SPIRELLI©. I SAW IT ONLINE...
GOOGLE STAR WARS KENNER GADGET SEARCH DARTH VADER IN STAINLESS STEEL SEARCH BABY ANIMAL VIDEOS SEARCH COOKING POTS
NAAAN...
SPIRELLI©... HMM...

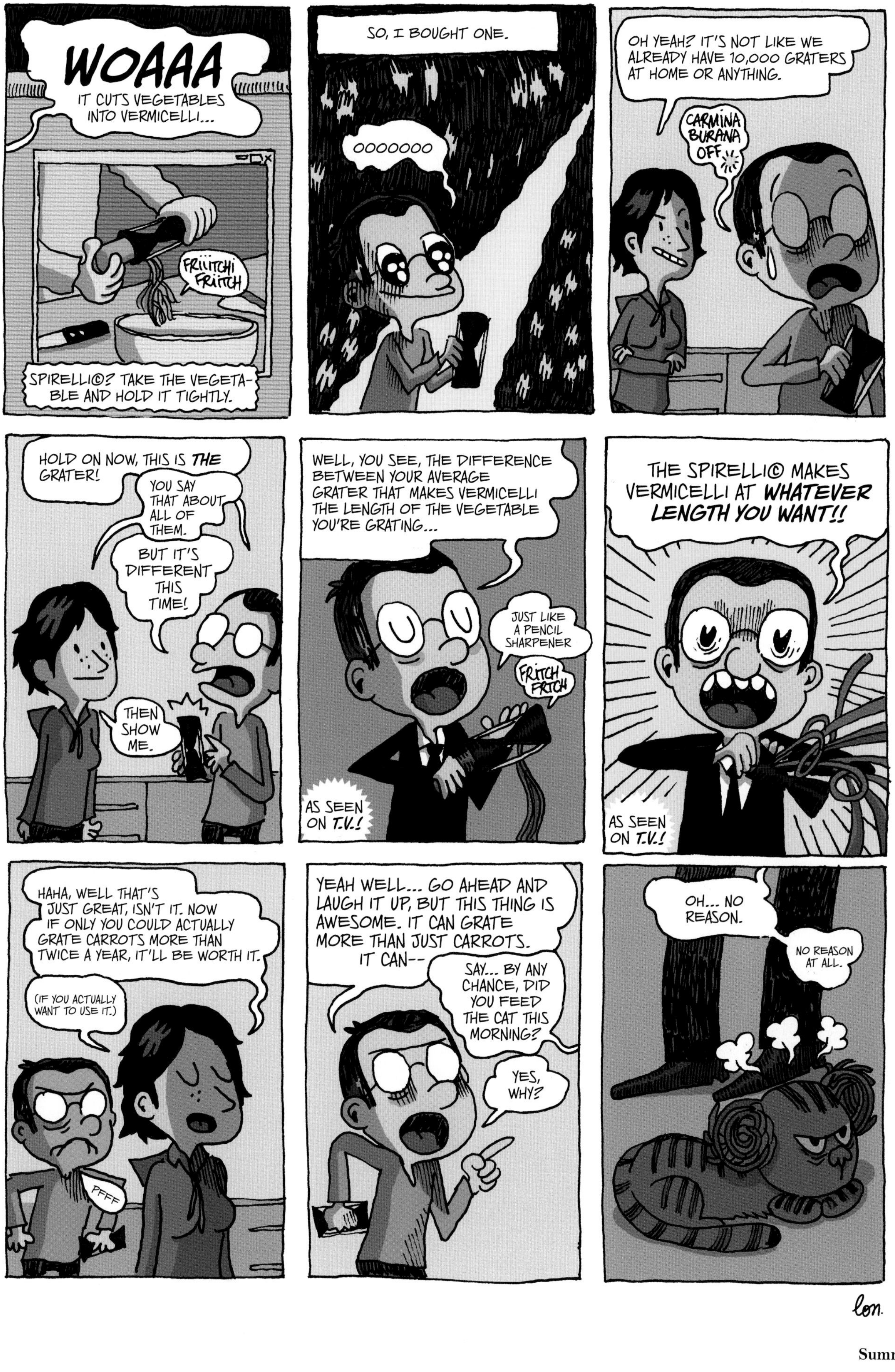
WOAAA
IT CUTS VEGETABLES INTO VERMICELLI...
FRIIITCHI FRITTCH
SPIRELLI©? TAKE THE VEGETABLE AND HOLD IT TIGHTLY.
SO, I BOUGHT ONE.
OOOOOOO
OH YEAH? IT'S NOT LIKE WE ALREADY HAVE 10,000 GRATERS AT HOME OR ANYTHING.
CARMINA BURANA OFF
HOLD ON NOW, THIS IS THE GRATER!
YOU SAY THAT ABOUT ALL OF THEM.
BUT IT'S DIFFERENT THIS TIME!
THEN SHOW ME.
WELL, YOU SEE, THE DIFFERENCE BETWEEN YOUR AVERAGE GRATER THAT MAKES VERMICELLI THE LENGTH OF THE VEGETABLE YOU'RE GRATING...
JUST LIKE A PENCIL SHARPENER
FRITCH FRITCH
AS SEEN ON T.V.!
THE SPIRELLI© MAKES VERMICELLI AT WHATEVER LENGTH YOU WANT!!
AS SEEN ON T.V.!
HAHA, WELL THAT'S JUST GREAT, ISN'T IT. NOW IF ONLY YOU COULD ACTUALLY GRATE CARROTS MORE THAN TWICE A YEAR, IT'LL BE WORTH IT.
(IF YOU ACTUALLY WANT TO USE IT.)
PFFF
YEAH WELL... GO AHEAD AND LAUGH IT UP, BUT THIS THING IS AWESOME. IT CAN GRATE MORE THAN JUST CARROTS. IT CAN--
SAY... BY ANY CHANCE, DID YOU FEED THE CAT THIS MORNING?
YES, WHY?
OH... NO REASON.
NO REASON AT ALL.
lon.

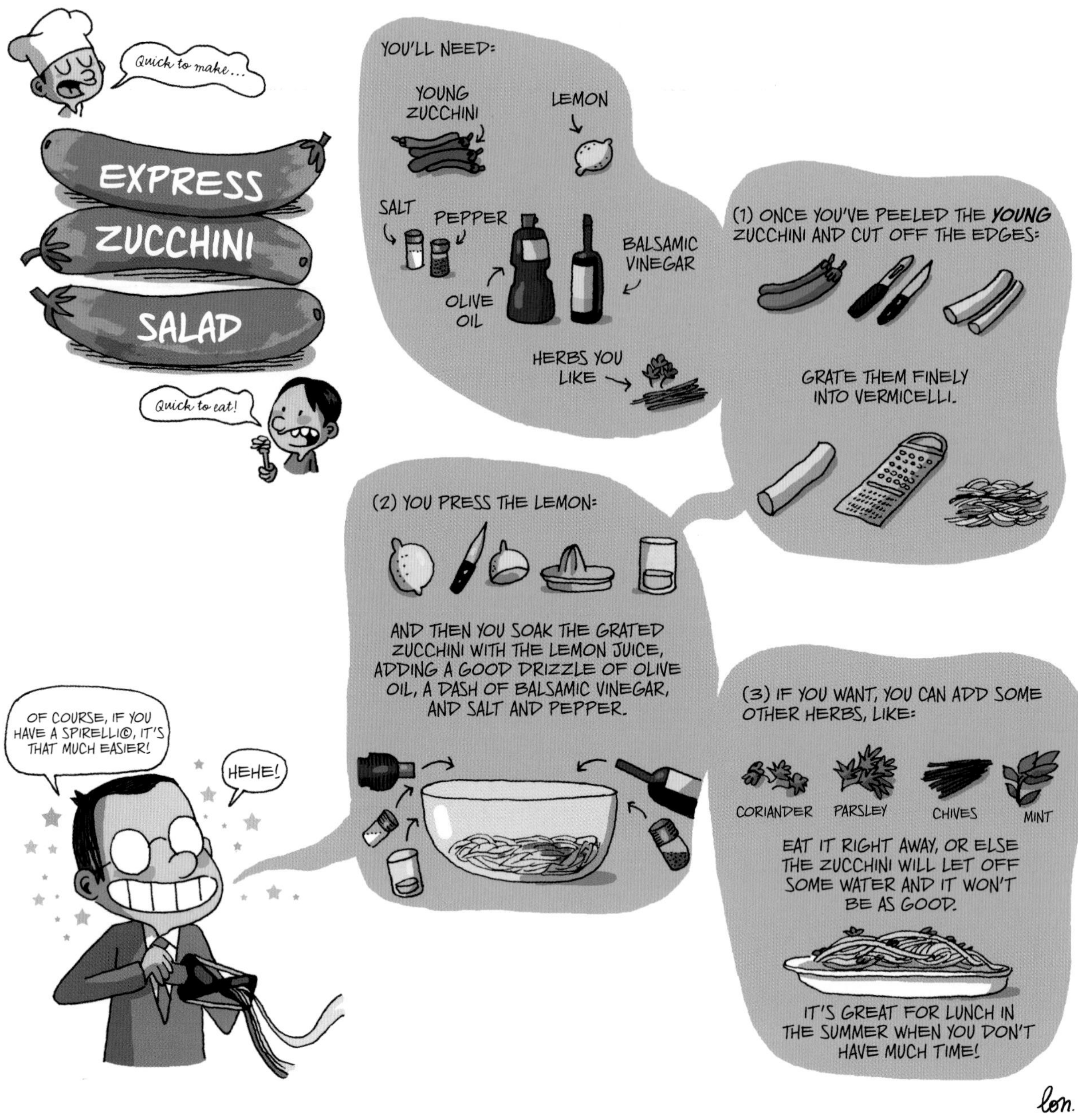
Quick to make...
EXPRESS ZUCCHINI SALAD
Quick to eat!
YOU'LL NEED:
YOUNG ZUCCHINI
LEMON
SALT
PEPPER
OLIVE OIL
BALSAMIC VINEGAR
HERBS YOU LIKE
(1) ONCE YOU'VE PEELED THE *YOUNG* ZUCCHINI AND CUT OFF THE EDGES:
GRATE THEM FINELY INTO VERMICELLI.
(2) YOU PRESS THE LEMON:
AND THEN YOU SOAK THE GRATED ZUCCHINI WITH THE LEMON JUICE, ADDING A GOOD DRIZZLE OF OLIVE OIL, A DASH OF BALSAMIC VINEGAR, AND SALT AND PEPPER.
OF COURSE, IF YOU HAVE A SPIRELLI©, IT'S THAT MUCH EASIER!
HEHE!
(3) IF YOU WANT, YOU CAN ADD SOME OTHER HERBS, LIKE:
CORIANDER
PARSLEY
CHIVES
MINT
EAT IT RIGHT AWAY, OR ELSE THE ZUCCHINI WILL LET OFF SOME WATER AND IT WON'T BE AS GOOD.
IT'S GREAT FOR LUNCH IN THE SUMMER WHEN YOU DON'T HAVE MUCH TIME!
lon.

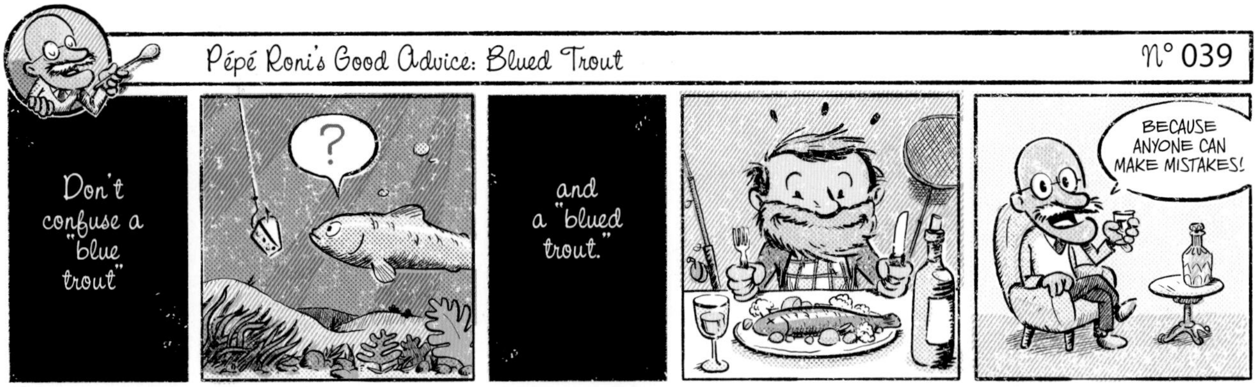
Pépé Roni's Good Advice: Blued Trout
N° 039
Don't confuse a "blue trout"
?
and a "blued trout."
BECAUSE ANYONE CAN MAKE MISTAKES!

Blued trout (truite au bleu): a way of cooking that involves plunging the fish rigorously while fresh so that it retains all of its mucus and then cooking it in a vinegar court-bouillon, which turns the fish blue.

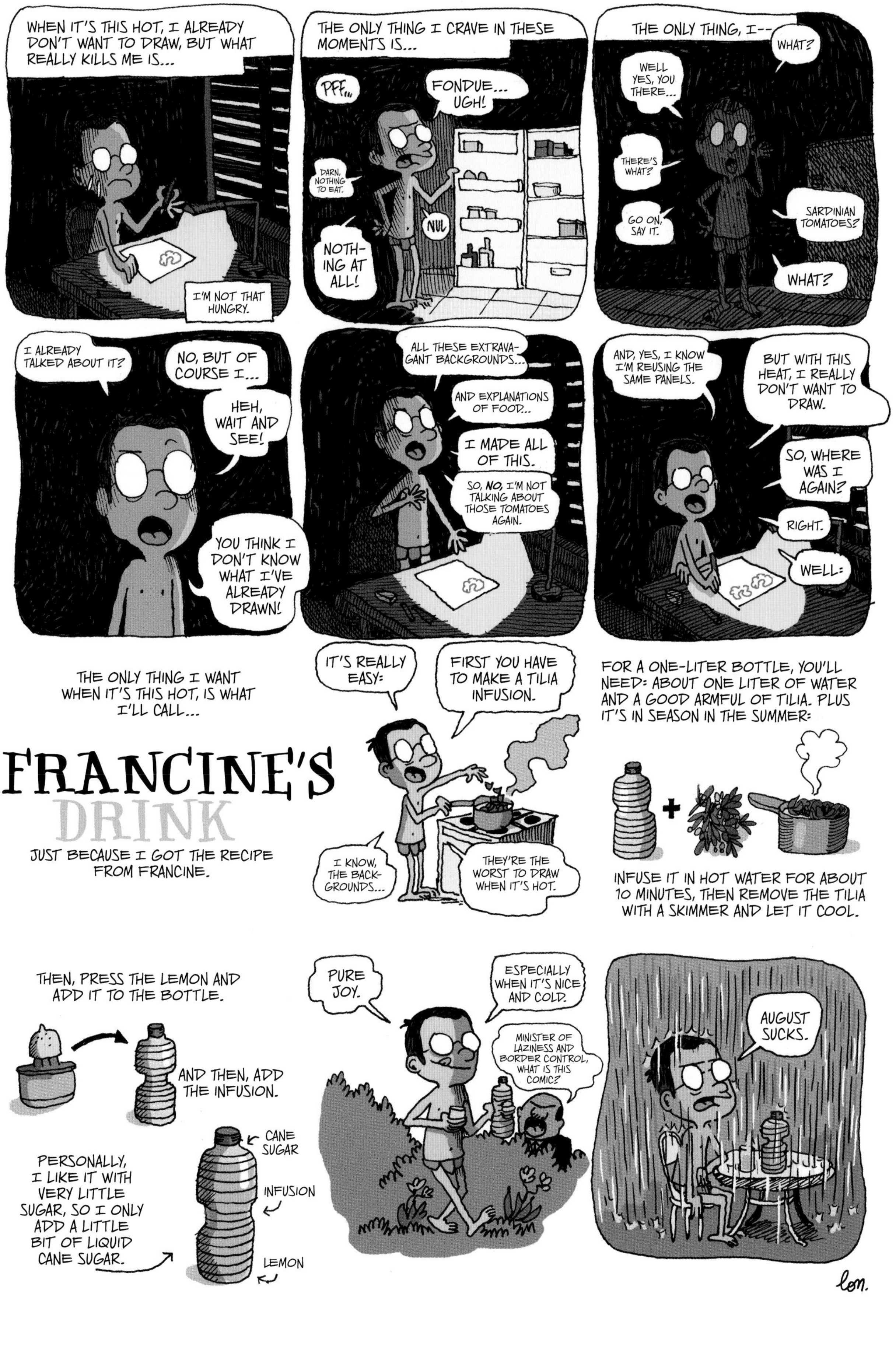
WHEN IT'S THIS HOT, I ALREADY DON'T WANT TO DRAW, BUT WHAT REALLY KILLS ME IS...
I'M NOT THAT HUNGRY.
THE ONLY THING I CRAVE IN THESE MOMENTS IS...
PFF...
FONDUE... UGH!
DARN, NOTHING TO EAT.
NUL
NOTHING AT ALL!
THE ONLY THING, I--
WHAT?
WELL YES, YOU THERE...
THERE'S WHAT?
GO ON, SAY IT.
SARDINIAN TOMATOES?
WHAT?
I ALREADY TALKED ABOUT IT?
NO, BUT OF COURSE I...
HEH, WAIT AND SEE!
YOU THINK I DON'T KNOW WHAT I'VE ALREADY DRAWN!
ALL THESE EXTRAVAGANT BACKGROUNDS...
AND EXPLANATIONS OF FOOD..
I MADE ALL OF THIS.
SO, NO, I'M NOT TALKING ABOUT THOSE TOMATOES AGAIN.
AND, YES, I KNOW I'M REUSING THE SAME PANELS.
BUT WITH THIS HEAT, I REALLY DON'T WANT TO DRAW.
SO, WHERE WAS I AGAIN?
RIGHT.
WELL:
THE ONLY THING I WANT WHEN IT'S THIS HOT, IS WHAT I'LL CALL...
FRANCINE'S DRINK
JUST BECAUSE I GOT THE RECIPE FROM FRANCINE.
IT'S REALLY EASY:
FIRST YOU HAVE TO MAKE A TILIA INFUSION.
I KNOW, THE BACKGROUNDS...
THEY'RE THE WORST TO DRAW WHEN IT'S HOT.
FOR A ONE-LITER BOTTLE, YOU'LL NEED: ABOUT ONE LITER OF WATER AND A GOOD ARMFUL OF TILIA. PLUS IT'S IN SEASON IN THE SUMMER:
INFUSE IT IN HOT WATER FOR ABOUT 10 MINUTES, THEN REMOVE THE TILIA WITH A SKIMMER AND LET IT COOL.
THEN, PRESS THE LEMON AND ADD IT TO THE BOTTLE.
AND THEN, ADD THE INFUSION.
PERSONALLY, I LIKE IT WITH VERY LITTLE SUGAR, SO I ONLY ADD A LITTLE BIT OF LIQUID CANE SUGAR.
CANE SUGAR
INFUSION
LEMON
PURE JOY.
ESPECIALLY WHEN IT'S NICE AND COLD.
MINISTER OF LAZINESS AND BORDER CONTROL, WHAT IS THIS COMIC?
AUGUST SUCKS.
lon.

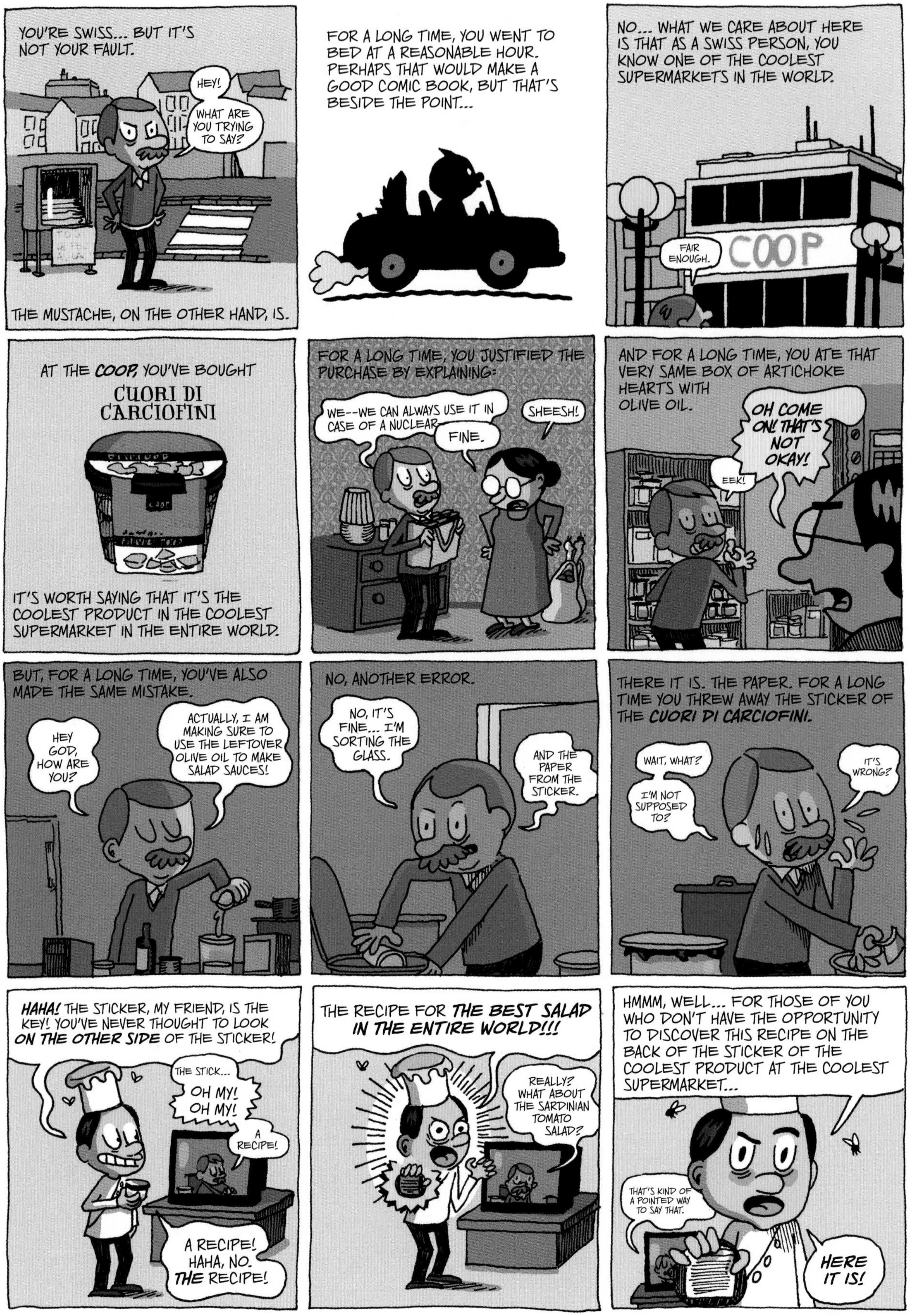
YOU'RE SWISS... BUT IT'S NOT YOUR FAULT.
HEY!
WHAT ARE YOU TRYING TO SAY?
THE MUSTACHE, ON THE OTHER HAND, IS.
FOR A LONG TIME, YOU WENT TO BED AT A REASONABLE HOUR. PERHAPS THAT WOULD MAKE A GOOD COMIC BOOK, BUT THAT'S BESIDE THE POINT...
NO... WHAT WE CARE ABOUT HERE IS THAT AS A SWISS PERSON, YOU KNOW ONE OF THE COOLEST SUPERMARKETS IN THE WORLD.
FAIR ENOUGH.
COOP
AT THE COOP, YOU'VE BOUGHT
CUORI DI CARCIOFINI
IT'S WORTH SAYING THAT IT'S THE COOLEST PRODUCT IN THE COOLEST SUPERMARKET IN THE ENTIRE WORLD.
FOR A LONG TIME, YOU JUSTIFIED THE PURCHASE BY EXPLAINING:
WE--WE CAN ALWAYS USE IT IN CASE OF A NUCLEAR
FINE.
SHEESH!
AND FOR A LONG TIME, YOU ATE THAT VERY SAME BOX OF ARTICHOKE HEARTS WITH OLIVE OIL.
OH COME ON! THAT'S NOT OKAY!
EEK!
BUT, FOR A LONG TIME, YOU'VE ALSO MADE THE SAME MISTAKE.
HEY GOD, HOW ARE YOU?
ACTUALLY, I AM MAKING SURE TO USE THE LEFTOVER OLIVE OIL TO MAKE SALAD SAUCES!
NO, ANOTHER ERROR.
NO, IT'S FINE... I'M SORTING THE GLASS.
AND THE PAPER FROM THE STICKER.
THERE IT IS. THE PAPER. FOR A LONG TIME YOU THREW AWAY THE STICKER OF THE CUORI DI CARCIOFINI.
WAIT, WHAT?
I'M NOT SUPPOSED TO?
IT'S WRONG?
HAHA! THE STICKER, MY FRIEND, IS THE KEY! YOU'VE NEVER THOUGHT TO LOOK ON THE OTHER SIDE OF THE STICKER!
THE STICK...
OH MY! OH MY!
A RECIPE!
A RECIPE! HAHA, NO. THE RECIPE!
THE RECIPE FOR THE BEST SALAD IN THE ENTIRE WORLD!!!
REALLY? WHAT ABOUT THE SARDINIAN TOMATO SALAD?
HMMM, WELL... FOR THOSE OF YOU WHO DON'T HAVE THE OPPORTUNITY TO DISCOVER THIS RECIPE ON THE BACK OF THE STICKER OF THE COOLEST PRODUCT AT THE COOLEST SUPERMARKET...
THAT'S KIND OF A POINTED WAY TO SAY THAT.
HERE IT IS!

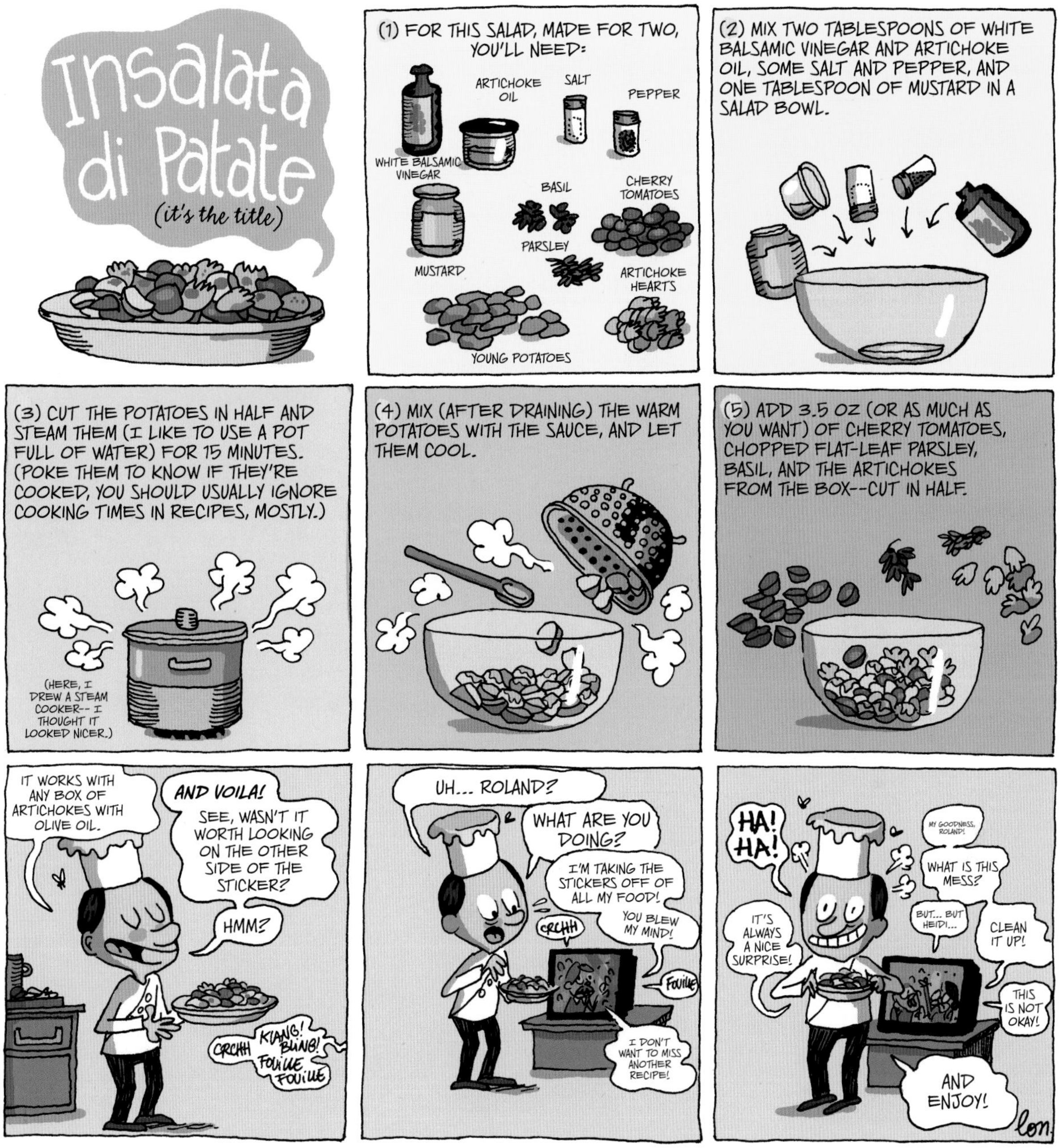
Insalata di Patate
(it's the title)
(1) FOR THIS SALAD, MADE FOR TWO, YOU'LL NEED:
ARTICHOKE OIL
SALT
PEPPER
WHITE BALSAMIC VINEGAR
BASIL
CHERRY TOMATOES
PARSLEY
MUSTARD
ARTICHOKE HEARTS
YOUNG POTATOES
(2) MIX TWO TABLESPOONS OF WHITE BALSAMIC VINEGAR AND ARTICHOKE OIL, SOME SALT AND PEPPER, AND ONE TABLESPOON OF MUSTARD IN A SALAD BOWL.
(3) CUT THE POTATOES IN HALF AND STEAM THEM (I LIKE TO USE A POT FULL OF WATER) FOR 15 MINUTES. (POKE THEM TO KNOW IF THEY'RE COOKED, YOU SHOULD USUALLY IGNORE COOKING TIMES IN RECIPES, MOSTLY.)
(HERE, I DREW A STEAM COOKER-- I THOUGHT IT LOOKED NICER.)
(4) MIX (AFTER DRAINING) THE WARM POTATOES WITH THE SAUCE, AND LET THEM COOL.
(5) ADD 3.5 OZ (OR AS MUCH AS YOU WANT) OF CHERRY TOMATOES, CHOPPED FLAT-LEAF PARSLEY, BASIL, AND THE ARTICHOKES FROM THE BOX--CUT IN HALF.
IT WORKS WITH ANY BOX OF ARTICHOKES WITH OLIVE OIL.
AND VOILA!
SEE, WASN'T IT WORTH LOOKING ON THE OTHER SIDE OF THE STICKER?
HMM?
CRCHH KLANG! BLING! FOUILLE FOUILLE
UH... ROLAND?
WHAT ARE YOU DOING?
I'M TAKING THE STICKERS OFF OF ALL MY FOOD!
YOU BLEW MY MIND!
CRCHH
FOUILLE
I DON'T WANT TO MISS ANOTHER RECIPE!
HA! HA!
MY GOODNESS, ROLAND!
WHAT IS THIS MESS?
IT'S ALWAYS A NICE SURPRISE!
BUT... BUT HEIDI...
CLEAN IT UP!
THIS IS NOT OKAY!
AND ENJOY!
lon

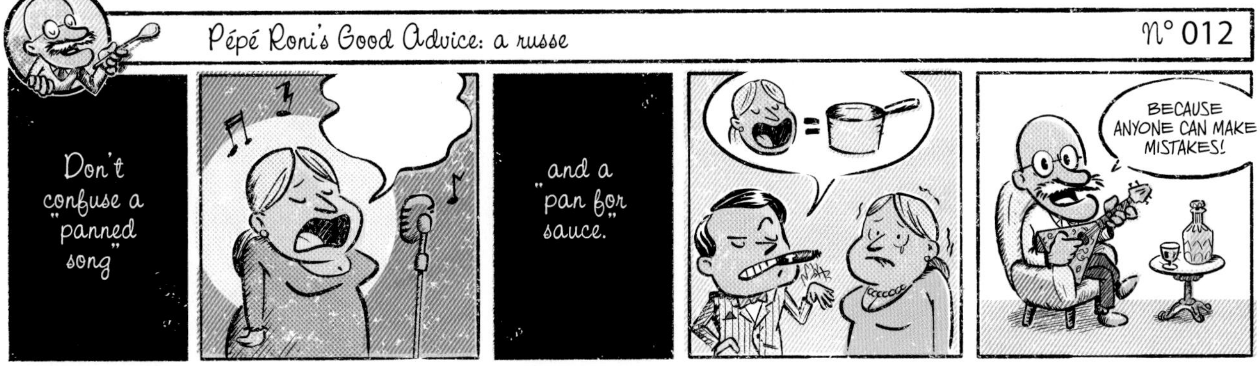
Pépé Roni's Good Advice: a russe
N° 012
Don't confuse a "panned song"
and a "pan for sauce."
BECAUSE ANYONE CAN MAKE MISTAKES!

A russe: a round, slanted pan for sauces.

Eggplant isn't that complicated

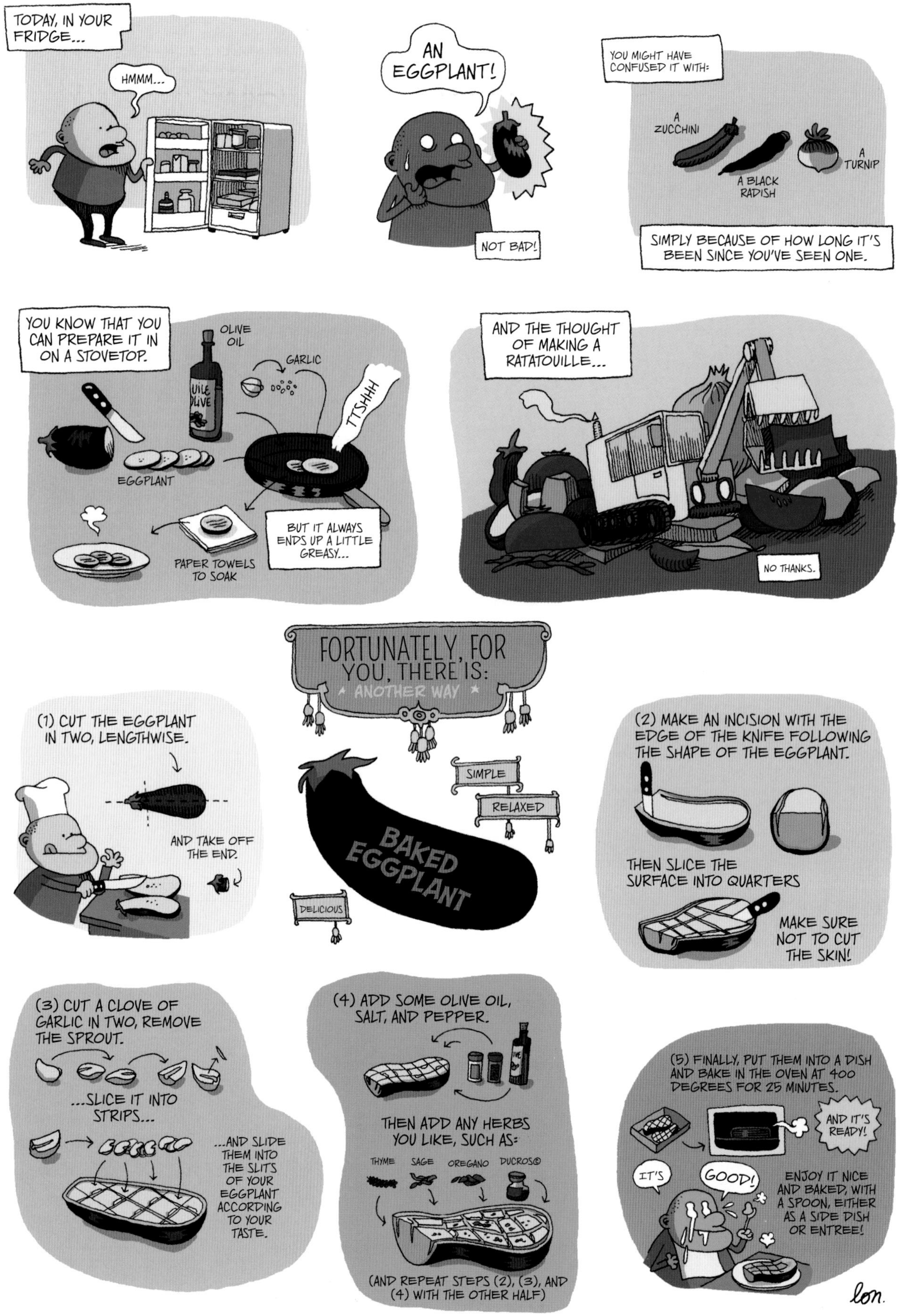

TODAY, IN YOUR FRIDGE...
HMMM...
AN EGGPLANT!
NOT BAD!
YOU MIGHT HAVE CONFUSED IT WITH:
A ZUCCHINI
A BLACK RADISH
A TURNIP
SIMPLY BECAUSE OF HOW LONG IT'S BEEN SINCE YOU'VE SEEN ONE.
YOU KNOW THAT YOU CAN PREPARE IT IN ON A STOVETOP.
OLIVE OIL
GARLIC
TTSHHH
EGGPLANT
PAPER TOWELS TO SOAK
BUT IT ALWAYS ENDS UP A LITTLE GREASY...
AND THE THOUGHT OF MAKING A RATATOUILLE...
NO THANKS.
FORTUNATELY, FOR YOU, THERE IS:
ANOTHER WAY
SIMPLE
RELAXED
BAKED EGGPLANT
DELICIOUS
(1) CUT THE EGGPLANT IN TWO, LENGTHWISE.
AND TAKE OFF THE END.
(2) MAKE AN INCISION WITH THE EDGE OF THE KNIFE FOLLOWING THE SHAPE OF THE EGGPLANT.
THEN SLICE THE SURFACE INTO QUARTERS
MAKE SURE NOT TO CUT THE SKIN!
(3) CUT A CLOVE OF GARLIC IN TWO, REMOVE THE SPROUT.
...SLICE IT INTO STRIPS...
...AND SLIDE THEM INTO THE SLITS OF YOUR EGGPLANT ACCORDING TO YOUR TASTE.
(4) ADD SOME OLIVE OIL, SALT, AND PEPPER.
THEN ADD ANY HERBS YOU LIKE, SUCH AS:
THYME
SAGE
OREGANO
DUCROS©
(AND REPEAT STEPS (2), (3), AND (4) WITH THE OTHER HALF)
(5) FINALLY, PUT THEM INTO A DISH AND BAKE IN THE OVEN AT 400 DEGREES FOR 25 MINUTES.
AND IT'S READY!
IT'S
GOOD!
ENJOY IT NICE AND BAKED, WITH A SPOON, EITHER AS A SIDE DISH OR ENTREE!
lon.

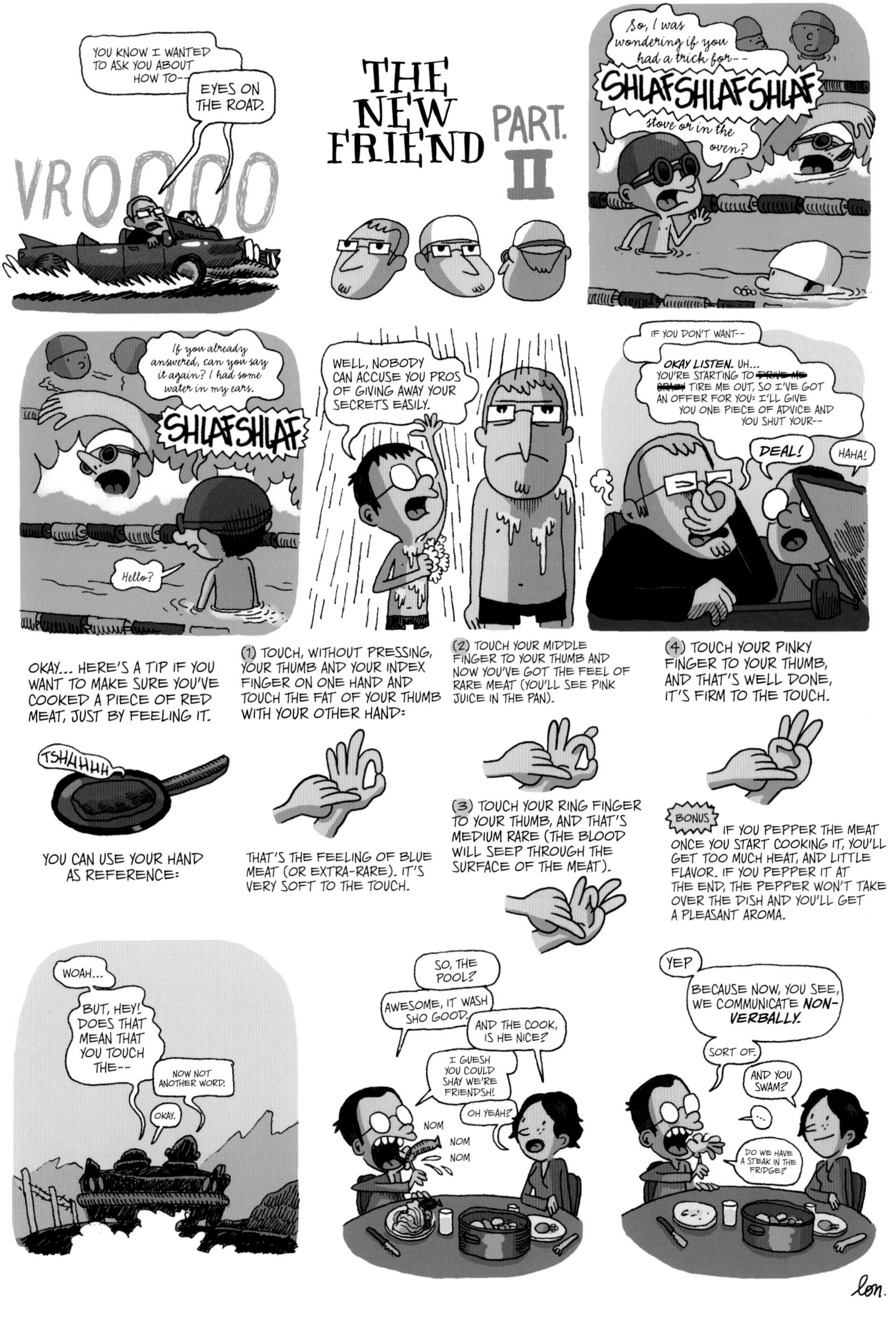
YOU KNOW I WANTED TO ASK YOU ABOUT HOW TO--
EYES ON THE ROAD.
VROOOO
THE NEW FRIEND PART. II
So, I was wondering if you had a trick for--
SHLAFSHLAFSHLAF
stove or in the oven?
If you already answered, can you say it again? I had some water in my ears.
SHLAFSHLAF
Hello?
WELL, NOBODY CAN ACCUSE YOU PROS OF GIVING AWAY YOUR SECRETS EASILY.
IF YOU DON'T WANT--
OKAY LISTEN. UH... YOU'RE STARTING TO ~~DRIVE ME CRAZY~~ TIRE ME OUT, SO I'VE GOT AN OFFER FOR YOU: I'LL GIVE YOU ONE PIECE OF ADVICE AND YOU SHUT YOUR--
DEAL!
HAHA!
OKAY... HERE'S A TIP IF YOU WANT TO MAKE SURE YOU'VE COOKED A PIECE OF RED MEAT, JUST BY FEELING IT.
TSHHHHH
YOU CAN USE YOUR HAND AS REFERENCE:
(1) TOUCH, WITHOUT PRESSING, YOUR THUMB AND YOUR INDEX FINGER ON ONE HAND AND TOUCH THE FAT OF YOUR THUMB WITH YOUR OTHER HAND:
THAT'S THE FEELING OF BLUE MEAT (OR EXTRA-RARE). IT'S VERY SOFT TO THE TOUCH.
(2) TOUCH YOUR MIDDLE FINGER TO YOUR THUMB AND NOW YOU'VE GOT THE FEEL OF RARE MEAT (YOU'LL SEE PINK JUICE IN THE PAN).
(3) TOUCH YOUR RING FINGER TO YOUR THUMB, AND THAT'S MEDIUM RARE (THE BLOOD WILL SEEP THROUGH THE SURFACE OF THE MEAT).
(4) TOUCH YOUR PINKY FINGER TO YOUR THUMB, AND THAT'S WELL DONE, IT'S FIRM TO THE TOUCH.
BONUS IF YOU PEPPER THE MEAT ONCE YOU START COOKING IT, YOU'LL GET TOO MUCH HEAT, AND LITTLE FLAVOR. IF YOU PEPPER IT AT THE END, THE PEPPER WON'T TAKE OVER THE DISH AND YOU'LL GET A PLEASANT AROMA.
WOAH...
BUT, HEY! DOES THAT MEAN THAT YOU TOUCH THE--
NOW NOT ANOTHER WORD.
OKAY.
SO, THE POOL?
AWESOME, IT WASH SHO GOOD.
AND THE COOK, IS HE NICE?
I GUESH YOU COULD SHAY WE'RE FRIENDSH!
OH YEAH?
NOM
NOM
NOM
YEP
BECAUSE NOW, YOU SEE, WE COMMUNICATE NON-VERBALLY.
SORT OF.
AND YOU SWAM?
...
DO WE HAVE A STEAK IN THE FRIDGE?
lon.

Egg heist II

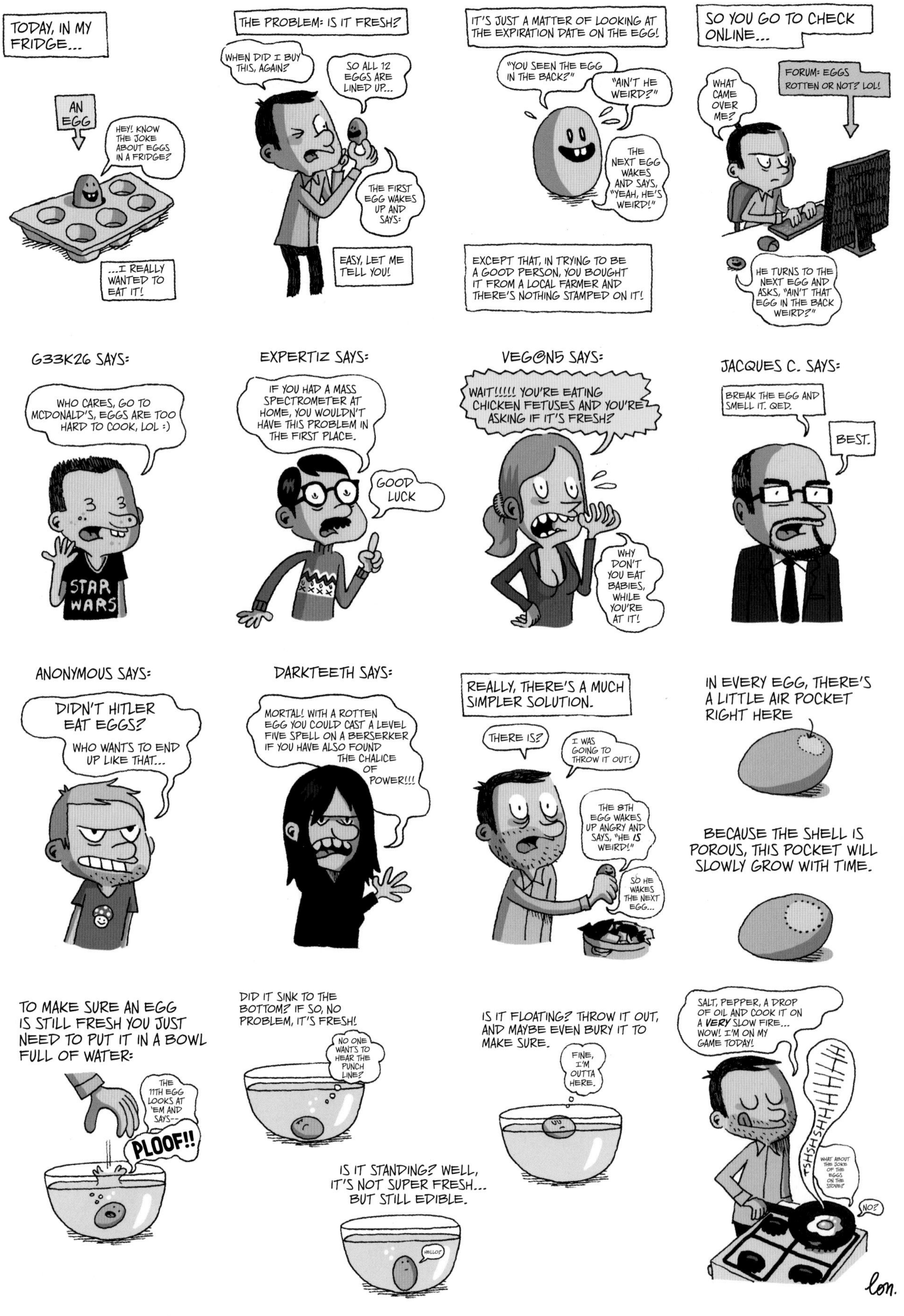

TODAY, IN MY FRIDGE...
AN EGG
HEY! KNOW THE JOKE ABOUT EGGS IN A FRIDGE?
...I REALLY WANTED TO EAT IT!
THE PROBLEM: IS IT FRESH?
WHEN DID I BUY THIS, AGAIN?
SO ALL 12 EGGS ARE LINED UP...
THE FIRST EGG WAKES UP AND SAYS:
EASY, LET ME TELL YOU!
IT'S JUST A MATTER OF LOOKING AT THE EXPIRATION DATE ON THE EGG!
"YOU SEEN THE EGG IN THE BACK?"
"AIN'T HE WEIRD?"
THE NEXT EGG WAKES AND SAYS, "YEAH, HE'S WEIRD!"
EXCEPT THAT, IN TRYING TO BE A GOOD PERSON, YOU BOUGHT IT FROM A LOCAL FARMER AND THERE'S NOTHING STAMPED ON IT!
SO YOU GO TO CHECK ONLINE...
WHAT CAME OVER ME?
FORUM: EGGS ROTTEN OR NOT? LOL!
HE TURNS TO THE NEXT EGG AND ASKS, "AIN'T THAT EGG IN THE BACK WEIRD?"
G33K26 SAYS:
WHO CARES, GO TO MCDONALD'S, EGGS ARE TOO HARD TO COOK, LOL :)
STAR WARS
EXPERTIZ SAYS:
IF YOU HAD A MASS SPECTROMETER AT HOME, YOU WOULDN'T HAVE THIS PROBLEM IN THE FIRST PLACE.
GOOD LUCK
VEG@N5 SAYS:
WAIT!!!!! YOU'RE EATING CHICKEN FETUSES AND YOU'RE ASKING IF IT'S FRESH?
WHY DON'T YOU EAT BABIES, WHILE YOU'RE AT IT!
JACQUES C. SAYS:
BREAK THE EGG AND SMELL IT. QED.
BEST.
ANONYMOUS SAYS:
DIDN'T HITLER EAT EGGS?
WHO WANTS TO END UP LIKE THAT...
DARKTEETH SAYS:
MORTAL! WITH A ROTTEN EGG YOU COULD CAST A LEVEL FIVE SPELL ON A BERSERKER IF YOU HAVE ALSO FOUND THE CHALICE OF POWER!!!
REALLY, THERE'S A MUCH SIMPLER SOLUTION.
THERE IS?
I WAS GOING TO THROW IT OUT!
THE 8TH EGG WAKES UP ANGRY AND SAYS, "HE IS WEIRD!"
SO HE WAKES THE NEXT EGG...
IN EVERY EGG, THERE'S A LITTLE AIR POCKET RIGHT HERE
BECAUSE THE SHELL IS POROUS, THIS POCKET WILL SLOWLY GROW WITH TIME.
TO MAKE SURE AN EGG IS STILL FRESH YOU JUST NEED TO PUT IT IN A BOWL FULL OF WATER:
THE 11TH EGG LOOKS AT 'EM AND SAYS--
PLOOF!!
DID IT SINK TO THE BOTTOM? IF SO, NO PROBLEM, IT'S FRESH!
NO ONE WANTS TO HEAR THE PUNCH LINE?
IS IT STANDING? WELL, IT'S NOT SUPER FRESH... BUT STILL EDIBLE.
HELLO?
IS IT FLOATING? THROW IT OUT, AND MAYBE EVEN BURY IT TO MAKE SURE.
FINE, I'M OUTTA HERE.
SALT, PEPPER, A DROP OF OIL AND COOK IT ON A VERY SLOW FIRE... WOW! I'M ON MY GAME TODAY!
TSHSHSHHHHHHHH
WHAT ABOUT THE JOKE OF THE EGGS ON THE STOVE?
NO?
lon.

TODAY LET'S ASK OURSELVES: WHAT DISH CAN PRIDE ITSELF ON BRINGING TOGETHER SOMEONE FROM INDIA, GREECE, SPAIN, AND MOROCCO?

MOVE YOUR BUTTS FOR THE MINISTERS, OR YOU CAN FORGET ABOUT YOUR ID'S!!!

¡JODER!

HAH! NO... I WAS ACTUALLY THINKING OF...

THE FETA WATERMELON SALAD

WATERMELON

CURRY

FETA

MINT

THE RECIPE IS IN THE INGREDIENTS!

(1) START BY CUTTING THE WATERMELON INTO SMALL PIECES:

AND MAKE SURE TO REMOVE THE SEEDS, OF COURSE.

(2) THEN DO THE SAME THING WITH THE FETA:

TIP: CUT THE FETA *IN* ITS PACKAGE (IF YOU BOUGHT IT IN A SUPERMARKET). IT WON'T FALL APART AS MUCH.

(3) MIX THE WATERMELON AND THE FETA IN A SALAD BOWL, CHOP THE MINT AND SPRINKLE IT ON TOP AND THEN SEASON IT WITH A LITTLE CURRY.

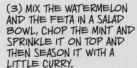

THEN PUT IT IN YOUR REFRIGERATOR FOR AN HOUR BEFORE SERVING IT.

OH NO! NO FETA FOR ME!

SOMEONE TOLD ME THAT CHEESE MAKES YOU FAT.

SEND IT BACK.

leon.

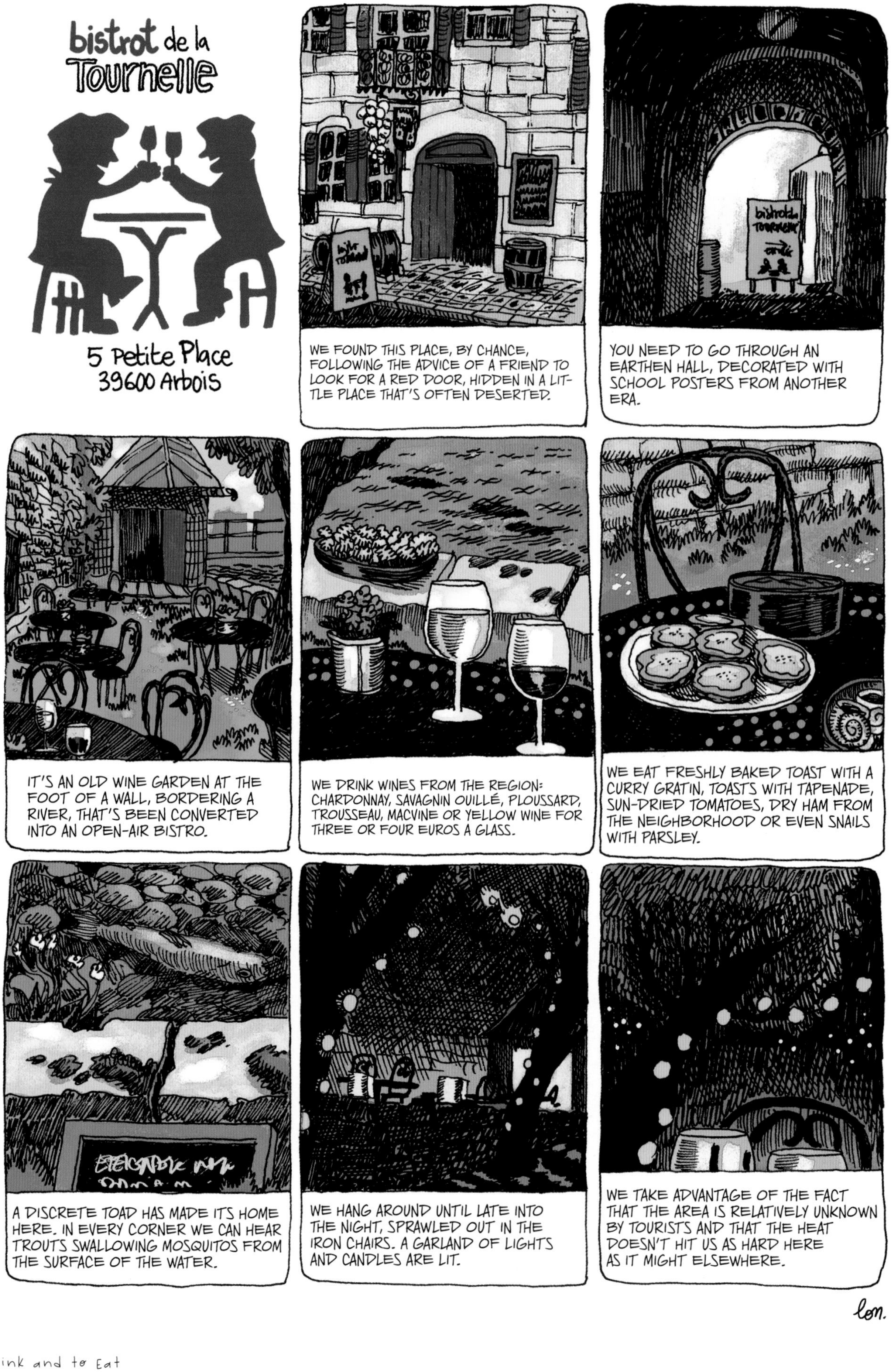
bistrot de la Tournelle
5 Petite Place
39600 Arbois
WE FOUND THIS PLACE, BY CHANCE, FOLLOWING THE ADVICE OF A FRIEND TO LOOK FOR A RED DOOR, HIDDEN IN A LITTLE PLACE THAT'S OFTEN DESERTED.
YOU NEED TO GO THROUGH AN EARTHEN HALL, DECORATED WITH SCHOOL POSTERS FROM ANOTHER ERA.
IT'S AN OLD WINE GARDEN AT THE FOOT OF A WALL, BORDERING A RIVER, THAT'S BEEN CONVERTED INTO AN OPEN-AIR BISTRO.
WE DRINK WINES FROM THE REGION: CHARDONNAY, SAVAGNIN OUILLÉ, PLOUSSARD, TROUSSEAU, MACVINE OR YELLOW WINE FOR THREE OR FOUR EUROS A GLASS.
WE EAT FRESHLY BAKED TOAST WITH A CURRY GRATIN, TOASTS WITH TAPENADE, SUN-DRIED TOMATOES, DRY HAM FROM THE NEIGHBORHOOD OR EVEN SNAILS WITH PARSLEY.
A DISCRETE TOAD HAS MADE ITS HOME HERE. IN EVERY CORNER WE CAN HEAR TROUTS SWALLOWING MOSQUITOS FROM THE SURFACE OF THE WATER.
WE HANG AROUND UNTIL LATE INTO THE NIGHT, SPRAWLED OUT IN THE IRON CHAIRS. A GARLAND OF LIGHTS AND CANDLES ARE LIT.
WE TAKE ADVANTAGE OF THE FACT THAT THE AREA IS RELATIVELY UNKNOWN BY TOURISTS AND THAT THE HEAT DOESN'T HIT US AS HARD HERE AS IT MIGHT ELSEWHERE.
lon.

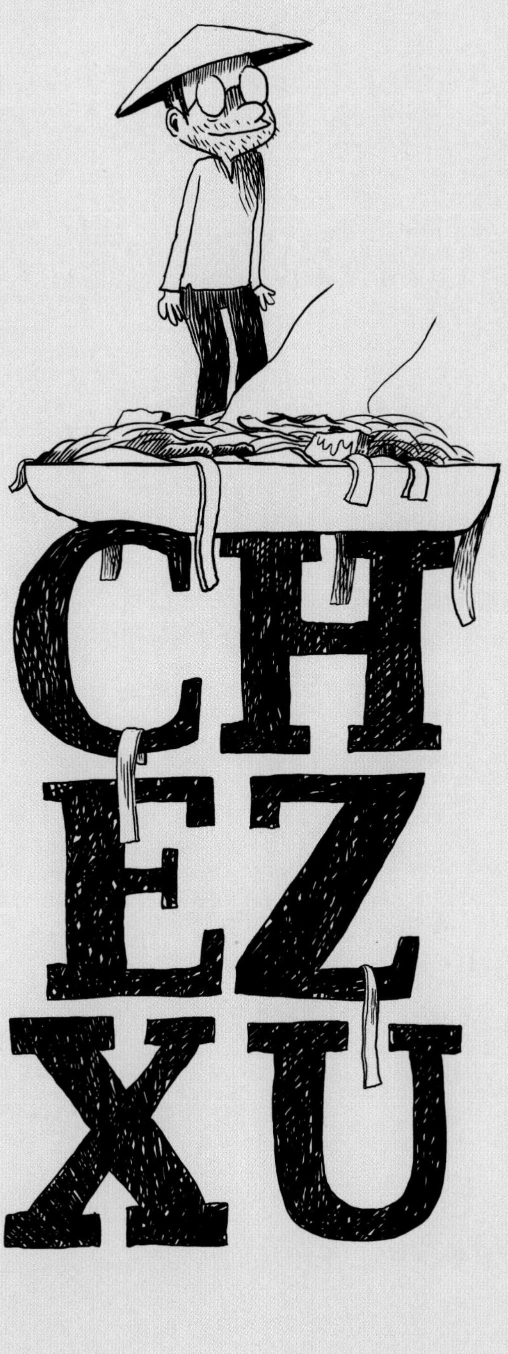
CHEZ XU

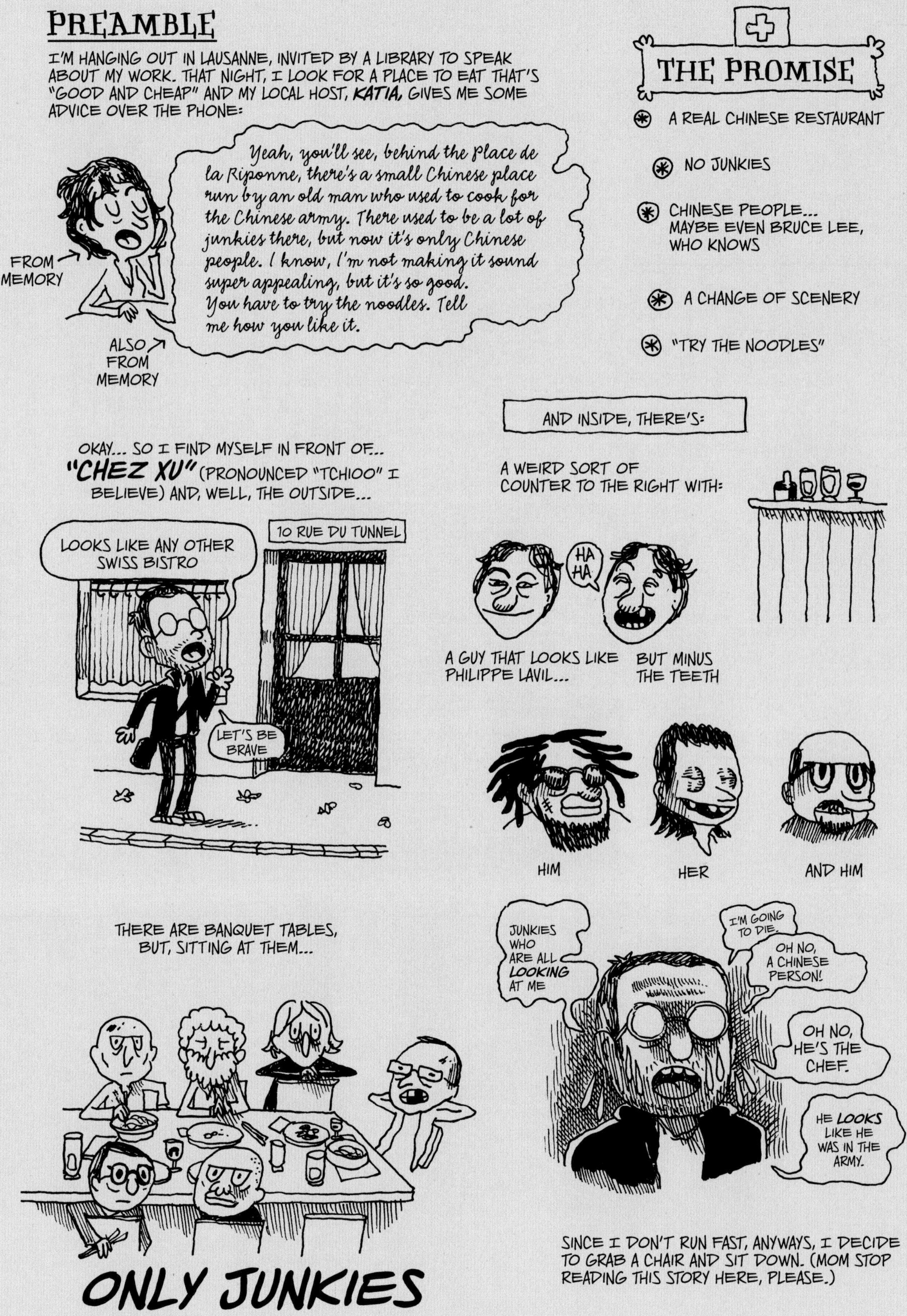
PREAMBLE
I'M HANGING OUT IN LAUSANNE, INVITED BY A LIBRARY TO SPEAK ABOUT MY WORK. THAT NIGHT, I LOOK FOR A PLACE TO EAT THAT'S "GOOD AND CHEAP" AND MY LOCAL HOST, KATIA, GIVES ME SOME ADVICE OVER THE PHONE:
Yeah, you'll see, behind the Place de la Riponne, there's a small Chinese place run by an old man who used to cook for the Chinese army. There used to be a lot of junkies there, but now it's only Chinese people. I know, I'm not making it sound super appealing, but it's so good. You have to try the noodles. Tell me how you like it.
FROM MEMORY
ALSO FROM MEMORY
THE PROMISE
A REAL CHINESE RESTAURANT
NO JUNKIES
CHINESE PEOPLE... MAYBE EVEN BRUCE LEE, WHO KNOWS
A CHANGE OF SCENERY
"TRY THE NOODLES"
OKAY... SO I FIND MYSELF IN FRONT OF.. "CHEZ XU" (PRONOUNCED "TCHIOO" I BELIEVE) AND, WELL, THE OUTSIDE...
10 RUE DU TUNNEL
LOOKS LIKE ANY OTHER SWISS BISTRO
LET'S BE BRAVE
AND INSIDE, THERE'S:
A WEIRD SORT OF COUNTER TO THE RIGHT WITH:
HA HA
A GUY THAT LOOKS LIKE PHILIPPE LAVIL...
BUT MINUS THE TEETH
HIM
HER
AND HIM
THERE ARE BANQUET TABLES, BUT, SITTING AT THEM...
ONLY JUNKIES
JUNKIES WHO ARE ALL LOOKING AT ME
I'M GOING TO DIE.
OH NO, A CHINESE PERSON!
OH NO, HE'S THE CHEF.
HE LOOKS LIKE HE WAS IN THE ARMY.
SINCE I DON'T RUN FAST, ANYWAYS, I DECIDE TO GRAB A CHAIR AND SIT DOWN. (MOM STOP READING THIS STORY HERE, PLEASE.)

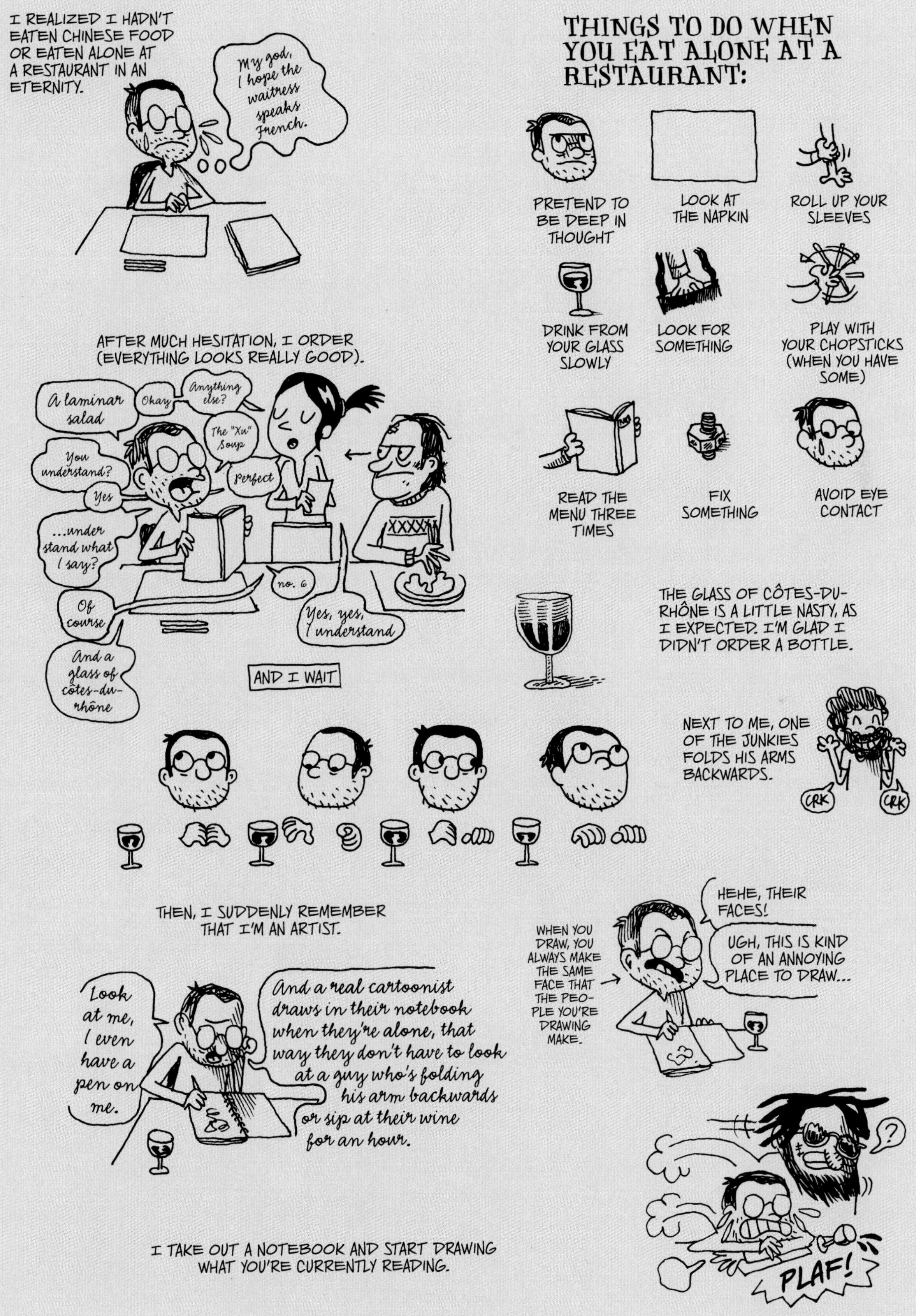

I REALIZED I HADN'T EATEN CHINESE FOOD OR EATEN ALONE AT A RESTAURANT IN AN ETERNITY.
My god, I hope the waitress speaks French.
THINGS TO DO WHEN YOU EAT ALONE AT A RESTAURANT:
PRETEND TO BE DEEP IN THOUGHT
LOOK AT THE NAPKIN
ROLL UP YOUR SLEEVES
DRINK FROM YOUR GLASS SLOWLY
LOOK FOR SOMETHING
PLAY WITH YOUR CHOPSTICKS (WHEN YOU HAVE SOME)
READ THE MENU THREE TIMES
FIX SOMETHING
AVOID EYE CONTACT
AFTER MUCH HESITATION, I ORDER (EVERYTHING LOOKS REALLY GOOD).
A laminar salad
Okay
Anything else?
The "Xu" Soup
You understand?
Perfect
Yes
...understand what I say?
no. 6
Of course
Yes, yes, I understand
And a glass of côtes-du-rhône
AND I WAIT
THE GLASS OF CÔTES-DU-RHÔNE IS A LITTLE NASTY, AS I EXPECTED. I'M GLAD I DIDN'T ORDER A BOTTLE.
NEXT TO ME, ONE OF THE JUNKIES FOLDS HIS ARMS BACKWARDS.
CRK
CRK
THEN, I SUDDENLY REMEMBER THAT I'M AN ARTIST.
Look at me, I even have a pen on me.
And a real cartoonist draws in their notebook when they're alone, that way they don't have to look at a guy who's folding his arm backwards or sip at their wine for an hour.
I TAKE OUT A NOTEBOOK AND START DRAWING WHAT YOU'RE CURRENTLY READING.
HEHE, THEIR FACES!
UGH, THIS IS KIND OF AN ANNOYING PLACE TO DRAW...
WHEN YOU DRAW, YOU ALWAYS MAKE THE SAME FACE THAT THE PEOPLE YOU'RE DRAWING MAKE.
?
PLAF!

TEN OR SO MINUTES LATER (I DON'T KNOW HOW LONG EXACTLY, I WAS DRAWING), THE FIRST DISH ARRIVES:

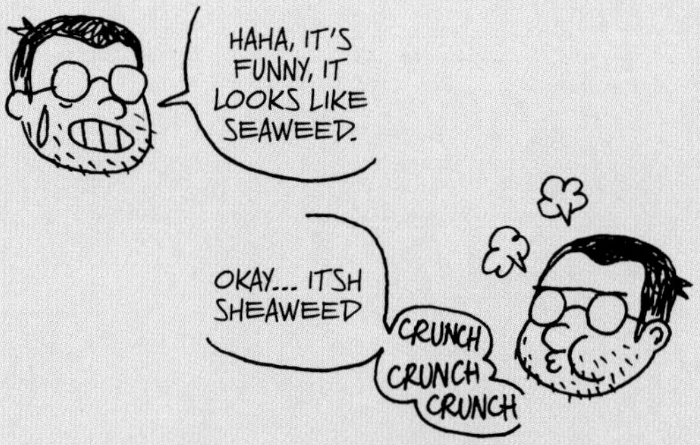
HAHA, IT'S FUNNY, IT LOOKS LIKE SEAWEED.
OKAY... ITSH SHEAWEED
CRUNCH
CRUNCH
CRUNCH

LAMINAR SALAD

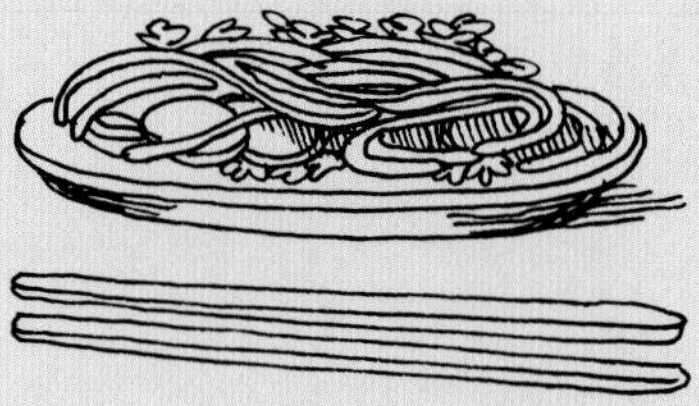

I'M SURPRISED BECAUSE I WAS EXPECTING THE LAMINAR TO BE MUSHROOMS (STRIPS OF THEM) BUT I HAVE TO ADMIT THAT IT'S ***VERY*** GOOD AND ***QUITE*** A LARGE PORTION. THE SOUP THAT'S ON IT'S WAY FREAKS ME OUT.

(NEXT TO ME, THE GUY WITH HIS ARMS BACKWARD IS HAVING A DISCUSSION WITH A FRIEND WHILE LAUGHING NERVOUSLY.)

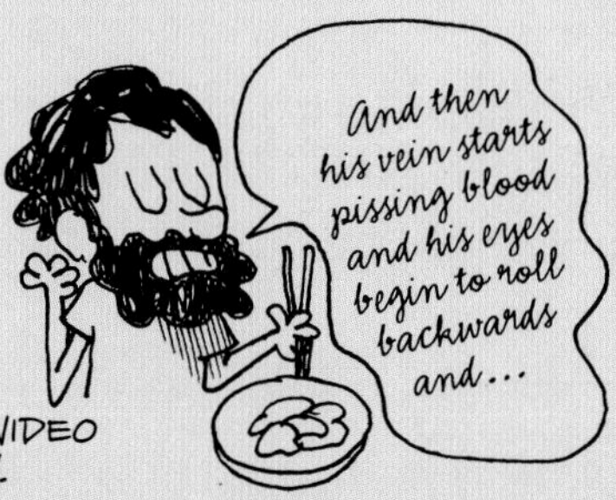
And then his vein starts pissing blood and his eyes begin to roll backwards and...

THEY'RE DISCUSSING A VIDEO GAME ABOUT SURGERY.

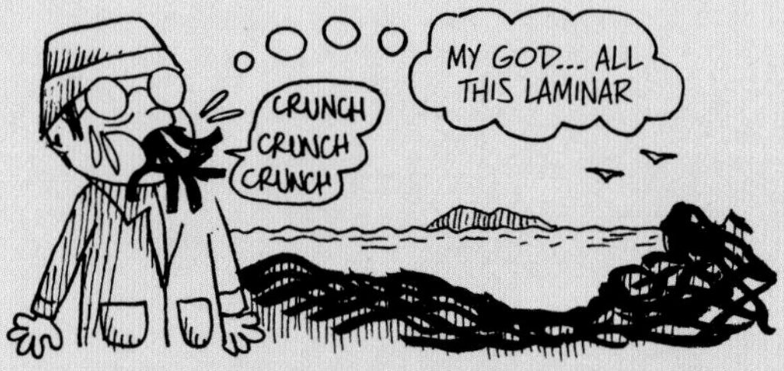
MY GOD... ALL THIS LAMINAR
CRUNCH
CRUNCH
CRUNCH

AND THEN, IT ARRIVES...

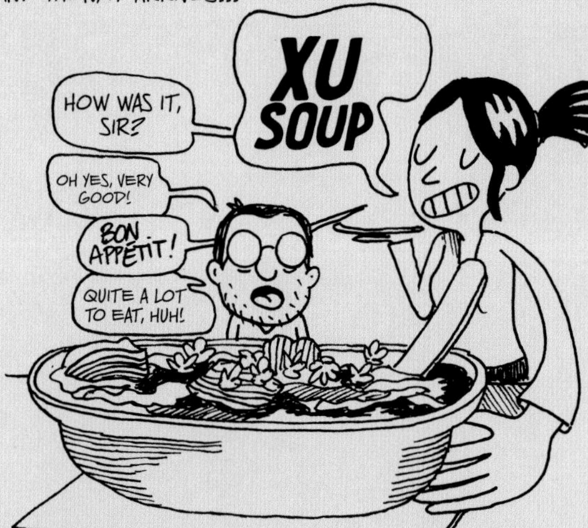
HOW WAS IT, SIR?
XU SOUP
OH YES, VERY GOOD!
BON APPÉTIT!
QUITE A LOT TO EAT, HUH!

THE SOUP IS VERY RUSTIC. IT FEELS LIKE THE SORT OF THING YOU'D EAT IN SOME VILLAGE IN THE MIDDLE OF NOWHERE IN CHINA: BOILED BEEF(1), CORIANDER(2), FLAT-LEAF PARSLEY(3), A FEW VEGETABLES(4), AND SOME HANDMADE NOODLES(5). A REAL CHINESE RESTAURANT, AS FAR AS I CAN TELL, ANYWAYS.

AND ALMOST AT THE SAME TIME (AROUND 8 P.M.) A BUNCH MORE HIP-LOOKING PEOPLE ARRIVE.

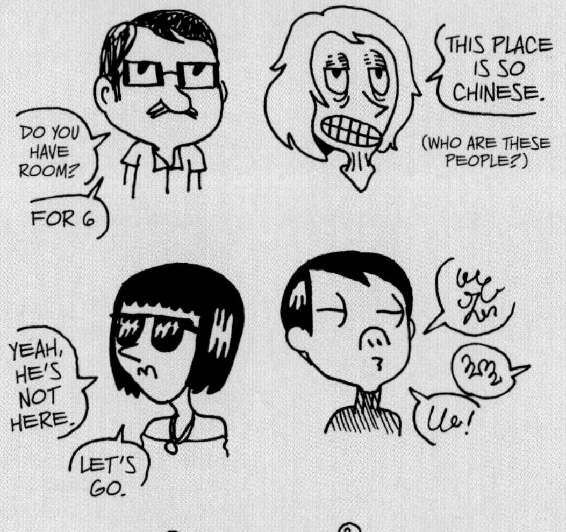
THIS PLACE IS SO CHINESE.
DO YOU HAVE ROOM?
(WHO ARE THESE PEOPLE?)
FOR 6
YEAH, HE'S NOT HERE.
LET'S GO.

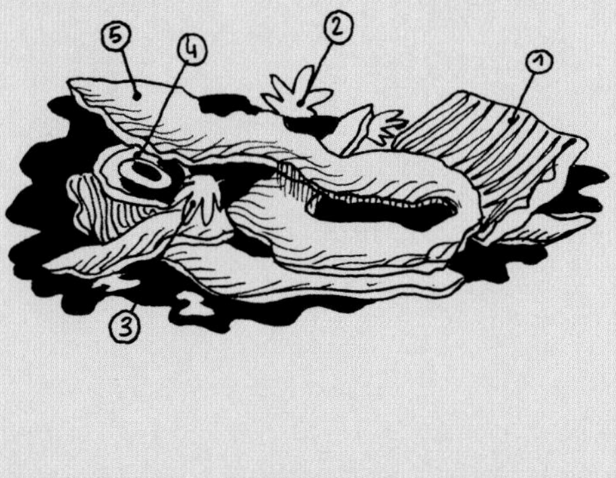
5
4
2
1
3

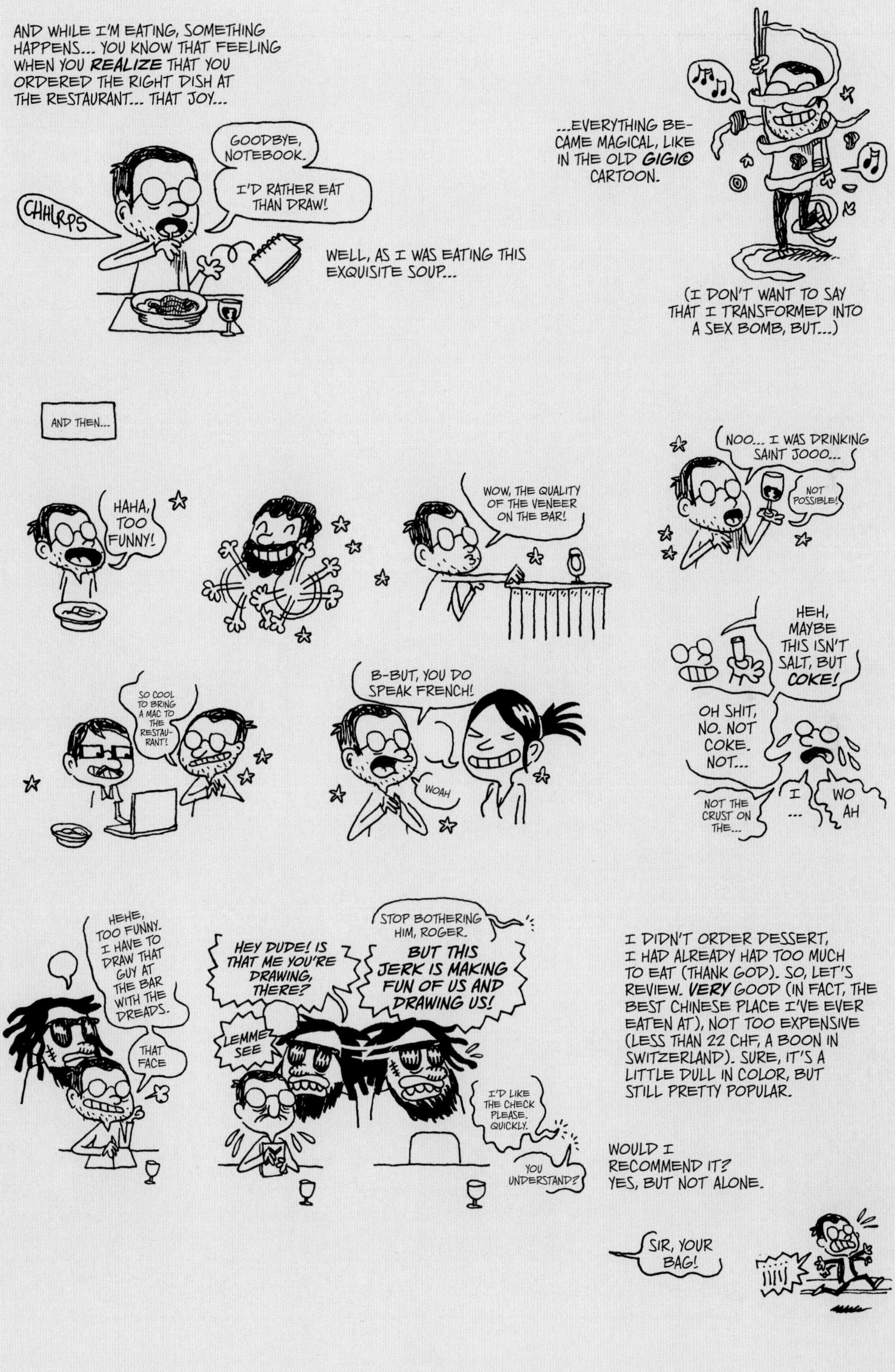
AND WHILE I'M EATING, SOMETHING HAPPENS... YOU KNOW THAT FEELING WHEN YOU REALIZE THAT YOU ORDERED THE RIGHT DISH AT THE RESTAURANT... THAT JOY...
GOODBYE, NOTEBOOK.
I'D RATHER EAT THAN DRAW!
CHHLRPS
WELL, AS I WAS EATING THIS EXQUISITE SOUP...
...EVERYTHING BECAME MAGICAL, LIKE IN THE OLD GIGI© CARTOON.
(I DON'T WANT TO SAY THAT I TRANSFORMED INTO A SEX BOMB, BUT...)
AND THEN...
HAHA, TOO FUNNY!
WOW, THE QUALITY OF THE VENEER ON THE BAR!
NOO... I WAS DRINKING SAINT JOOO...
NOT POSSIBLE!
SO COOL TO BRING A MAC TO THE RESTAURANT!
B-BUT, YOU DO SPEAK FRENCH!
WOAH
HEH, MAYBE THIS ISN'T SALT, BUT COKE!
OH SHIT, NO. NOT COKE. NOT...
NOT THE CRUST ON THE...
I ...
WO AH
HEHE, TOO FUNNY. I HAVE TO DRAW THAT GUY AT THE BAR WITH THE DREADS.
THAT FACE
HEY DUDE! IS THAT ME YOU'RE DRAWING, THERE?
STOP BOTHERING HIM, ROGER.
BUT THIS JERK IS MAKING FUN OF US AND DRAWING US!
LEMME SEE
I'D LIKE THE CHECK PLEASE. QUICKLY.
YOU UNDERSTAND?
I DIDN'T ORDER DESSERT, I HAD ALREADY HAD TOO MUCH TO EAT (THANK GOD). SO, LET'S REVIEW. VERY GOOD (IN FACT, THE BEST CHINESE PLACE I'VE EVER EATEN AT), NOT TOO EXPENSIVE (LESS THAN 22 CHF, A BOON IN SWITZERLAND). SURE, IT'S A LITTLE DULL IN COLOR, BUT STILL PRETTY POPULAR.
WOULD I RECOMMEND IT? YES, BUT NOT ALONE.
SIR, YOUR BAG!

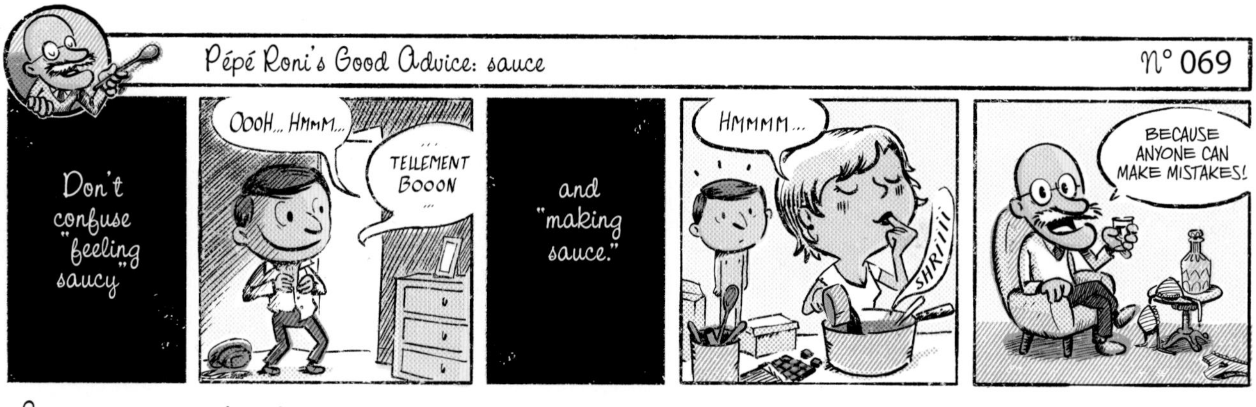
Pépé Roni's Good Advice: sauce
N° 069
Don't confuse "feeling saucy"
OOOH... HMMM...
... TELLEMENT BOOON ...
and "making sauce."
HMMMM...
SHRIIII
BECAUSE ANYONE CAN MAKE MISTAKES!

Sauce: a cream or liquid served on or used in preparing other foods.

Fall

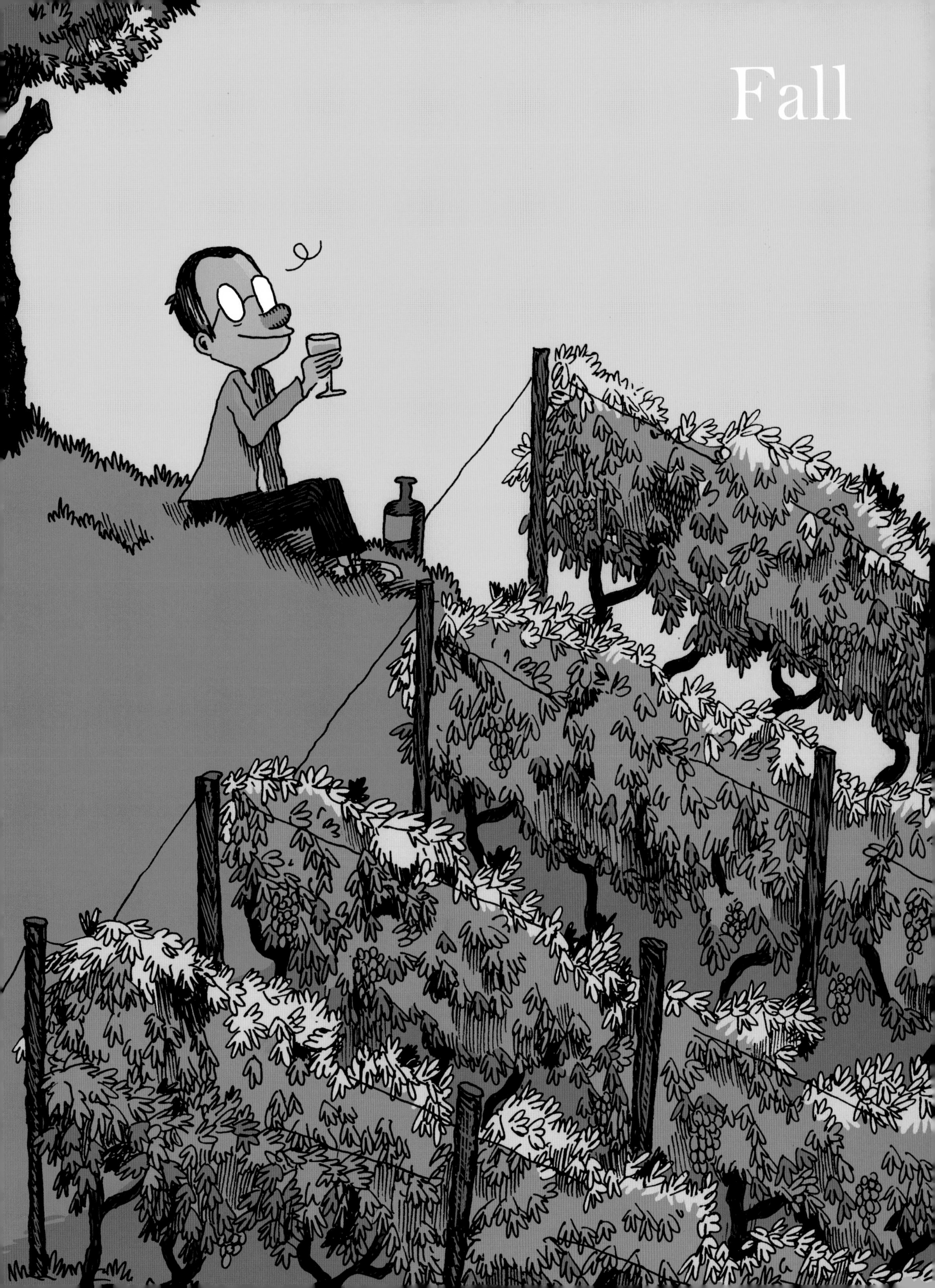

THE OTHER DAY IN THE SUPERMARKET, YOU HAD A FLASH, A MOMENT OF WEAKNESS--OF CRAZINESS-- DURING WHICH YOU ENTERED THE FOURTH DIMENSION...

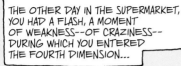

THAT IS TO SAY, YOU BOUGHT...

SOME BROCCOLI

PLEASE!

NOW, ALONE IN YOUR KITCHEN, YOU HAVE RETURNED TO REASON, AND YOU ASK YOURSELF:

SHIIIIT

WHY DID I BUY THIS THING?

DON'T WORRY, IT'S ONLY NORMAL...

YOU RECALL MEMORIES OF SOFT, LUKE-WARM BROCCOLI, FULL OF WATER...

THE VAGUE TASTE OF MOLDY CABBAGE...

WELL, GOOD NEWS: BROCCOLI CAN BE VERY DELICIOUS AND EVEN COOL!

BUT YOU'LL NEED:

BROCCOLI (CAN'T AVOID THAT)

SOY SAUCE

AND MAYBE SOME WASABI PASTE

THEN, YOU NEED TO CUT THE BROCCOLI LIKE THIS:

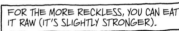

FOR THE MORE RECKLESS, YOU CAN EAT IT RAW (IT'S SLIGHTLY STRONGER).

I CAN'T BELIEVE I'M GOING TO EAT BROCCOLI!

OR YOU CAN COOK IT IN BOILING WATER FOR TWO OR THREE MINUTES.

BUT IT HAS TO STAY "AL DENTE."

FINALLY YOU SET THE CUT VEGETABLES ONTO A DISH, AND ACCOMPANY IT WITH SAUCERS FULL OF SOY SAUCE, TO WHICH YOU CAN ADD A *LITTLE* WASABI.

TO EAT WARM OR COLD

NOW, **DO NOT** THROW AWAY THE STEM OF THE BROCCOLI! YOU CAN USE IT AS "BONE MARROW" IN A SOUP, OR MIX IT WITH MASHED POTATOES. IT'S DELICIOUS!

OH REALLY?

SO I KEEP EVERYTHING.

LAST PIECE OF ADVICE, AVOID TALKING ABOUT BROCCOLI WHEN YOU SERVE THIS DISH (AS A SIDE TO SOME COLD ROAST BEEF, FOR EXAMPLE) TO YOUR FRIENDS... INSTEAD, INVENT A COOLER NAME LIKE:

THE *BROCOLOUNGE©.*

YOU'LL SEE HOW WELL THE TASTE COMPLEMENTS THE SOY SAUCE!

WOW! IT LOOKS LIKE BROCCOLI!

WOAH!

IS IT FROM NEW YORK?

THIS WAS A MESSAGE

FROM THE ASSOCIATION "TURNIPS, CELERY, SPINACH, BRUSSEL SPROUTS, AND OTHER UNFORTUNATE VEGETABLES THAT CAN BE DELICIOUS)"

(T.C.S.B.S.A.O.U.V.T.C.B.D.)

THANK YOU FOR TUNING IN.

leon.

In the cupboards

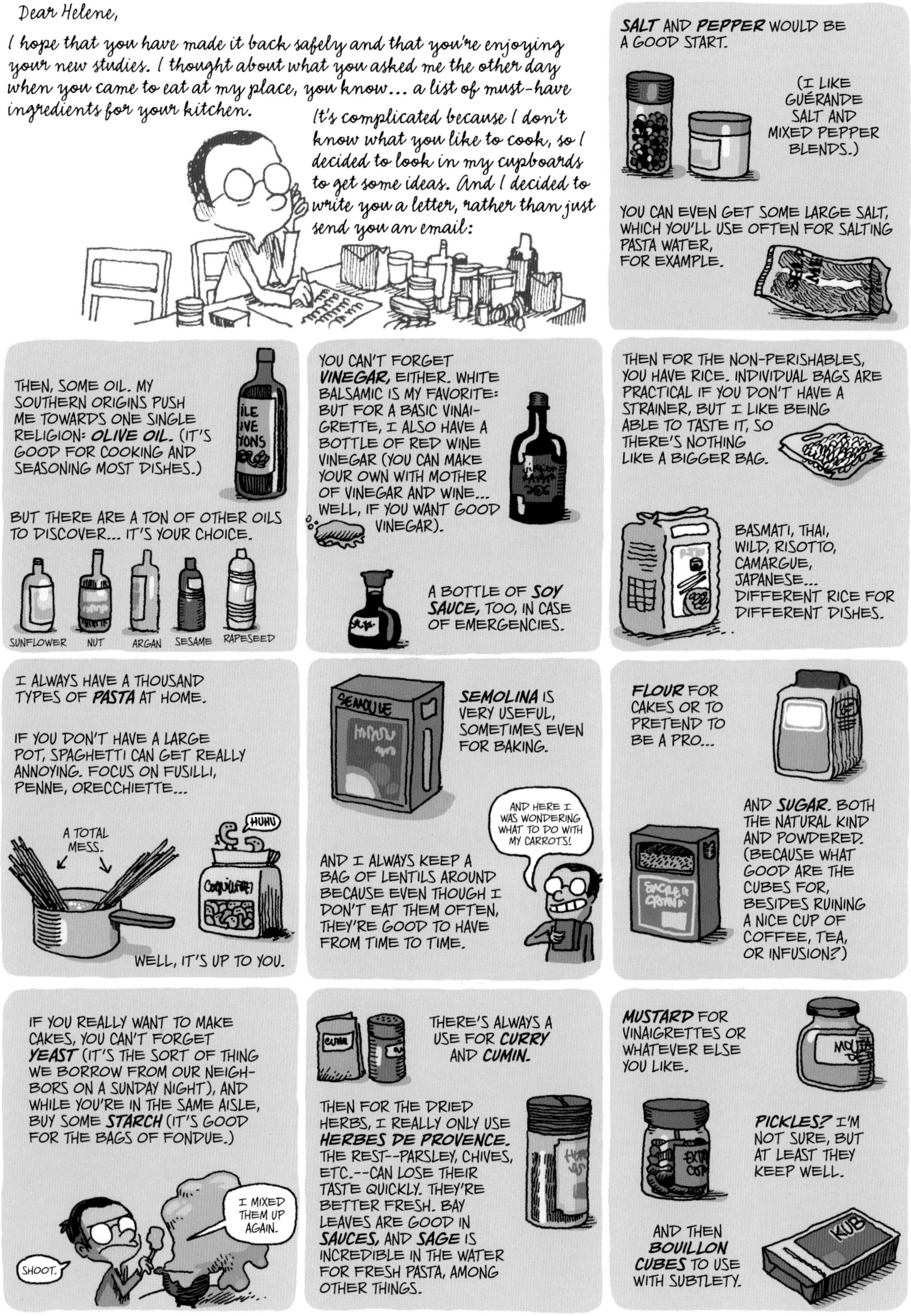
Dear Helene,
I hope that you have made it back safely and that you're enjoying your new studies. I thought about what you asked me the other day when you came to eat at my place, you know... a list of must-have ingredients for your kitchen.
(It's complicated because I don't know what you like to cook, so I decided to look in my cupboards to get some ideas. And I decided to write you a letter, rather than just send you an email:
SALT AND PEPPER WOULD BE A GOOD START.
(I LIKE GUÉRANDE SALT AND MIXED PEPPER BLENDS.)
YOU CAN EVEN GET SOME LARGE SALT, WHICH YOU'LL USE OFTEN FOR SALTING PASTA WATER, FOR EXAMPLE.
THEN, SOME OIL. MY SOUTHERN ORIGINS PUSH ME TOWARDS ONE SINGLE RELIGION: OLIVE OIL. (IT'S GOOD FOR COOKING AND SEASONING MOST DISHES.)
BUT THERE ARE A TON OF OTHER OILS TO DISCOVER... IT'S YOUR CHOICE.
SUNFLOWER
NUT
ARGAN
SESAME
RAPESEED
YOU CAN'T FORGET VINEGAR, EITHER. WHITE BALSAMIC IS MY FAVORITE: BUT FOR A BASIC VINAIGRETTE, I ALSO HAVE A BOTTLE OF RED WINE VINEGAR (YOU CAN MAKE YOUR OWN WITH MOTHER OF VINEGAR AND WINE... WELL, IF YOU WANT GOOD VINEGAR).
A BOTTLE OF SOY SAUCE, TOO, IN CASE OF EMERGENCIES.
THEN FOR THE NON-PERISHABLES, YOU HAVE RICE. INDIVIDUAL BAGS ARE PRACTICAL IF YOU DON'T HAVE A STRAINER, BUT I LIKE BEING ABLE TO TASTE IT, SO THERE'S NOTHING LIKE A BIGGER BAG.
BASMATI, THAI, WILD, RISOTTO, CAMARGUE, JAPANESE... DIFFERENT RICE FOR DIFFERENT DISHES.
I ALWAYS HAVE A THOUSAND TYPES OF PASTA AT HOME.
IF YOU DON'T HAVE A LARGE POT, SPAGHETTI CAN GET REALLY ANNOYING. FOCUS ON FUSILLI, PENNE, ORECCHIETTE...
A TOTAL MESS.
HUHU
WELL, IT'S UP TO YOU.
SEMOULE
SEMOLINA IS VERY USEFUL, SOMETIMES EVEN FOR BAKING.
AND I ALWAYS KEEP A BAG OF LENTILS AROUND BECAUSE EVEN THOUGH I DON'T EAT THEM OFTEN, THEY'RE GOOD TO HAVE FROM TIME TO TIME.
AND HERE I WAS WONDERING WHAT TO DO WITH MY CARROTS!
FLOUR FOR CAKES OR TO PRETEND TO BE A PRO...
AND SUGAR. BOTH THE NATURAL KIND AND POWDERED. (BECAUSE WHAT GOOD ARE THE CUBES FOR, BESIDES RUINING A NICE CUP OF COFFEE, TEA, OR INFUSION?)
IF YOU REALLY WANT TO MAKE CAKES, YOU CAN'T FORGET YEAST (IT'S THE SORT OF THING WE BORROW FROM OUR NEIGHBORS ON A SUNDAY NIGHT), AND WHILE YOU'RE IN THE SAME AISLE, BUY SOME STARCH (IT'S GOOD FOR THE BAGS OF FONDUE.)
I MIXED THEM UP AGAIN.
SHOOT.
THERE'S ALWAYS A USE FOR CURRY AND CUMIN.
THEN FOR THE DRIED HERBS, I REALLY ONLY USE HERBES DE PROVENCE. THE REST--PARSLEY, CHIVES, ETC.--CAN LOSE THEIR TASTE QUICKLY. THEY'RE BETTER FRESH. BAY LEAVES ARE GOOD IN SAUCES, AND SAGE IS INCREDIBLE IN THE WATER FOR FRESH PASTA, AMONG OTHER THINGS.
MUSTARD FOR VINAIGRETTES OR WHATEVER ELSE YOU LIKE.
PICKLES? I'M NOT SURE, BUT AT LEAST THEY KEEP WELL.
AND THEN BOUILLON CUBES TO USE WITH SUBTLETY.
KUB

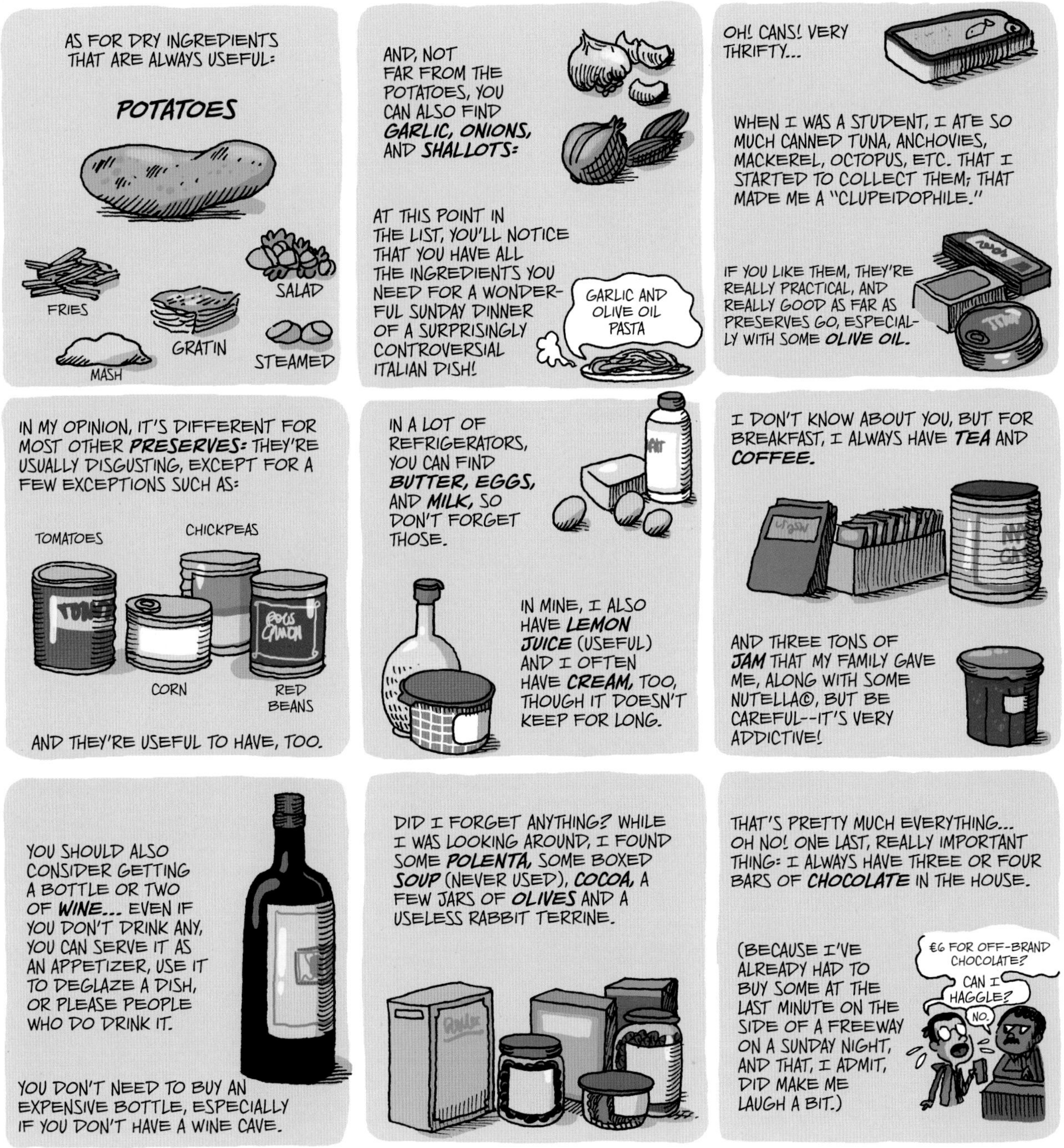
AS FOR DRY INGREDIENTS THAT ARE ALWAYS USEFUL:
POTATOES
FRIES
MASH
GRATIN
SALAD
STEAMED
AND, NOT FAR FROM THE POTATOES, YOU CAN ALSO FIND GARLIC, ONIONS, AND SHALLOTS:
AT THIS POINT IN THE LIST, YOU'LL NOTICE THAT YOU HAVE ALL THE INGREDIENTS YOU NEED FOR A WONDERFUL SUNDAY DINNER OF A SURPRISINGLY CONTROVERSIAL ITALIAN DISH!
GARLIC AND OLIVE OIL PASTA
OH! CANS! VERY THRIFTY...
WHEN I WAS A STUDENT, I ATE SO MUCH CANNED TUNA, ANCHOVIES, MACKEREL, OCTOPUS, ETC. THAT I STARTED TO COLLECT THEM; THAT MADE ME A "CLUPEIDOPHILE."
IF YOU LIKE THEM, THEY'RE REALLY PRACTICAL, AND REALLY GOOD AS FAR AS PRESERVES GO, ESPECIALLY WITH SOME OLIVE OIL.
IN MY OPINION, IT'S DIFFERENT FOR MOST OTHER PRESERVES: THEY'RE USUALLY DISGUSTING, EXCEPT FOR A FEW EXCEPTIONS SUCH AS:
TOMATOES
CHICKPEAS
CORN
RED BEANS
AND THEY'RE USEFUL TO HAVE, TOO.
IN A LOT OF REFRIGERATORS, YOU CAN FIND BUTTER, EGGS, AND MILK, SO DON'T FORGET THOSE.
IN MINE, I ALSO HAVE LEMON JUICE (USEFUL) AND I OFTEN HAVE CREAM, TOO, THOUGH IT DOESN'T KEEP FOR LONG.
I DON'T KNOW ABOUT YOU, BUT FOR BREAKFAST, I ALWAYS HAVE TEA AND COFFEE.
AND THREE TONS OF JAM THAT MY FAMILY GAVE ME, ALONG WITH SOME NUTELLA©, BUT BE CAREFUL--IT'S VERY ADDICTIVE!
YOU SHOULD ALSO CONSIDER GETTING A BOTTLE OR TWO OF WINE... EVEN IF YOU DON'T DRINK ANY, YOU CAN SERVE IT AS AN APPETIZER, USE IT TO DEGLAZE A DISH, OR PLEASE PEOPLE WHO DO DRINK IT.
YOU DON'T NEED TO BUY AN EXPENSIVE BOTTLE, ESPECIALLY IF YOU DON'T HAVE A WINE CAVE.
DID I FORGET ANYTHING? WHILE I WAS LOOKING AROUND, I FOUND SOME POLENTA, SOME BOXED SOUP (NEVER USED), COCOA, A FEW JARS OF OLIVES AND A USELESS RABBIT TERRINE.
THAT'S PRETTY MUCH EVERYTHING... OH NO! ONE LAST, REALLY IMPORTANT THING: I ALWAYS HAVE THREE OR FOUR BARS OF CHOCOLATE IN THE HOUSE.
(BECAUSE I'VE ALREADY HAD TO BUY SOME AT THE LAST MINUTE ON THE SIDE OF A FREEWAY ON A SUNDAY NIGHT, AND THAT, I ADMIT, DID MAKE ME LAUGH A BIT.)
€6 FOR OFF-BRAND CHOCOLATE?
CAN I HAGGLE?
NO.

There... I hope that this list helps you a little with your groceries. I've done my best not to forget anything, but I'm sure you'll find some things I haven't thought about.

And you'll see, fall is a great season to start cooking. You can still find summer vegetables, next to the new arrivals: squash, mushrooms, chestnuts, cabbage, etc.

I wish you a good start to your new life, and nothing but the best for the rest.
Affectionately,

Guillaume

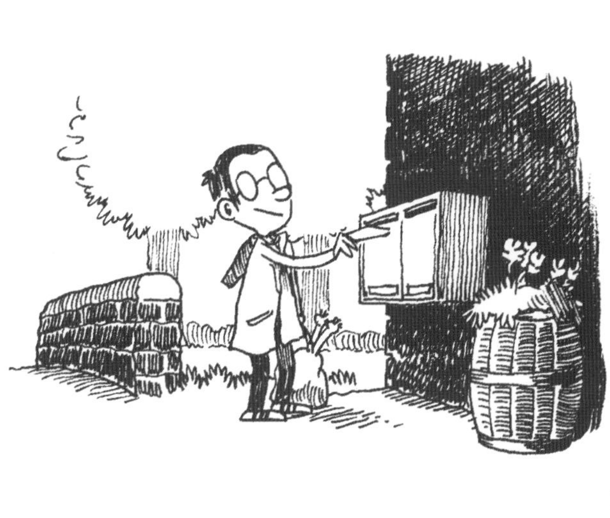

Bitter (sweet) life

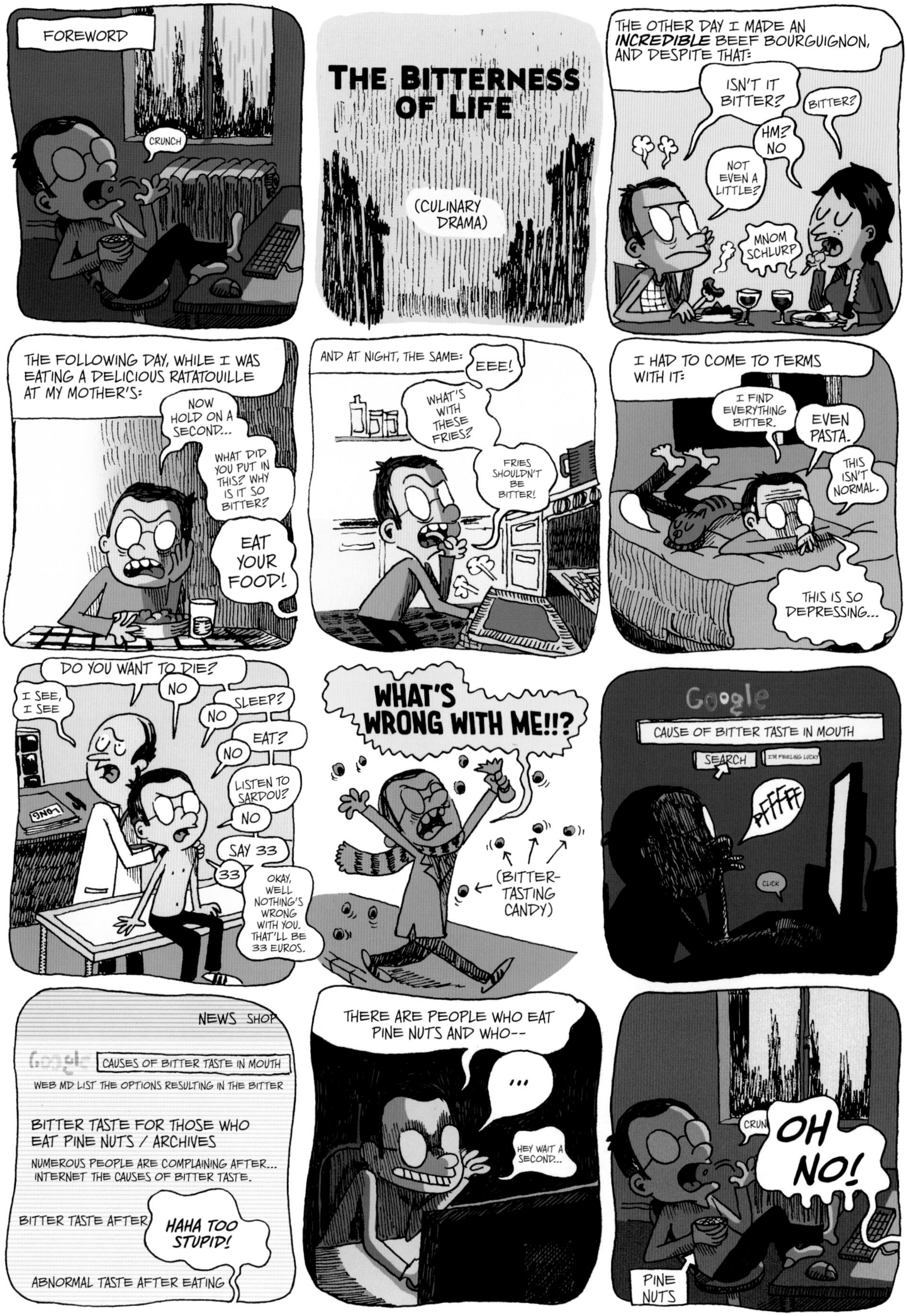

FOREWORD
CRUNCH
THE BITTERNESS OF LIFE
(CULINARY DRAMA)
THE OTHER DAY I MADE AN INCREDIBLE BEEF BOURGUIGNON, AND DESPITE THAT:
ISN'T IT BITTER?
BITTER?
HM? NO
NOT EVEN A LITTLE?
MNOM SCHLURP
THE FOLLOWING DAY, WHILE I WAS EATING A DELICIOUS RATATOUILLE AT MY MOTHER'S:
NOW HOLD ON A SECOND...
WHAT DID YOU PUT IN THIS? WHY IS IT SO BITTER?
EAT YOUR FOOD!
AND AT NIGHT, THE SAME:
EEE!
WHAT'S WITH THESE FRIES?
FRIES SHOULDN'T BE BITTER!
I HAD TO COME TO TERMS WITH IT:
I FIND EVERYTHING BITTER.
EVEN PASTA.
THIS ISN'T NORMAL.
THIS IS SO DEPRESSING...
DO YOU WANT TO DIE?
I SEE, I SEE
NO
SLEEP?
NO
EAT?
NO
LISTEN TO SARDOU?
NO
SAY 33
33
OKAY, WELL NOTHING'S WRONG WITH YOU. THAT'LL BE 33 EUROS.
WHAT'S WRONG WITH ME!!?
(BITTER-TASTING CANDY)
Google
CAUSE OF BITTER TASTE IN MOUTH
SEARCH
I'M FEELING LUCKY
PFFFF
CLICK
NEWS SHOP
CAUSES OF BITTER TASTE IN MOUTH
WEB MD LIST THE OPTIONS RESULTING IN THE BITTER
BITTER TASTE FOR THOSE WHO EAT PINE NUTS / ARCHIVES
NUMEROUS PEOPLE ARE COMPLAINING AFTER...
INTERNET THE CAUSES OF BITTER TASTE.
BITTER TASTE AFTER
HAHA TOO STUPID!
ABNORMAL TASTE AFTER EATING
THERE ARE PEOPLE WHO EAT PINE NUTS AND WHO--
...
HEY WAIT A SECOND...
CRUN
OH NO!
PINE NUTS

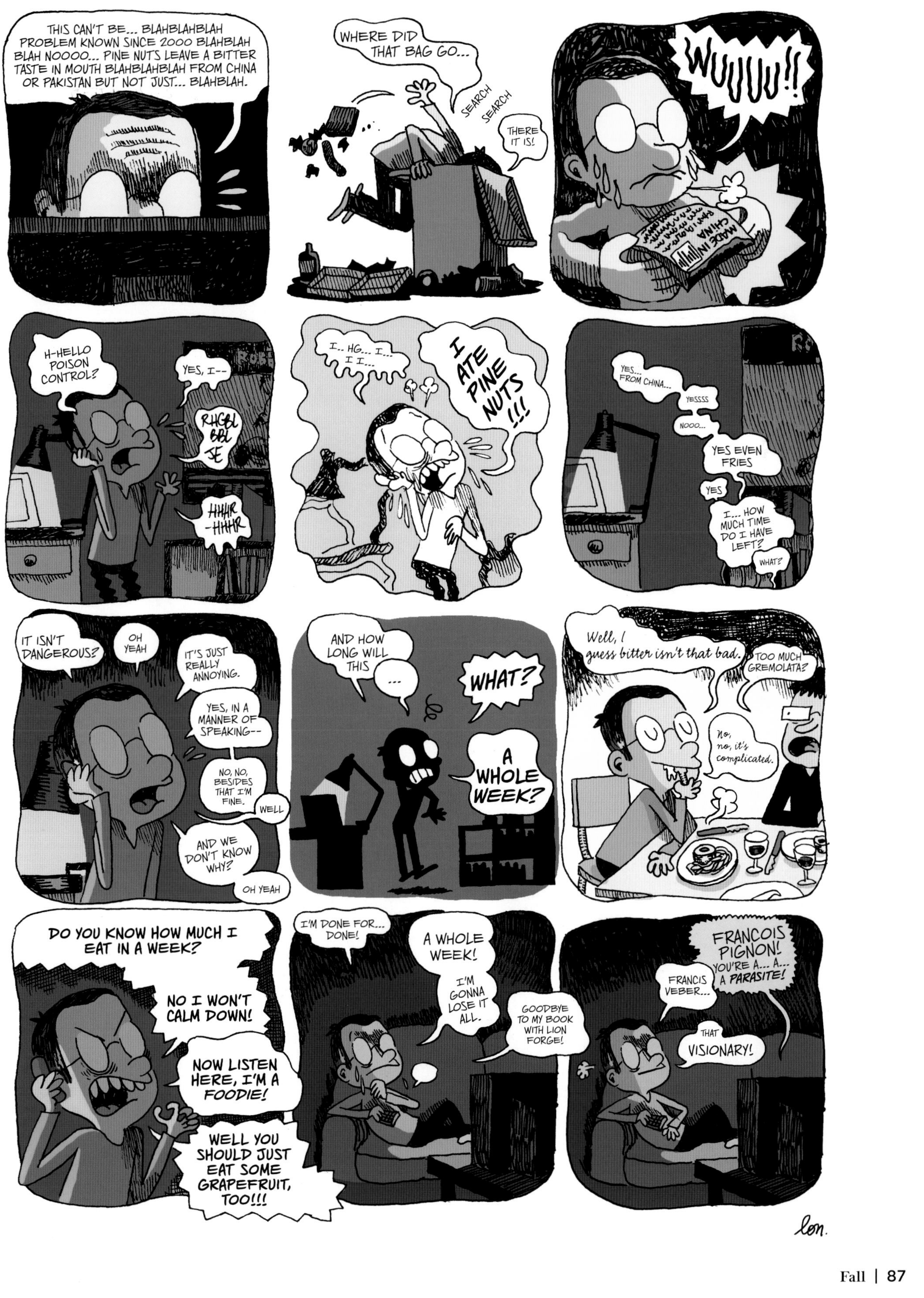
THIS CAN'T BE... BLAHBLAHBLAH PROBLEM KNOWN SINCE 2000 BLAHBLAH BLAH NOOOO... PINE NUTS LEAVE A BITTER TASTE IN MOUTH BLAHBLAHBLAH FROM CHINA OR PAKISTAN BUT NOT JUST... BLAHBLAH.
WHERE DID THAT BAG GO...
SEARCH
SEARCH
THERE IT IS!
WUUUU!!
H-HELLO POISON CONTROL?
YES, I--
RHGBL BBL JE
HHHR -HHHR
I.. HG... I... I I...
I ATE PINE NUTS!!!
YES... FROM CHINA...
YESSSS
NOOO...
YES EVEN FRIES
YES
I... HOW MUCH TIME DO I HAVE LEFT?
WHAT?
IT ISN'T DANGEROUS?
OH YEAH
IT'S JUST REALLY ANNOYING.
YES, IN A MANNER OF SPEAKING--
NO, NO, BESIDES THAT I'M FINE.
WELL
AND WE DON'T KNOW WHY?
OH YEAH
AND HOW LONG WILL THIS
...
WHAT?
A WHOLE WEEK?
Well, I guess bitter isn't that bad.
TOO MUCH GREMOLATA?
No, no, it's complicated.
DO YOU KNOW HOW MUCH I EAT IN A WEEK?
NO I WON'T CALM DOWN!
NOW LISTEN HERE, I'M A FOODIE!
WELL YOU SHOULD JUST EAT SOME GRAPEFRUIT, TOO!!!
I'M DONE FOR... DONE!
A WHOLE WEEK!
I'M GONNA LOSE IT ALL.
GOODBYE TO MY BOOK WITH LION FORGE!
FRANCOIS PIGNON! YOU'RE A... A... A PARASITE!
FRANCIS VEBER...
THAT VISIONARY!
lon.

Stay the course

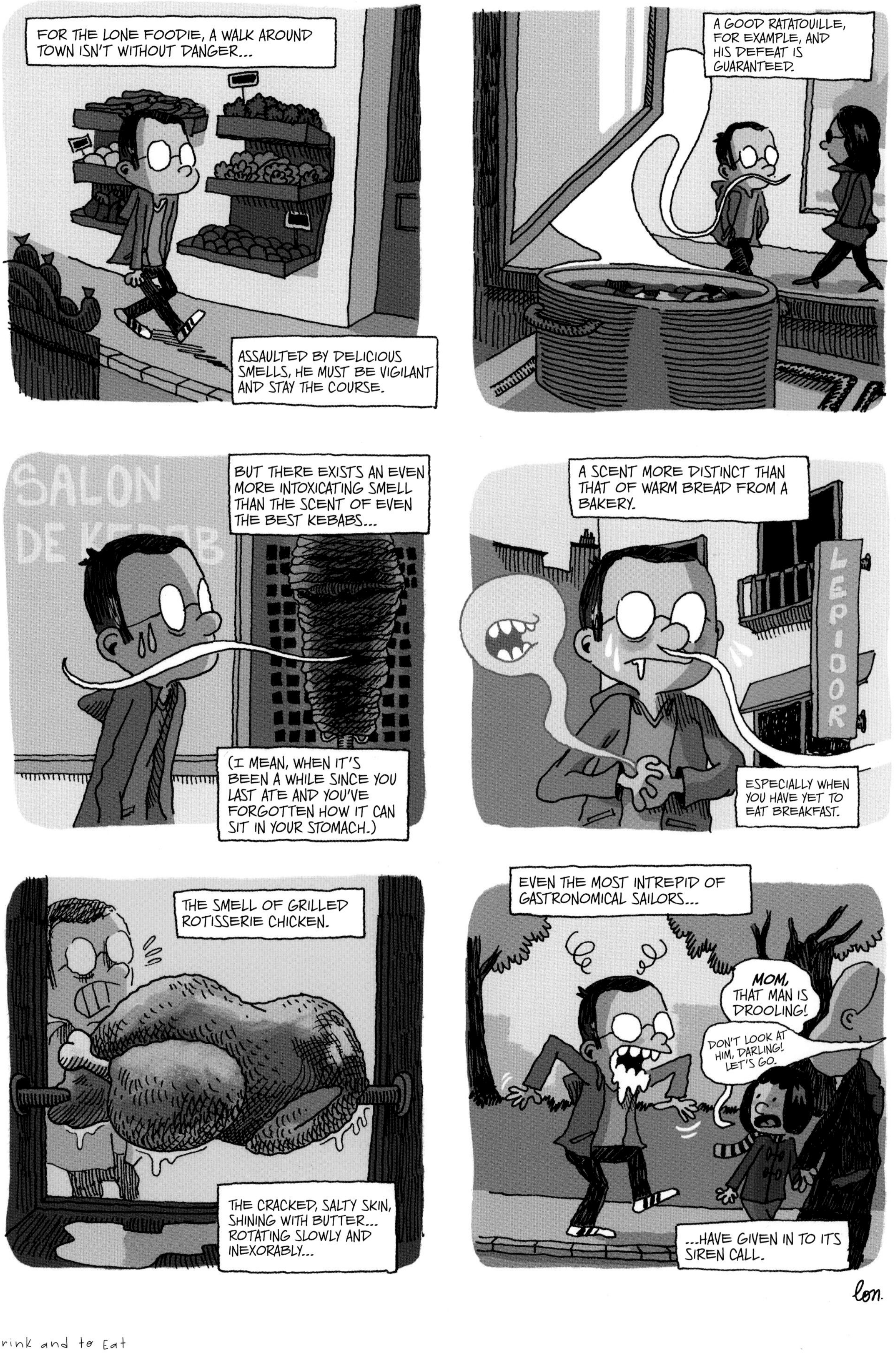
FOR THE LONE FOODIE, A WALK AROUND TOWN ISN'T WITHOUT DANGER...
ASSAULTED BY DELICIOUS SMELLS, HE MUST BE VIGILANT AND STAY THE COURSE.
A GOOD RATATOUILLE, FOR EXAMPLE, AND HIS DEFEAT IS GUARANTEED.
SALON DE KEBAB
BUT THERE EXISTS AN EVEN MORE INTOXICATING SMELL THAN THE SCENT OF EVEN THE BEST KEBABS...
(I MEAN, WHEN IT'S BEEN A WHILE SINCE YOU LAST ATE AND YOU'VE FORGOTTEN HOW IT CAN SIT IN YOUR STOMACH.)
A SCENT MORE DISTINCT THAN THAT OF WARM BREAD FROM A BAKERY.
LEPIDOR
ESPECIALLY WHEN YOU HAVE YET TO EAT BREAKFAST.
THE SMELL OF GRILLED ROTISSERIE CHICKEN.
THE CRACKED, SALTY SKIN, SHINING WITH BUTTER... ROTATING SLOWLY AND INEXORABLY...
EVEN THE MOST INTREPID OF GASTRONOMICAL SAILORS...
MOM, THAT MAN IS DROOLING!
DON'T LOOK AT HIM, DARLING! LET'S GO.
...HAVE GIVEN IN TO ITS SIREN CALL.
lon.

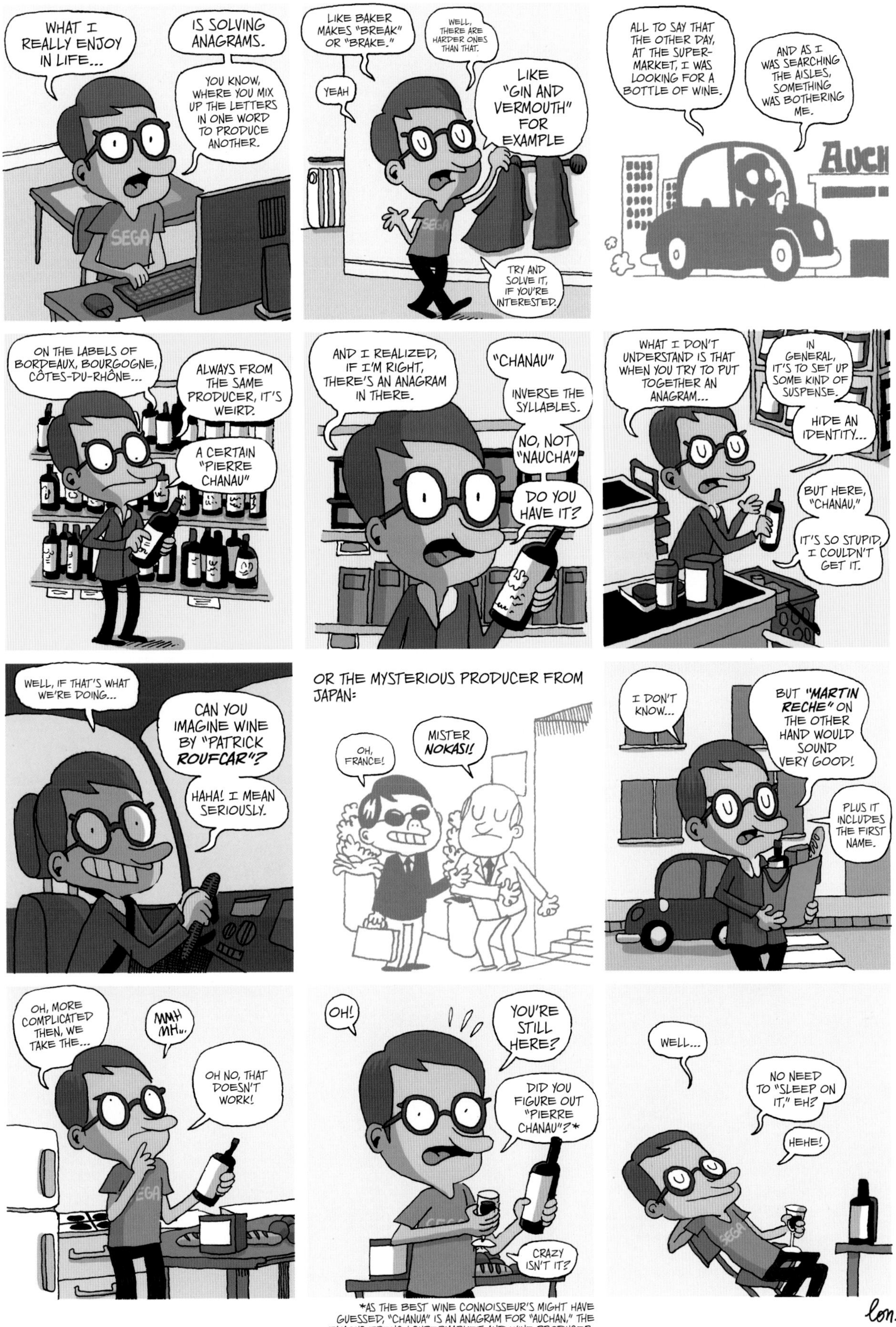
WHAT I REALLY ENJOY IN LIFE...
IS SOLVING ANAGRAMS.
YOU KNOW, WHERE YOU MIX UP THE LETTERS IN ONE WORD TO PRODUCE ANOTHER.
LIKE BAKER MAKES "BREAK" OR "BRAKE."
YEAH
WELL, THERE ARE HARDER ONES THAN THAT.
LIKE "GIN AND VERMOUTH" FOR EXAMPLE
TRY AND SOLVE IT, IF YOU'RE INTERESTED.
ALL TO SAY THAT THE OTHER DAY, AT THE SUPER-MARKET, I WAS LOOKING FOR A BOTTLE OF WINE.
AND AS I WAS SEARCHING THE AISLES, SOMETHING WAS BOTHERING ME.
AUCH
ON THE LABELS OF BORDEAUX, BOURGOGNE, CÔTES-DU-RHÔNE...
ALWAYS FROM THE SAME PRODUCER, IT'S WEIRD.
A CERTAIN "PIERRE CHANAU"
AND I REALIZED, IF I'M RIGHT, THERE'S AN ANAGRAM IN THERE.
"CHANAU"
INVERSE THE SYLLABLES.
NO, NOT "NAUCHA"
DO YOU HAVE IT?
WHAT I DON'T UNDERSTAND IS THAT WHEN YOU TRY TO PUT TOGETHER AN ANAGRAM...
IN GENERAL, IT'S TO SET UP SOME KIND OF SUSPENSE.
HIDE AN IDENTITY...
BUT HERE, "CHANAU,"
IT'S SO STUPID, I COULDN'T GET IT.
WELL, IF THAT'S WHAT WE'RE DOING...
CAN YOU IMAGINE WINE BY "PATRICK ROUFCAR"?
HAHA! I MEAN SERIOUSLY.
OR THE MYSTERIOUS PRODUCER FROM JAPAN:
OH, FRANCE!
MISTER NOKASI!
I DON'T KNOW...
BUT "MARTIN RECHE" ON THE OTHER HAND WOULD SOUND VERY GOOD!
PLUS IT INCLUDES THE FIRST NAME.
OH, MORE COMPLICATED THEN, WE TAKE THE...
MMH MH...
OH NO, THAT DOESN'T WORK!
OH!
YOU'RE STILL HERE?
DID YOU FIGURE OUT "PIERRE CHANAU"?*
CRAZY ISN'T IT?
WELL...
NO NEED TO "SLEEP ON IT," EH?
HEHE!
lon.

*AS THE BEST WINE CONNOISSEUR'S MIGHT HAVE GUESSED, "CHANUA" IS AN ANAGRAM FOR "AUCHAN," THE FAMOUS FRENCH SUPERMARKET AND WINE PRODUCER.

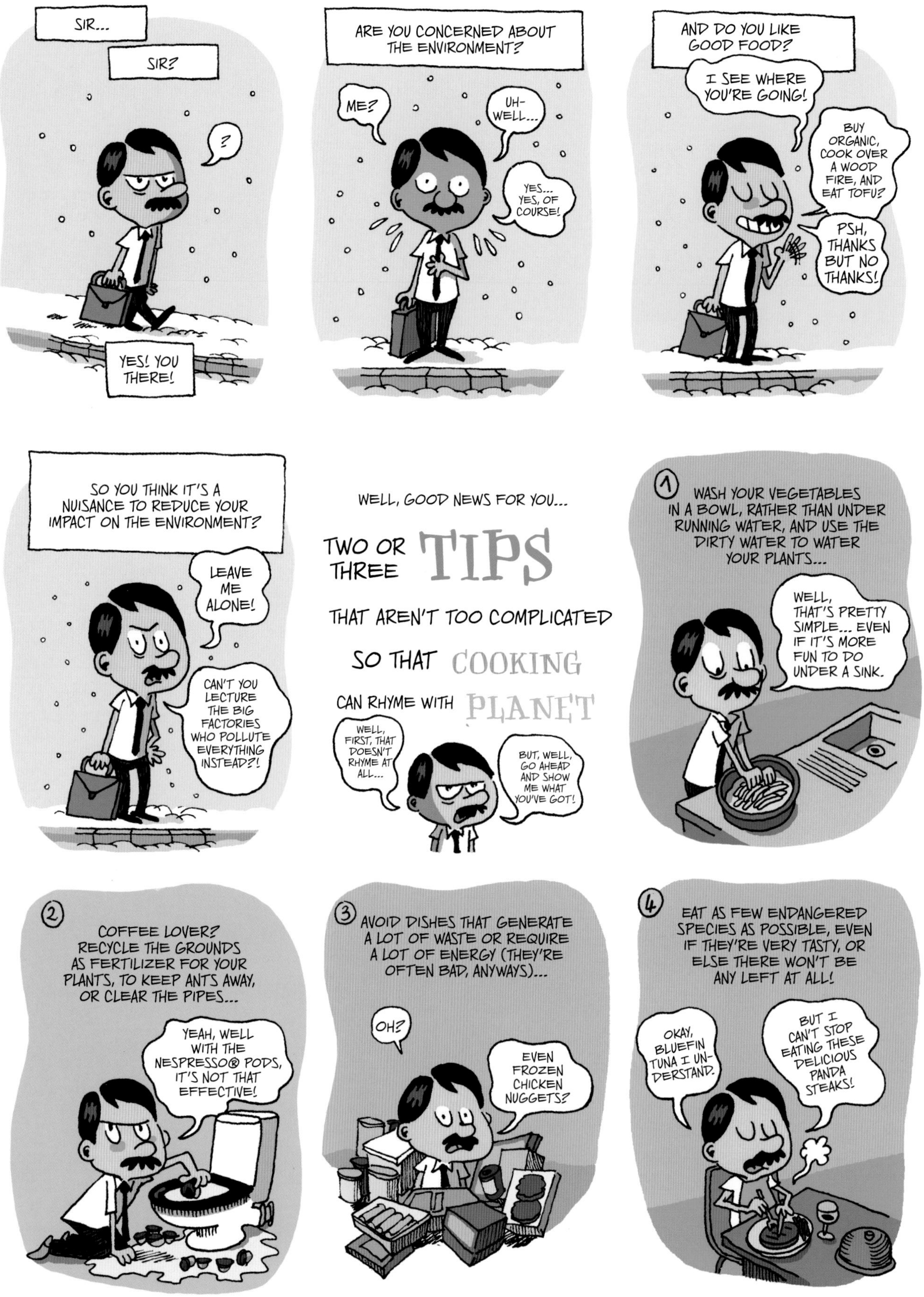
SIR...
SIR?
?
YES! YOU THERE!
ARE YOU CONCERNED ABOUT THE ENVIRONMENT?
ME?
UH- WELL...
YES... YES, OF COURSE!
AND DO YOU LIKE GOOD FOOD?
I SEE WHERE YOU'RE GOING!
BUY ORGANIC, COOK OVER A WOOD FIRE, AND EAT TOFU?
PSH, THANKS BUT NO THANKS!
SO YOU THINK IT'S A NUISANCE TO REDUCE YOUR IMPACT ON THE ENVIRONMENT?
LEAVE ME ALONE!
CAN'T YOU LECTURE THE BIG FACTORIES WHO POLLUTE EVERYTHING INSTEAD?!
WELL, GOOD NEWS FOR YOU...
TWO OR THREE TIPS
THAT AREN'T TOO COMPLICATED
SO THAT COOKING
CAN RHYME WITH PLANET
WELL, FIRST, THAT DOESN'T RHYME AT ALL...
BUT, WELL, GO AHEAD AND SHOW ME WHAT YOU'VE GOT!
1 WASH YOUR VEGETABLES IN A BOWL, RATHER THAN UNDER RUNNING WATER, AND USE THE DIRTY WATER TO WATER YOUR PLANTS...
WELL, THAT'S PRETTY SIMPLE... EVEN IF IT'S MORE FUN TO DO UNDER A SINK.
2 COFFEE LOVER? RECYCLE THE GROUNDS AS FERTILIZER FOR YOUR PLANTS, TO KEEP ANTS AWAY, OR CLEAR THE PIPES...
YEAH, WELL WITH THE NESPRESSO® PODS, IT'S NOT THAT EFFECTIVE!
3 AVOID DISHES THAT GENERATE A LOT OF WASTE OR REQUIRE A LOT OF ENERGY (THEY'RE OFTEN BAD, ANYWAYS)...
OH?
EVEN FROZEN CHICKEN NUGGETS?
4 EAT AS FEW ENDANGERED SPECIES AS POSSIBLE, EVEN IF THEY'RE VERY TASTY, OR ELSE THERE WON'T BE ANY LEFT AT ALL!
OKAY, BLUEFIN TUNA I UNDERSTAND.
BUT I CAN'T STOP EATING THESE DELICIOUS PANDA STEAKS!

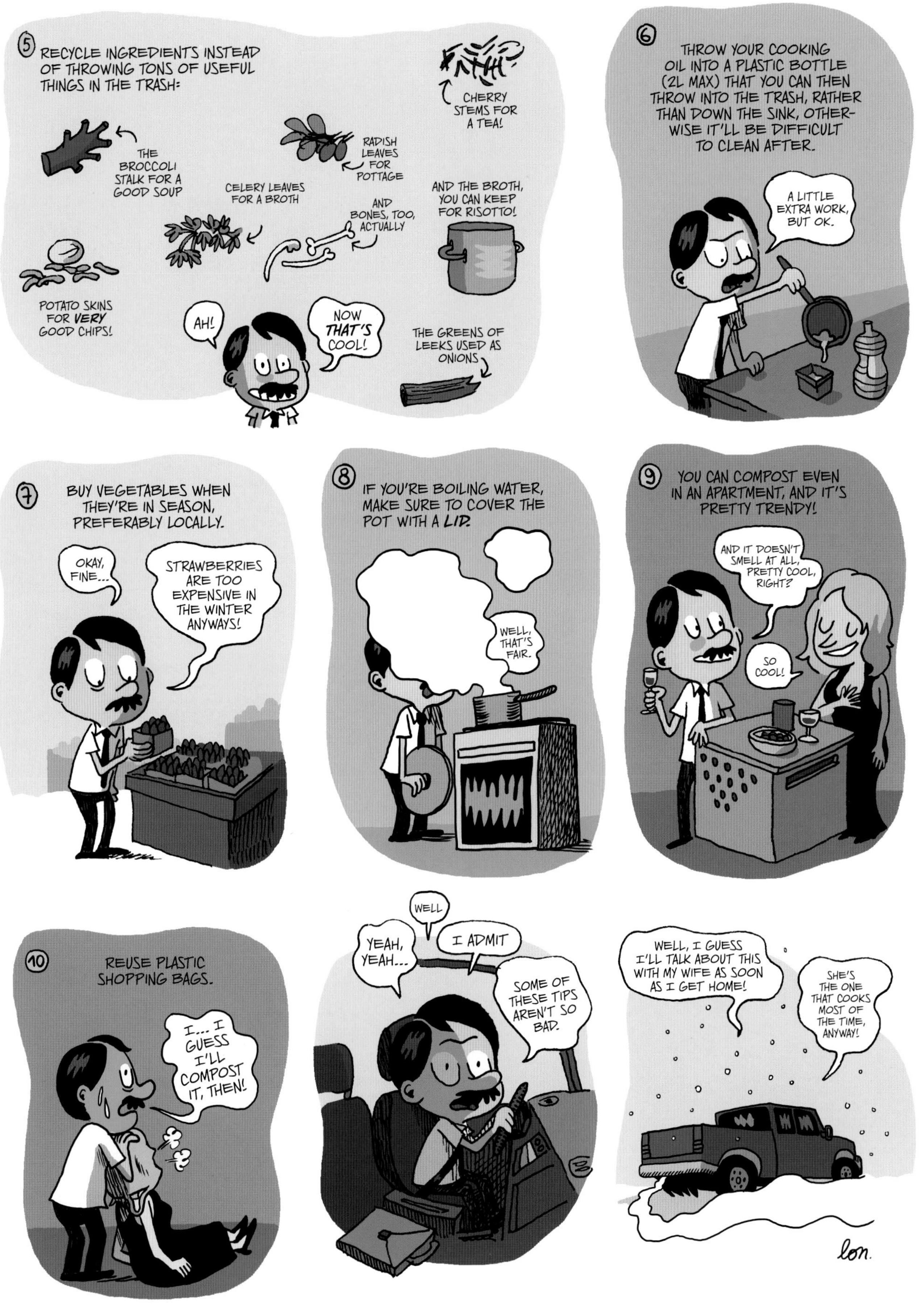
5 RECYCLE INGREDIENTS INSTEAD OF THROWING TONS OF USEFUL THINGS IN THE TRASH:
CHERRY STEMS FOR A TEA!
THE BROCCOLI STALK FOR A GOOD SOUP
RADISH LEAVES FOR POTTAGE
CELERY LEAVES FOR A BROTH
AND BONES, TOO, ACTUALLY
AND THE BROTH, YOU CAN KEEP FOR RISOTTO!
POTATO SKINS FOR VERY GOOD CHIPS!
AH!
NOW THAT'S COOL!
THE GREENS OF LEEKS USED AS ONIONS
6 THROW YOUR COOKING OIL INTO A PLASTIC BOTTLE (2L MAX) THAT YOU CAN THEN THROW INTO THE TRASH, RATHER THAN DOWN THE SINK, OTHERWISE IT'LL BE DIFFICULT TO CLEAN AFTER.
A LITTLE EXTRA WORK, BUT OK.
7 BUY VEGETABLES WHEN THEY'RE IN SEASON, PREFERABLY LOCALLY.
OKAY, FINE...
STRAWBERRIES ARE TOO EXPENSIVE IN THE WINTER ANYWAYS!
8 IF YOU'RE BOILING WATER, MAKE SURE TO COVER THE POT WITH A LID.
WELL, THAT'S FAIR.
9 YOU CAN COMPOST EVEN IN AN APARTMENT, AND IT'S PRETTY TRENDY!
AND IT DOESN'T SMELL AT ALL, PRETTY COOL, RIGHT?
SO COOL!
10 REUSE PLASTIC SHOPPING BAGS.
I... I GUESS I'LL COMPOST IT, THEN!
YEAH, YEAH...
WELL
I ADMIT
SOME OF THESE TIPS AREN'T SO BAD.
WELL, I GUESS I'LL TALK ABOUT THIS WITH MY WIFE AS SOON AS I GET HOME!
SHE'S THE ONE THAT COOKS MOST OF THE TIME, ANYWAY!
lon.

The egg song

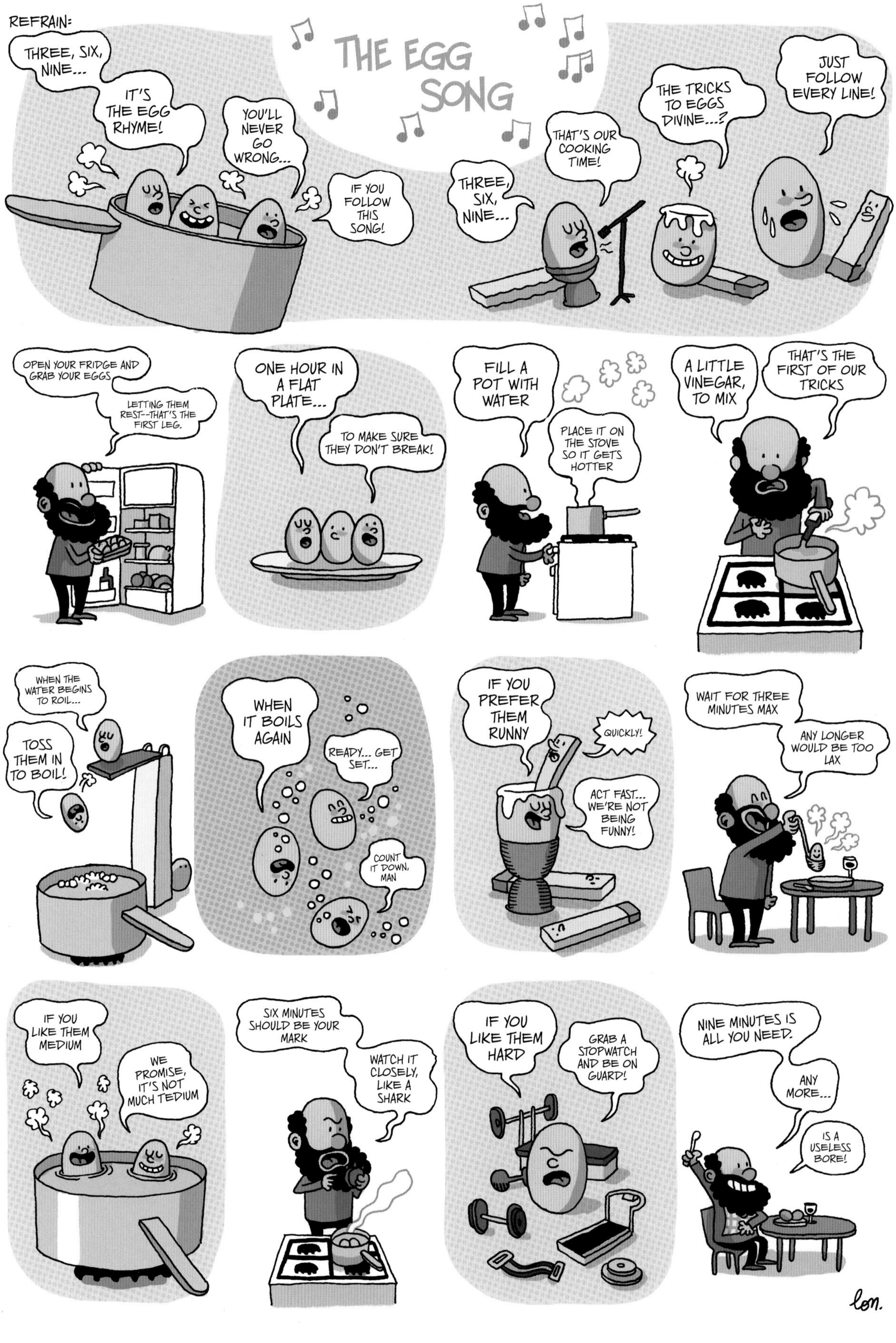
REFRAIN:
THE EGG SONG
THREE, SIX, NINE...
IT'S THE EGG RHYME!
YOU'LL NEVER GO WRONG...
IF YOU FOLLOW THIS SONG!
THREE, SIX, NINE...
THAT'S OUR COOKING TIME!
THE TRICKS TO EGGS DIVINE...?
JUST FOLLOW EVERY LINE!
OPEN YOUR FRIDGE AND GRAB YOUR EGGS
LETTING THEM REST--THAT'S THE FIRST LEG.
ONE HOUR IN A FLAT PLATE...
TO MAKE SURE THEY DON'T BREAK!
FILL A POT WITH WATER
PLACE IT ON THE STOVE SO IT GETS HOTTER
A LITTLE VINEGAR, TO MIX
THAT'S THE FIRST OF OUR TRICKS
WHEN THE WATER BEGINS TO ROIL...
TOSS THEM IN TO BOIL!
WHEN IT BOILS AGAIN
READY... GET SET...
COUNT IT DOWN, MAN
IF YOU PREFER THEM RUNNY
QUICKLY!
ACT FAST... WE'RE NOT BEING FUNNY!
WAIT FOR THREE MINUTES MAX
ANY LONGER WOULD BE TOO LAX
IF YOU LIKE THEM MEDIUM
WE PROMISE, IT'S NOT MUCH TEDIUM
SIX MINUTES SHOULD BE YOUR MARK
WATCH IT CLOSELY, LIKE A SHARK
IF YOU LIKE THEM HARD
GRAB A STOPWATCH AND BE ON GUARD!
NINE MINUTES IS ALL YOU NEED.
ANY MORE...
IS A USELESS BORE!
lon.

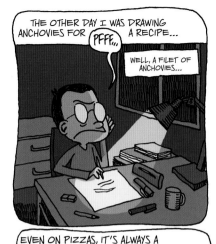

THE OTHER DAY I WAS DRAWING ANCHOVIES FOR A RECIPE...

PFFF...

WELL, A FILET OF ANCHOVIES...

WELL, LET ME TELL YOU: DRAWING AN ANCHOVY FILET IS THE MOST BORING THING IN THE WORLD

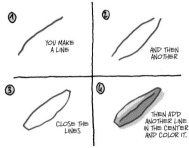

① YOU MAKE A LINE

② AND THEN ANOTHER

③ CLOSE THE LINES

④ THEN ADD ANOTHER LINE IN THE CENTER AND COLOR IT.

YOU DON'T EVEN NEED TO SKETCH IT OUT BEFOREHAND.

NOW, I HAVE TO ADMIT THAT ANCHOVIES HAVE KIND OF A BAD REPUTATION.

WHAT'S A SADDER APPETIZER THAN A BOWL OF OLIVES STUFFED WITH ANCHOVIES?

I CAN

SPEAKING OF BAKED OLIVES... WELL... NEVERMIND.

NO, NOT PEANUTS!

ME ME!

EVEN ON PIZZAS, IT'S ALWAYS A LITTLE DECEIVING.

FULLY STOCKED ANCHOVIES

WELL, UH... A NEAPOLITAN.

BUT WITHOUT ANCHOVIES.

TAKE MY FRIEND CAROLINE, FOR EXAMPLE: WELL, SHE HATES THEM!

I REFUSE TO EVEN TASTE THEM!

YES I KNOW YOU DON'T CARE THAT I HAVE A FRIEND NAMED CAROLINE, BUT SHE LIKES BEING IN MY COMICS, SO THIS WAS THE RIGHT OPPORTUNITY.

WELL, TOO BAD FOR HER, AND ALL THE OTHERS WHO WILL NEVER KNOW THE PLEASURE:

Orecchiette alla Barese

A PUGLIAN RECIPE

VIVA ITALIA!

FOR THE INGREDIENTS, IT'S SIMPLE, YOU'LL NEED:

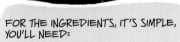
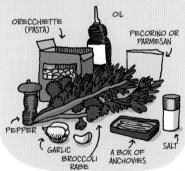

ORECCHIETTE (PASTA)

OIL

PECORINO OR PARMESAN

PEPPER

GARLIC

BROCCOLI RABE

A BOX OF ANCHOVIES

SALT

ANNOUNCEMENT: BROCCOLI RABE IS A VEGETABLE PRIMARILY GROWN IN PUGLIA (SOUTHERN ITALY), BUT YOU CAN REPLACE IT WITH... BROCCOLI!

WOW!

THIS IS GREAT! I ALREADY LIKE THIS RECIPE!

PRESIDENT OF THE T.C.S.B.S. A.O.U.V.T. C.B.D.

(1) YOU NEED TO SORT THE BROCCOLI RABE (IT'S THE MOST TIME-CONSUMING PART) AND ONLY KEEP THE LEAVES, THE TENDER STEMS, AND THE FLOWERS.

AND IF YOU'RE COOKING WITH BROCCOLI, WE ONLY KEEP THE FLORETS.

FOR FOUR PEOPLE, YOU'LL NEED ABOUT TWO LBS OF BROCCOLI RABE, OR ONE LB OF BROCCOLI.

AFTERWARD, YOU BOIL SALTED WATER AND COOK THE ORECCHIETTE.

(2) YOU CUT GARLIC AND ANCHOVIES INTO SMALL PIECES, AND GRATE THE PECORINO (IF YOU HAVE THE TIME)...

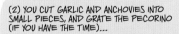

BECAUSE FIVE MINUTES BEFORE THE PASTA IS COOKED, YOU HAVE TO BE READY TO THROW THE BROCCOLI RABE (OR THE BROCCOLI) INTO THE SAME POT!

(DON'T PANIC, IT'LL REDUCE)

(3) WHILE THE ORECCHIETTE AND THE BROCCOLI RABE FINISH COOKING, BROWN THE GARLIC (SLOWLY SO IT DOESN'T BURN) IN OLIVE OIL ON A STOVETOP.

(USE 5 OR 6 CLOVES FOR 4 PEOPLE)

TSHHHHHH

THEN, WITH THE HEAT TURNED OFF, MELT THE ANCHOVIES WHILE STIRRING (COUNT TEN FILETS FOR FOUR PEOPLE).

(4) STRAIN THE ORECCHIETTE AND BROCCOLI RABE, THEN CONTINUE TO COOK THEM OVER A LOW FLAME FOR TWO MINUTES, WHILE CRUSHING THE VEGETABLES WITH A WOODEN SPOON AND ADDING THE CONTENTS OF THE OTHER PAN AND THE PEPPER.

FCHHHHHH

SERVE WARM, WITH A STRONG GLASS OF RED WINE (WHY NOT A GLASS OF ETNA?) BECAUSE THIS SIMPLE DISH HAS QUITE A STRONG TASTE.

leon.

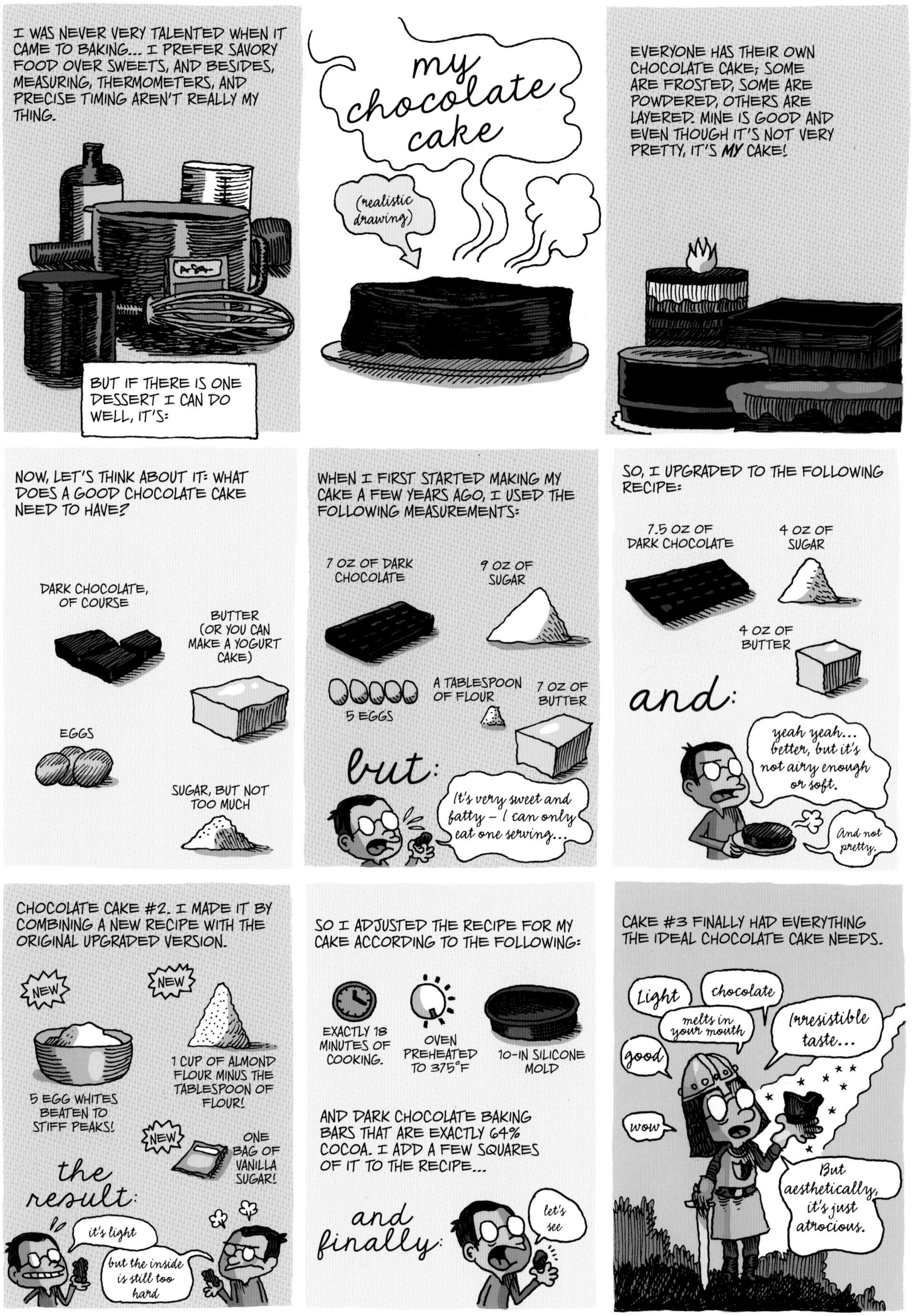
I WAS NEVER VERY TALENTED WHEN IT CAME TO BAKING... I PREFER SAVORY FOOD OVER SWEETS, AND BESIDES, MEASURING, THERMOMETERS, AND PRECISE TIMING AREN'T REALLY MY THING.
BUT IF THERE IS ONE DESSERT I CAN DO WELL, IT'S:
my chocolate cake
(realistic drawing)
EVERYONE HAS THEIR OWN CHOCOLATE CAKE; SOME ARE FROSTED, SOME ARE POWDERED, OTHERS ARE LAYERED. MINE IS GOOD AND EVEN THOUGH IT'S NOT VERY PRETTY, IT'S MY CAKE!
NOW, LET'S THINK ABOUT IT: WHAT DOES A GOOD CHOCOLATE CAKE NEED TO HAVE?
DARK CHOCOLATE, OF COURSE
BUTTER (OR YOU CAN MAKE A YOGURT CAKE)
EGGS
SUGAR, BUT NOT TOO MUCH
WHEN I FIRST STARTED MAKING MY CAKE A FEW YEARS AGO, I USED THE FOLLOWING MEASUREMENTS:
7 OZ OF DARK CHOCOLATE
9 OZ OF SUGAR
5 EGGS
A TABLESPOON OF FLOUR
7 OZ OF BUTTER
but:
It's very sweet and fatty – I can only eat one serving...
SO, I UPGRADED TO THE FOLLOWING RECIPE:
7.5 OZ OF DARK CHOCOLATE
4 OZ OF SUGAR
4 OZ OF BUTTER
and:
yeah yeah... better, but it's not airy enough or soft.
And not pretty.
CHOCOLATE CAKE #2. I MADE IT BY COMBINING A NEW RECIPE WITH THE ORIGINAL UPGRADED VERSION.
NEW
5 EGG WHITES BEATEN TO STIFF PEAKS!
NEW
1 CUP OF ALMOND FLOUR MINUS THE TABLESPOON OF FLOUR!
NEW
ONE BAG OF VANILLA SUGAR!
the result:
it's light
but the inside is still too hard
SO I ADJUSTED THE RECIPE FOR MY CAKE ACCORDING TO THE FOLLOWING:
EXACTLY 18 MINUTES OF COOKING.
OVEN PREHEATED TO 375°F
10-IN SILICONE MOLD
AND DARK CHOCOLATE BAKING BARS THAT ARE EXACTLY 64% COCOA. I ADD A FEW SQUARES OF IT TO THE RECIPE...
and finally:
let's see
CAKE #3 FINALLY HAD EVERYTHING THE IDEAL CHOCOLATE CAKE NEEDS.
Light
chocolate
melts in your mouth
Irresistible taste...
good
wow
But aesthetically, it's just atrocious.

My chocolate cake

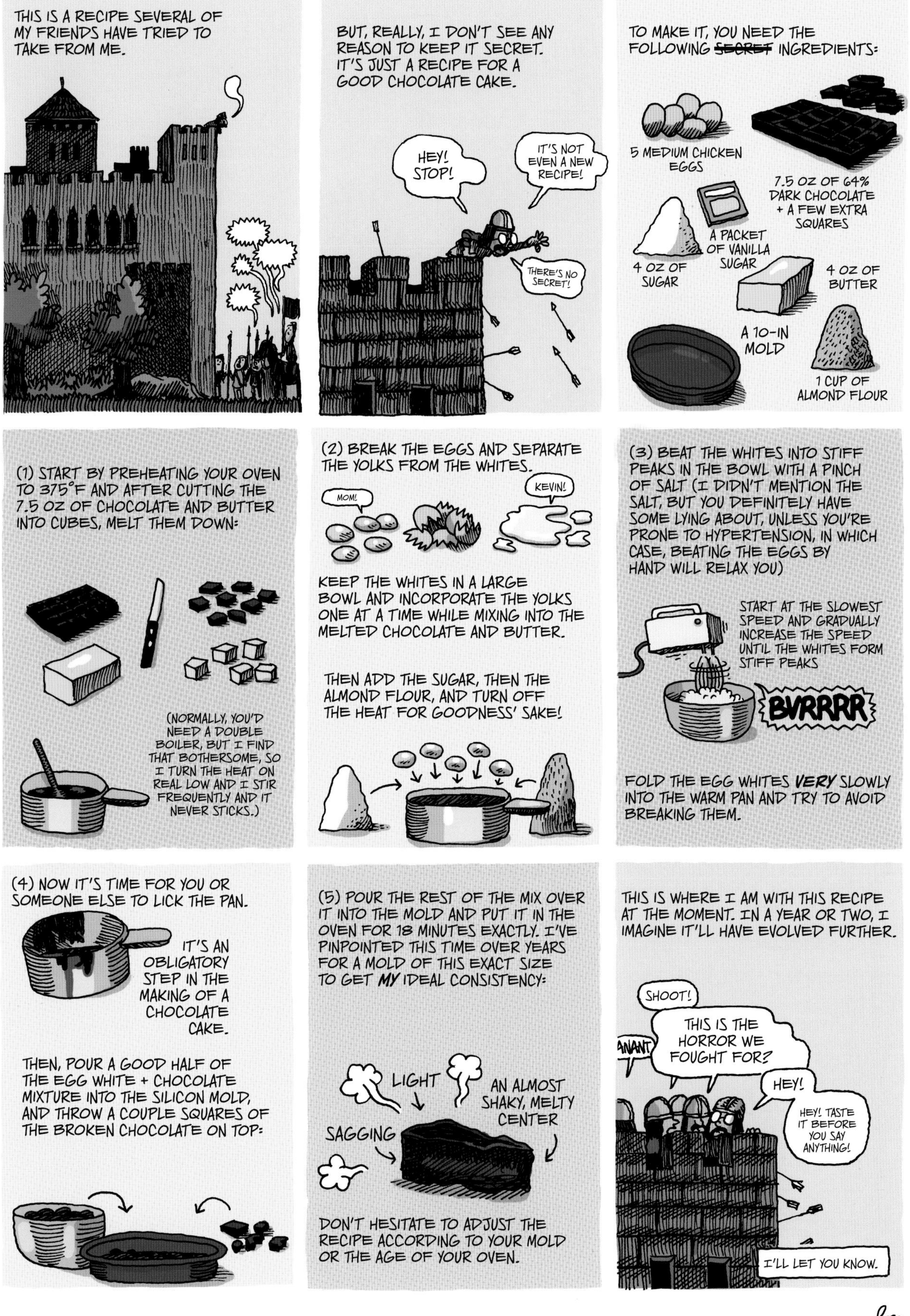

THIS IS A RECIPE SEVERAL OF MY FRIENDS HAVE TRIED TO TAKE FROM ME.
BUT, REALLY, I DON'T SEE ANY REASON TO KEEP IT SECRET. IT'S JUST A RECIPE FOR A GOOD CHOCOLATE CAKE.
HEY! STOP!
IT'S NOT EVEN A NEW RECIPE!
THERE'S NO SECRET!
TO MAKE IT, YOU NEED THE FOLLOWING ~~SECRET~~ INGREDIENTS:
5 MEDIUM CHICKEN EGGS
7.5 OZ OF 64% DARK CHOCOLATE + A FEW EXTRA SQUARES
A PACKET OF VANILLA SUGAR
4 OZ OF SUGAR
4 OZ OF BUTTER
A 10-IN MOLD
1 CUP OF ALMOND FLOUR
(1) START BY PREHEATING YOUR OVEN TO 375°F AND AFTER CUTTING THE 7.5 OZ OF CHOCOLATE AND BUTTER INTO CUBES, MELT THEM DOWN:
(NORMALLY, YOU'D NEED A DOUBLE BOILER, BUT I FIND THAT BOTHERSOME, SO I TURN THE HEAT ON REAL LOW AND I STIR FREQUENTLY AND IT NEVER STICKS.)
(2) BREAK THE EGGS AND SEPARATE THE YOLKS FROM THE WHITES.
MOM!
KEVIN!
KEEP THE WHITES IN A LARGE BOWL AND INCORPORATE THE YOLKS ONE AT A TIME WHILE MIXING INTO THE MELTED CHOCOLATE AND BUTTER.
THEN ADD THE SUGAR, THEN THE ALMOND FLOUR, AND TURN OFF THE HEAT FOR GOODNESS' SAKE!
(3) BEAT THE WHITES INTO STIFF PEAKS IN THE BOWL WITH A PINCH OF SALT (I DIDN'T MENTION THE SALT, BUT YOU DEFINITELY HAVE SOME LYING ABOUT, UNLESS YOU'RE PRONE TO HYPERTENSION, IN WHICH CASE, BEATING THE EGGS BY HAND WILL RELAX YOU)
START AT THE SLOWEST SPEED AND GRADUALLY INCREASE THE SPEED UNTIL THE WHITES FORM STIFF PEAKS
BVRRRR
FOLD THE EGG WHITES ***VERY*** SLOWLY INTO THE WARM PAN AND TRY TO AVOID BREAKING THEM.
(4) NOW IT'S TIME FOR YOU OR SOMEONE ELSE TO LICK THE PAN.
IT'S AN OBLIGATORY STEP IN THE MAKING OF A CHOCOLATE CAKE.
THEN, POUR A GOOD HALF OF THE EGG WHITE + CHOCOLATE MIXTURE INTO THE SILICON MOLD, AND THROW A COUPLE SQUARES OF THE BROKEN CHOCOLATE ON TOP:
(5) POUR THE REST OF THE MIX OVER IT INTO THE MOLD AND PUT IT IN THE OVEN FOR 18 MINUTES EXACTLY. I'VE PINPOINTED THIS TIME OVER YEARS FOR A MOLD OF THIS EXACT SIZE TO GET ***MY*** IDEAL CONSISTENCY:
LIGHT
AN ALMOST SHAKY, MELTY CENTER
SAGGING
DON'T HESITATE TO ADJUST THE RECIPE ACCORDING TO YOUR MOLD OR THE AGE OF YOUR OVEN.
THIS IS WHERE I AM WITH THIS RECIPE AT THE MOMENT. IN A YEAR OR TWO, I IMAGINE IT'LL HAVE EVOLVED FURTHER.
SHOOT!
THIS IS THE HORROR WE FOUGHT FOR?
HEY!
HEY! TASTE IT BEFORE YOU SAY ANYTHING!
I'LL LET YOU KNOW.
lon.

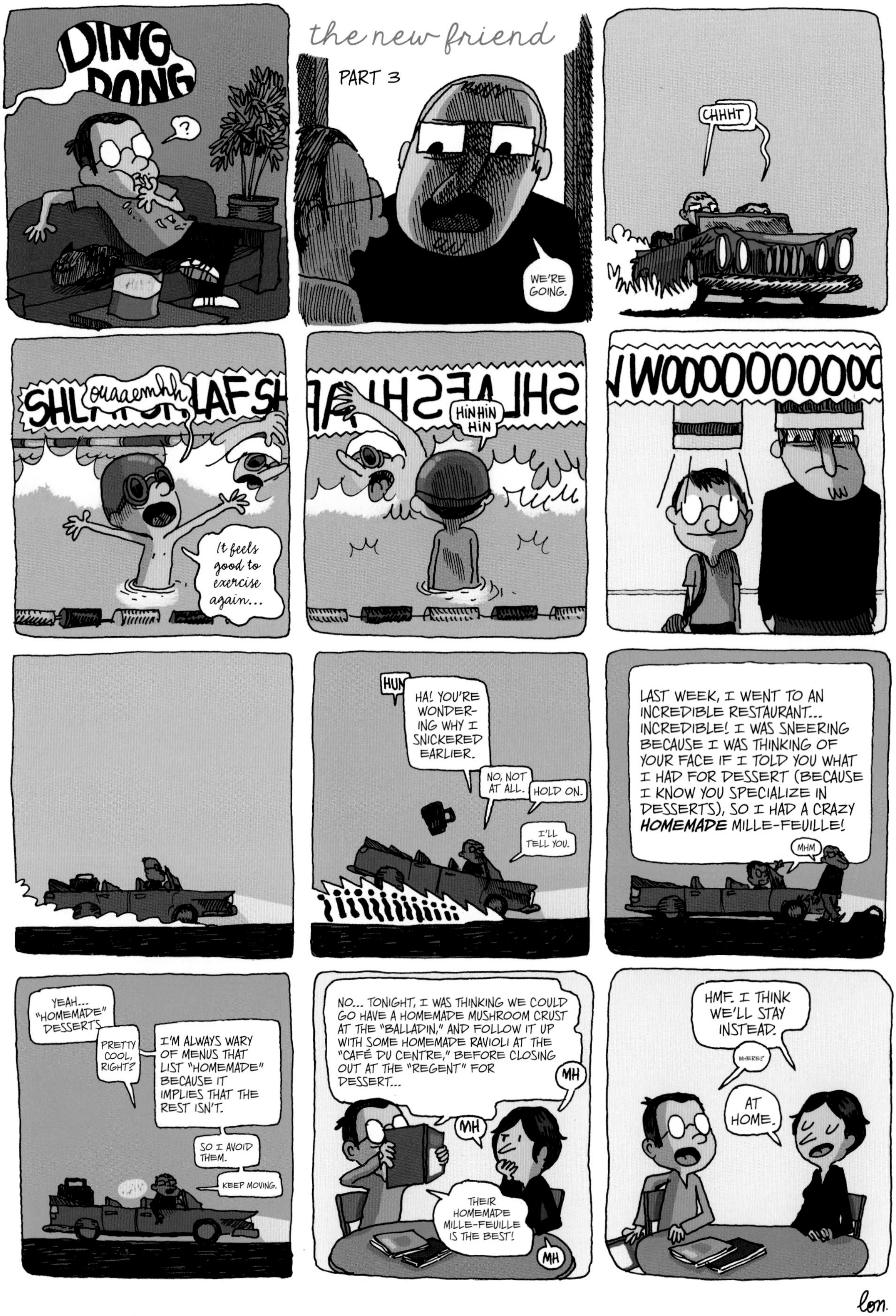
DING DONG
?
the new friend
PART 3
WE'RE GOING.
CHHHT
ouaaemhh
It feels good to exercise again...
HIN HIN HIN
WOOOOOOOOOO
HUN
HA! YOU'RE WONDERING WHY I SNICKERED EARLIER.
NO, NOT AT ALL.
HOLD ON.
I'LL TELL YOU.
LAST WEEK, I WENT TO AN INCREDIBLE RESTAURANT... INCREDIBLE! I WAS SNEERING BECAUSE I WAS THINKING OF YOUR FACE IF I TOLD YOU WHAT I HAD FOR DESSERT (BECAUSE I KNOW YOU SPECIALIZE IN DESSERTS), SO I HAD A CRAZY ***HOMEMADE*** MILLE-FEUILLE!
MHM
YEAH... "HOMEMADE" DESSERTS.
PRETTY COOL, RIGHT?
I'M ALWAYS WARY OF MENUS THAT LIST "HOMEMADE" BECAUSE IT IMPLIES THAT THE REST ISN'T.
SO I AVOID THEM.
KEEP MOVING.
NO... TONIGHT, I WAS THINKING WE COULD GO HAVE A HOMEMADE MUSHROOM CRUST AT THE "BALLADIN," AND FOLLOW IT UP WITH SOME HOMEMADE RAVIOLI AT THE "CAFÉ DU CENTRE," BEFORE CLOSING OUT AT THE "REGENT" FOR DESSERT...
MH
MH
THEIR HOMEMADE MILLE-FEUILLE IS THE BEST!
MH
HMF. I THINK WE'LL STAY INSTEAD.
WHERE?
AT HOME.

lon.

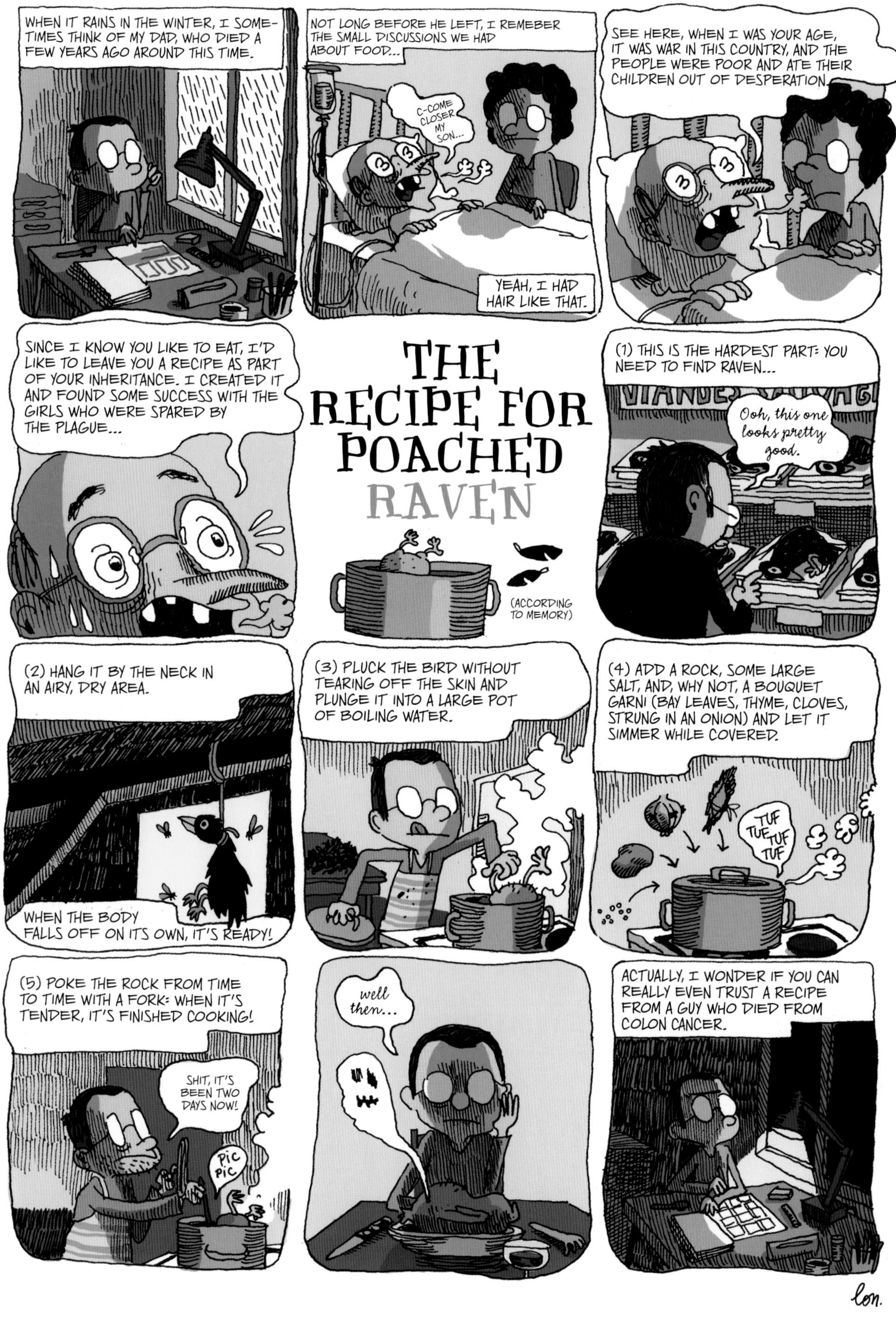
WHEN IT RAINS IN THE WINTER, I SOMETIMES THINK OF MY DAD, WHO DIED A FEW YEARS AGO AROUND THIS TIME.
NOT LONG BEFORE HE LEFT, I REMEBER THE SMALL DISCUSSIONS WE HAD ABOUT FOOD...
C-COME CLOSER MY SON...
YEAH, I HAD HAIR LIKE THAT.
SEE HERE, WHEN I WAS YOUR AGE, IT WAS WAR IN THIS COUNTRY, AND THE PEOPLE WERE POOR AND ATE THEIR CHILDREN OUT OF DESPERATION.
SINCE I KNOW YOU LIKE TO EAT, I'D LIKE TO LEAVE YOU A RECIPE AS PART OF YOUR INHERITANCE. I CREATED IT AND FOUND SOME SUCCESS WITH THE GIRLS WHO WERE SPARED BY THE PLAGUE...
THE RECIPE FOR POACHED RAVEN
(ACCORDING TO MEMORY)
(1) THIS IS THE HARDEST PART: YOU NEED TO FIND RAVEN...
Ooh, this one looks pretty good.
(2) HANG IT BY THE NECK IN AN AIRY, DRY AREA.
WHEN THE BODY FALLS OFF ON ITS OWN, IT'S READY!
(3) PLUCK THE BIRD WITHOUT TEARING OFF THE SKIN AND PLUNGE IT INTO A LARGE POT OF BOILING WATER.
(4) ADD A ROCK, SOME LARGE SALT, AND, WHY NOT, A BOUQUET GARNI (BAY LEAVES, THYME, CLOVES, STRUNG IN AN ONION) AND LET IT SIMMER WHILE COVERED.
TUF TUF TUF TUF
(5) POKE THE ROCK FROM TIME TO TIME WITH A FORK: WHEN IT'S TENDER, IT'S FINISHED COOKING!
SHIT, IT'S BEEN TWO DAYS NOW!
PIC PIC
well then...
ACTUALLY, I WONDER IF YOU CAN REALLY EVEN TRUST A RECIPE FROM A GUY WHO DIED FROM COLON CANCER.
lon.

Pépé Roni's Good Advice: blanching — n° 073

Don't confuse "blanching"

and "blanching."

BECAUSE ANYONE CAN MAKE MISTAKES!

Blanching: scalding a raw ingredient in boiling water, to clean it, tenderize it, or remove excess salt.

TRIP TO VENICE

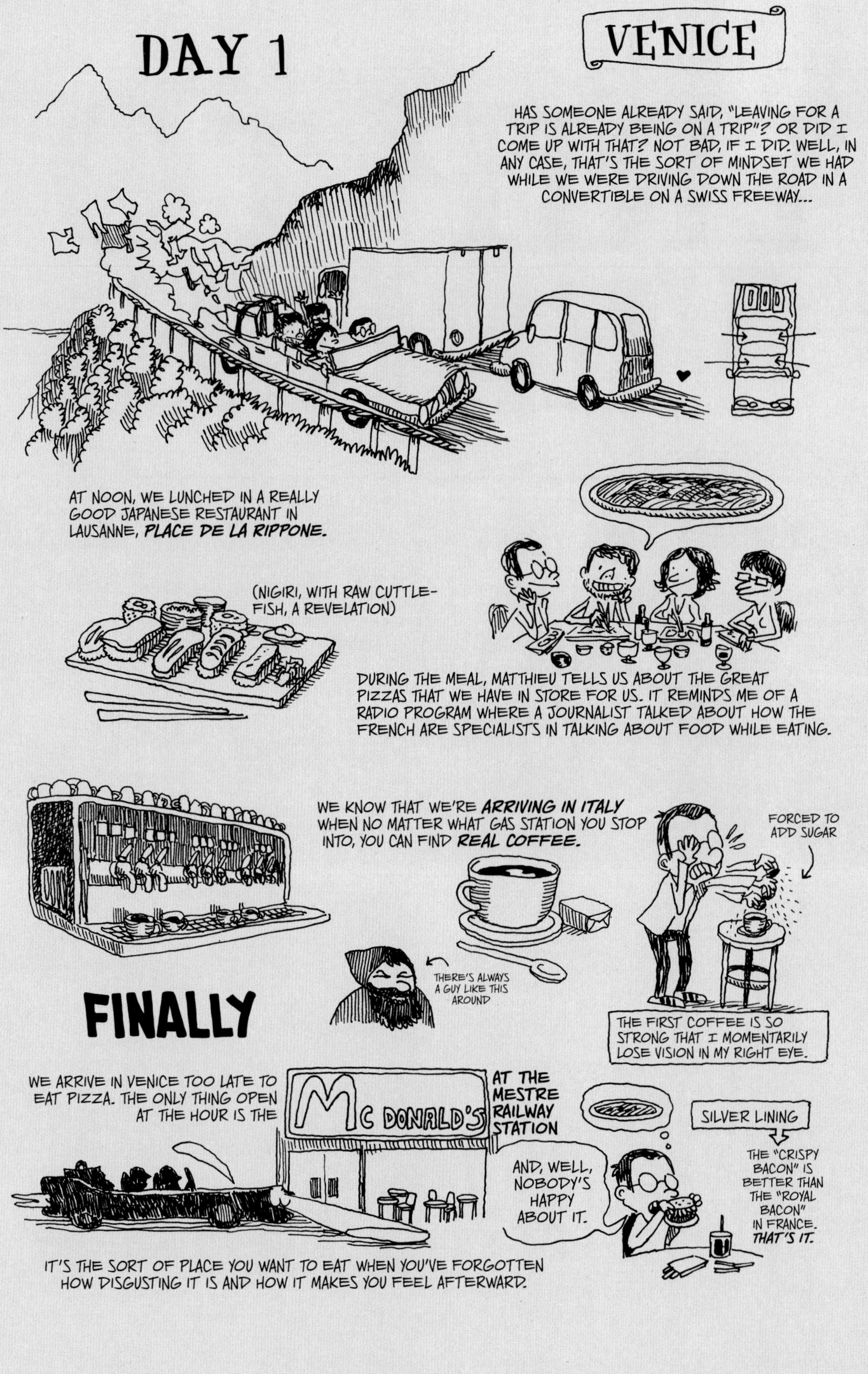
DAY 1
VENICE
HAS SOMEONE ALREADY SAID, "LEAVING FOR A TRIP IS ALREADY BEING ON A TRIP"? OR DID I COME UP WITH THAT? NOT BAD, IF I DID. WELL, IN ANY CASE, THAT'S THE SORT OF MINDSET WE HAD WHILE WE WERE DRIVING DOWN THE ROAD IN A CONVERTIBLE ON A SWISS FREEWAY...
AT NOON, WE LUNCHED IN A REALLY GOOD JAPANESE RESTAURANT IN LAUSANNE, PLACE DE LA RIPPONE.
(NIGIRI, WITH RAW CUTTLE-FISH, A REVELATION)
DURING THE MEAL, MATTHIEU TELLS US ABOUT THE GREAT PIZZAS THAT WE HAVE IN STORE FOR US. IT REMINDS ME OF A RADIO PROGRAM WHERE A JOURNALIST TALKED ABOUT HOW THE FRENCH ARE SPECIALISTS IN TALKING ABOUT FOOD WHILE EATING.
WE KNOW THAT WE'RE ARRIVING IN ITALY WHEN NO MATTER WHAT GAS STATION YOU STOP INTO, YOU CAN FIND REAL COFFEE.
FORCED TO ADD SUGAR
THERE'S ALWAYS A GUY LIKE THIS AROUND
FINALLY
THE FIRST COFFEE IS SO STRONG THAT I MOMENTARILY LOSE VISION IN MY RIGHT EYE.
WE ARRIVE IN VENICE TOO LATE TO EAT PIZZA. THE ONLY THING OPEN AT THE HOUR IS THE
Mc DONALD'S
AT THE MESTRE RAILWAY STATION
AND, WELL, NOBODY'S HAPPY ABOUT IT.
SILVER LINING
THE "CRISPY BACON" IS BETTER THAN THE "ROYAL BACON" IN FRANCE. THAT'S IT.
IT'S THE SORT OF PLACE YOU WANT TO EAT WHEN YOU'VE FORGOTTEN HOW DISGUSTING IT IS AND HOW IT MAKES YOU FEEL AFTERWARD.

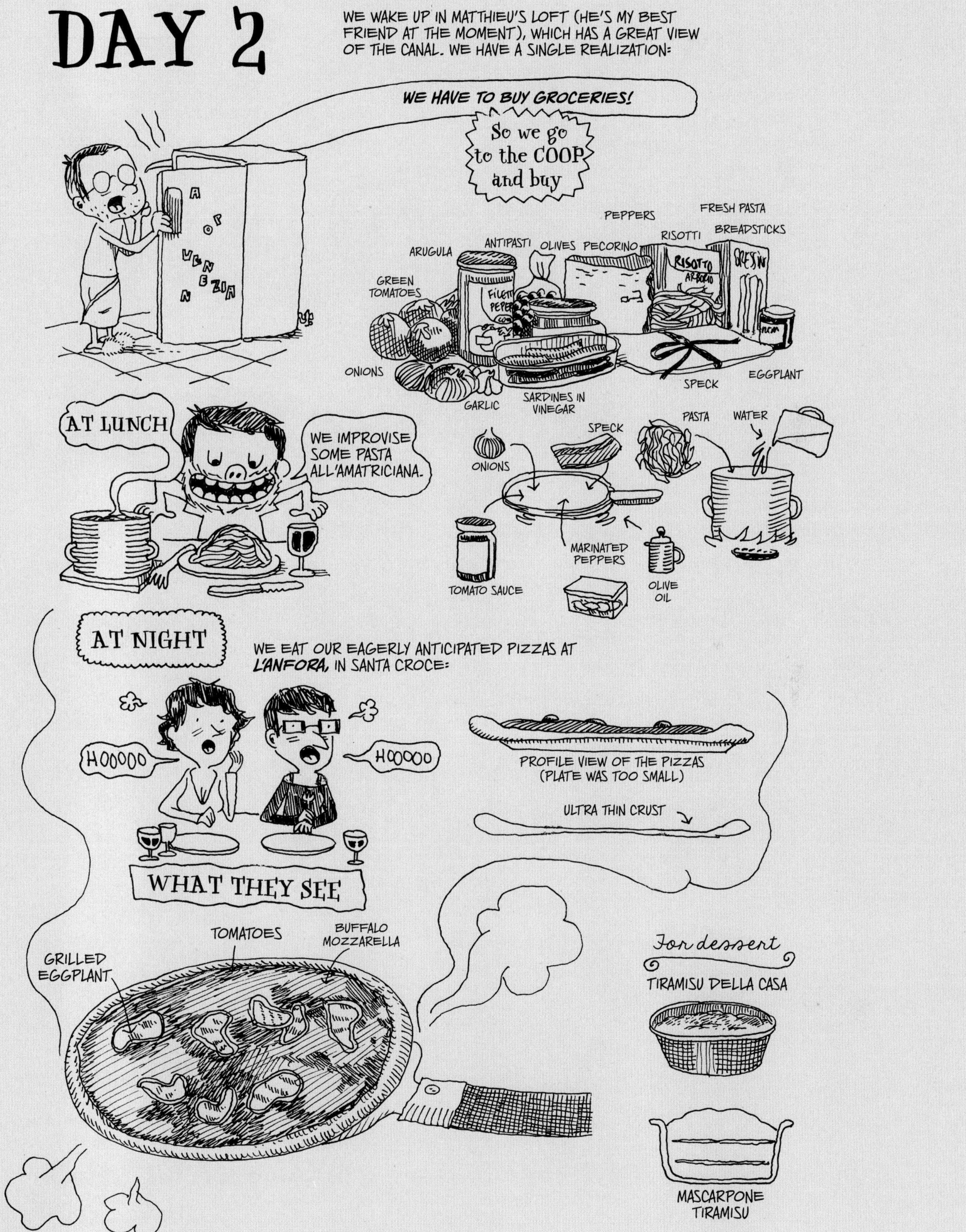
DAY 2
WE WAKE UP IN MATTHIEU'S LOFT (HE'S MY BEST FRIEND AT THE MOMENT), WHICH HAS A GREAT VIEW OF THE CANAL. WE HAVE A SINGLE REALIZATION:
WE HAVE TO BUY GROCERIES!
So we go to the COOP and buy
PEPPERS
FRESH PASTA
ANTIPASTI
OLIVES
PECORINO
RISOTTI
BREADSTICKS
ARUGULA
GREEN TOMATOES
ONIONS
GARLIC
SARDINES IN VINEGAR
SPECK
EGGPLANT
AT LUNCH
WE IMPROVISE SOME PASTA ALL'AMATRICIANA.
ONIONS
SPECK
PASTA
WATER
TOMATO SAUCE
MARINATED PEPPERS
OLIVE OIL
AT NIGHT
WE EAT OUR EAGERLY ANTICIPATED PIZZAS AT L'ANFORA, IN SANTA CROCE:
HOOOOO
HOOOOO
PROFILE VIEW OF THE PIZZAS (PLATE WAS TOO SMALL)
ULTRA THIN CRUST
WHAT THEY SEE
GRILLED EGGPLANT
TOMATOES
BUFFALO MOZZARELLA
For dessert
TIRAMISU DELLA CASA
MASCARPONE TIRAMISU

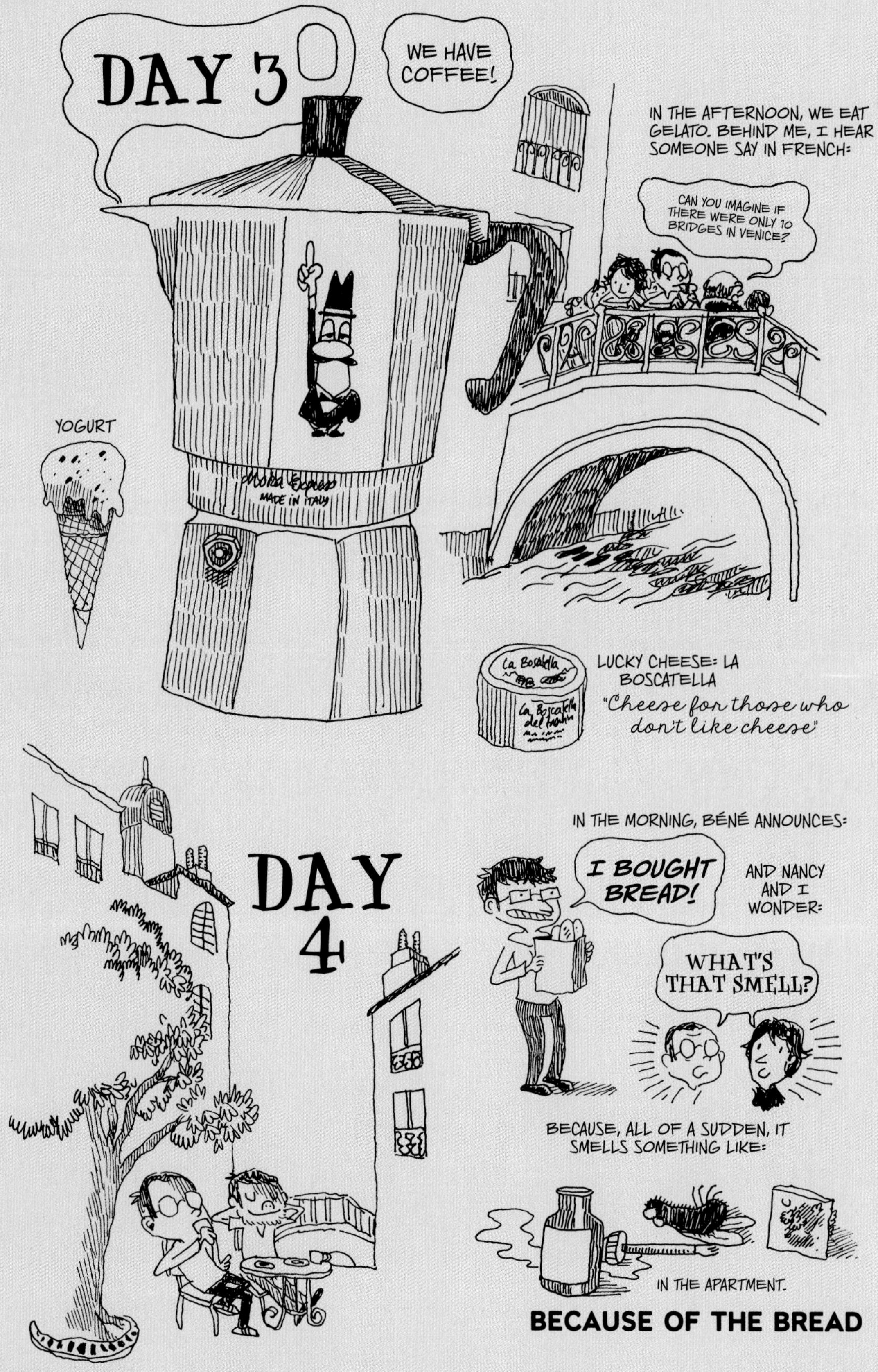
DAY 3
WE HAVE COFFEE!
IN THE AFTERNOON, WE EAT GELATO. BEHIND ME, I HEAR SOMEONE SAY IN FRENCH:
CAN YOU IMAGINE IF THERE WERE ONLY 10 BRIDGES IN VENICE?
YOGURT
MADE IN ITALY
LUCKY CHEESE: LA BOSCATELLA
"Cheese for those who don't like cheese"
DAY 4
IN THE MORNING, BÉNÉ ANNOUNCES:
I BOUGHT BREAD!
AND NANCY AND I WONDER:
WHAT'S THAT SMELL?
BECAUSE, ALL OF A SUDDEN, IT SMELLS SOMETHING LIKE:
IN THE APARTMENT.
BECAUSE OF THE BREAD

I THINK THAT THIS OLIVE BREAD WAS PREPARED IN THE FOLLOWING WAY:

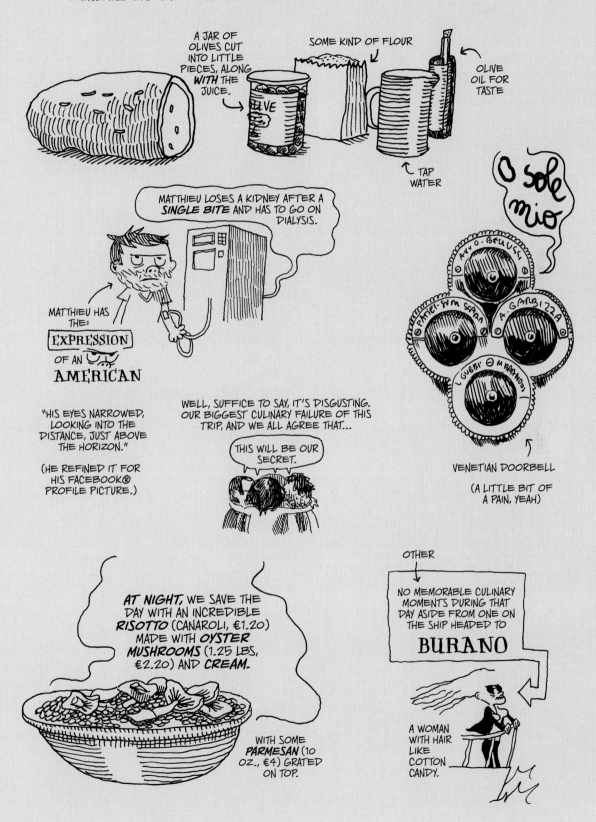

A JAR OF OLIVES CUT INTO LITTLE PIECES, ALONG **WITH** THE JUICE.

SOME KIND OF FLOUR

OLIVE OIL FOR TASTE

TAP WATER

O sole mio

MATTHIEU LOSES A KIDNEY AFTER A **SINGLE BITE** AND HAS TO GO ON DIALYSIS.

MATTHIEU HAS THE: EXPRESSION OF AN AMERICAN

"HIS EYES NARROWED, LOOKING INTO THE DISTANCE, JUST ABOVE THE HORIZON."

(HE REFINED IT FOR HIS FACEBOOK® PROFILE PICTURE.)

WELL, SUFFICE TO SAY, IT'S DISGUSTING. OUR BIGGEST CULINARY FAILURE OF THIS TRIP, AND WE ALL AGREE THAT...

THIS WILL BE OUR SECRET.

VENETIAN DOORBELL

(A LITTLE BIT OF A PAIN, YEAH)

AT NIGHT, WE SAVE THE DAY WITH AN INCREDIBLE **RISOTTO** (CANAROLI, €1.20) MADE WITH **OYSTER MUSHROOMS** (1.25 LBS, €2.20) AND **CREAM.**

WITH SOME **PARMESAN** (10 OZ., €4) GRATED ON TOP.

OTHER

NO MEMORABLE CULINARY MOMENTS DURING THAT DAY ASIDE FROM ONE ON THE SHIP HEADED TO BURANO

A WOMAN WITH HAIR LIKE COTTON CANDY.

DAY 5

THE *RIALTO* MARKET

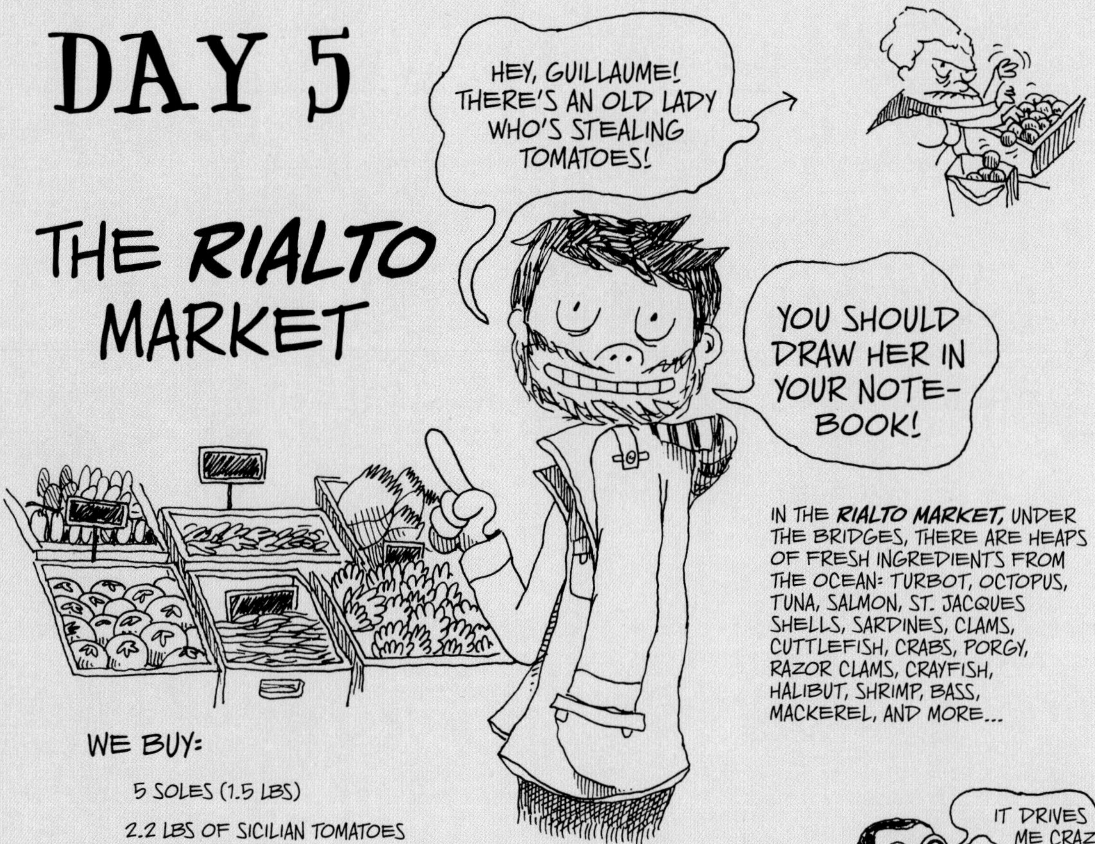
HEY, GUILLAUME! THERE'S AN OLD LADY WHO'S STEALING TOMATOES!
YOU SHOULD DRAW HER IN YOUR NOTE-BOOK!

IN THE ***RIALTO MARKET,*** UNDER THE BRIDGES, THERE ARE HEAPS OF FRESH INGREDIENTS FROM THE OCEAN: TURBOT, OCTOPUS, TUNA, SALMON, ST. JACQUES SHELLS, SARDINES, CLAMS, CUTTLEFISH, CRABS, PORGY, RAZOR CLAMS, CRAYFISH, HALIBUT, SHRIMP, BASS, MACKEREL, AND MORE...

WE BUY:

- 5 SOLES (1.5 LBS)
- 2.2 LBS OF SICILIAN TOMATOES
- 1 LB RAZOR CLAMS
- 2.2 LBS MIXED SALAD (ARUGULA, MESCLUN, ETC.)
- 1 BOX OF PARSLEY
- 4–5 SMALL LEEKS
- 2.2 LBS OF WHITE RAISINS

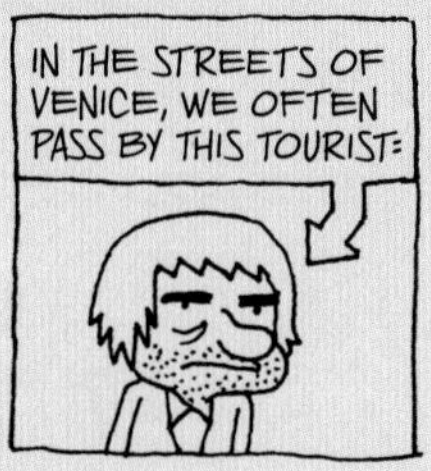
IN THE STREETS OF VENICE, WE OFTEN PASS BY THIS TOURIST:

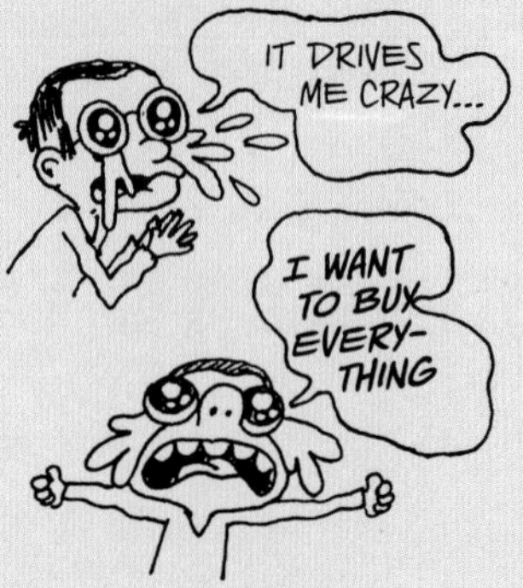
IT DRIVES ME CRAZY...
I WANT TO BUY EVERY-THING

FOR LUNCH, WE MAKE:

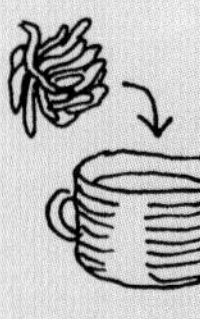

1) BOIL WATER TO COOK THE FRESH PASTA.

2) DISGORGE THE RAZOR CLAMS IN WATER.

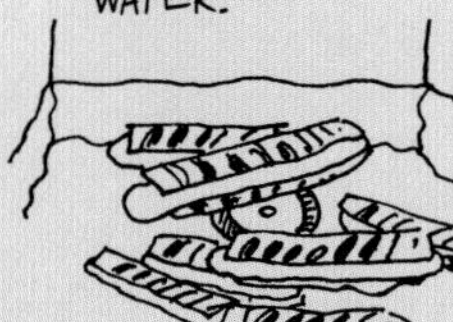

3) HEAT THE RAZOR CLAMS FOR 2 MINUTES IN A PAN SO THEY OPEN UP.

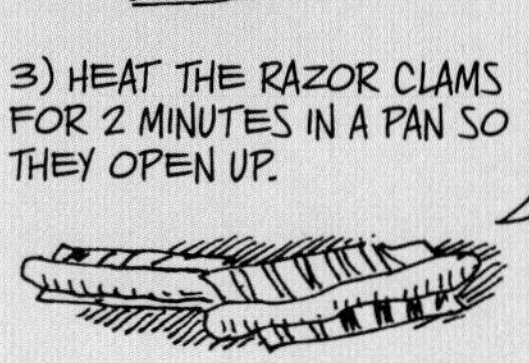
TSHIIIII

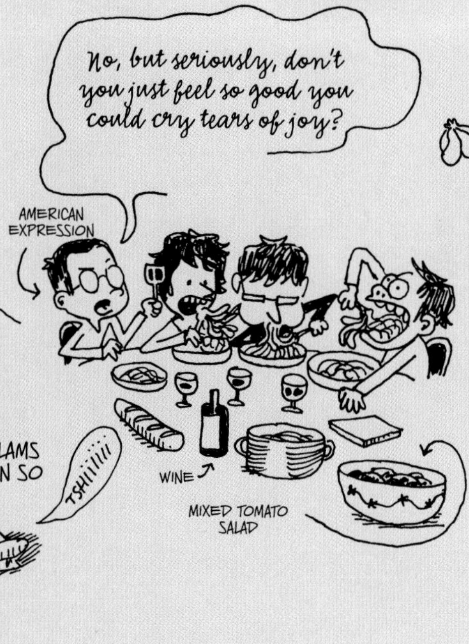
No, but seriously, don't you just feel so good you could cry tears of joy?
AMERICAN EXPRESSION
WINE
MIXED TOMATO SALAD

4) COOK GARLIC AND PARSLEY IN OLIVE OIL FOR 1 MINUTE. MEANWHILE DESHELL THE RAZOR CLAMS.

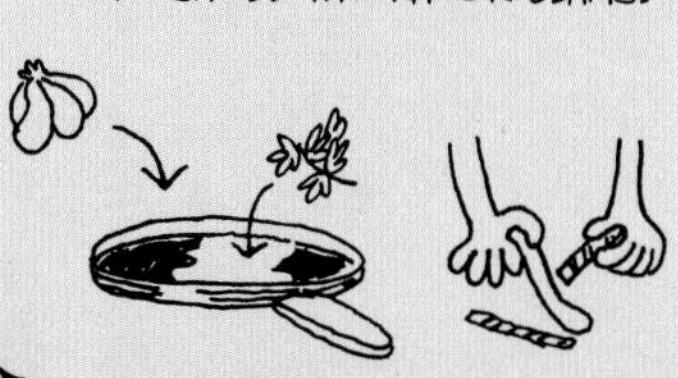

5) FOR 3 MINUTES, COOK THE RAZOR CLAMS WITH THE GARLIC AND PARLSEY, WHILE THE PASTA COOKS.

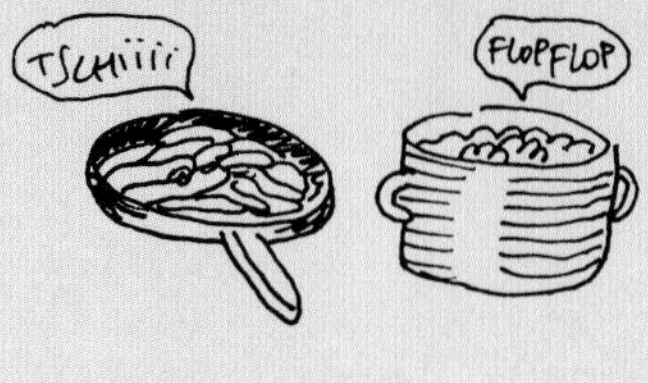
TSCHIIII
FLOPFLOP

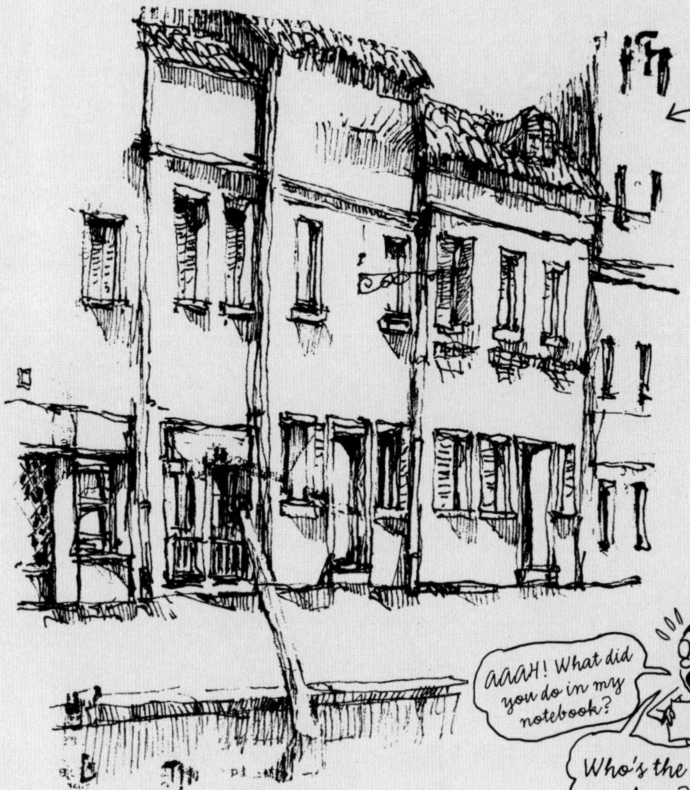

NANCY DIDN'T BRING HER SKETCHBOOK, SO SHE USES MINE (AND SHE DRAWS SO MUCH BETTER THAN ME IT HURTS).

I FIND SOME **MARTELLI©** PASTA IN A SHOP, AND IF YOU WANT TO KNOW HOW I FEEL, WELL, IT'S LIKE WHEN INDIANA JONES FINDS THE HOLY GRAIL IN THE THIRD MOVIE (EXCEPT THAT PASTA DOESN'T MAKE YOU AGE FASTER).

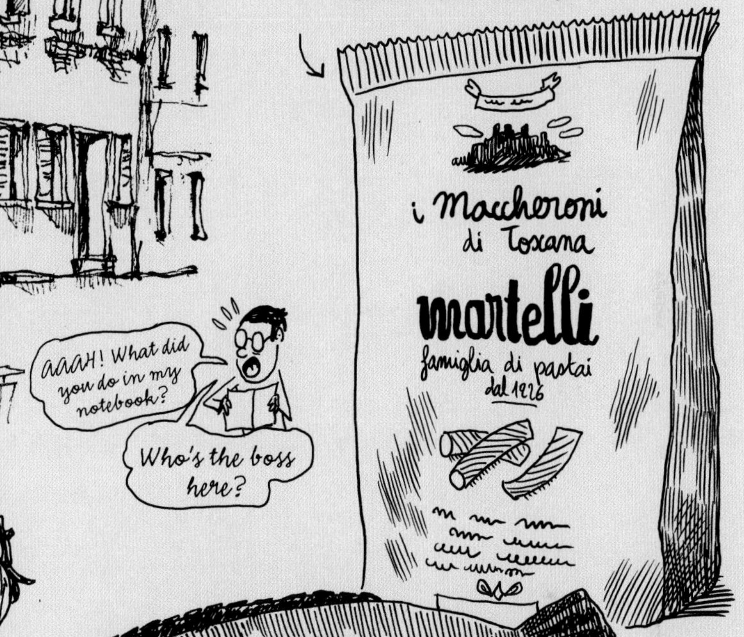
i Maccheroni
di Toscana
martelli
famiglia di pastai
dal 1926
AAAH! What did you do in my notebook?
Who's the boss here?

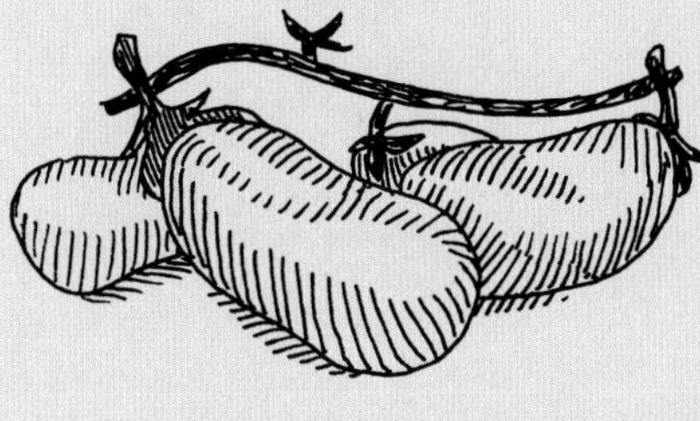

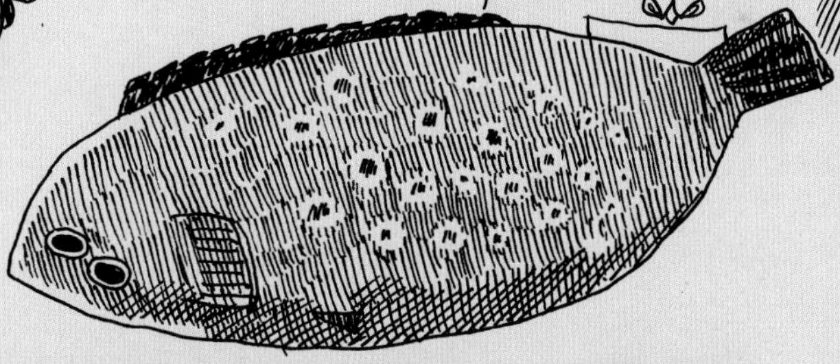

TO FINISH SHARING MY ACCOUNT OF THAT DAY, I HAVE TO SPEAK OF THE NIGHT WE SPENT ON THE TERRACE LOOKING AT THE BARGES ON THE CANAL WHILE EATING LEMON-BUTTER GRILLED SOLE, ALONGSIDE A LITTLE RISOTTO WITH SOME SOFT LEEKS, BUT MOST IMPORTANTLY: I'D HAVE TO BE A HELL OF A WRITER TO DESCRIBE, IN JUST A FEW WORDS, EXACTLY HOW DELICIOUS SICILIAN TOMATOES ARE.

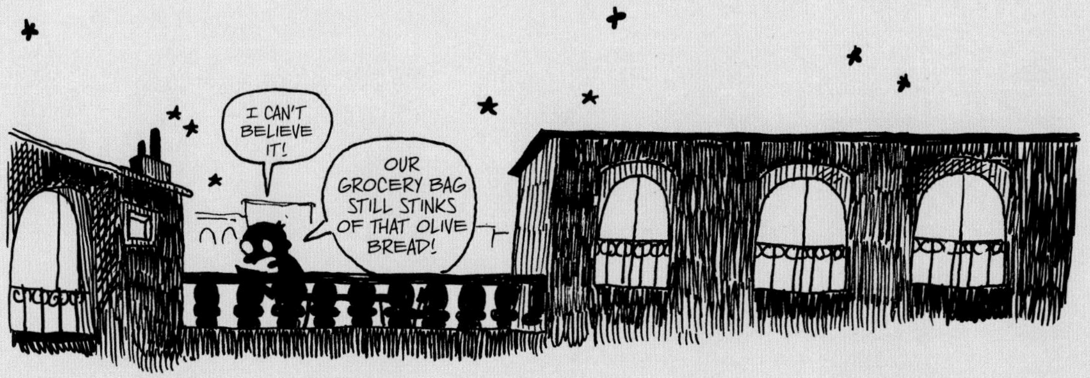
I CAN'T BELIEVE IT!
OUR GROCERY BAG STILL STINKS OF THAT OLIVE BREAD!

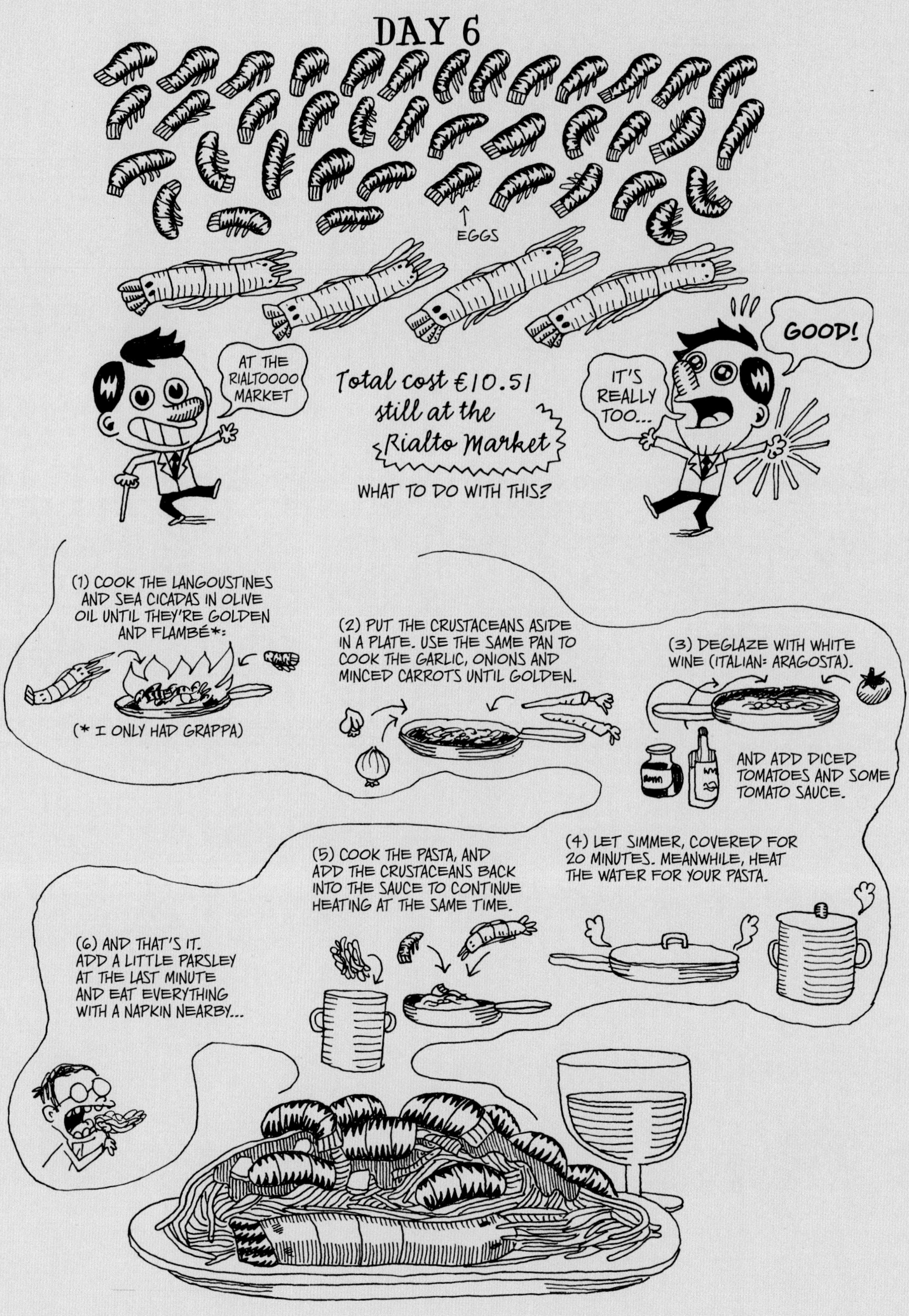

DAY 6
EGGS
AT THE RIALTOOOO MARKET
Total cost €10.51 still at the Rialto Market
IT'S REALLY TOO...
GOOD!
WHAT TO DO WITH THIS?
(1) COOK THE LANGOUSTINES AND SEA CICADAS IN OLIVE OIL UNTIL THEY'RE GOLDEN AND FLAMBÉ*:
(* I ONLY HAD GRAPPA)
(2) PUT THE CRUSTACEANS ASIDE IN A PLATE. USE THE SAME PAN TO COOK THE GARLIC, ONIONS AND MINCED CARROTS UNTIL GOLDEN.
(3) DEGLAZE WITH WHITE WINE (ITALIAN: ARAGOSTA).
AND ADD DICED TOMATOES AND SOME TOMATO SAUCE.
(4) LET SIMMER, COVERED FOR 20 MINUTES. MEANWHILE, HEAT THE WATER FOR YOUR PASTA.
(5) COOK THE PASTA, AND ADD THE CRUSTACEANS BACK INTO THE SAUCE TO CONTINUE HEATING AT THE SAME TIME.
(6) AND THAT'S IT. ADD A LITTLE PARSLEY AT THE LAST MINUTE AND EAT EVERYTHING WITH A NAPKIN NEARBY...

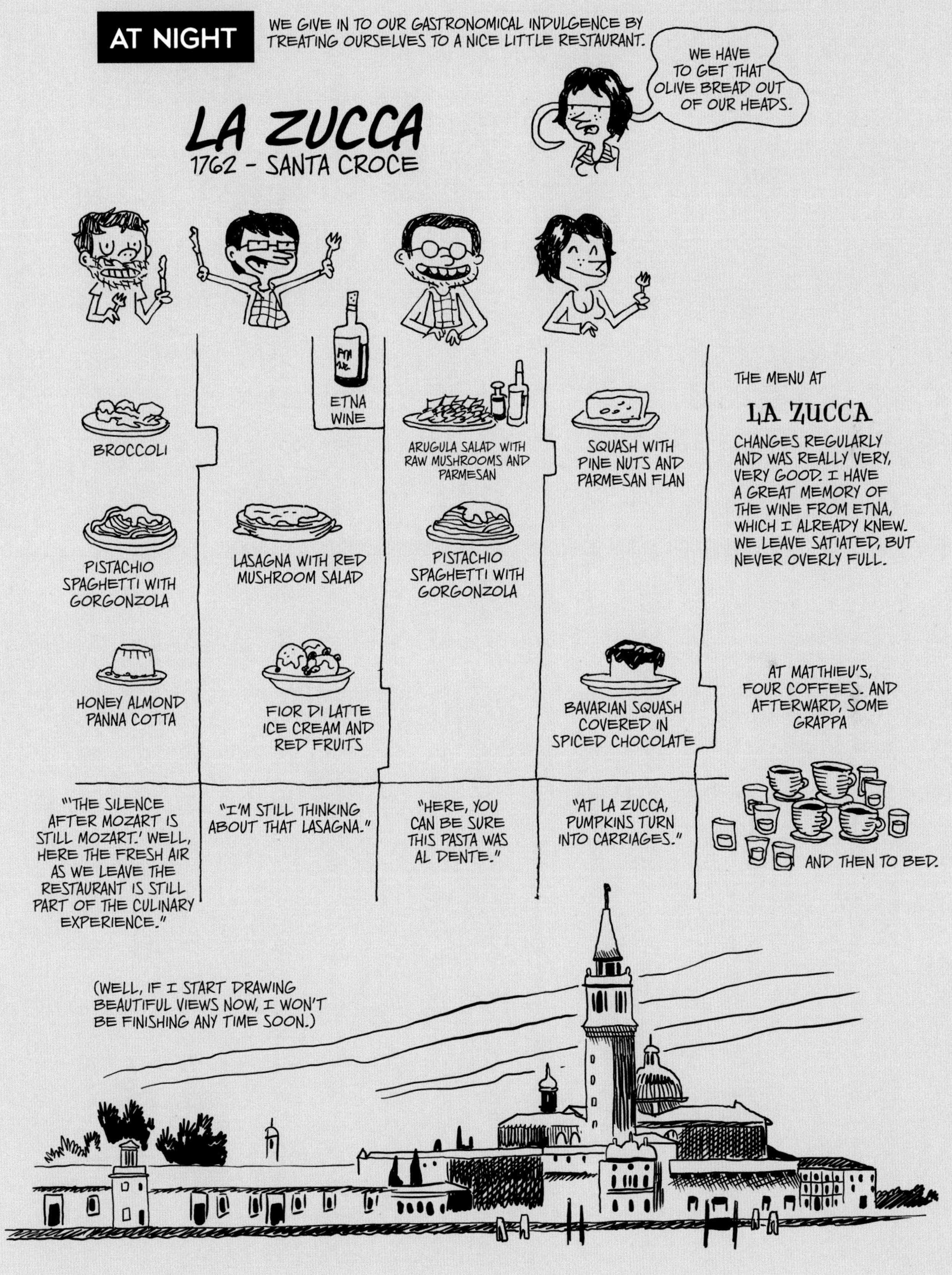
AT NIGHT
WE GIVE IN TO OUR GASTRONOMICAL INDULGENCE BY TREATING OURSELVES TO A NICE LITTLE RESTAURANT.
WE HAVE TO GET THAT OLIVE BREAD OUT OF OUR HEADS.
LA ZUCCA
1762 - SANTA CROCE
ETNA WINE
BROCCOLI
ARUGULA SALAD WITH RAW MUSHROOMS AND PARMESAN
SQUASH WITH PINE NUTS AND PARMESAN FLAN
THE MENU AT LA ZUCCA CHANGES REGULARLY AND WAS REALLY VERY, VERY GOOD. I HAVE A GREAT MEMORY OF THE WINE FROM ETNA, WHICH I ALREADY KNEW. WE LEAVE SATIATED, BUT NEVER OVERLY FULL.
PISTACHIO SPAGHETTI WITH GORGONZOLA
LASAGNA WITH RED MUSHROOM SALAD
PISTACHIO SPAGHETTI WITH GORGONZOLA
HONEY ALMOND PANNA COTTA
FIOR DI LATTE ICE CREAM AND RED FRUITS
BAVARIAN SQUASH COVERED IN SPICED CHOCOLATE
AT MATTHIEU'S, FOUR COFFEES. AND AFTERWARD, SOME GRAPPA
"'THE SILENCE AFTER MOZART IS STILL MOZART.' WELL, HERE THE FRESH AIR AS WE LEAVE THE RESTAURANT IS STILL PART OF THE CULINARY EXPERIENCE."
"I'M STILL THINKING ABOUT THAT LASAGNA."
"HERE, YOU CAN BE SURE THIS PASTA WAS AL DENTE."
"AT LA ZUCCA, PUMPKINS TURN INTO CARRIAGES."
AND THEN TO BED.
(WELL, IF I START DRAWING BEAUTIFUL VIEWS NOW, I WON'T BE FINISHING ANY TIME SOON.)

BUT HOW DID WE GET HERE? *AI GRECI*, A TOURISTY
RESTAURANT IN THE *CASTELLO* NEIGHBORHOOD. I WANT TO DIE.
THE WAITERS LOOK INDIAN, SPEAK ENGLISH, FRENCH, SPANISH,
GERMAN, AND ITALIAN, AND THERE'S A BUDDHA IN THE CORNER.

DAY 7

IT SMELLS LIKE MOLDY BREAD FOR SIX MILES AROUND,
AND I'M FEELING A LITTLE BUMMED OUT, BECAUSE I KNOW
IT'S MY SECOND TO LAST MEAL IN VENICE AND YESTERDAY
WAS AN EXCEPTIONALLY DELICIOUS DAY... ALL BECAUSE:

(BEHIND US THERE'S A FRENCH FAMILY WHO ARE VERY PLEASED WITH THEIR MEAL.)

WOW! LOOK AT THE SIZE OF THE PIZZAS!

IT'S ITALY!

5.5 INCHES IN DIAMETER, 3 DEAD FISH ON TOP.

THE GIRL SAYS:

THIS IS THE BEST PIZZA I'VE EVER HAD!

THE PIZZA IN QUESTION IS VERY STIFF AND STRAIGHT.

3 DAYS AGO
I WANT PASTA AL NERO DI SEPIA

2 DAYS AGO
I WANT PASTA AL NERO DI SE

YESTERDAY
PASTA AL NERO DI SEP

SO MATTHIEU SAYS, "OKAY, WE'RE GOING TO EAT THE BEST PASTA AL NERO DI SEPPIA*, ACCORDING TO MY DAD."

* SQUID INK PASTA

EXCEPT THAT THEN, MATTHIEU CALLS HIS FATHER TO BE SURE HE'S GOT THE RIGHT ADDRESS.

AND STILL THAT AMERICAN EXPRESSION...

You're sure of yourself, right?

Because this place looks terrible.

Yeah, Castello, that's it.

AND FINALLY:

IT'S GOOD

BUT IT'S THE ONLY THING WE CAN ORDER.

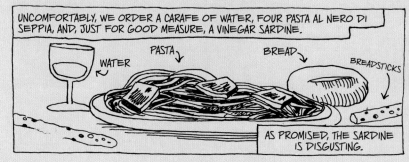

UNCOMFORTABLY, WE ORDER A CARAFE OF WATER, FOUR PASTA AL NERO DI SEPPIA, AND, JUST FOR GOOD MEASURE, A VINEGAR SARDINE.

WATER

PASTA

BREAD

BREADSTICKS

AS PROMISED, THE SARDINE IS DISGUSTING.

BUT
THE PASTA'S DEFINITIVELY DELICIOUS, SO IT WAS WORTH THE RISK.

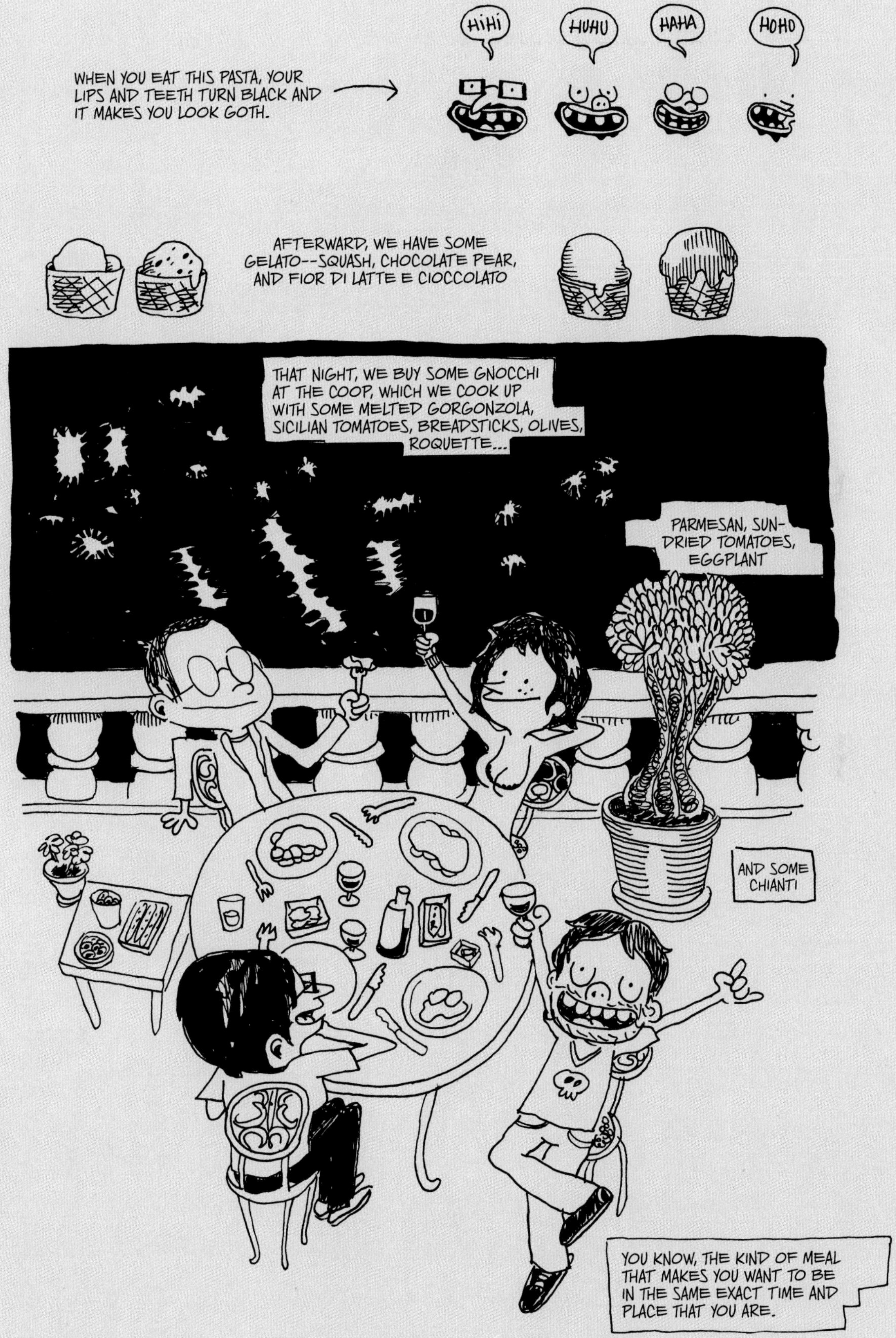
WHEN YOU EAT THIS PASTA, YOUR LIPS AND TEETH TURN BLACK AND IT MAKES YOU LOOK GOTH.
HIHI
HUHU
HAHA
HOHO
AFTERWARD, WE HAVE SOME GELATO--SQUASH, CHOCOLATE PEAR, AND FIOR DI LATTE E CIOCCOLATO
THAT NIGHT, WE BUY SOME GNOCCHI AT THE COOP, WHICH WE COOK UP WITH SOME MELTED GORGONZOLA, SICILIAN TOMATOES, BREADSTICKS, OLIVES, ROQUETTE...
PARMESAN, SUN-DRIED TOMATOES, EGGPLANT
AND SOME CHIANTI
YOU KNOW, THE KIND OF MEAL THAT MAKES YOU WANT TO BE IN THE SAME EXACT TIME AND PLACE THAT YOU ARE.

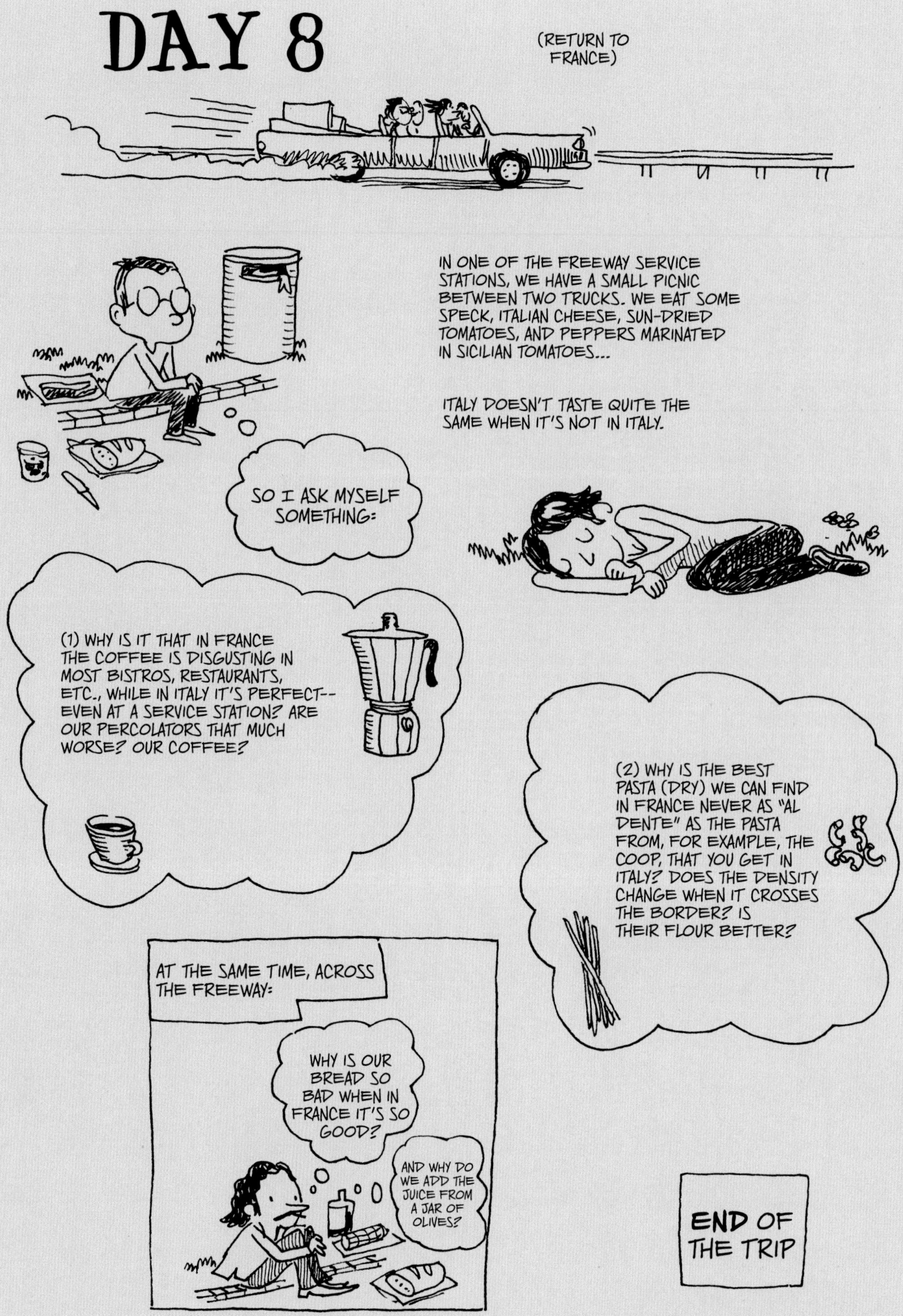
DAY 8
(RETURN TO FRANCE)
IN ONE OF THE FREEWAY SERVICE STATIONS, WE HAVE A SMALL PICNIC BETWEEN TWO TRUCKS. WE EAT SOME SPECK, ITALIAN CHEESE, SUN-DRIED TOMATOES, AND PEPPERS MARINATED IN SICILIAN TOMATOES...
ITALY DOESN'T TASTE QUITE THE SAME WHEN IT'S NOT IN ITALY.
SO I ASK MYSELF SOMETHING:
(1) WHY IS IT THAT IN FRANCE THE COFFEE IS DISGUSTING IN MOST BISTROS, RESTAURANTS, ETC., WHILE IN ITALY IT'S PERFECT--EVEN AT A SERVICE STATION? ARE OUR PERCOLATORS THAT MUCH WORSE? OUR COFFEE?
(2) WHY IS THE BEST PASTA (DRY) WE CAN FIND IN FRANCE NEVER AS "AL DENTE" AS THE PASTA FROM, FOR EXAMPLE, THE COOP, THAT YOU GET IN ITALY? DOES THE DENSITY CHANGE WHEN IT CROSSES THE BORDER? IS THEIR FLOUR BETTER?
AT THE SAME TIME, ACROSS THE FREEWAY:
WHY IS OUR BREAD SO BAD WHEN IN FRANCE IT'S SO GOOD?
AND WHY DO WE ADD THE JUICE FROM A JAR OF OLIVES?
END OF THE TRIP

Winter

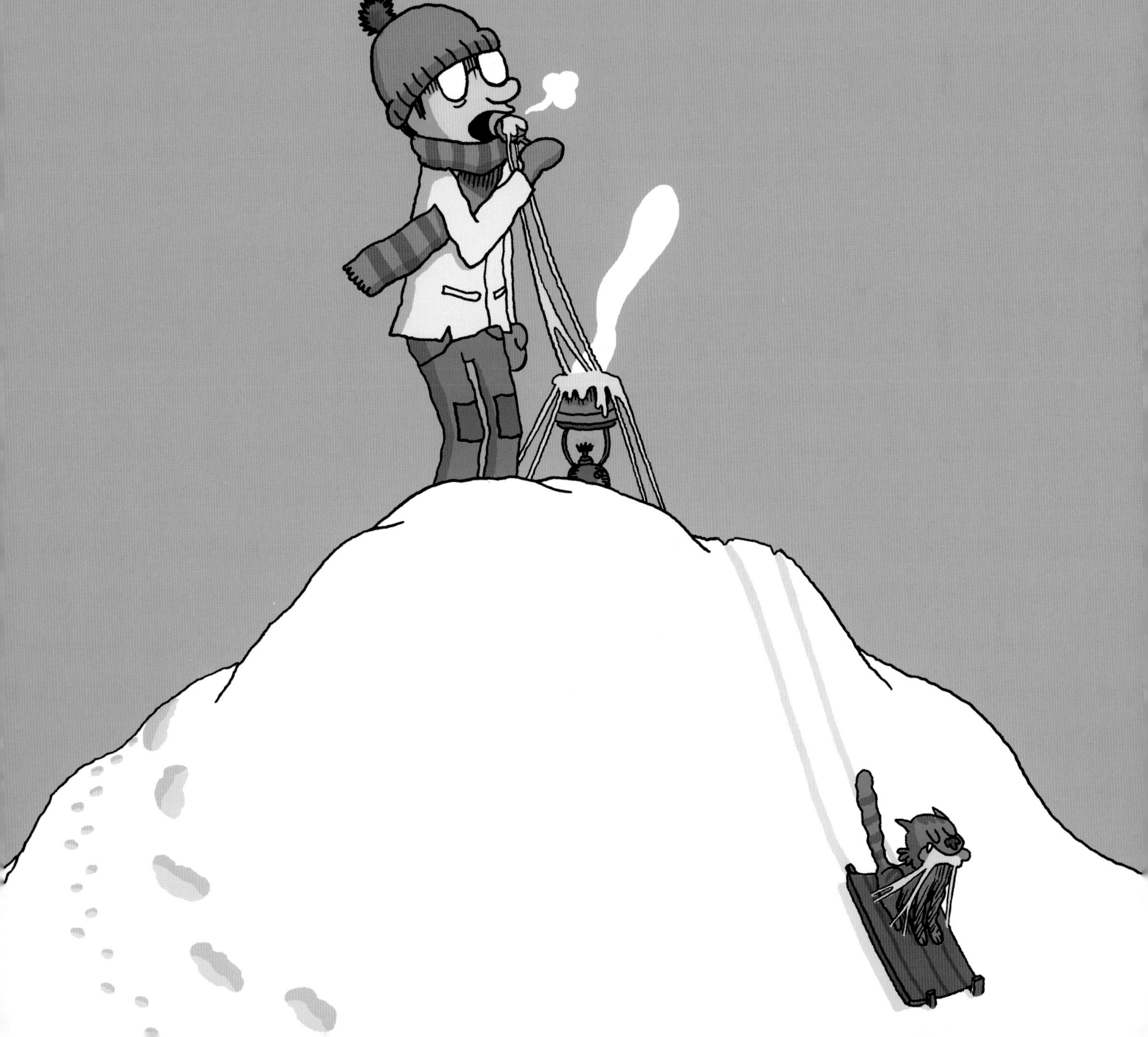

YOU'VE BEEN AT THIS DINNER PARTY FOR SOME TIME, FILLING YOUR BELLY WITH A GLASS IN YOUR HAND.

EVERYONE SEEMS TO HAVE FORGOTTEN YOU.

SO YOU TAKE A SIP, NOTHING UNUSUAL...

AND SUDDENLY...

LOOK AT JEAN-MICHEL!

THAT'S TERRIBLE!

HIM AGAIN!

HEY!! WE HAVEN'T CHEERS'D YET!

JEAN-MICHEL SUCKS

THAT'S REALLY IMPO-LITE!

SHIT, I CAN'T BELIEVE

PLUS, YOUR NAME IS JEAN-MICHEL.

HELLO, REGULARS!

TODAY, WE'RE TALKING ABOUT APERITIFS AND, IN PARTICULAR...

WHY WE CHEERS

TCHIN TCHIN

IT HAS TO DO WITH A VERY OLD TRADITION...

THAT GOES BACK ALL THE WAY TO A TIME THAT WAS QUITE MEDIEVAL...

ESPECIALLY FOR FOOD.

IN THAT TIME, POISONINGS WERE COMMON.

EVERYWHERE, ALL THE TIME... IT WAS PRACTICALLY COOL!

HEHE

SEEMS LIKE THE HIPPOCRAS HAS BEEN TAMPERED WITH!

BUT THIS TREND WAS CAUSING A HELL OF A MESS...

WOW! I GUESS BROCOLOUNGE WASN'T THE ONLY THING THE BARON WAS SERVING LAST NIGHT!

SO WE STARTED TO CHEERS. WHEN YOU WOULD CHEERS, A LITTLE BIT OF LIQUID WOULD GO INTO YOUR NEIGHBORS CUP, AND VICE VERSA ("TCHIN-TCHIN" IS THE NOISE OF THAT EXCHANGE). AND SO, IF THE PERSON WAS WILLING TO CHEERS WITH YOU...

...IT WAS ONLY LOGICAL THAT THEY WEREN'T TRYING TO POISON YOU!

THAT'S WHY IT WAS IMPORTANT FOR YOU TO LOOK EACH OTHER IN THE EYES (IN CASE THE OTHER PERSON WAS SUICIDAL).

AND THE MOST PARANOID WOULD EVEN SAY: "TO YOUR HEALTH!"

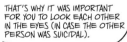

THAT'S WHY YOU HAVE TO CHEERS WITH YOUR FRIENDS, JEAN-MICHEL!

EVEN IF I CAN'T IMAGINE YOU HAVING ANY INTENTION OF POISONING... JEAN-MICHEL?

I... I... I HAD ENOUGH OF MY FRIENDS MAKING FUN OF MY NAME...

THEY ALWAYS LAUGHED AS THEY SAID IT!

THEY EVEN MADE A FACEBOOK® GROUP!

leon.

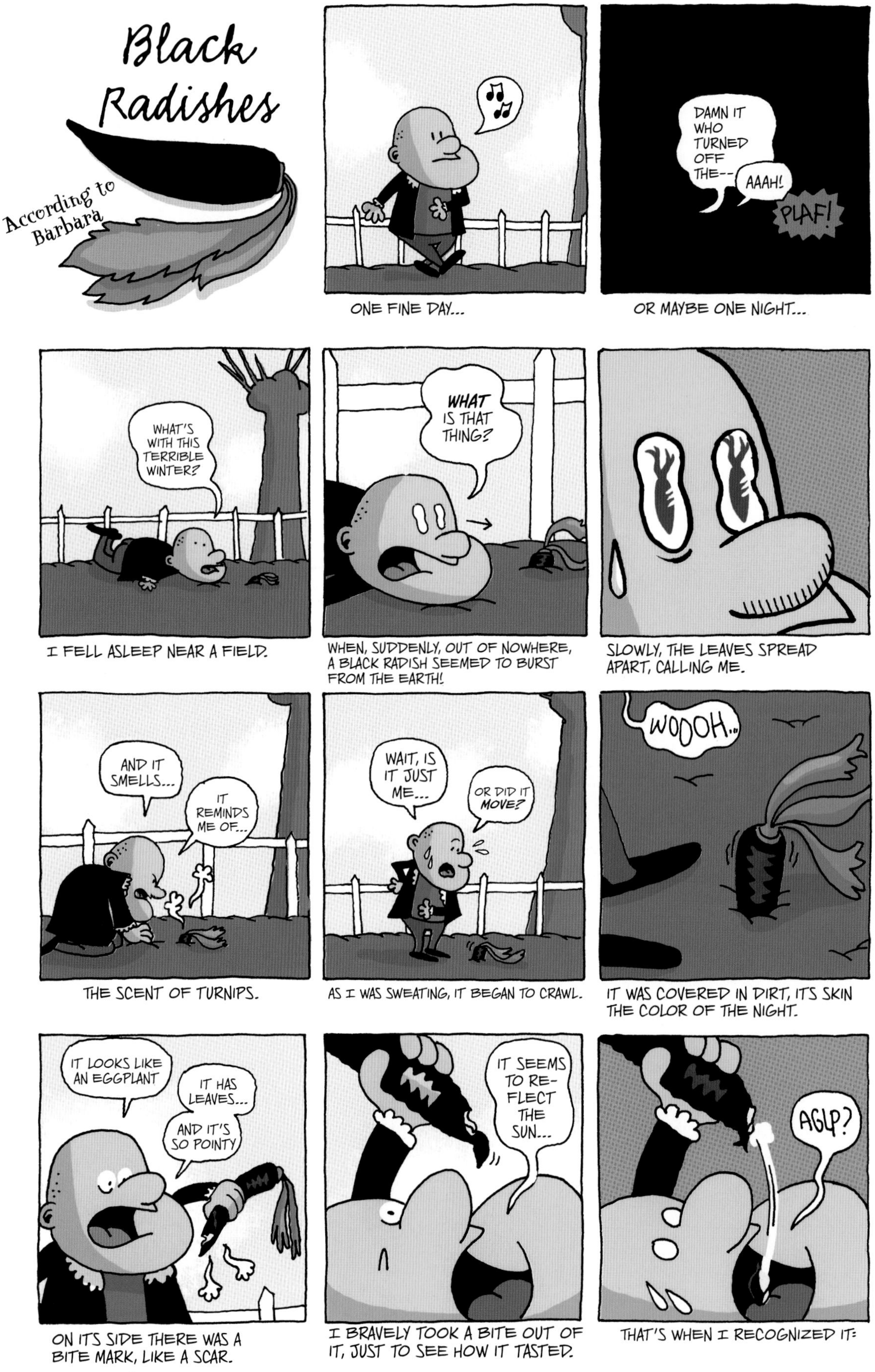
Black Radishes
According to Barbara
ONE FINE DAY...
DAMN IT WHO TURNED OFF THE--
AAAH!
PLAF!
OR MAYBE ONE NIGHT...
WHAT'S WITH THIS TERRIBLE WINTER?
I FELL ASLEEP NEAR A FIELD.
WHAT IS THAT THING?
WHEN, SUDDENLY, OUT OF NOWHERE, A BLACK RADISH SEEMED TO BURST FROM THE EARTH!
SLOWLY, THE LEAVES SPREAD APART, CALLING ME.
AND IT SMELLS...
IT REMINDS ME OF...
THE SCENT OF TURNIPS.
WAIT, IS IT JUST ME...
OR DID IT MOVE?
AS I WAS SWEATING, IT BEGAN TO CRAWL.
WOOOH..
IT WAS COVERED IN DIRT, ITS SKIN THE COLOR OF THE NIGHT.
IT LOOKS LIKE AN EGGPLANT
IT HAS LEAVES...
AND IT'S SO POINTY
ON ITS SIDE THERE WAS A BITE MARK, LIKE A SCAR.
IT SEEMS TO RE-FLECT THE SUN...
I BRAVELY TOOK A BITE OUT OF IT, JUST TO SEE HOW IT TASTED.
AGLP?
THAT'S WHEN I RECOGNIZED IT:

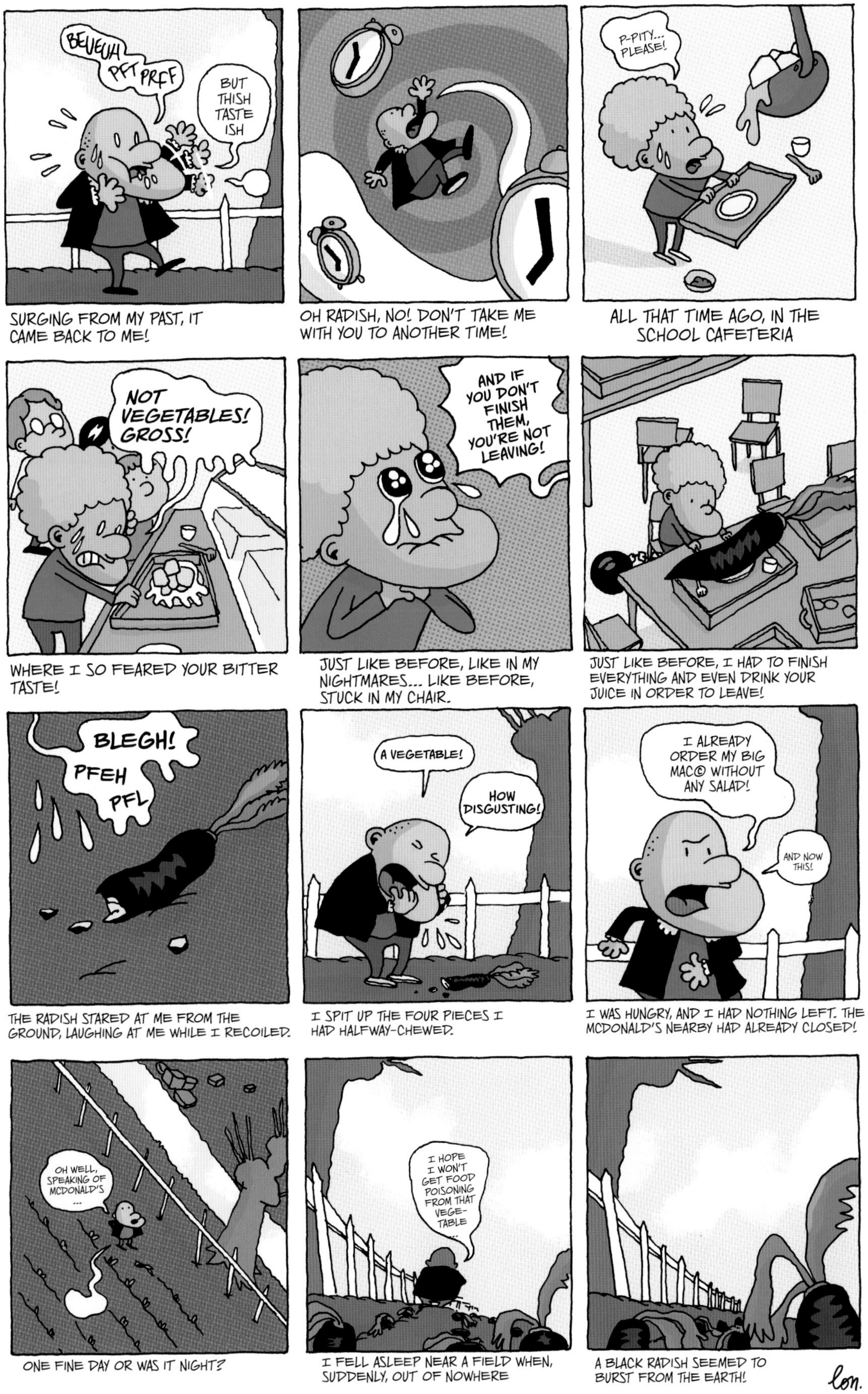
BEVEUH PFT PRFF
BUT THISH TASTE ISH
SURGING FROM MY PAST, IT CAME BACK TO ME!
OH RADISH, NO! DON'T TAKE ME WITH YOU TO ANOTHER TIME!
P-PITY... PLEASE!
ALL THAT TIME AGO, IN THE SCHOOL CAFETERIA
NOT VEGETABLES! GROSS!
WHERE I SO FEARED YOUR BITTER TASTE!
AND IF YOU DON'T FINISH THEM, YOU'RE NOT LEAVING!
JUST LIKE BEFORE, LIKE IN MY NIGHTMARES... LIKE BEFORE, STUCK IN MY CHAIR.
JUST LIKE BEFORE, I HAD TO FINISH EVERYTHING AND EVEN DRINK YOUR JUICE IN ORDER TO LEAVE!
BLEGH!
PFEH
PFL
THE RADISH STARED AT ME FROM THE GROUND, LAUGHING AT ME WHILE I RECOILED.
A VEGETABLE!
HOW DISGUSTING!
I SPIT UP THE FOUR PIECES I HAD HALFWAY-CHEWED.
I ALREADY ORDER MY BIG MAC© WITHOUT ANY SALAD!
AND NOW THIS!
I WAS HUNGRY, AND I HAD NOTHING LEFT. THE MCDONALD'S NEARBY HAD ALREADY CLOSED!
OH WELL, SPEAKING OF MCDONALD'S ...
ONE FINE DAY OR WAS IT NIGHT?
I HOPE I WON'T GET FOOD POISONING FROM THAT VEGE-TABLE ...
I FELL ASLEEP NEAR A FIELD WHEN, SUDDENLY, OUT OF NOWHERE
A BLACK RADISH SEEMED TO BURST FROM THE EARTH!
lon.

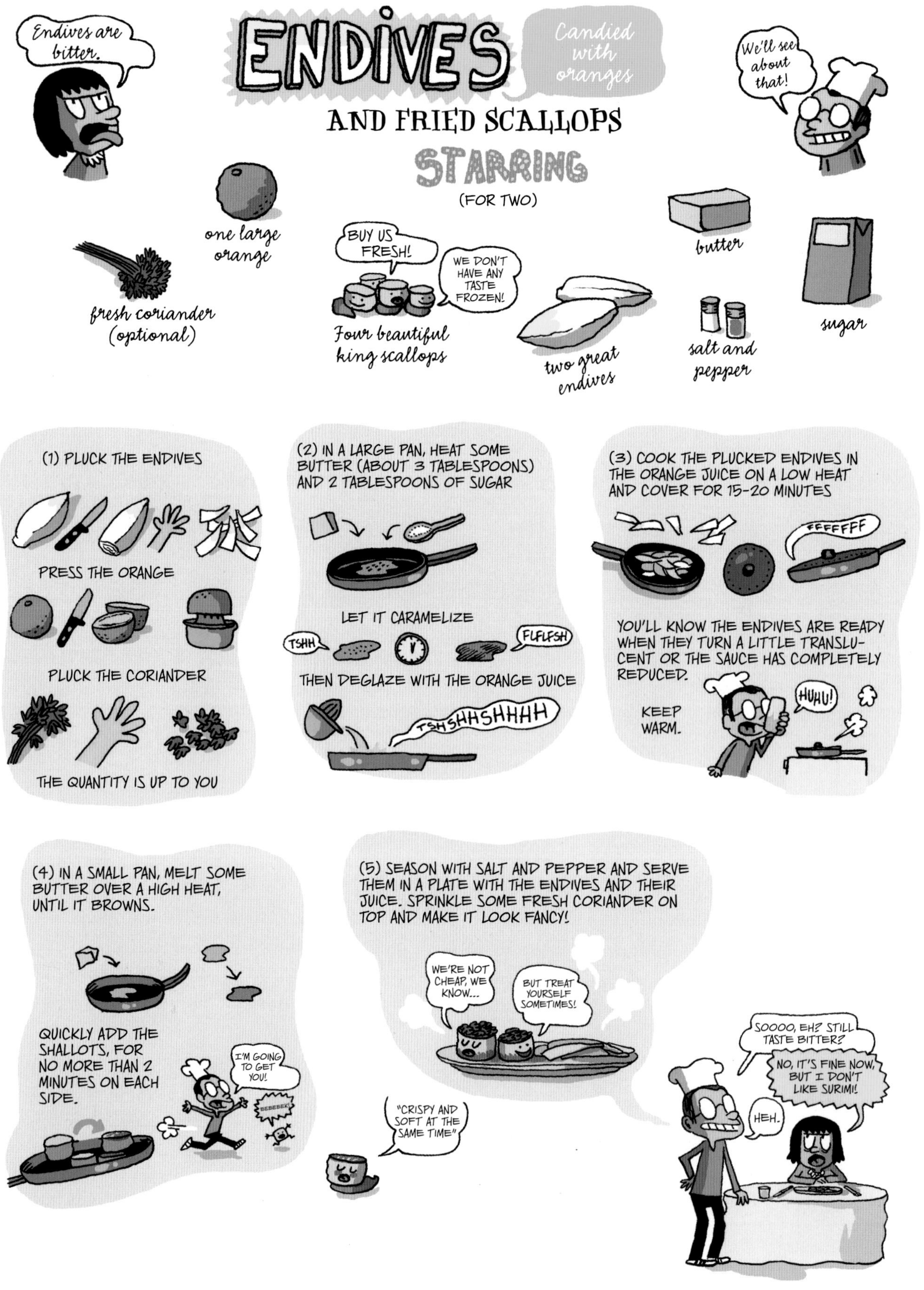
Endives are bitter.
ENDIVES
Candied with oranges
AND FRIED SCALLOPS
We'll see about that!
STARRING
(FOR TWO)
one large orange
fresh coriander (optional)
BUY US FRESH!
WE DON'T HAVE ANY TASTE FROZEN!
Four beautiful king scallops
two great endives
butter
salt and pepper
sugar
(1) PLUCK THE ENDIVES
PRESS THE ORANGE
PLUCK THE CORIANDER
THE QUANTITY IS UP TO YOU
(2) IN A LARGE PAN, HEAT SOME BUTTER (ABOUT 3 TABLESPOONS) AND 2 TABLESPOONS OF SUGAR
LET IT CARAMELIZE
TSHH
FLFLFSH
THEN DEGLAZE WITH THE ORANGE JUICE
TSHSHHSHHHH
(3) COOK THE PLUCKED ENDIVES IN THE ORANGE JUICE ON A LOW HEAT AND COVER FOR 15-20 MINUTES
FFFFFFF
YOU'LL KNOW THE ENDIVES ARE READY WHEN THEY TURN A LITTLE TRANSLUCENT OR THE SAUCE HAS COMPLETELY REDUCED.
KEEP WARM.
HUHU!
(4) IN A SMALL PAN, MELT SOME BUTTER OVER A HIGH HEAT, UNTIL IT BROWNS.
QUICKLY ADD THE SHALLOTS, FOR NO MORE THAN 2 MINUTES ON EACH SIDE.
I'M GOING TO GET YOU!
BEBEBEK!
(5) SEASON WITH SALT AND PEPPER AND SERVE THEM IN A PLATE WITH THE ENDIVES AND THEIR JUICE. SPRINKLE SOME FRESH CORIANDER ON TOP AND MAKE IT LOOK FANCY!
WE'RE NOT CHEAP, WE KNOW...
BUT TREAT YOURSELF SOMETIMES!
"CRISPY AND SOFT AT THE SAME TIME"
SOOOO, EH? STILL TASTE BITTER?
NO, IT'S FINE NOW, BUT I DON'T LIKE SURIMI!
HEH.

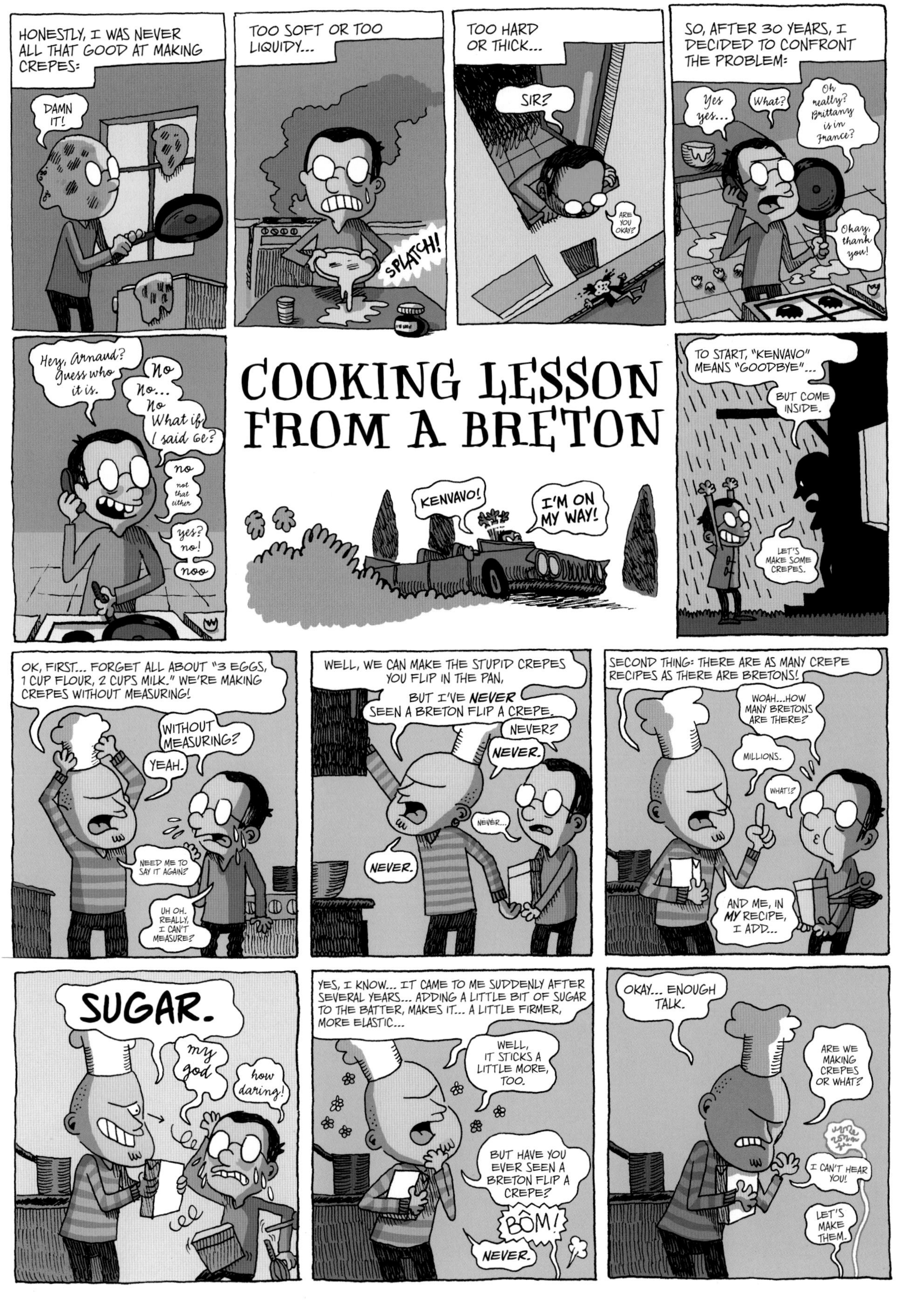
HONESTLY, I WAS NEVER ALL THAT GOOD AT MAKING CREPES:
DAMN IT!
TOO SOFT OR TOO LIQUIDY...
SPLATCH!
TOO HARD OR THICK...
SIR?
ARE YOU OKAY?
SO, AFTER 30 YEARS, I DECIDED TO CONFRONT THE PROBLEM:
Yes yes...
What?
Oh really? Brittany is in France?
Okay, thank you!
Hey, Arnaud? Guess who it is.
No
No... No
What if I said 6e?
no
not that either
yes? no!
noo
COOKING LESSON FROM A BRETON
KENVAVO!
I'M ON MY WAY!
TO START, "KENVAVO" MEANS "GOODBYE"...
BUT COME INSIDE.
LET'S MAKE SOME CREPES.
OK, FIRST... FORGET ALL ABOUT "3 EGGS, 1 CUP FLOUR, 2 CUPS MILK." WE'RE MAKING CREPES WITHOUT MEASURING!
WITHOUT MEASURING?
YEAH.
NEED ME TO SAY IT AGAIN?
UH OH. REALLY, I CAN'T MEASURE?
WELL, WE CAN MAKE THE STUPID CREPES YOU FLIP IN THE PAN,
BUT I'VE NEVER SEEN A BRETON FLIP A CREPE.
NEVER?
NEVER.
NEVER...
NEVER.
SECOND THING: THERE ARE AS MANY CREPE RECIPES AS THERE ARE BRETONS!
WOAH...HOW MANY BRETONS ARE THERE?
MILLIONS.
WHAT!?
AND ME, IN MY RECIPE, I ADD...
SUGAR.
my god
how daring!
YES, I KNOW... IT CAME TO ME SUDDENLY AFTER SEVERAL YEARS... ADDING A LITTLE BIT OF SUGAR TO THE BATTER, MAKES IT... A LITTLE FIRMER, MORE ELASTIC...
WELL, IT STICKS A LITTLE MORE, TOO.
BUT HAVE YOU EVER SEEN A BRETON FLIP A CREPE?
BÔM!
NEVER.
OKAY... ENOUGH TALK.
ARE WE MAKING CREPES OR WHAT?
I CAN'T HEAR YOU!
LET'S MAKE THEM.

Without measuring

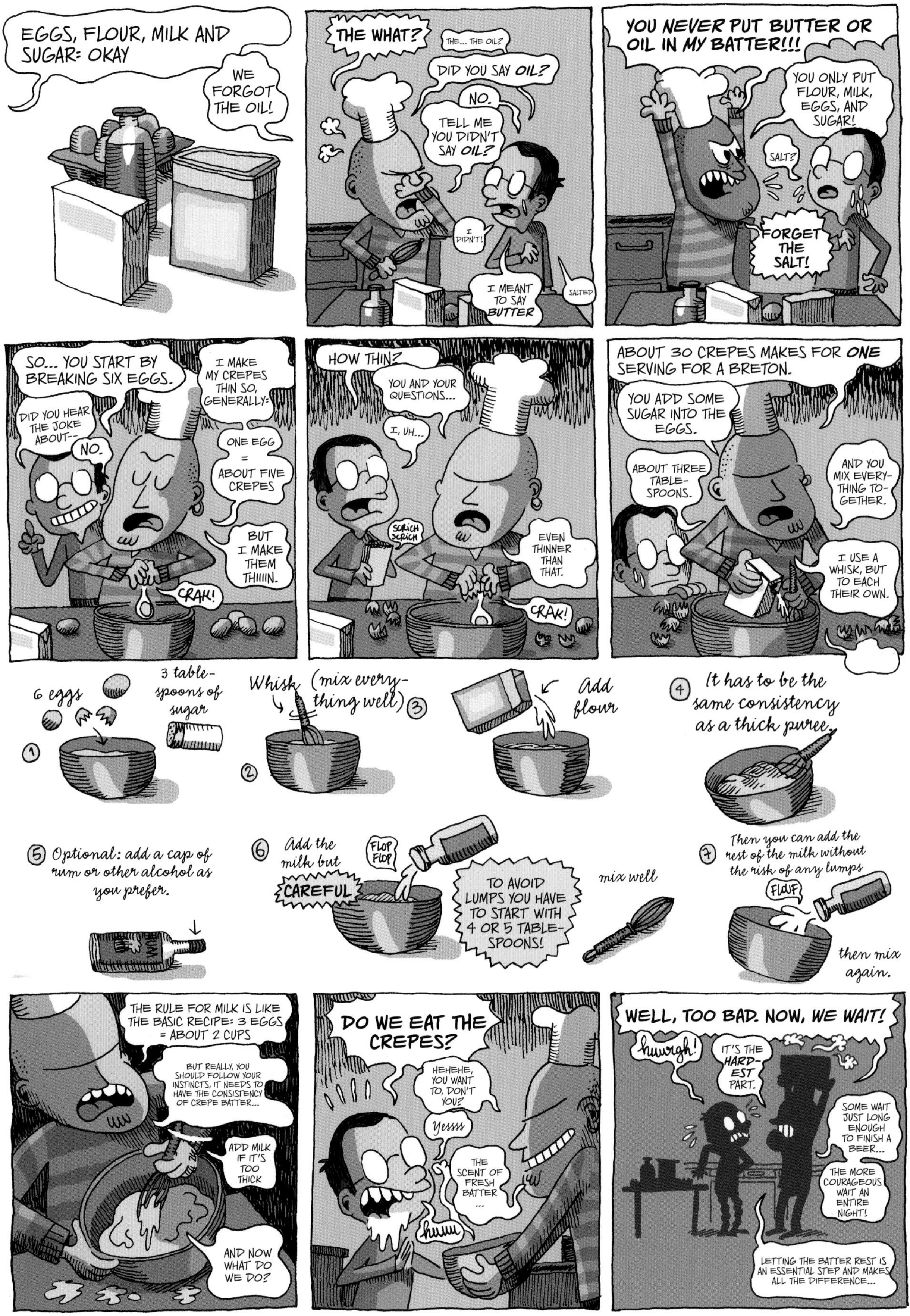

EGGS, FLOUR, MILK AND SUGAR: OKAY
WE FORGOT THE OIL!
THE WHAT?
THE... THE OIL?
DID YOU SAY OIL?
NO.
TELL ME YOU DIDN'T SAY OIL?
I DIDN'T!
I MEANT TO SAY BUTTER
SALTED
YOU NEVER PUT BUTTER OR OIL IN MY BATTER!!!
YOU ONLY PUT FLOUR, MILK, EGGS, AND SUGAR!
SALT?
FORGET THE SALT!
SO... YOU START BY BREAKING SIX EGGS.
I MAKE MY CREPES THIN SO, GENERALLY:
DID YOU HEAR THE JOKE ABOUT--
NO.
ONE EGG = ABOUT FIVE CREPES
BUT I MAKE THEM THIIIIN.
CRAK!
HOW THIN?
YOU AND YOUR QUESTIONS...
I, UH...
SCRICH SCRICH
EVEN THINNER THAN THAT.
CRAK!
ABOUT 30 CREPES MAKES FOR ONE SERVING FOR A BRETON.
YOU ADD SOME SUGAR INTO THE EGGS.
ABOUT THREE TABLE-SPOONS.
AND YOU MIX EVERY-THING TO-GETHER.
I USE A WHISK, BUT TO EACH THEIR OWN.
6 eggs
3 table-spoons of sugar
1
Whisk (mix every-thing well)
2
3
Add flour
4 It has to be the same consistency as a thick puree.
5 Optional: add a cap of rum or other alcohol as you prefer.
6 Add the milk but
CAREFUL
FLOP FLOP
TO AVOID LUMPS YOU HAVE TO START WITH 4 OR 5 TABLE-SPOONS!
mix well
7 Then you can add the rest of the milk without the risk of any lumps
FLOUF
then mix again.
THE RULE FOR MILK IS LIKE THE BASIC RECIPE: 3 EGGS = ABOUT 2 CUPS
BUT REALLY, YOU SHOULD FOLLOW YOUR INSTINCTS, IT NEEDS TO HAVE THE CONSISTENCY OF CREPE BATTER...
ADD MILK IF IT'S TOO THICK
AND NOW WHAT DO WE DO?
DO WE EAT THE CREPES?
HEHEHE, YOU WANT TO, DON'T YOU?
Yessss
THE SCENT OF FRESH BATTER ...
huuu
WELL, TOO BAD. NOW, WE WAIT!
huurgh!
IT'S THE HARD-EST PART.
SOME WAIT JUST LONG ENOUGH TO FINISH A BEER...
THE MORE COURAGEOUS WAIT AN ENTIRE NIGHT!
LETTING THE BATTER REST IS AN ESSENTIAL STEP AND MAKES ALL THE DIFFERENCE...

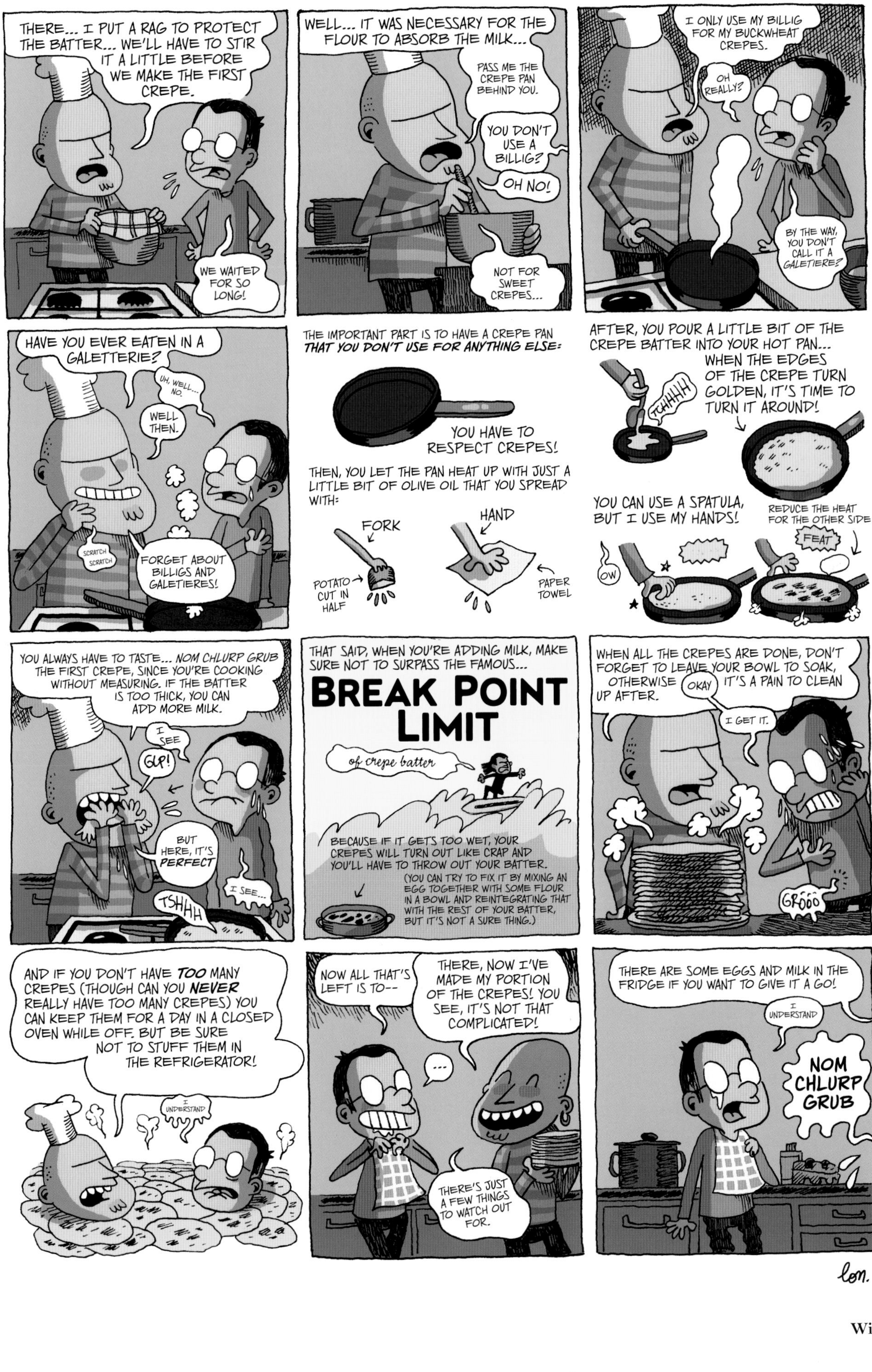
THERE... I PUT A RAG TO PROTECT THE BATTER... WE'LL HAVE TO STIR IT A LITTLE BEFORE WE MAKE THE FIRST CREPE.
WE WAITED FOR SO LONG!
WELL... IT WAS NECESSARY FOR THE FLOUR TO ABSORB THE MILK...
PASS ME THE CREPE PAN BEHIND YOU.
YOU DON'T USE A BILLIG?
OH NO!
NOT FOR SWEET CREPES...
I ONLY USE MY BILLIG FOR MY BUCKWHEAT CREPES.
OH REALLY?
BY THE WAY, YOU DON'T CALL IT A GALETIERE?
HAVE YOU EVER EATEN IN A GALETTERIE?
UH, WELL... NO.
WELL THEN.
SCRATCH SCRATCH
FORGET ABOUT BILLIGS AND GALETIERES!
THE IMPORTANT PART IS TO HAVE A CREPE PAN *THAT YOU DON'T USE FOR ANYTHING ELSE:*
YOU HAVE TO RESPECT CREPES!
THEN, YOU LET THE PAN HEAT UP WITH JUST A LITTLE BIT OF OLIVE OIL THAT YOU SPREAD WITH:
FORK
POTATO CUT IN HALF
HAND
PAPER TOWEL
AFTER, YOU POUR A LITTLE BIT OF THE CREPE BATTER INTO YOUR HOT PAN...
TSHHHH
WHEN THE EDGES OF THE CREPE TURN GOLDEN, IT'S TIME TO TURN IT AROUND!
YOU CAN USE A SPATULA, BUT I USE MY HANDS!
REDUCE THE HEAT FOR THE OTHER SIDE
OW
FEAT
YOU ALWAYS HAVE TO TASTE... NOM CHLURP GRUB THE FIRST CREPE, SINCE YOU'RE COOKING WITHOUT MEASURING. IF THE BATTER IS TOO THICK, YOU CAN ADD MORE MILK.
I SEE
GLP!
BUT HERE, IT'S *PERFECT*
I SEE...
TSHHH
THAT SAID, WHEN YOU'RE ADDING MILK, MAKE SURE NOT TO SURPASS THE FAMOUS...
BREAK POINT LIMIT
of crepe batter
BECAUSE IF IT GETS TOO WET, YOUR CREPES WILL TURN OUT LIKE CRAP AND YOU'LL HAVE TO THROW OUT YOUR BATTER.
(YOU CAN TRY TO FIX IT BY MIXING AN EGG TOGETHER WITH SOME FLOUR IN A BOWL AND REINTEGRATING THAT WITH THE REST OF YOUR BATTER, BUT IT'S NOT A SURE THING.)
WHEN ALL THE CREPES ARE DONE, DON'T FORGET TO LEAVE YOUR BOWL TO SOAK, OTHERWISE IT'S A PAIN TO CLEAN UP AFTER.
OKAY
I GET IT.
GRÔÔÔ
AND IF YOU DON'T HAVE *TOO* MANY CREPES (THOUGH CAN YOU *NEVER* REALLY HAVE TOO MANY CREPES) YOU CAN KEEP THEM FOR A DAY IN A CLOSED OVEN WHILE OFF. BUT BE SURE NOT TO STUFF THEM IN THE REFRIGERATOR!
I UNDERSTAND
NOW ALL THAT'S LEFT IS TO--
THERE, NOW I'VE MADE MY PORTION OF THE CREPES! YOU SEE, IT'S NOT THAT COMPLICATED!
...
THERE'S JUST A FEW THINGS TO WATCH OUT FOR.
THERE ARE SOME EGGS AND MILK IN THE FRIDGE IF YOU WANT TO GIVE IT A GO!
I UNDERSTAND
NOM CHLURP GRUB
lon.

Radish to remember

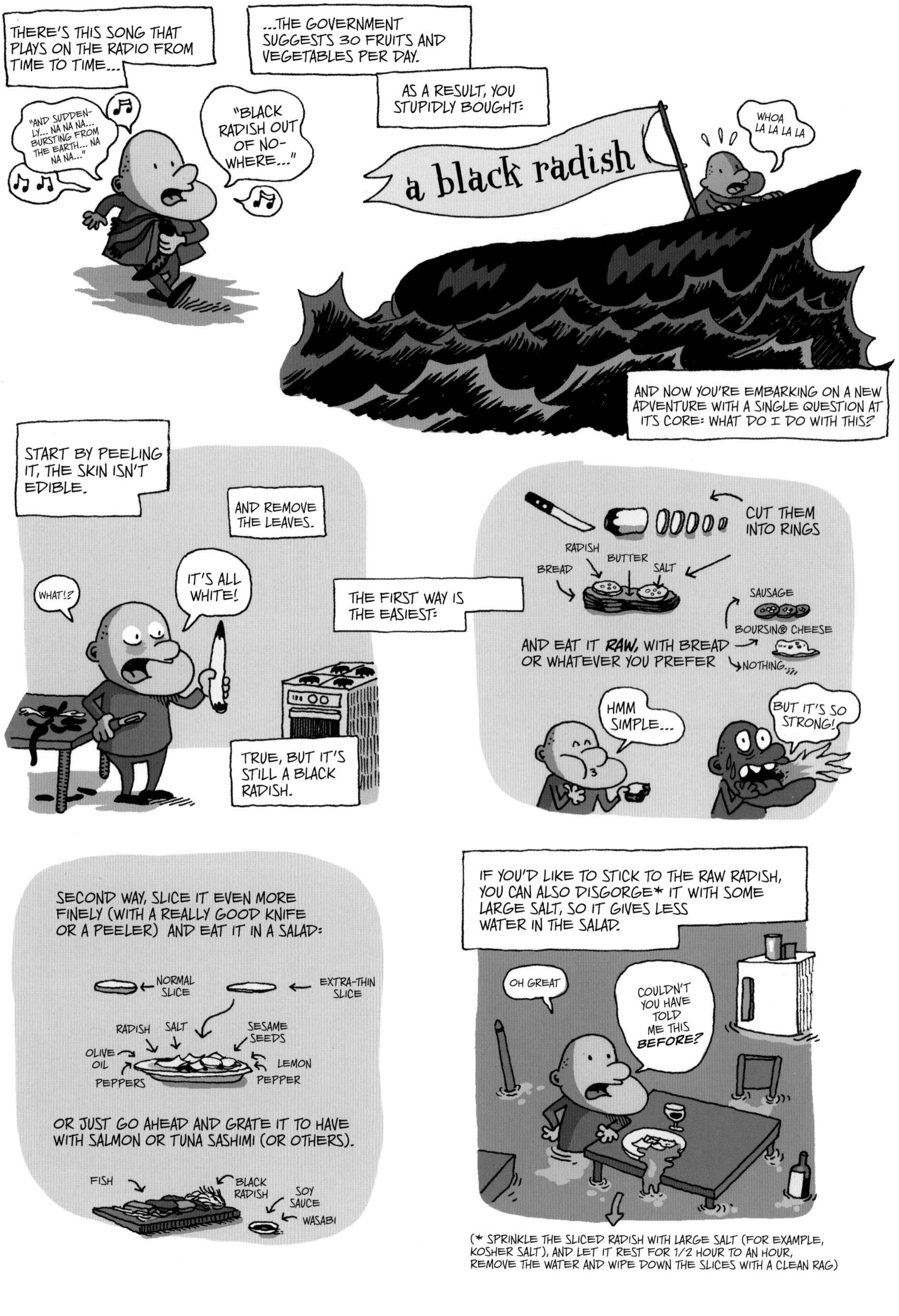

THERE'S THIS SONG THAT PLAYS ON THE RADIO FROM TIME TO TIME...
"AND SUDDEN-LY... NA NA NA... BURSTING FROM THE EARTH... NA NA NA..."
"BLACK RADISH OUT OF NO-WHERE..."
...THE GOVERNMENT SUGGESTS 30 FRUITS AND VEGETABLES PER DAY.
AS A RESULT, YOU STUPIDLY BOUGHT:
a black radish
WHOA LA LA LA LA
AND NOW YOU'RE EMBARKING ON A NEW ADVENTURE WITH A SINGLE QUESTION AT ITS CORE: WHAT DO I DO WITH THIS?
START BY PEELING IT, THE SKIN ISN'T EDIBLE.
AND REMOVE THE LEAVES.
WHAT!?
IT'S ALL WHITE!
TRUE, BUT IT'S STILL A BLACK RADISH.
THE FIRST WAY IS THE EASIEST:
CUT THEM INTO RINGS
RADISH
BUTTER
BREAD
SALT
SAUSAGE
BOURSIN® CHEESE
AND EAT IT RAW, WITH BREAD OR WHATEVER YOU PREFER
NOTHING...
HMM SIMPLE...
BUT IT'S SO STRONG!
SECOND WAY, SLICE IT EVEN MORE FINELY (WITH A REALLY GOOD KNIFE OR A PEELER) AND EAT IT IN A SALAD:
NORMAL SLICE
EXTRA-THIN SLICE
RADISH
SALT
SESAME SEEDS
OLIVE OIL
LEMON
PEPPERS
PEPPER
OR JUST GO AHEAD AND GRATE IT TO HAVE WITH SALMON OR TUNA SASHIMI (OR OTHERS).
FISH
BLACK RADISH
SOY SAUCE
WASABI
IF YOU'D LIKE TO STICK TO THE RAW RADISH, YOU CAN ALSO DISGORGE* IT WITH SOME LARGE SALT, SO IT GIVES LESS WATER IN THE SALAD.
OH GREAT
COULDN'T YOU HAVE TOLD ME THIS BEFORE?
(* SPRINKLE THE SLICED RADISH WITH LARGE SALT (FOR EXAMPLE, KOSHER SALT), AND LET IT REST FOR 1/2 HOUR TO AN HOUR, REMOVE THE WATER AND WIPE DOWN THE SLICES WITH A CLEAN RAG)

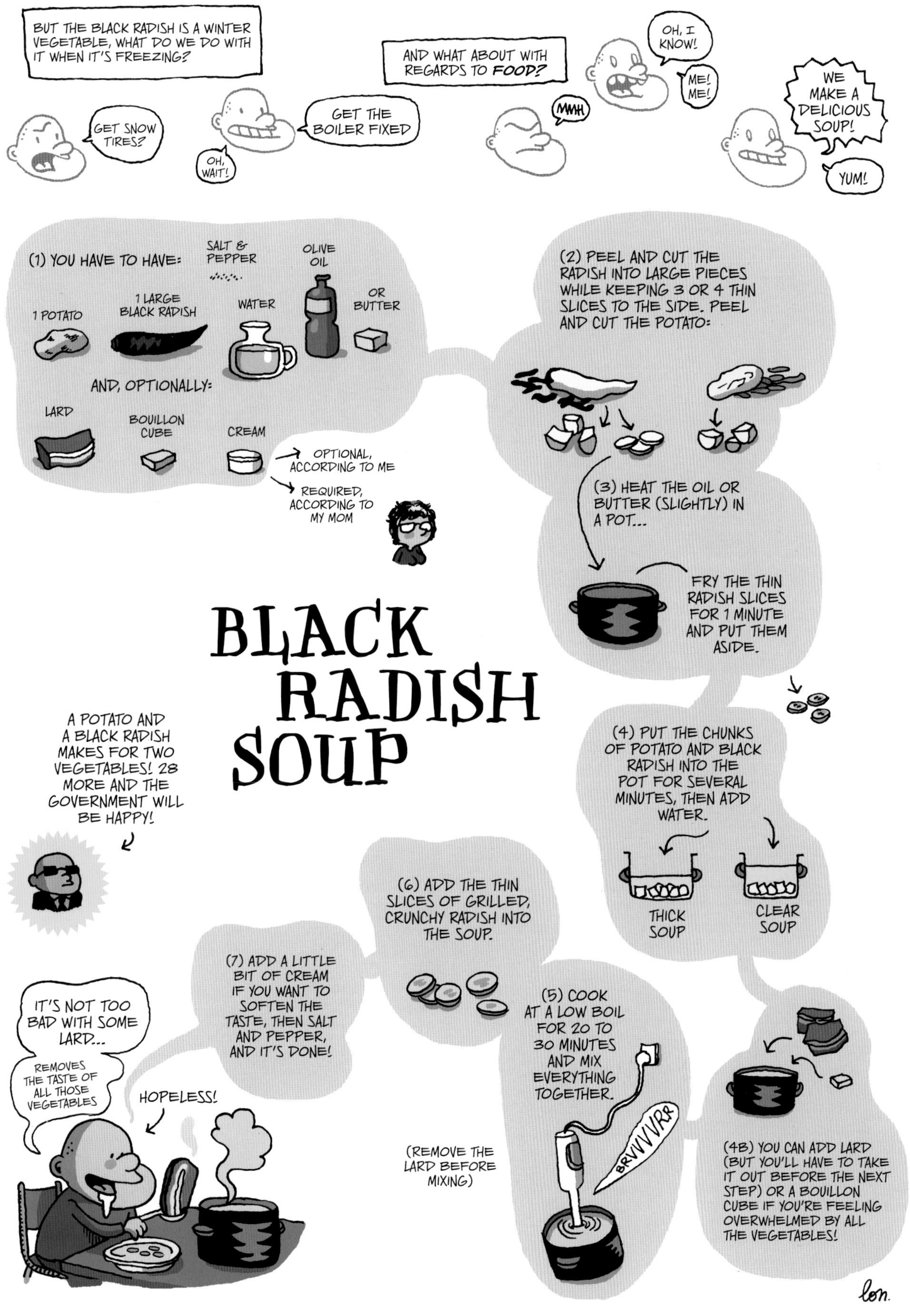
BUT THE BLACK RADISH IS A WINTER VEGETABLE, WHAT DO WE DO WITH IT WHEN IT'S FREEZING?
GET SNOW TIRES?
GET THE BOILER FIXED
OH, WAIT!
AND WHAT ABOUT WITH REGARDS TO FOOD?
MMH
OH, I KNOW!
ME! ME!
WE MAKE A DELICIOUS SOUP!
YUM!
BLACK RADISH SOUP
(1) YOU HAVE TO HAVE:
SALT & PEPPER
OLIVE OIL
1 POTATO
1 LARGE BLACK RADISH
WATER
OR BUTTER
AND, OPTIONALLY:
LARD
BOUILLON CUBE
CREAM
OPTIONAL, ACCORDING TO ME
REQUIRED, ACCORDING TO MY MOM
(2) PEEL AND CUT THE RADISH INTO LARGE PIECES WHILE KEEPING 3 OR 4 THIN SLICES TO THE SIDE. PEEL AND CUT THE POTATO:
(3) HEAT THE OIL OR BUTTER (SLIGHTLY) IN A POT...
FRY THE THIN RADISH SLICES FOR 1 MINUTE AND PUT THEM ASIDE.
(4) PUT THE CHUNKS OF POTATO AND BLACK RADISH INTO THE POT FOR SEVERAL MINUTES, THEN ADD WATER.
THICK SOUP
CLEAR SOUP
(4B) YOU CAN ADD LARD (BUT YOU'LL HAVE TO TAKE IT OUT BEFORE THE NEXT STEP) OR A BOUILLON CUBE IF YOU'RE FEELING OVERWHELMED BY ALL THE VEGETABLES!
(5) COOK AT A LOW BOIL FOR 20 TO 30 MINUTES AND MIX EVERYTHING TOGETHER.
BRVVVRR
(REMOVE THE LARD BEFORE MIXING)
(6) ADD THE THIN SLICES OF GRILLED, CRUNCHY RADISH INTO THE SOUP.
(7) ADD A LITTLE BIT OF CREAM IF YOU WANT TO SOFTEN THE TASTE, THEN SALT AND PEPPER, AND IT'S DONE!
A POTATO AND A BLACK RADISH MAKES FOR TWO VEGETABLES! 28 MORE AND THE GOVERNMENT WILL BE HAPPY!
IT'S NOT TOO BAD WITH SOME LARD...
REMOVES THE TASTE OF ALL THOSE VEGETABLES
HOPELESS!
lon.

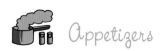

YOU'RE TIRED OF THOSE LAME APPETIZERS YOU'RE USUALLY SERVED. YOU'VE HAD ENOUGH OF MIXED NUTS, CASHEWS, AND EVEN GRILLED PEANUTS. THEY'RE NOT WHAT THEY USED TO BE. YOU'RE TIRED OF THE VERRINES, "TRENDY" AMUSE-BOUCHES, AND, IN ANY CASE, THEY TAKE TOO LONG TO MAKE FOR AN APPETIZER!

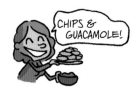

CHIPS & GUACAMOLE!

WELL, ***GOOD NEWS*** FOR YOU. HERE ARE A FEW IDEAS TO HELP YOU MAKE SOME DELICIOUS APPETIZERS QUICKLY AND WITH JUST A FEW INGREDIENTS.

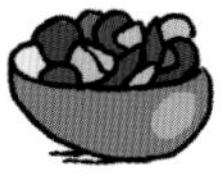

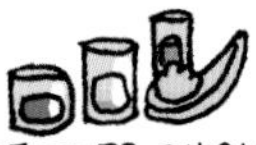

A FEW QUICK APPETIZERS THAT DON'T TAKE LONG TO MAKE

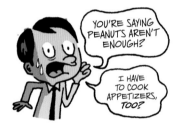

YOU'RE SAYING PEANUTS AREN'T ENOUGH?
I HAVE TO COOK APPETIZERS, *TOO?*

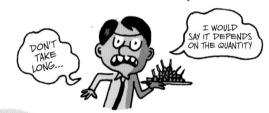

DON'T TAKE LONG...
I WOULD SAY IT DEPENDS ON THE QUANTITY

1
CUT THE ENDS OFF THE ZUCCHINI
(NO NEED TO PEEL)
CUT INTO THIN STRIPS WITH A MANDOLINE
RAW HAM
CUT INTO STRIPS
ASSEMBLE HAM AND ZUCCHINI
ONE TEASPOON OF PESTO
ROLL
TOOTHPICKS

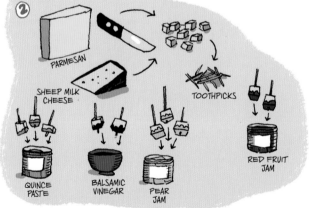

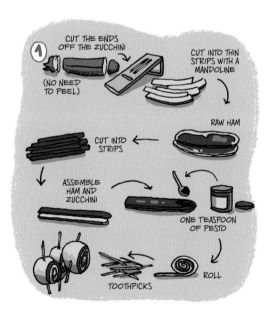

(WARNING: EAT IMMEDIATELY BECAUSE IT GIVES OFF QUITE A LOT OF WATER. OF COURSE, IF YOU'D LIKE, YOU CAN SWEAT AND SALT THE ZUCCHINI BEFOREHAND TO DISGORGE IT, AND THEN PUT IT IN THE OVEN TO DRY, BUT WHY BOTHER? IT'S SO MUCH BETTER FRESH!)

2
PARMESAN
SHEEP MILK CHEESE
TOOTHPICKS
QUINCE PASTE
BALSAMIC VINEGAR
PEAR JAM
RED FRUIT JAM

3
WHITE CHEESE
SHALLOTS
CHIVES
PARSLEY
PEPPER
GARLIC
SALT
CAULIFLOWER
CARROTS
CUCUMBER
BROCOLOUNGE

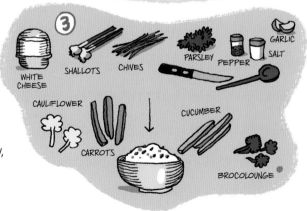

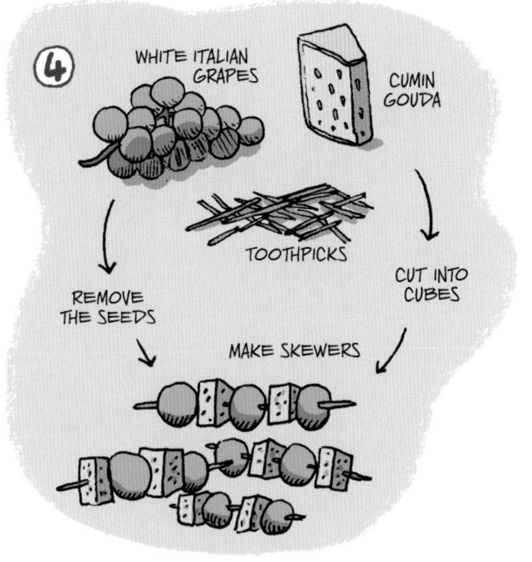
4
WHITE ITALIAN GRAPES
CUMIN GOUDA
TOOTHPICKS
REMOVE THE SEEDS
CUT INTO CUBES
MAKE SKEWERS

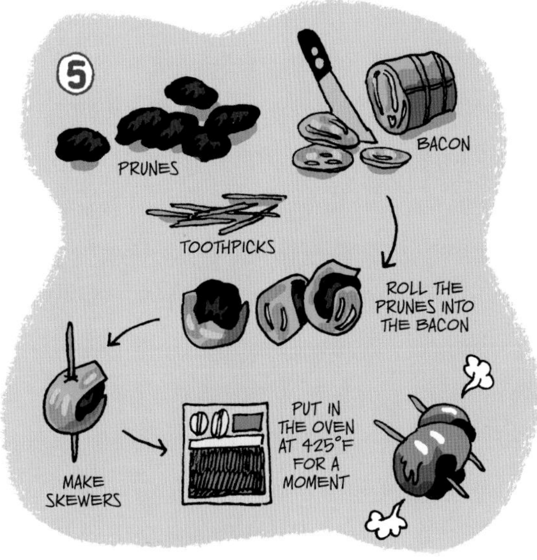
5
PRUNES
BACON
TOOTHPICKS
ROLL THE PRUNES INTO THE BACON
MAKE SKEWERS
PUT IN THE OVEN AT 425°F FOR A MOMENT

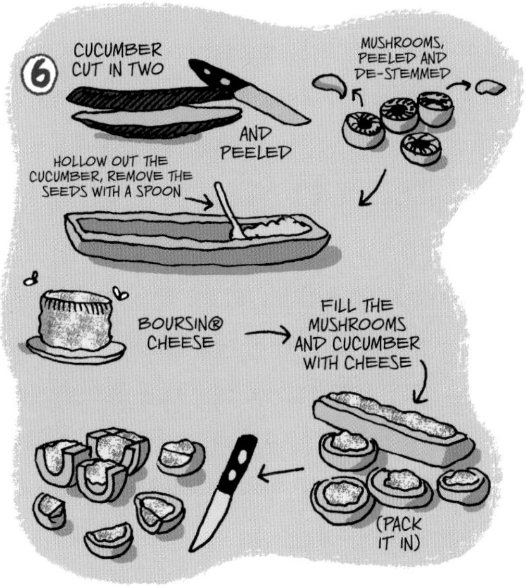
6
CUCUMBER CUT IN TWO
AND PEELED
MUSHROOMS, PEELED AND DE-STEMMED
HOLLOW OUT THE CUCUMBER, REMOVE THE SEEDS WITH A SPOON
BOURSIN® CHEESE
FILL THE MUSHROOMS AND CUCUMBER WITH CHEESE
(PACK IT IN)

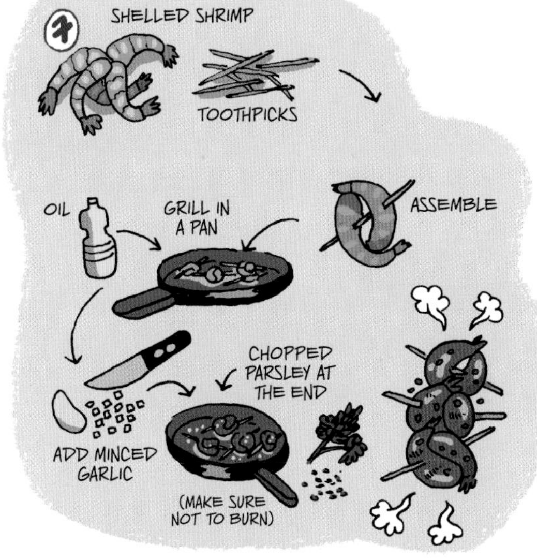
7
SHELLED SHRIMP
TOOTHPICKS
OIL
GRILL IN A PAN
ASSEMBLE
CHOPPED PARSLEY AT THE END
ADD MINCED GARLIC
(MAKE SURE NOT TO BURN)

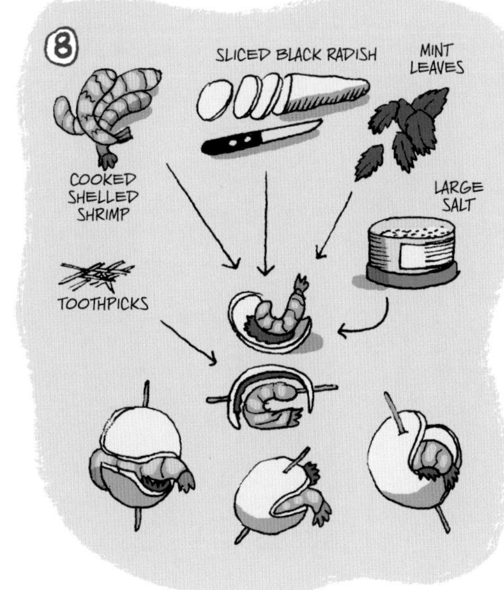
8
SLICED BLACK RADISH
MINT LEAVES
COOKED SHELLED SHRIMP
LARGE SALT
TOOTHPICKS

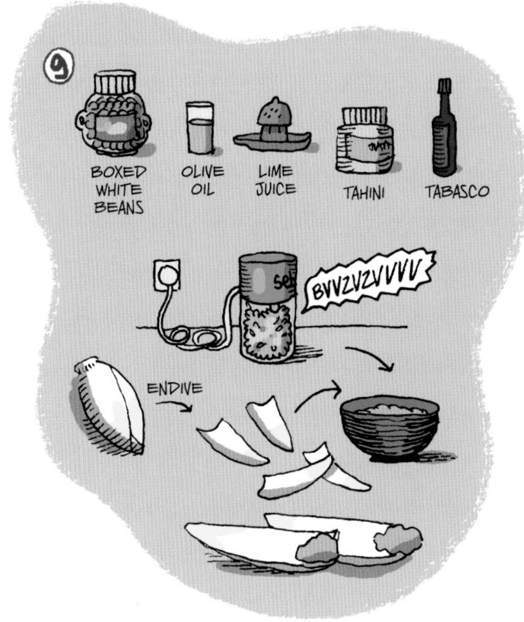
9
BOXED WHITE BEANS
OLIVE OIL
LIME JUICE
TAHINI
TABASCO
BVVZVZVVVV
ENDIVE

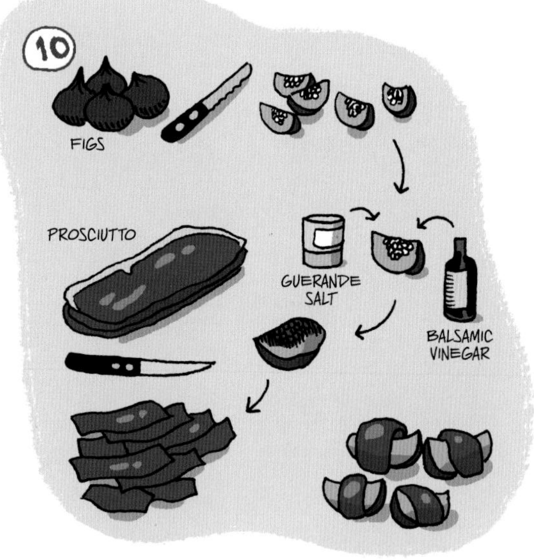
10
FIGS
PROSCIUTTO
GUERANDE SALT
BALSAMIC VINEGAR

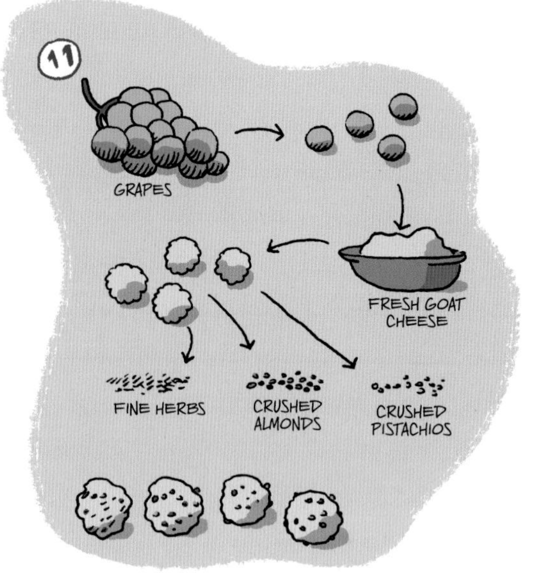
11
GRAPES
FRESH GOAT CHEESE
FINE HERBS
CRUSHED ALMONDS
CRUSHED PISTACHIOS

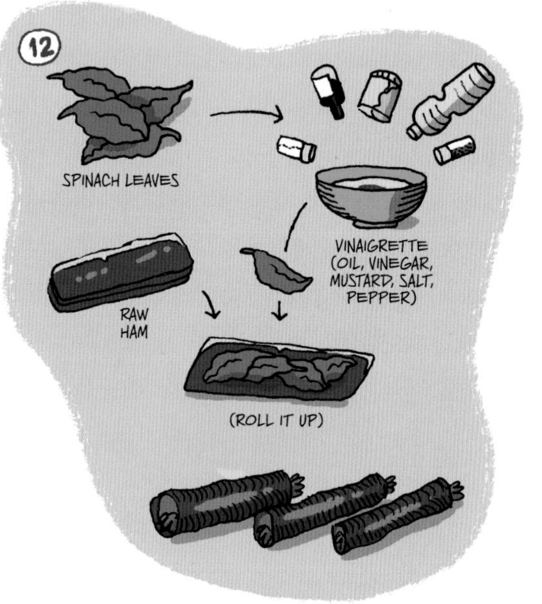
12
SPINACH LEAVES
VINAIGRETTE (OIL, VINEGAR, MUSTARD, SALT, PEPPER)
RAW HAM
(ROLL IT UP)

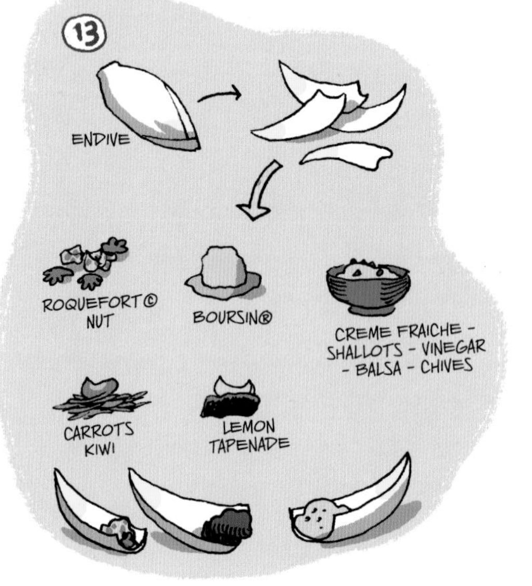
13
ENDIVE
ROQUEFORT© NUT
BOURSIN®
CREME FRAICHE - SHALLOTS - VINEGAR - BALSA - CHIVES
CARROTS KIWI
LEMON TAPENADE

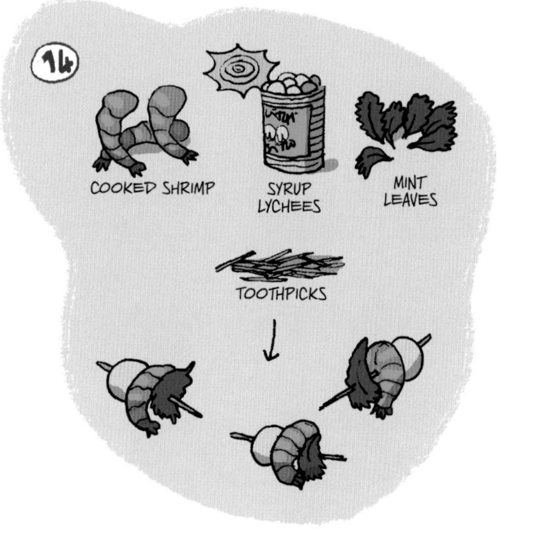
14
COOKED SHRIMP
SYRUP LYCHEES
MINT LEAVES
TOOTHPICKS

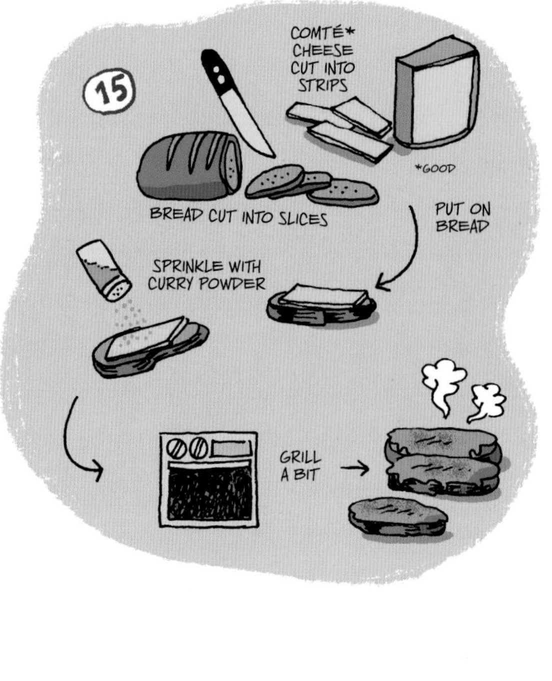
15
COMTÉ* CHEESE CUT INTO STRIPS
*GOOD
BREAD CUT INTO SLICES
PUT ON BREAD
SPRINKLE WITH CURRY POWDER
GRILL A BIT

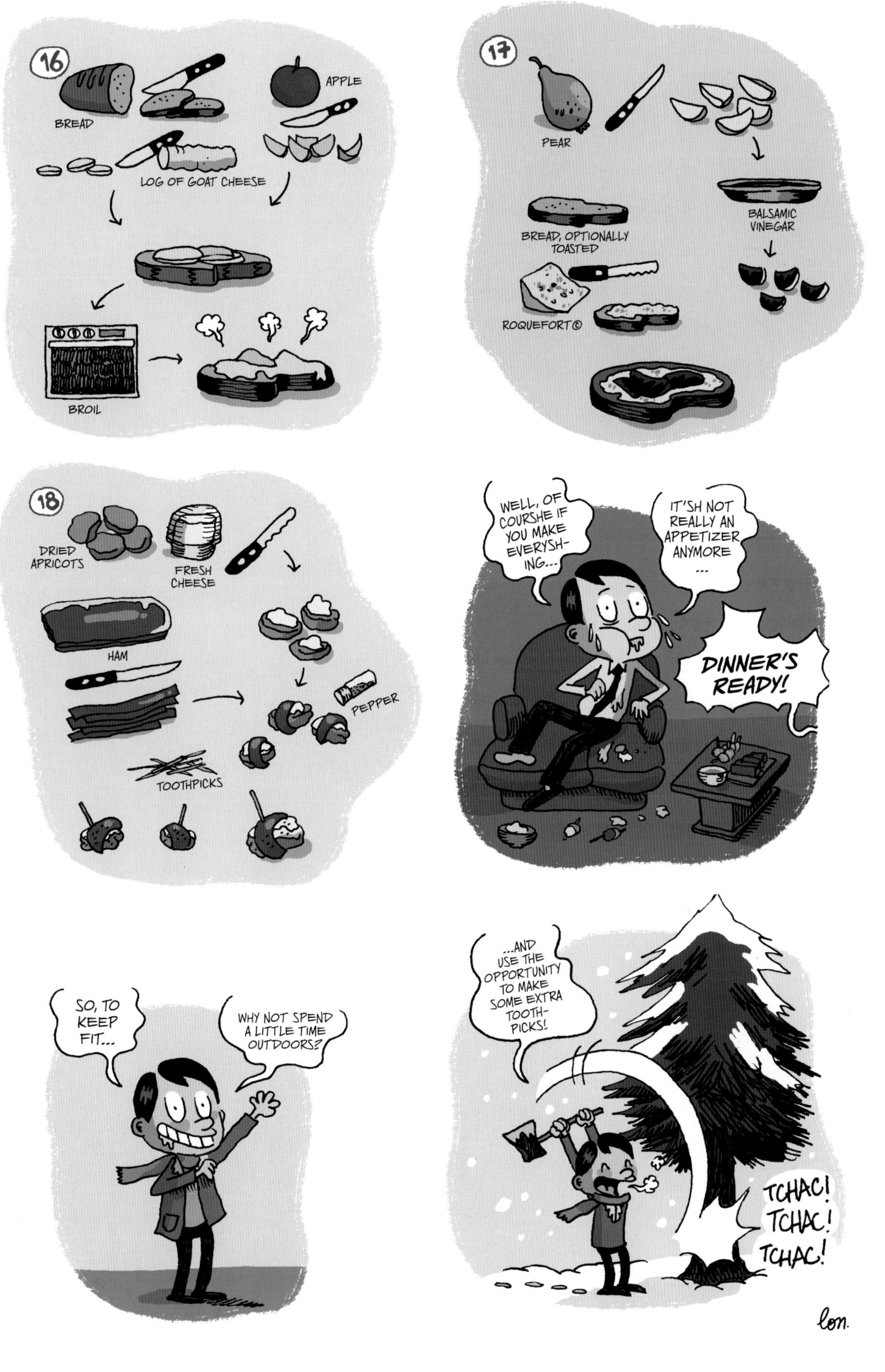
16
BREAD
APPLE
LOG OF GOAT CHEESE
BROIL
17
PEAR
BREAD, OPTIONALLY TOASTED
BALSAMIC VINEGAR
ROQUEFORT©
18
DRIED APRICOTS
FRESH CHEESE
HAM
PEPPER
TOOTHPICKS
WELL, OF COURSHE IF YOU MAKE EVERYSH-ING...
IT'SH NOT REALLY AN APPETIZER ANYMORE ...
DINNER'S READY!
SO, TO KEEP FIT...
WHY NOT SPEND A LITTLE TIME OUTDOORS?
...AND USE THE OPPORTUNITY TO MAKE SOME EXTRA TOOTH-PICKS!
TCHAC! TCHAC! TCHAC!
lon.

MID-MARCH IS FERA SEASON. SO, STUPIDLY, YOU SAY:

I'LL HAVE SOME FERA TO...

HiNHiN

TO UH... MAKE A... TARTAR!

AND HERE, EQUALLY STUPIDLY, THE FISHMONGER (YES, THE FERA IS A FISH) WILL SAY:

HERE'S YOUR FERA.

BON APPETIT

IN EFFECT, NEITHER OF YOU REALIZE HOW DIFFICULT IT IS TO FIND FERA FOR THE SIMPLE REASON THAT...

FERA NO LONGER EXISTS!

OH REALLY?

WHAT DID I BUY THEN?

EH?

TO ANSWER THIS QUESTION, LET US TAKE LOOK BACK IN TIME TO THE MONTH OF DECEMBER OF AN UNKNOWN YEAR WHEN THE FERA ENJOYS ITS DAYS IN SWITZERLAND IN LAKE GENEVA'S GLACIAL WATERS...

Merry Christmas, Jean-Jacques

500 KILOMETERS FROM HERE, IN DECEMBER OF THE YEAR 1930, JEAN FERRAT WAS BORN... NO RELATION, BUT HERE COMES THE UNNECESSARY WORDPLAY...

AND YET...

QUICKLY, HE FINDS SUCCESS BY SINGING A FEW POPULAR SONGS.

POURTAAANT♪

QUE LA MONTAGN'EST BEÊUEU

THE FERA, ON THE OTHER HAND, DOESN'T SING, OR SINGS POORLY. IT'S HARD TO TELL UNDERWATER:

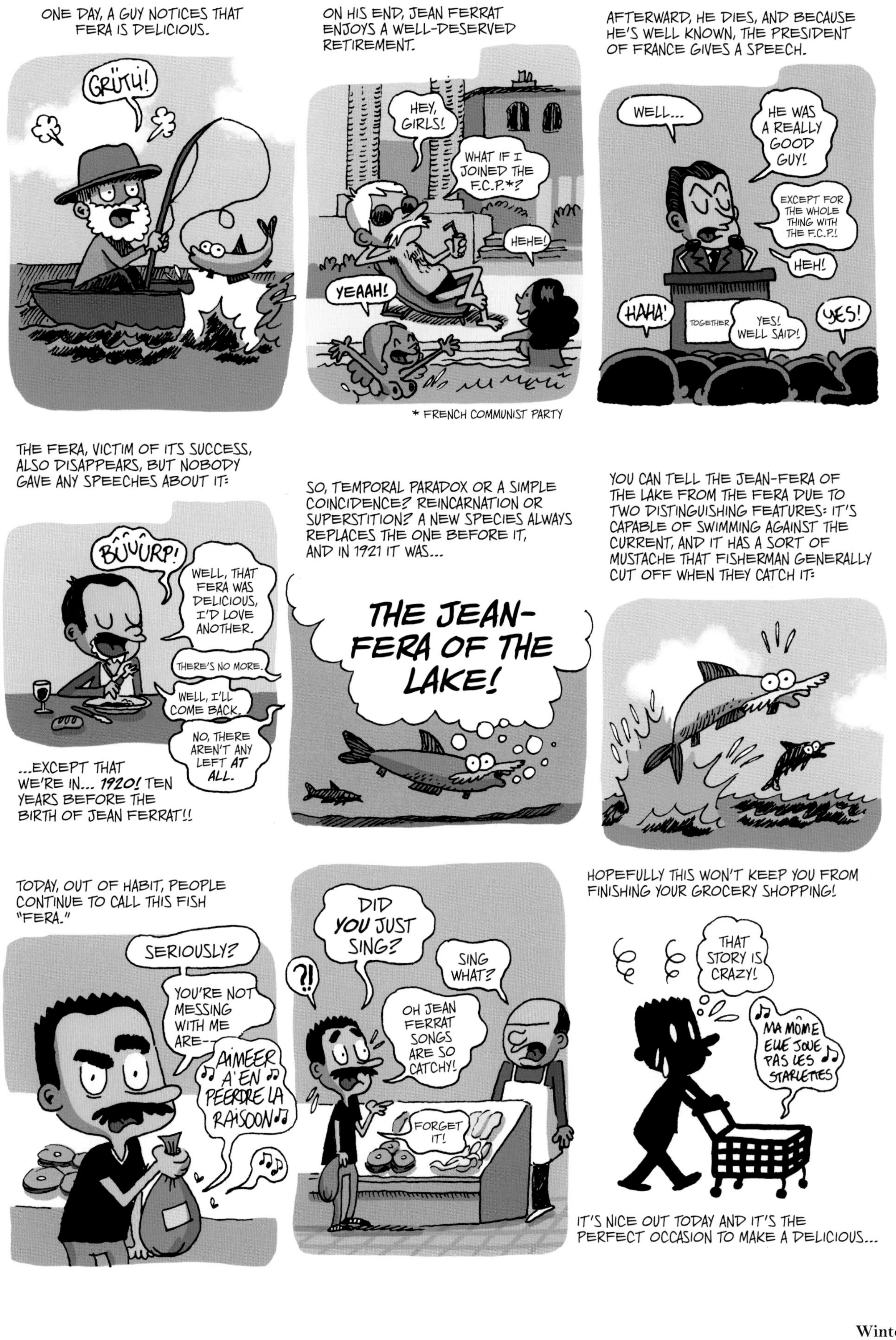
ONE DAY, A GUY NOTICES THAT FERA IS DELICIOUS.
GRÜTLI!
ON HIS END, JEAN FERRAT ENJOYS A WELL-DESERVED RETIREMENT.
HEY, GIRLS!
WHAT IF I JOINED THE F.C.P.*?
HEHE!
YEAAH!
* FRENCH COMMUNIST PARTY
AFTERWARD, HE DIES, AND BECAUSE HE'S WELL KNOWN, THE PRESIDENT OF FRANCE GIVES A SPEECH.
WELL...
HE WAS A REALLY GOOD GUY!
EXCEPT FOR THE WHOLE THING WITH THE F.C.P.!
HEH!
HAHA!
TOGETHER
YES! WELL SAID!
YES!
THE FERA, VICTIM OF ITS SUCCESS, ALSO DISAPPEARS, BUT NOBODY GAVE ANY SPEECHES ABOUT IT:
BÛÛURP!
WELL, THAT FERA WAS DELICIOUS, I'D LOVE ANOTHER.
THERE'S NO MORE.
WELL, I'LL COME BACK.
NO, THERE AREN'T ANY LEFT AT ALL.
...EXCEPT THAT WE'RE IN... 1920! TEN YEARS BEFORE THE BIRTH OF JEAN FERRAT!!
SO, TEMPORAL PARADOX OR A SIMPLE COINCIDENCE? REINCARNATION OR SUPERSTITION? A NEW SPECIES ALWAYS REPLACES THE ONE BEFORE IT, AND IN 1921 IT WAS...
THE JEAN-FERA OF THE LAKE!
YOU CAN TELL THE JEAN-FERA OF THE LAKE FROM THE FERA DUE TO TWO DISTINGUISHING FEATURES: IT'S CAPABLE OF SWIMMING AGAINST THE CURRENT, AND IT HAS A SORT OF MUSTACHE THAT FISHERMAN GENERALLY CUT OFF WHEN THEY CATCH IT:
TODAY, OUT OF HABIT, PEOPLE CONTINUE TO CALL THIS FISH "FERA."
SERIOUSLY?
YOU'RE NOT MESSING WITH ME ARE--
AIMEER A'EN PEERDRE LA RAISOON
DID YOU JUST SING?
?!
SING WHAT?
OH JEAN FERRAT SONGS ARE SO CATCHY!
FORGET IT!
HOPEFULLY THIS WON'T KEEP YOU FROM FINISHING YOUR GROCERY SHOPPING!
THAT STORY IS CRAZY!
MA MÔME ELLE JOUE PAS LES STARLETTES
IT'S NICE OUT TODAY AND IT'S THE PERFECT OCCASION TO MAKE A DELICIOUS...

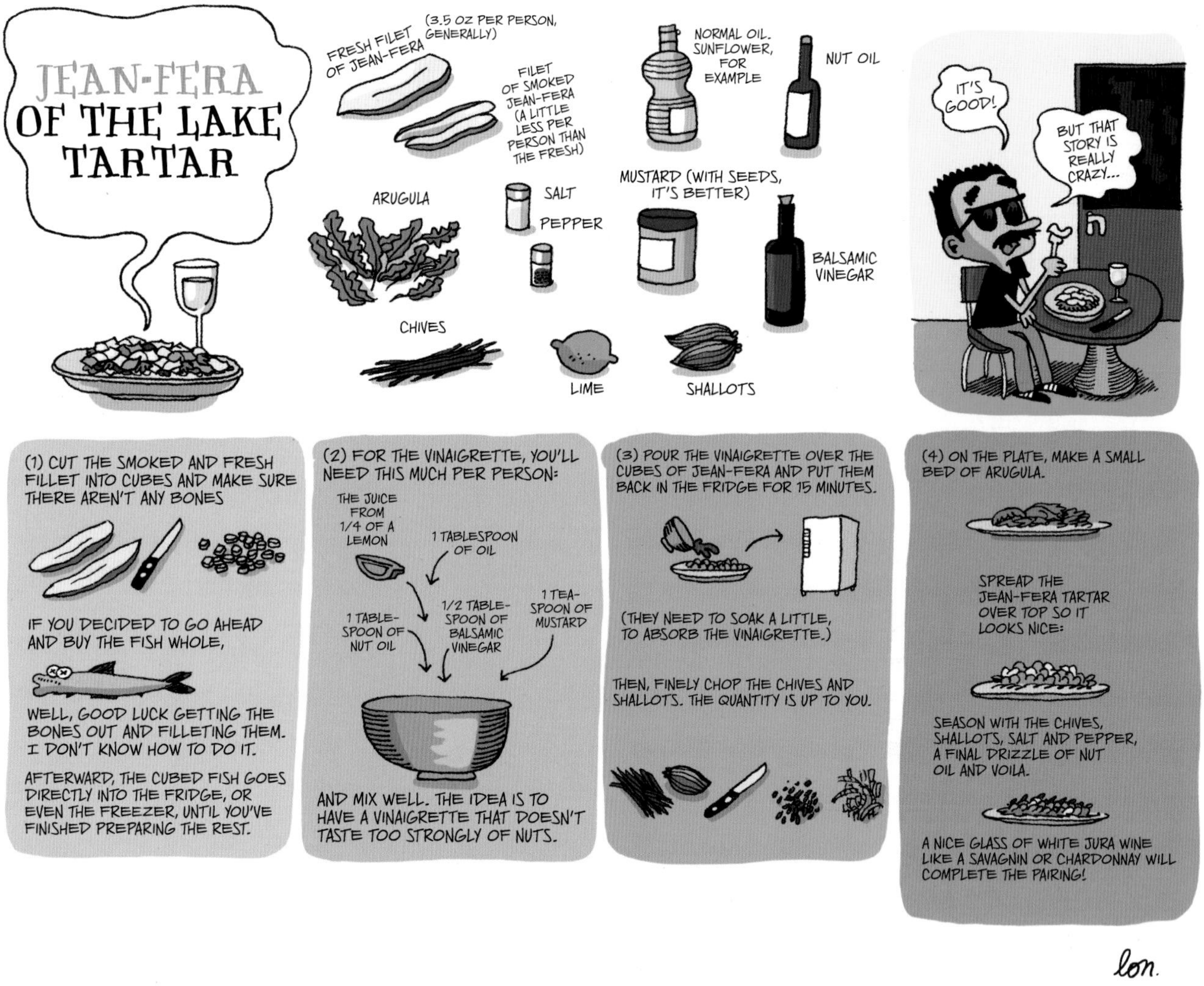
JEAN-FERA OF THE LAKE TARTAR
FRESH FILET OF JEAN-FERA
(3.5 OZ PER PERSON, GENERALLY)
FILET OF SMOKED JEAN-FERA (A LITTLE LESS PER PERSON THAN THE FRESH)
NORMAL OIL. SUNFLOWER, FOR EXAMPLE
NUT OIL
ARUGULA
SALT
PEPPER
MUSTARD (WITH SEEDS, IT'S BETTER)
BALSAMIC VINEGAR
CHIVES
LIME
SHALLOTS
IT'S GOOD!
BUT THAT STORY IS REALLY CRAZY...
(1) CUT THE SMOKED AND FRESH FILLET INTO CUBES AND MAKE SURE THERE AREN'T ANY BONES
IF YOU DECIDED TO GO AHEAD AND BUY THE FISH WHOLE,
WELL, GOOD LUCK GETTING THE BONES OUT AND FILLETING THEM. I DON'T KNOW HOW TO DO IT.
AFTERWARD, THE CUBED FISH GOES DIRECTLY INTO THE FRIDGE, OR EVEN THE FREEZER, UNTIL YOU'VE FINISHED PREPARING THE REST.
(2) FOR THE VINAIGRETTE, YOU'LL NEED THIS MUCH PER PERSON:
THE JUICE FROM 1/4 OF A LEMON
1 TABLESPOON OF OIL
1 TABLE-SPOON OF NUT OIL
1/2 TABLE-SPOON OF BALSAMIC VINEGAR
1 TEA-SPOON OF MUSTARD
AND MIX WELL. THE IDEA IS TO HAVE A VINAIGRETTE THAT DOESN'T TASTE TOO STRONGLY OF NUTS.
(3) POUR THE VINAIGRETTE OVER THE CUBES OF JEAN-FERA AND PUT THEM BACK IN THE FRIDGE FOR 15 MINUTES.
(THEY NEED TO SOAK A LITTLE, TO ABSORB THE VINAIGRETTE.)
THEN, FINELY CHOP THE CHIVES AND SHALLOTS. THE QUANTITY IS UP TO YOU.
(4) ON THE PLATE, MAKE A SMALL BED OF ARUGULA.
SPREAD THE JEAN-FERA TARTAR OVER TOP SO IT LOOKS NICE:
SEASON WITH THE CHIVES, SHALLOTS, SALT AND PEPPER, A FINAL DRIZZLE OF NUT OIL AND VOILA.
A NICE GLASS OF WHITE JURA WINE LIKE A SAVAGNIN OR CHARDONNAY WILL COMPLETE THE PAIRING!
lon.

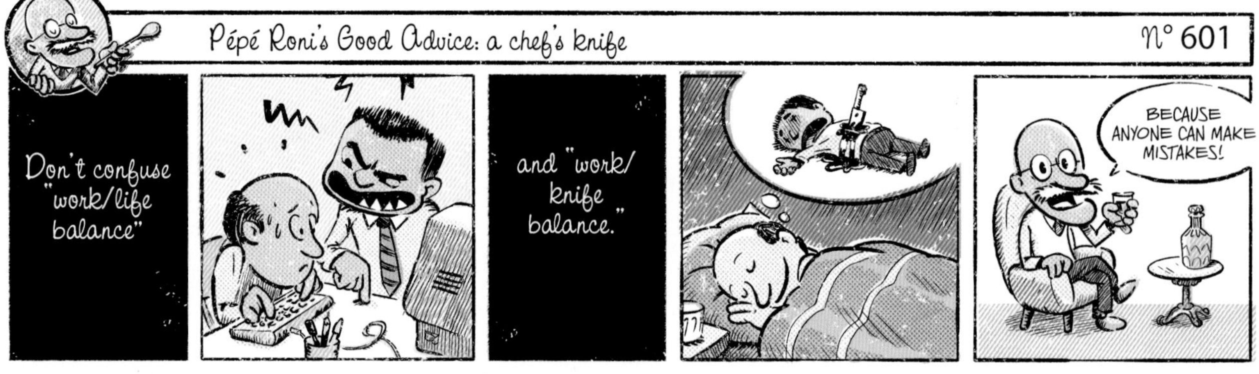
Pépé Roni's Good Advice: a chef's knife
N° 601
Don't confuse "work/life balance"
and "work/knife balance."
BECAUSE ANYONE CAN MAKE MISTAKES!

A chef's knife: knife most commonly used by chefs in the kitchen. good for cutting both meats and vegetables.

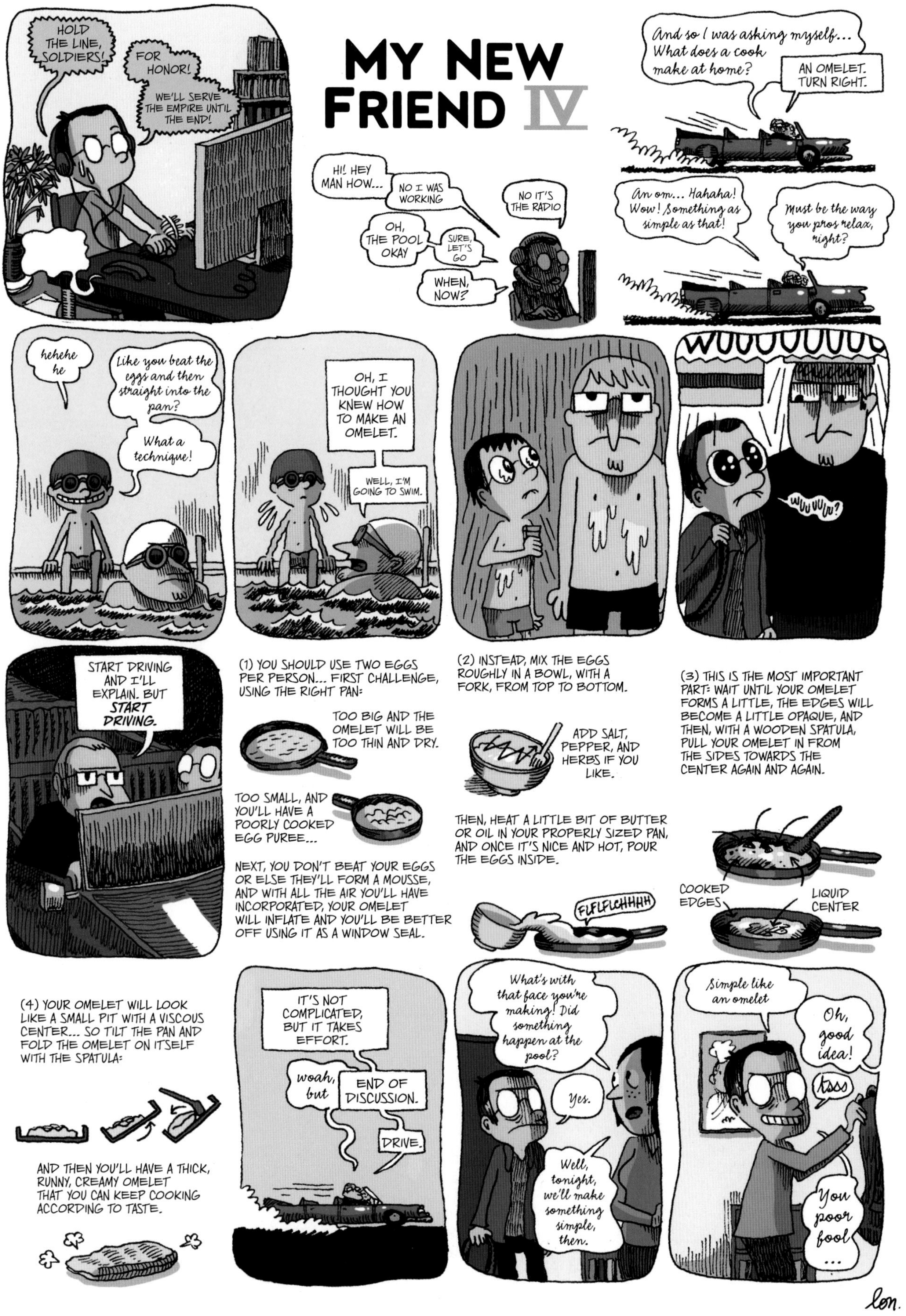
HOLD THE LINE, SOLDIERS!
FOR HONOR!
WE'LL SERVE THE EMPIRE UNTIL THE END!
MY NEW FRIEND IV
HI! HEY MAN HOW...
NO I WAS WORKING
NO IT'S THE RADIO
OH, THE POOL OKAY
SURE, LET'S GO
WHEN, NOW?
And so I was asking myself... What does a cook make at home?
AN OMELET. TURN RIGHT.
An om... Hahaha! Wow! Something as simple as that!
Must be the way you pros relax, right?
hehehe he
Like you beat the eggs and then straight into the pan?
What a technique!
OH, I THOUGHT YOU KNEW HOW TO MAKE AN OMELET.
WELL, I'M GOING TO SWIM.
WUUUUUUU
WUUUUU?
START DRIVING AND I'LL EXPLAIN. BUT START DRIVING.
(1) YOU SHOULD USE TWO EGGS PER PERSON... FIRST CHALLENGE, USING THE RIGHT PAN:
TOO BIG AND THE OMELET WILL BE TOO THIN AND DRY.
TOO SMALL, AND YOU'LL HAVE A POORLY COOKED EGG PUREE...
NEXT, YOU DON'T BEAT YOUR EGGS OR ELSE THEY'LL FORM A MOUSSE, AND WITH ALL THE AIR YOU'LL HAVE INCORPORATED, YOUR OMELET WILL INFLATE AND YOU'LL BE BETTER OFF USING IT AS A WINDOW SEAL.
(2) INSTEAD, MIX THE EGGS ROUGHLY IN A BOWL, WITH A FORK, FROM TOP TO BOTTOM.
ADD SALT, PEPPER, AND HERBS IF YOU LIKE.
THEN, HEAT A LITTLE BIT OF BUTTER OR OIL IN YOUR PROPERLY SIZED PAN, AND ONCE IT'S NICE AND HOT, POUR THE EGGS INSIDE.
FLFLFLCHHHH
(3) THIS IS THE MOST IMPORTANT PART: WAIT UNTIL YOUR OMELET FORMS A LITTLE, THE EDGES WILL BECOME A LITTLE OPAQUE, AND THEN, WITH A WOODEN SPATULA, PULL YOUR OMELET IN FROM THE SIDES TOWARDS THE CENTER AGAIN AND AGAIN.
COOKED EDGES
LIQUID CENTER
(4) YOUR OMELET WILL LOOK LIKE A SMALL PIT WITH A VISCOUS CENTER... SO TILT THE PAN AND FOLD THE OMELET ON ITSELF WITH THE SPATULA:
AND THEN YOU'LL HAVE A THICK, RUNNY, CREAMY OMELET THAT YOU CAN KEEP COOKING ACCORDING TO TASTE.
IT'S NOT COMPLICATED, BUT IT TAKES EFFORT.
woah, but
END OF DISCUSSION.
DRIVE.
What's with that face you're making! Did something happen at the pool?
Yes.
Well, tonight, we'll make something simple, then.
Simple like an omelet
Oh, good idea!
tsss
You poor fool ...
lon.

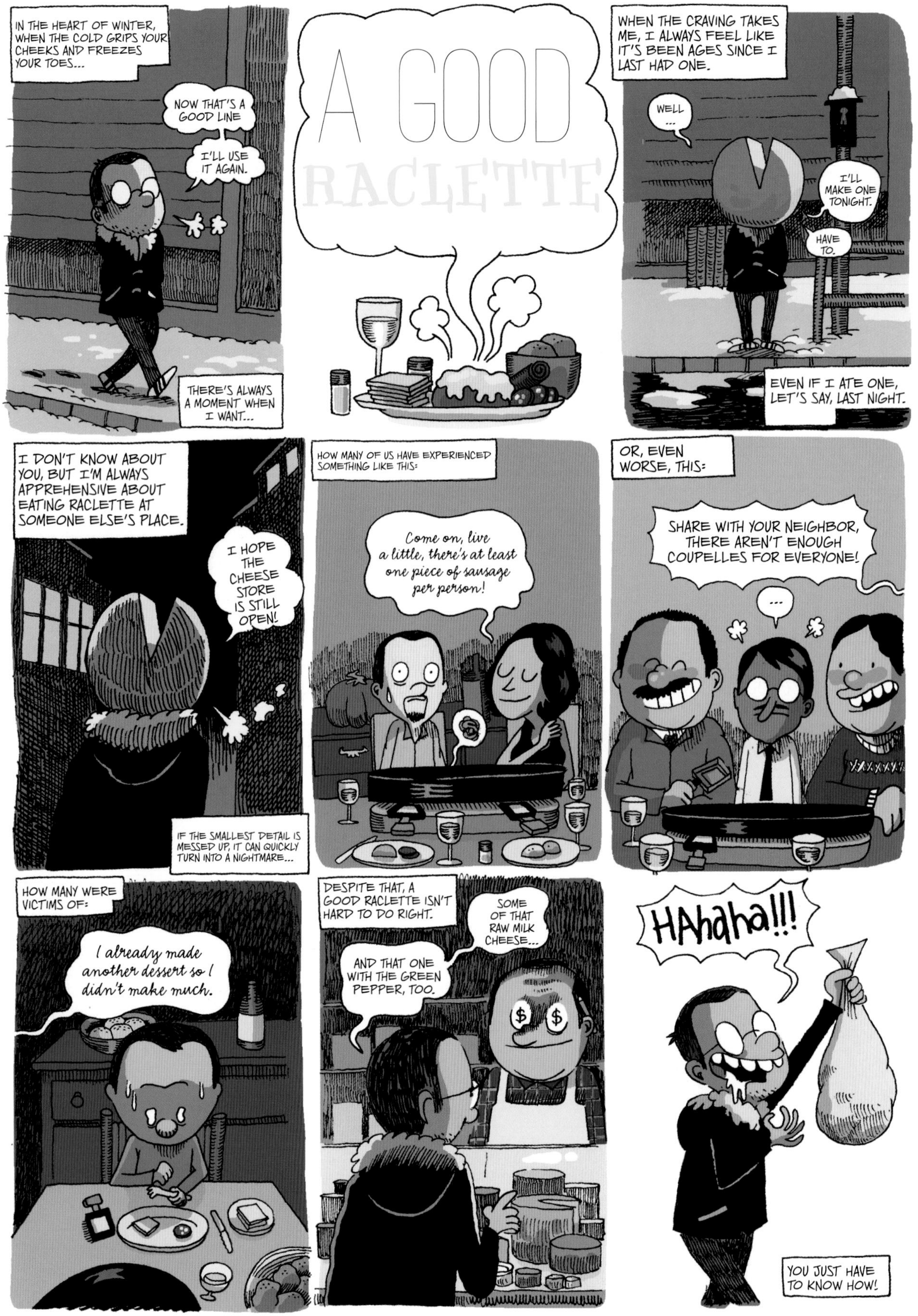
IN THE HEART OF WINTER, WHEN THE COLD GRIPS YOUR CHEEKS AND FREEZES YOUR TOES...
NOW THAT'S A GOOD LINE
I'LL USE IT AGAIN.
THERE'S ALWAYS A MOMENT WHEN I WANT...
A GOOD
RACLETTE
WHEN THE CRAVING TAKES ME, I ALWAYS FEEL LIKE IT'S BEEN AGES SINCE I LAST HAD ONE.
WELL ...
I'LL MAKE ONE TONIGHT.
HAVE TO.
EVEN IF I ATE ONE, LET'S SAY, LAST NIGHT.
I DON'T KNOW ABOUT YOU, BUT I'M ALWAYS APPREHENSIVE ABOUT EATING RACLETTE AT SOMEONE ELSE'S PLACE.
I HOPE THE CHEESE STORE IS STILL OPEN!
IF THE SMALLEST DETAIL IS MESSED UP, IT CAN QUICKLY TURN INTO A NIGHTMARE...
HOW MANY OF US HAVE EXPERIENCED SOMETHING LIKE THIS:
Come on, live a little, there's at least one piece of sausage per person!
OR, EVEN WORSE, THIS:
SHARE WITH YOUR NEIGHBOR, THERE AREN'T ENOUGH COUPELLES FOR EVERYONE!
...
HOW MANY WERE VICTIMS OF:
I already made another dessert so I didn't make much.
DESPITE THAT, A GOOD RACLETTE ISN'T HARD TO DO RIGHT.
SOME OF THAT RAW MILK CHEESE...
AND THAT ONE WITH THE GREEN PEPPER, TOO.
HAhaha!!!
YOU JUST HAVE TO KNOW HOW!

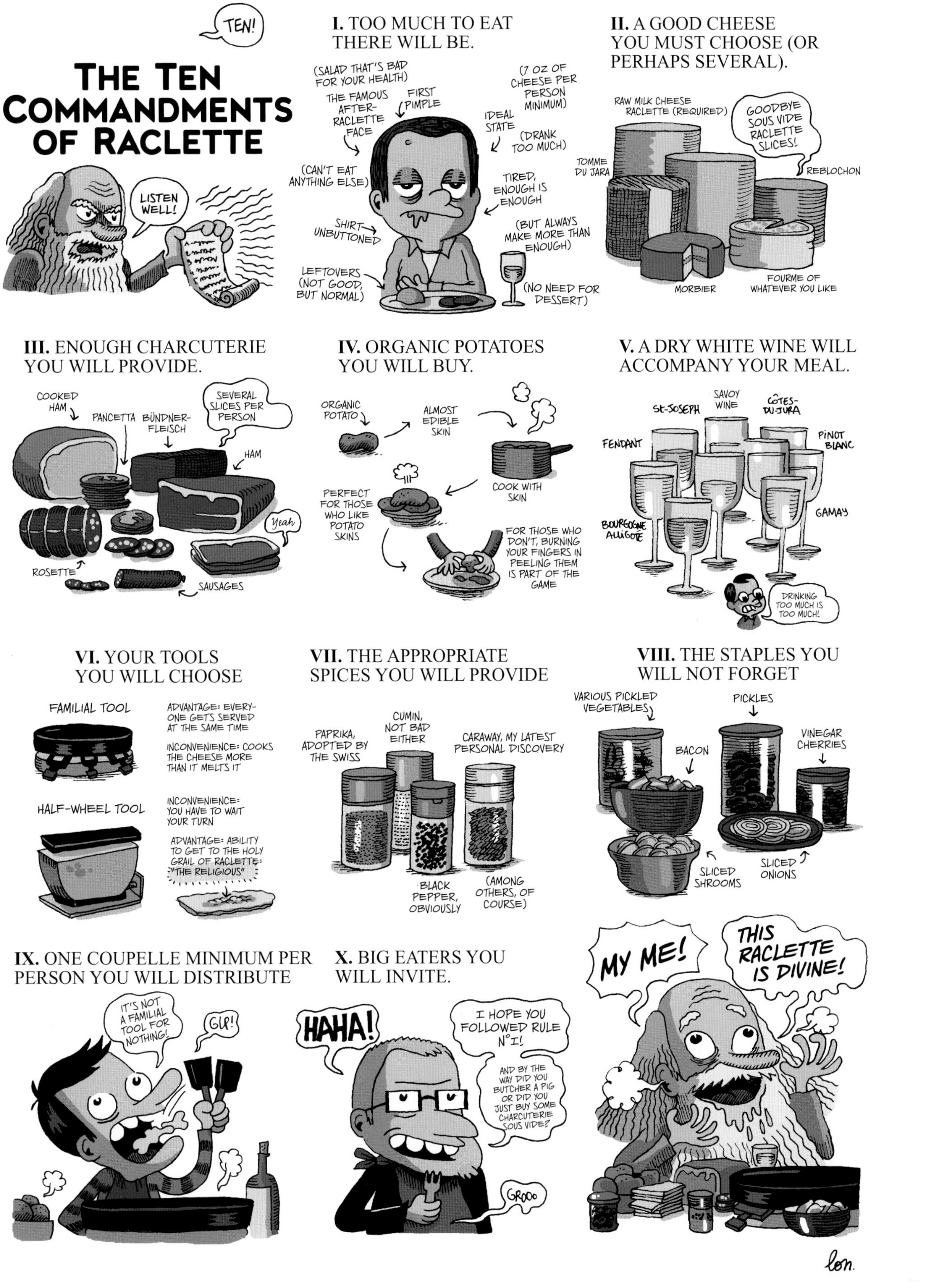
TEN!
THE TEN COMMANDMENTS OF RACLETTE
LISTEN WELL!
I. TOO MUCH TO EAT THERE WILL BE.
(SALAD THAT'S BAD FOR YOUR HEALTH)
THE FAMOUS AFTER-RACLETTE FACE
FIRST PIMPLE
(7 OZ OF CHEESE PER PERSON MINIMUM)
IDEAL STATE
(DRANK TOO MUCH)
(CAN'T EAT ANYTHING ELSE)
TIRED, ENOUGH IS ENOUGH
SHIRT UNBUTTONED
(BUT ALWAYS MAKE MORE THAN ENOUGH)
LEFTOVERS (NOT GOOD, BUT NORMAL)
(NO NEED FOR DESSERT)
II. A GOOD CHEESE YOU MUST CHOOSE (OR PERHAPS SEVERAL).
RAW MILK CHEESE RACLETTE (REQUIRED)
GOODBYE SOUS VIDE RACLETTE SLICES!
TOMME DU JARA
REBLOCHON
MORBIER
FOURME OF WHATEVER YOU LIKE
III. ENOUGH CHARCUTERIE YOU WILL PROVIDE.
COOKED HAM
PANCETTA
BÜNDNER-FLEISCH
SEVERAL SLICES PER PERSON
HAM
Yeah
ROSETTE
SAUSAGES
IV. ORGANIC POTATOES YOU WILL BUY.
ORGANIC POTATO
ALMOST EDIBLE SKIN
COOK WITH SKIN
PERFECT FOR THOSE WHO LIKE POTATO SKINS
FOR THOSE WHO DON'T, BURNING YOUR FINGERS IN PEELING THEM IS PART OF THE GAME
V. A DRY WHITE WINE WILL ACCOMPANY YOUR MEAL.
St-JOSEPH
SAVOY WINE
CÔTES-DU-JURA
FENDANT
PINOT BLANC
GAMAY
BOURGOGNE ALIGOTÉ
DRINKING TOO MUCH IS TOO MUCH!
VI. YOUR TOOLS YOU WILL CHOOSE
FAMILIAL TOOL
ADVANTAGE: EVERYONE GETS SERVED AT THE SAME TIME
INCONVENIENCE: COOKS THE CHEESE MORE THAN IT MELTS IT
HALF-WHEEL TOOL
INCONVENIENCE: YOU HAVE TO WAIT YOUR TURN
ADVANTAGE: ABILITY TO GET TO THE HOLY GRAIL OF RACLETTE: "THE RELIGIOUS"
VII. THE APPROPRIATE SPICES YOU WILL PROVIDE
PAPRIKA, ADOPTED BY THE SWISS
CUMIN, NOT BAD EITHER
CARAWAY, MY LATEST PERSONAL DISCOVERY
BLACK PEPPER, OBVIOUSLY
(AMONG OTHERS, OF COURSE)
VIII. THE STAPLES YOU WILL NOT FORGET
VARIOUS PICKLED VEGETABLES
PICKLES
BACON
VINEGAR CHERRIES
SLICED SHROOMS
SLICED ONIONS
IX. ONE COUPELLE MINIMUM PER PERSON YOU WILL DISTRIBUTE
IT'S NOT A FAMILIAL TOOL FOR NOTHING!
GLP!
X. BIG EATERS YOU WILL INVITE.
HAHA!
I HOPE YOU FOLLOWED RULE N°I!
AND BY THE WAY DID YOU BUTCHER A PIG OR DID YOU JUST BUY SOME CHARCUTERIE SOUS VIDE?
GROOO
MY ME!
THIS RACLETTE IS DIVINE!
lon.

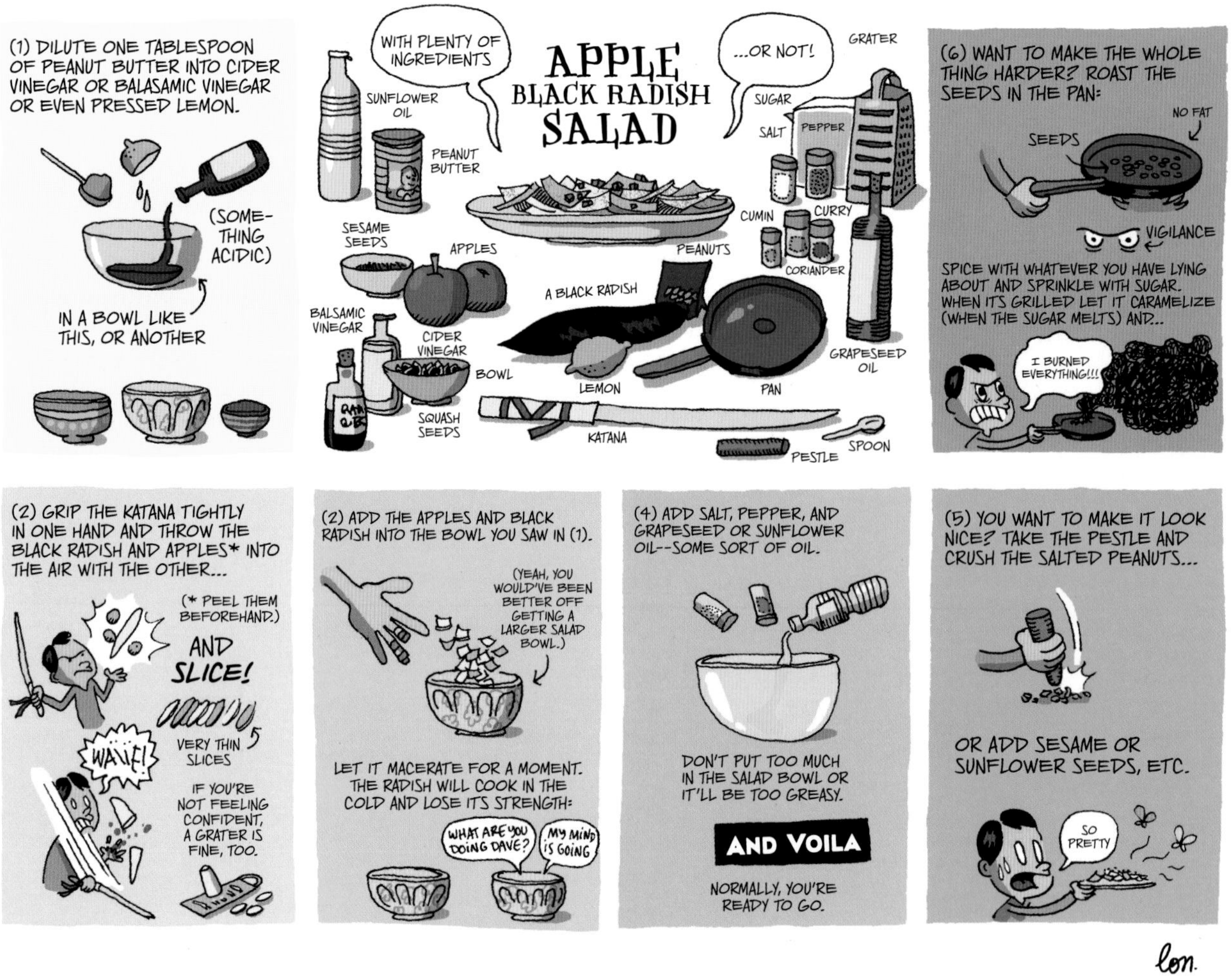
(1) DILUTE ONE TABLESPOON OF PEANUT BUTTER INTO CIDER VINEGAR OR BALASAMIC VINEGAR OR EVEN PRESSED LEMON.
(SOME-THING ACIDIC)
IN A BOWL LIKE THIS, OR ANOTHER
WITH PLENTY OF INGREDIENTS
APPLE BLACK RADISH SALAD
...OR NOT!
SUNFLOWER OIL
PEANUT BUTTER
SESAME SEEDS
APPLES
BALSAMIC VINEGAR
CIDER VINEGAR
BOWL
SQUASH SEEDS
A BLACK RADISH
LEMON
KATANA
PEANUTS
PAN
PESTLE
SPOON
GRATER
SUGAR
SALT
PEPPER
CUMIN
CURRY
CORIANDER
GRAPESEED OIL
(6) WANT TO MAKE THE WHOLE THING HARDER? ROAST THE SEEDS IN THE PAN:
SEEDS
NO FAT
VIGILANCE
SPICE WITH WHATEVER YOU HAVE LYING ABOUT AND SPRINKLE WITH SUGAR. WHEN ITS GRILLED LET IT CARAMELIZE (WHEN THE SUGAR MELTS) AND...
I BURNED EVERYTHING!!!
(2) GRIP THE KATANA TIGHTLY IN ONE HAND AND THROW THE BLACK RADISH AND APPLES* INTO THE AIR WITH THE OTHER...
(* PEEL THEM BEFOREHAND.)
AND SLICE!
WAH!
VERY THIN SLICES
IF YOU'RE NOT FEELING CONFIDENT, A GRATER IS FINE, TOO.
(2) ADD THE APPLES AND BLACK RADISH INTO THE BOWL YOU SAW IN (1).
(YEAH, YOU WOULD'VE BEEN BETTER OFF GETTING A LARGER SALAD BOWL.)
LET IT MACERATE FOR A MOMENT. THE RADISH WILL COOK IN THE COLD AND LOSE ITS STRENGTH:
WHAT ARE YOU DOING DAVE?
MY MIND IS GOING
(4) ADD SALT, PEPPER, AND GRAPESEED OR SUNFLOWER OIL--SOME SORT OF OIL.
DON'T PUT TOO MUCH IN THE SALAD BOWL OR IT'LL BE TOO GREASY.
AND VOILA
NORMALLY, YOU'RE READY TO GO.
(5) YOU WANT TO MAKE IT LOOK NICE? TAKE THE PESTLE AND CRUSH THE SALTED PEANUTS...
OR ADD SESAME OR SUNFLOWER SEEDS, ETC.
SO PRETTY
Lon.

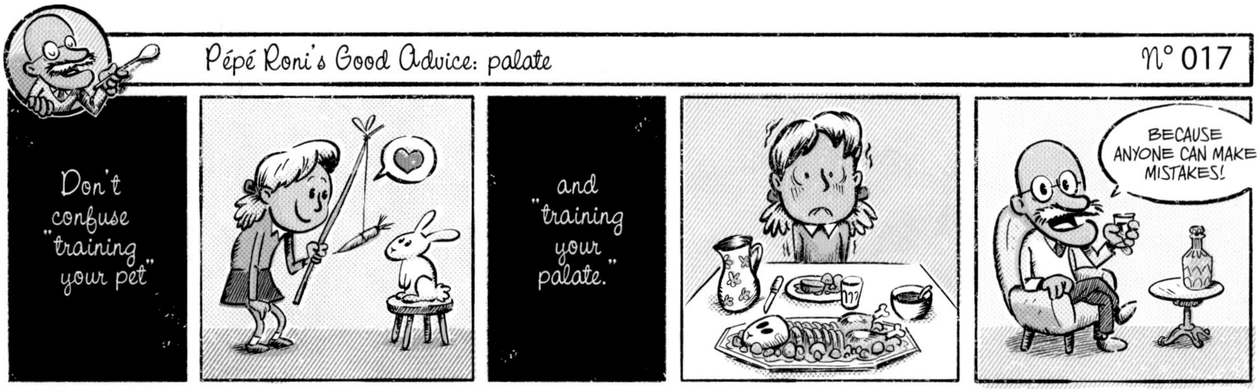
Pépé Roni's Good Advice: palate
N° 017
Don't confuse "training your pet"
and "training your palate."
BECAUSE ANYONE CAN MAKE MISTAKES!

Palate: your appreciation of taste and flavor

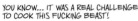
PARIS CITY, 2023

IN FRONT OF THE RESTAURANT **STAR PALACE**, THERE IS AN EVERGROWING CROWD AFTER TODAY'S INCREDIBLE DISCOVERY!

STAY CALM.

WARNING: REAL BULLETS.

STAY CALM.

IN EFFECT, THE CAPTURE OF A 650 POUND SPECIMEN FROM A BYGONE ERA, WHICH HAS SENT THE FOODIES OF THE WORLD INTO A PANIC... THE **STAR PALACE** MAY MAKE A PROFIT OF SEVERAL MILLION ROUPIDOLLARS... THE CROWD COULD BREAK OUT INTO A RIOT AT ANY MOMENT!

YOU KNOW... IT WAS A REAL CHALLENGE TO COOK THIS FUCKING BEAST!

I PLAYED IT VERY SIMPLE TO RESPECT THE CRAZY TASTE!

ANTONIN P., HEAD CHEF OF **STAR PALACE**

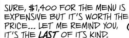

SURE, $1,400 FOR THE MENU IS EXPENSIVE BUT IT'S WORTH THE PRICE... LET ME REMIND YOU, IT'S THE **LAST** OF ITS KIND.

E. BESSON REPLICANT II, MINISTER OF THE ALLIANCE

LISTEN... AFTER MY 45TH BIRTHDAY THERE'S NOT MUCH TO LOOK FORWARD TO BEFORE DEATH, SO I WANTED TO TASTE IT ONE MORE TIME!

IT'S INCREDIBLE THERE'S STILL ANOTHER ONE!

INCREDIBLE, YES! HOW DID WE GET TO THIS POINT WITHOUT EVEN SEEING IT COMING? MANKIND IS CRAZY!

FRANCE, MARCH 2010
WHAT?!
NO WAY!

WUUUiii!!!

SO, IS IT TRUE, CAN I?
YOU CAN. I GOT THEM THIS MORNING.
WOO...
WOO...
FRESH
HOW MUCH?
2 LBS!

WAH! THIS IS THE BEST DAY OF MY LIFE!
POISS

RED... RED TUNA FROM THE MEDITERRANEAN?
ARE YOU MESSING WITH ME, OR WHAT?

IT'S FINE: WE **CAN!** BAH, DON'T YOU READ THE PAPERS? JAPAN AND QATAR ALREADY SAID THAT TUNA ISN'T ENDANGERED **AT ALL!**
NOT AT ALL?
AT ALL!
WE WERE WRONG!

PARIS CITY, 2023
CAN YOU BELIEVE THAT AT ONE TIME WE COULD HAVE AVOIDED ALL THIS... YOU KNOW, BACK WHEN THE INTERNET WAS STILL A THING, ALL IT TOOK WAS A COUPLE IDIOTS SAYING THAT TUNA WASN'T ENDANGERED, AND POOF! IT DISAPPEARED!
I DON'T KNOW WHERE THAT CAME FROM, BECAUSE TUNA HAS ALWAYS BEEN ENDANGERED.
OF COURSE, THE FAKE TUNA'S FINE, BUT THE TEXTURE JUST ISN'T THE SAME.

leon.

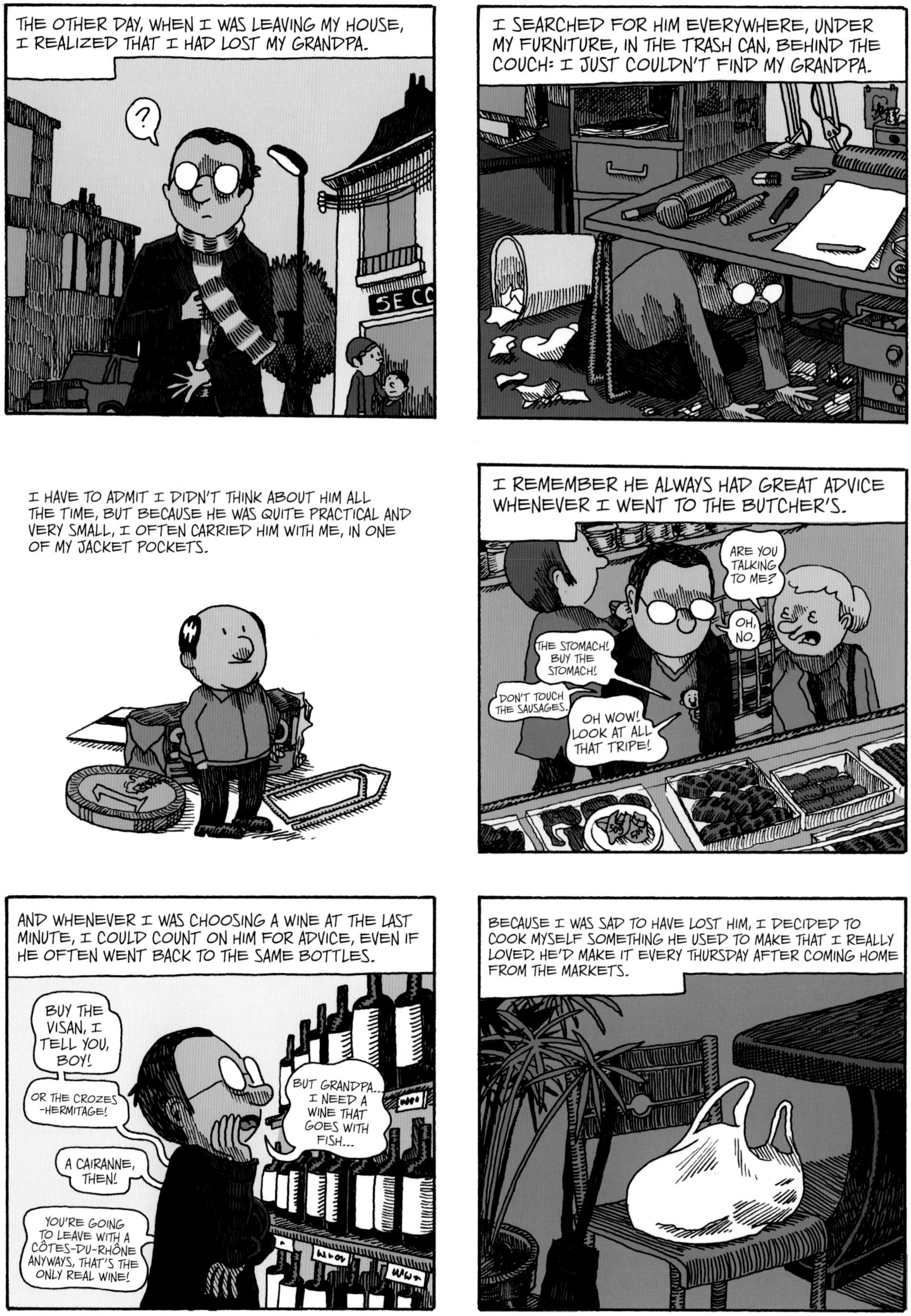
THE OTHER DAY, WHEN I WAS LEAVING MY HOUSE, I REALIZED THAT I HAD LOST MY GRANDPA.
?
I SEARCHED FOR HIM EVERYWHERE, UNDER MY FURNITURE, IN THE TRASH CAN, BEHIND THE COUCH: I JUST COULDN'T FIND MY GRANDPA.
I HAVE TO ADMIT I DIDN'T THINK ABOUT HIM ALL THE TIME, BUT BECAUSE HE WAS QUITE PRACTICAL AND VERY SMALL, I OFTEN CARRIED HIM WITH ME, IN ONE OF MY JACKET POCKETS.
I REMEMBER HE ALWAYS HAD GREAT ADVICE WHENEVER I WENT TO THE BUTCHER'S.
ARE YOU TALKING TO ME?
OH, NO.
THE STOMACH! BUY THE STOMACH!
DON'T TOUCH THE SAUSAGES.
OH WOW! LOOK AT ALL THAT TRIPE!
AND WHENEVER I WAS CHOOSING A WINE AT THE LAST MINUTE, I COULD COUNT ON HIM FOR ADVICE, EVEN IF HE OFTEN WENT BACK TO THE SAME BOTTLES.
BUY THE VISAN, I TELL YOU, BOY!
OR THE CROZES -HERMITAGE!
BUT GRANDPA... I NEED A WINE THAT GOES WITH FISH...
A CAIRANNE, THEN!
YOU'RE GOING TO LEAVE WITH A CÔTES-DU-RHÔNE ANYWAYS, THAT'S THE ONLY REAL WINE!
BECAUSE I WAS SAD TO HAVE LOST HIM, I DECIDED TO COOK MYSELF SOMETHING HE USED TO MAKE THAT I REALLY LOVED. HE'D MAKE IT EVERY THURSDAY AFTER COMING HOME FROM THE MARKETS.

IT'S KIND OF A GREASY DISH AND IT'S NOT THAT COMPLICATED, BUT IT WAS MY GRANDFATHER'S.

NOW, TIME FOR THIS RACK OF LAMB... WITH GARLIC AND PARSLEY!

IT'S A GOOD THING YOU NEVER JUST HEATED UP CANNED FOOD FOR ME, ISN'T IT GRANDPA?

(1) TO MAKE THIS DISH, YOU'LL NEED...

OLIVE OIL

PEPPER

HERBES DE PROVENCE

SALT

PARSLEY

GARLIC

RACK OF LAMB, IN PIECES, PREPARED BY THE BUTCHER.

(2) HEAT THE OIL (MY GRANDPA ALWAYS PUT AT LEAST A LITER) IN A PAN, BROWN THE LAMB, AND SPRINKLE WITH HERBES DE PROVENCE:

WHILE IT COOKS, PEEL AND SLICE TWO OR THREE CLOVES OF GARLIC (REMOVE THE STEM).

(3) CUT THE PARSLEY LEAVES AND CHOP THEM COARSELY:

WHEN THE LAMB IS ALMOST COOKED AND WELL GRILLED, THROW THE GARLIC INTO THE PAN, BROWN IT BEFORE SERVING IT, TOP WITH PARSLEY, SALT AND PEPPER: AND IT'S READY.

AND WHILE I WAS EATING THE LAMB, LIKE I USED TO, A TON OF MEMORIES CAME BACK TO ME AND I ALMOST CHOKED!

?

Hey! I can't believe this!

IT WAS MY GRANDPA! THERE HE WAS, PERCHED ON MY FORK: I WAS RELIEVED TO FIND HIM. MY LIFE COULD CONTINUE.

HAHAHA!

SO, KIDDO, YOU'RE COOKING RACK OF LAMB?

SURPRISE!

DID YOU USE ENOUGH OIL?

I HOPE YOU'RE HAVING A GOOD CHATE-ANEUF-DU-PAPE WITH IT!

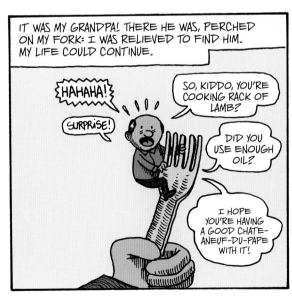

len.

Pépé Roni's Good Advice: deglazing   n° 024

Don't confuse "debasing"

and "deglazing."

SHIIII

BECAUSE ANYONE CAN MAKE MISTAKES!

Deglazing: diluting the caramelized juices at the bottom of a pan or a still-warm dish by adding a liquid in order to make a sauce.

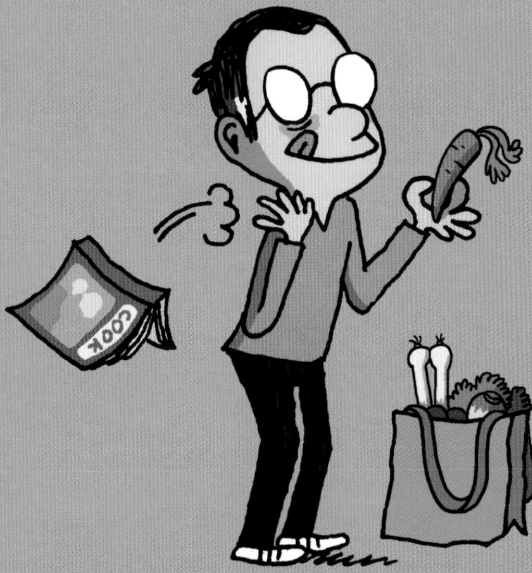
COOK

Table of Recipes

Appetizers

Entrees

Desserts

Index

* Pépé Roni's Good Advice

Acknowledgments

At the beginning, Martin gave this project the impetus it needed to get started. Then Boris, Nicolas, Alexis, and Celia at *Le Monde* trusted me enough and that was a gift. Yannick believed in this project—he's a wonderful guy. Now Thierry, Nicolas, Caroline, Muriel, Sandrine, and Olivier at Gallimard are going above and beyond, and I hope to work with them for a long time to come.

The blog readers have been so supportive; I'm very lucky. Matthieu has a great place in Venice. Francois-Regis is truly charming. Katia and Yoann know Lausanne and vegetables, respectively, like the back of their hands. My mother still knows how to cook well and my *pépé* knew how to appreciate the pleasure of food. Celine always saves me at the end. Roland and I talk often—that means more than you think, believe me.

On the blog, talented authors generously gave their unedited stories: Anne Montel, Daniel Blancou, Dorothee de Monfreid, Frederik Peeters, Guillaume Plantevin, Greg Shaw, Hervé Bourhis, Lison Bernet, Leslie Plée, Louis-Bertrand Devaud, Martin Vidberg, Mathias Martin, Nancy Penna, Pochep, Terruer Graphique, Thibaut, Soulcie, one and two.

This book owes much to Florian. And Nancy is a really cool girl.

Thank you.

Bon Appétit